Traditional Classics on Leadership

The International Library of Leadership

Editors: J. Thomas Wren
Associate Professor of Leadership Studies
Jepson School of Leadership Studies, University of Richmond, USA

Douglas A. Hicks
Associate Professor of Leadership Studies and Religion
Jepson School of Leadership Studies, University of Richmond, USA

Terry L. Price
Associate Professor of Leadership Studies
Jepson School of Leadership Studies, University of Richmond, USA

1 Traditional Classics on Leadership

2 Modern Classics on Leadership

3 New Perspectives on Leadership

For a list of all Edward Elgar published titles visit our site on the World Wide Web at
www.e-elgar.com

Traditional Classics on Leadership

Edited by

J. Thomas Wren

Associate Professor of Leadership Studies
Jepson School of Leadership Studies, University of Richmond, USA

Douglas A. Hicks

Associate Professor of Leadership Studies and Religion
Jepson School of Leadership Studies, University of Richmond, USA

and

Terry L. Price

Associate Professor of Leadership Studies
Jepson School of Leadership Studies, University of Richmond, USA

THE INTERNATIONAL LIBRARY OF LEADERSHIP

An Elgar Reference Collection
Cheltenham, UK • Northampton, MA, USA

Published by
Edward Elgar Publishing Limited
The Lypiatts
15 Lansdown Road
Cheltenham
Glos GL50 2JA
UK

Edward Elgar Publishing, Inc.
William Pratt House
9 Dewey Court
Northampton
Massachusetts 01060
USA

Paperback edition 2005

A catalogue record for this book
is available from the British Library

Library of Congress Cataloguing in Publication Data

The international library of leadership / editors, J. Thomas Wren, Douglas A. Hicks, Terry L. Price.
    p. cm. – (Elgar mini series)
  Includes Index.
  1.   Leadership. I. Wren, J. Thomas, 1950- II. Hicks, Douglas A. III. Price, Terry L., 1966- IV. Series

  HD57.7.I577 2004
  303.3'4—dc22

2004043429

ISBN 978 1 84376 401 4 (cased)
     978 1 84376 151 8 (paperback)

Printed and bound in Great Britain by Marston Book Services Limited, Didcot

Contents

Acknowledgements

The editors and publishers wish to thank the authors and the following publishers who have kindly given permission for the use of copyright material.

Cambridge University Press for excerpt: Immanuel Kant (1784/1970), 'An Answer to the Question: "What is Enlightenment?"', in Hans Reiss (ed.), *Kant's Political Writings*, Translated by H.B. Nisbet, 54–60, 192–3.

Free Press, an imprint of Simon and Schuster Adult Publishing Group for excerpt: John Dewey (1916/1922), 'The Democratic Conception in Education', in *Democracy and Education: An Introduction to the Philosophy of Education*, Chapter VII, 94–116.

Harcourt, Inc. and the Society of Authors for excerpt: Virginia Woolf (1929/1981), excerpt from *A Room of One's Own*, Chapter 6, 95–114.

Harvard University Press and the President and Fellows of Harvard College for excerpt: King James VI and I (1616/1918), 'The Trew Law of Free Monarchies: Or the Reciprock and Mvtvall Dvetie betwixt a Free King, and His Naturall Subjects', in Charles Howard McIlwain (ed.), *The Political Works of James I*, 53–70.

Charles H. Kerr Publishing Co. for excerpt: Karl Marx and Frederick Engels (1848/ 1906), excerpt from Frederick Engels (ed.), *Manifesto of the Communist Party*, translated by Samuel Moore, 11–47.

Alfred A. Knopf, a division of Random House, Inc. for excerpt: Sigmund Freud (1939), excerpt from 'Moses, His People, and Monotheistic Religion', in *Moses and Monotheism*, Translated by Katherine Jones, Part III, Section II, I–IV, 162–82.

Oxford University Press for excerpts: Plato (1941/1962), 'Thrasymachus: Justice as the Interest of the Stronger', in *The Republic of Plato*, Translated with Introduction and Notes by Francis MacDonald Cornford, Book I, Chapter III, 14–29; Plato (1941/1962), 'The Paradox: Philosophers Must Be Kings', 'The Philosopher's Fitness to Rule', 'Why the Philosophic Nature is Useless or Corrupted in Existing Society' and 'A Philosophic Ruler is not an Impossibility', in *The Republic of Plato*, Translated with Introduction and Notes by Francis MacDonald Cornford, Books 5 and 6, Chapters XVIII, XX–XXII, 175–9, 189–211.

Persea Books, Inc. for excerpt: Christine de Pizan (1406/1989), 'Which Shows How the Good Princess Wishes to Attract Virtue to Her', 'Wherein it is Explained How the Good and Wise Princess will Attempt to Make Peace Between the Prince and the Barons if There is any Difficulty Between Them' and 'Which Speaks of the Paths of Devout Charity Which are to be Followed by a Good Princess', in Madeleine Pelner Cosman (ed.), *A Medieval Woman's Mirror of Honor: The Treasury of the City of Ladies*, translated by Charity Caron Willard, Chapters 8–10, 83–90.

University of Pennsylvania Press for excerpt: Ptolemy of Lucca with portions attributed to Thomas Aquinas (c. 1301/1997), excerpt from *On the Government of Rulers: De Regimine Principum*, Translated by James M. Blythe, Book I (attributed to Thomas Aquinas), Prologue and Chapters 1–4, 60–70.

Authors' Acknowledgements

Completing a collection of this sort requires many hands and minds, and the editors are deeply grateful to a number of people who made it possible. Noreen Cullen and Nancy Vick in the interlibrary loan office at Boatwright Memorial Library at the University of Richmond processed literally hundreds of requests with unfailing good humor. Eric Wilson, Christopher Griffin, John Armstrong, Jonathan Wight, Dean Simpson, and Juliette Landphair provided guidance by suggesting readings for the collection, helping with translations, and offering interpretations of selections that bettered those of the editors. Gill Hickman, Richard Couto, and Elizabeth Faier, faculty colleagues at the Jepson School of Leadership Studies at the University of Richmond, were constant sources of ideas and inspiration. Fred Jablin as Acting Dean of the Jepson School provided considerable institutional support and personal encouragement. Joanne Ciulla, another faculty colleague, and Bruce Avolio read all or parts of the results of our efforts and offered useful advice and criticism along the way.

In the actual production of the work we were fortunate to enjoy superb editorial and administrative assistance. Nicola Mills at Edward Elgar Publishing spearheaded this project from the beginning, and graciously accommodated the whims of her sometimes cranky editors. Edward Elgar himself never failed to respond quickly and creatively to our occasionally unorthodox requests. We also thank Caroline McLin and Clare Arnold at Edward Elgar for their fine work in the production phase. At the University of Richmond, Kathy Bradley, Judy Mable, Sue Murphy, Jackie Duresky, Melissa Foster, Michael Frankston, Emily Latshaw, and Kristina Lam provided helpful administrative and technological support.

Our research assistant, Cassie King, deserves special mention and appreciation. She devoted untold hours to this project. Not only did she do the bulk of the legwork, but it is safe to say that nary a word or a comma in this entire collection has escaped her meticulous attention. This work is as much hers as it is our own.

Of course, our families contributed to this endeavor in the way that the families of academics always contribute: in the missed opportunities for shared time together, and in their toleration of distracted spouses and fathers. For that we thank, with love, Catherine, Noah, Lori, Harper, Suzanne, and Jack.

Preface

J. Thomas Wren, Douglas A. Hicks and Terry L. Price

This book is one of a three-volume set devoted to bringing together in one place the most significant writings and scholarship on leadership. When Edward Elgar Publishing first contacted the editors about creating a reference collection pertaining to leadership, an opportunity presented itself to reshape the traditional formulation of leadership studies and to suggest a deeper and more fundamental understanding of the phenomenon. In scholarly circles, the term *leadership studies* has often been used to connote a rather narrow corpus of social science analyses, chiefly from the fields of social psychology and management science. Such studies have contributed mightily to our understanding of leadership, yet they are limited in scope and purpose. On the other hand, the recent popularity of 'leadership' has spurred an outpouring of publications in the trade press. These popular treatments are almost invariably simplistic and shallow.

The premise underlying this collection is that the phenomenon of leadership is too important and too complex to leave the field to these champions alone. Our view of leadership is that it is a universal component of the human condition. It is the process by which and through which groups, organizations, and societies seek to achieve their perceived needs and objectives. As such, leadership has occupied center stage throughout human history. It embraces far more than the mere running of modern formal organizations, and it is much too complex to summarize neatly in a short paperback. Fortunately, because leadership has played such a central role in the human endeavor, it has not lacked for study and analysis. Indeed, the greatest minds in history have considered its implications, probed its dilemmas, and prescribed solutions for its problems.

The goal of this collection is to make readily available to the serious student of leadership a compilation of sources the editors think are representative of the best insights into this important phenomenon. The selections contained in these volumes, it should be noted, come solely from Western traditions. Many works from other cultural traditions are obviously relevant, but constraints of space would limit our inclusion of them to anecdotal status. Such works deserve fuller treatment, perhaps in a future Edward Elgar collection.

Volume I, *Traditional Classics on Leadership*, contains our version of the most insightful and important writings on leadership from ancient times to the dawn of the twentieth century. Moreover, the selections are arranged according to what we believe have been the key leadership issues in the preindustrial age. The volume begins with the central question of the moral purpose of leadership. The selections in this section – from Plato, Aristotle, Rousseau, Kant, Madison, and Nietzsche – suggest the sort of intellectual capital that has been brought to bear upon our topics. Other issues that the volume addresses include: What is the nature of ideal leadership? What constitutes legitimate authority? What is the role of followers? How might one go about challenging authority? We have taken care to include voices that have traditionally been out of the mainstream: women such as Christine de Pizan, Mary Wollstonecraft, Elizabeth Cady Stanton, and Virginia Woolf, and men of color such as David Walker and W.E.B. Du Bois. Taken together, the selections in this volume provide a rich and textured reference collection for an initial understanding of some of the central issues of leadership.

Volume II we have labeled *Modern Classics on Leadership*. It is here that we collect for the reader the seminal articles and chapters that have shaped what is commonly known as the modern field of leadership studies. With the rise of the modern business corporation (and other precedent-shattering developments such as modern warfare), there was an increasing perception that the role of leadership needed closer study. Concurrent with this was the rise of professional academic disciplines in the social sciences. Thus began a fortuitous pairing of leadership with serious academic scholarship that has spawned enormous insights. This volume seeks to bring together the best of that work. Beginning with the paradigm-shaping work of Frederick Winslow Taylor early in the twentieth century, this volume traces the field of leadership studies as it evolved throughout the twentieth century and became a sophisticated scholarship of considerable influence. We place at the reader's disposal the path-breaking studies that led to trait theory, behavior theory, contingency theories of leadership, transformational leadership, charismatic leadership, cognitive approaches to leadership, and studies of power. We also trace the insights that social scientists have brought to the study of followers, organizational culture, and such specific leadership issues as the role of gender. Thus, this volume provides in one place the 'giants' of modern social science leadership literature.

Volume III we call *New Perspectives on Leadership*. Here we seek to demonstrate how the insights of many intellectual approaches contribute to an understanding of current leadership issues. In this volume you will find writings by contemporary philosophers, management scientists, political scientists, social and political activists, and others. We have sought to organize these writings around the questions and themes that we believe most pertain to the study of leadership in the postmodern age. The questions include how leadership should be conceptualized; the role of power and authority; and questions of values, morality, and ethics. The themes that this volume explores reflect what we believe are the most important for our contemporary society: leadership and service, social change, democratic leadership and inclusion, and international leadership. Volume III of the Edward Elgar collection, then, should provide an important intellectual foundation for anyone interested in the current challenges of leadership.

If one were to take a step back and look at the Edward Elgar *International Library of Leadership* collection as a whole, it is our hope that the view thus gained would be one of coherence. It has been our goal in this editing project to do more than just collate good writings on leadership. Our aim has been one of integration. The challenges of our modern world make an understanding of leadership too important to leave to happenstance or haphazard experience. We have sought to make it possible for those serious about leadership to have easy access to the best thinking of the great minds of past and present. Moreover, we have arranged these selections around what we believe are the central issues that modern leaders continue to confront. Many of the selections in these volumes are not an easy read. But they represent what the editors believe to be the most important collection of sources on leadership now available. The 'unity' we have sought is the unity of a common subject matter that has, through the ages, occupied the attention of the brightest luminaries. We hope that this collection may serve as the steppingstone toward a better understanding of the subject of leadership and, in the process, a better world.

Introduction

J. Thomas Wren, Douglas A. Hicks and Terry L. Price

Leadership might be thought of as the process that facilitates the achievement of societal objectives. As such, it has been at the center of learned reflection and debate since such reflection began. This volume draws together in one place some of the best thinking on leadership from great minds of Western traditions. From earliest times, philosophers, religious leaders, political theorists, and reformers have struggled with (and argued about) the ends of leadership, how individuals and societies can best go about achieving those ends, and what role leaders and followers play in the process. Some of the most incisive thinking about leadership has sprung from the maelstrom of societal conflict, as those faced with the frustration of their ideals groped for ways to nudge (or push) their society on to the correct track. What follows is a thematic tour of what the editors believe is the best of such commentaries on leadership.

Since the chosen selections represent some of the greatest minds of history, they often contain arguments of a sophisticated and complex nature. It has been the editors' conscious decision to include sufficient portions of each writer's argument so as to allow the reader the opportunity to gain a firsthand acquaintance with the author's position. Accordingly, each selection is as long as the constraints of space will allow, and, whenever possible, our editing has been minimal, so that each selection represents contiguous portions of the primary source material. The editors also chose to retain the original spelling and punctuation of the sources. Readers of all three volumes in this collection, published by Edward Elgar under the title *The International Library of Leadership*, will note that the typeface for *Traditional Classics on Leadership* differs from that of its compatriots. This is due to idiosyncratic editing decisions relating to this volume that required its contents to be reset in different type.

The purpose of this Introduction is to provide the reader with a succinct overview of the arguments of each contributor, together with a narrative of how the respective selections interrelate with one another, and thus provide a sense of the development of the historical argument. There follows, then, our guide to the source material of *Traditional Classics on Leadership*.

The Moral Purpose of Leadership

Perhaps the most important debate in which any society engages is that which determines its ultimate ends and objectives. The resolution of that debate, in turn, fundamentally shapes how it goes about seeking to achieve those ends and objectives – in other words, how leadership will and should operate. The contributors in this initial section reflect deeply upon the desired ends of leadership in a society. Their arguments are moral arguments in the classic sense of the term: they are debates over fundamental principles of the good society.

As in so many other realms, an appropriate starting point is the thinking of Plato. The first selection, from his *Republic*, finds Plato debating with friends about the nature of justice. When Thrasymachus argues that 'might makes right,' Plato (through the voice of Socrates in the selection) responds with a ringing affirmation of his view of the proper end of leadership and relationship between leaders and followers. A ruler (and a state) will have but one end in mind: 'All that he says and does will be said and done with a view to what is good and proper for the subject for whom he practises his art.' The motivation for leadership should never be money or honor. Rather, the focus for Plato is the good of the people. His ultimate recommendation – to be pursued in the next section of this volume – is the establishment of government under the rule of a virtuous elite, his 'philosopher kings.'

Aristotle takes a slightly different tack. The desired end of government is not all that different from that of Plato. 'A state exists,' argues Aristotle, 'for the sake of a good life.' This can be achieved through the auspices of a good state – a community of common interest dedicated to virtue and justice. Aristotle differs from Plato in his implementation, however. According to Aristotle, how such a state might be structured can vary, although a strong argument can be made that the multitude, taken as a collective, possesses more virtue and wisdom than the few. Nonetheless, Aristotle is no particular friend of unbridled democracy. Only when there are wise and virtuous leaders, ruling in conjunction with the participation of the people (defined in such a way as to exclude women, slaves, and those with an insufficient stake in society), will a state be likely to achieve the desired end.

If Plato and Aristotle set out the initial parameters of the discussion, Jean-Jacques Rousseau weighs in on the conceptions put forth by the earlier writers. He agrees with Plato that might does not make right. Indeed, society is formed in an effort to thwart that principle. The problem is 'to find a form of association which shall defend and protect with the public force the person and property of each associate . . . .' The challenge is to do so while protecting one's freedom. This is achieved by means of a social contract, in which each individual alienates his natural liberty to the community, which will, under the guidance of the 'general will,' establish notions of justice and morality and protect one's civil liberty. Through the exercise of the general will, man acquires 'moral liberty,' an improvement over the state of nature. In principle, then, Rousseau gives the people power in governing, as they deliberate to determine the general will.

Although each of the contributors thus far has addressed the issue in his particular terms, each is seeking answers to essentially the same question: What is the purpose of the state, and how does the state go about achieving it? The next selection, by Immanuel Kant, is less direct but no less substantive. Kant picks up on Rousseau's theme of liberty while indirectly addressing Aristotle's discussion of the role of the people. He discusses liberty in terms of 'enlightenment.' To Kant, to be enlightened is to have the ability to use one's own understanding in all matters, without the guidance of another. This applies to all realms, including the political. To have enlightened citizens one needs enlightened rulers, who permit the citizens the freedom to reason. These citizens, then, have the opportunity to think for themselves and to criticize policy. The duty of the leader is to protect and support this process. *[handwritten: not present in Tyranny]*

James Madison also addresses issues relating to the role of the people in a state and the role of leaders in a state purporting to rest upon popular power. Madison's concerns have to do with the proper ends of political society, which he thinks is the achieving of the common good – the 'permanent and aggregate interests of the community.' In the face of challenges to this objective created by democratic majorities run amok, Madison suggests a new structure of government – a large republic – that would make it difficult for the majority to organize and oppress the rights of others. Such a republic would also lead to the selection of virtuous leaders who would keep the larger interests of the community in view.

In one form or another, all of the contributors thus far can be said to take benevolent views of the ends of the state and the contributions of leaders. Whether the ends of the state are follower interests, virtue and justice, freedom, or the common good, the state appears dedicated to the betterment of society. Likewise, the role of leaders has generally been to foster similar goals. This section ends on a provocative note. In the last selection Friedrich Nietzsche takes quite a different stance regarding the purpose of the state and the role of the leader. Nietzsche provides a narrative of the state and its leaders that is at once a creative and conflicted tale of oppositions and a call for the freedom of self-creation. Rejecting Rousseau's contract notions of the origins of the state, Nietzsche suggests the state began when 'a herd of blonde beasts of prey, a race of conquerors and masters which with all its warlike organisation … pounces with its terrible claws on a population….' These leaders know nothing of responsibility or consideration and instead have an 'instinct of freedom,' or 'the will to power.' Ironically, as time passed, the oppressed generated what Nietzsche considers a monstrous swing to the other extreme. In the process, the powerful group of initial leaders became deified, and with the rise of religion (Christianity) came notions of guilt, duty, and even concern for others. Nietzsche calls for a new leader or leaders to free us from this sickness. What must come, he argues, is another warlike and savage leader who will again liberate the will to power. *[handwritten: doesn't think leaders should care about others?]* His goal is not so much totalitarian rule but the overcoming of any value system that stifles philosophical/artistic creativity by leveling man to a herd mentality. Clearly Nietzsche begins from differing premises than the others, and it is not without reason that he is linked to some of the evil developments of the twentieth century. Nevertheless, his aspirations for the creative freedom that accompanies the will to power are not lacking in their attractions.

It is obvious from our last selection that debates about the desired ends of the state and its leaders do not necessarily lead one to happy outcomes. This is all the more reason for those interested in the study of leadership to consider fully such first principles when engaging in an analysis of leadership. If this section has helped to begin that process, the next should place a finer point on what comprises good leadership.

Ideal Leadership

Closely related to the moral purpose of leadership is the question of what constitutes ideal leadership. This question has also been the subject of considerable discussion and much insight. Here, again, it is appropriate to begin with the insights of Plato.

Plato's solution to the problems of the state is justly famous. He turns to a very special type of leader, the philosopher king. 'Unless either philosophers become kings in their countries or those who are now called kings and rulers come to be sufficiently inspired with a genuine desire for wisdom; unless, that is to say, political power and philosophy meet together ... there can be no rest from troubles ....' Such a leader will love truth, be magnanimous, and be known for justice, courage, and temperance. Plato acknowledges that implementing such a rule will be difficult. Although followers should defer to such wisdom, the masses have not always shown a propensity to do so. In his later writings – in his *Statesman*, *Laws*, and *Letters* – Plato suggests that laws can help achieve such appropriate rule. Nevertheless, Plato holds out hope that, if such a leader can be put into place, the public will recognize his abilities and follow him.

In a later epoch, Thomas Aquinas had reason to reflect upon ideal leadership. Aquinas was much influenced by his reading of Aristotle, and hence echoes him in speaking of the need for political society and in giving his typology of the various forms such government could take. The contribution of Aquinas is in his focus upon the criterion for distinguishing between good and bad leadership and his choice of the appropriate leadership structure. A good leader is one who governs 'for the common good of the multitude and not his own profit.' Under this criterion, Aquinas finds monarchy to be the best form of government because it is most efficient in securing the common good. Democracy is the worst, since it is most inefficient at the same task.

If Plato and Aquinas portray ideal leadership as a benevolent despot whose objective is to achieve the happiness of society, Niccolo Machiavelli's *The Prince* provides a dramatically different sort of ideal. For Machiavelli, the goal of leadership is to maintain 'the prince' in power. Machiavelli's work is, in effect, a handbook to accomplish just that. In the selection included in this volume, he argues that 'a prince who wishes to maintain his power ought therefore to learn that he should not be always good, and must use that knowledge as circumstances and the exigencies of his own affairs may seem to require.' The prince should be both 'the fox and the lion,' and 'have a spirit disposed to change as the winds of fortune and variations of things command him.'

Perhaps because of the dark possibilities of leadership, the Scottish moral philosopher Adam Smith takes a more cautionary approach. He shares with Plato and Thomas Aquinas a commitment to the general welfare but has less faith in leaders. In this selection from *The Theory of Moral Sentiments*, Smith addresses the dilemma leaders face when society loses equilibrium and faces social and political challenges. He advises leaders to attempt to avoid such difficulties by balancing interests within society. But if discontent arises, the leader faces a real balancing act. He should be open to moderate reform, because thereby society can be improved. Yet fundamental change, particularly that championed by ideologues, should be avoided at all costs. Such movements usually lead to fanaticism and evil. Instead, the leader of public spirit should advocate moderation and be content with what pragmatic changes are possible within the system. Smith thus argues for a conservative response to societal and political change, even as his moral philosophy upholds justice, benevolence, and virtue.

If Smith prefers a careful and pragmatic approach to leadership over some ideal system with perfectionist ends, John Stuart Mill is even more skeptical of the notion of some ideal leader presiding over society. Indeed, he challenges that very premise. Mill holds that a benevolent despot is not a realistic solution. Even if it were possible to secure such rule, it would still be undesirable, because any despotism quashes the realization of human possibilities. What is needed is a government grounded in the people. This will assure that the interests of all will be addressed in efforts to achieve sound policy for the good of the community. Mill acknowledges that direct democracy is not always feasible and champions representative government as the means to a just and free society.

For all their differences, Plato, Aquinas, Smith, and Mill represent a body of writings that address ideal leadership in structural terms; that is, each seeks to construct a leadership structure that will ultimately secure the moral ends of society. The remaining selections in this section address ideal leadership in behavioral and cognitive terms. In effect, they advocate proper leader behavior or suggest ways of thinking about leadership that will lead to desirable results. The first of these selections harks back to the Middle Ages to capture a rare woman's voice from that time period, that of Christine de Pizan. Her text is a reminder that the formal leadership roles thus far under debate were applied exclusively to men. Yet women played important roles as informal leaders nonetheless. De Pizan, writing advice to one who aspires to be a 'good princess,' sets out several guidelines. The good princess should be humble, kind, gracious, merciful, and charitable. 'The benevolent princess ... will celebrate other people's worthiness as greater than her own and rejoice in their welfare as if it were her own.' Moreover, there are times when she should add her counsel to the man's work of her husband, the prince. Specifically, she should counsel against avoidable war because of the harm it inflicts upon the people. She should go so far as to be a peacemaker, if possible. Although it might seem dated to our modern sensibilities, this piece suggests that both men and women always had leadership roles to play, and each had attendant expectations. Despite their socially imposed restrictions, elite women were able to exercise substantial public influence.

In contrast to de Pizan's portrayal of the behavioral attributes of the ideal (female) leader, Virginia Woolf, in her classic *A Room of One's Own*, takes a more cognitive approach. In this selection, Woolf, although ostensibly thinking about the challenges that women writers face, nevertheless makes an important point about our thinking about ideal leadership. Having reflected upon the distinctive ways that men and women approach thinking and writing (as well as the lack of opportunities for women), Woolf suggests that the 'androgynous mind,' one that combines the best of male and female characteristics, would lead best. There is much to learn from each other. Her view of ideal leadership, then, would entail including perspectives and people who were currently outside the formal leadership process. In contrast to Adam Smith, of course, this calls for more fundamental social change.

Our final selection in this section, by Sigmund Freud, also takes a cognitive – in this case psychological – approach to the notion of the ideal leader. Freud asks how it is possible for one man to be considered 'great,' and to be perceived as a leader. Using Moses and the Jews as a case study, Freud finds that followers are drawn to such a leader due to their need for authority; specifically, by their longing for a father figure. Thus the great man has the traits of a father. His followers admire and trust him but also fear him. Moses is the perfect example of such an ideal leader.

The initial sections have introduced the reader to alternative idealized ends and means of leadership. Leadership, however, is almost by definition grounded in everyday life, and some of the great leadership tracts in history have sprung from quite pragmatic public issues. The next section traces one of the most important of these debates.

The Nature of Legitimate Authority

Virtually all of the important writings about leadership, prior to the twentieth century, at any rate, had to do with 'public' or political leadership. This makes sense, since the private corporation, which became the focus of so much modern leadership attention, did not rise to prominence until the late nineteenth century. Prior to that time, it was the great public events that spurred the important intellectual outpourings related to leadership. So it was that events of the Early Modern Age – that is, from the fifteenth to eighteenth centuries – generated one of the more profound debates related to leadership. The specific catalytic events varied, ranging from the Reformation to political upheavals in England and on the continent, but the resulting intellectual ferment surrounded a single issue: What are the source and nature of legitimate authority in a polity? The selections that we have ranged before you in this section provide some of the chief answers to this central leadership query.

John Calvin was the principal founder of the Reformed Protestant tradition and a bold experimenter in political and religious affairs in Geneva. In his *Institutes of the Christian Religion*, he articulates his thinking about legitimate government. In this selection, Calvin acknowledges that the source of authority is a sovereign God and that the responsibility of the state is to be a deputy of God's society by maintaining order and justice. Within that purview leaders have a rather wide discretion as vicars of God, but all laws must be based upon equity. Followers are expected to show deference to rulers and be obedient to them, even if they are unjust. Calvin adds the caveat that lesser magistrates can resist a leader who is unjust and that no one can obey a leader if it means disobedience to God.

James I of England, partly in response to a restive Parliament, goes one better than Calvin and champions the divine right of kings. James quotes the biblical King David when he says that 'kings are called Gods.' They arose before laws, and therefore all laws derive from kings, and the king himself is above all law. While kings should keep the interests of subjects in mind, these leaders are a law unto themselves, and followers are out of line to question the monarch. Consequently, no such resistance is ever justified.

The breakdown of English royal government under James's son Charles I in the 1640s led to some of the most radical political writings prior to the modern era. In the midst of this intellectual ferment, a group called the Levellers articulated a basis for governmental legitimacy that would have profound implications in a later era. Government secures its legitimacy, the Levellers say, from the people. Moreover – and it is this that made them so radical – the people never surrender that sovereignty to government. The Levellers give considerable powers to members of Parliament, but the power of these representatives is 'inferiour only to theirs who chuse them.' Thus we have a line drawn in the sand regarding the issue of the source of legitimacy regarding leadership. The final selections, written in the century after the 'Agreement of the People,' represent some sophisticated attempts at a resolution.

Thomas Hobbes, although his conclusion is a Leviathan of leadership that echoes earlier absolutist writings, nevertheless grounds the legitimacy of government upon a quite different basis. Hobbes imagines a state of nature in which there is 'a condition of warre of every man against every man.' In this state of nature, life is, in Hobbes's famous phrase, 'solitary, poor, nasty, brutish, and short.' As a result, men covenant together to place restraints upon themselves in the form of commonwealth. The only way to do this successfully is 'to confer all their power and strength upon one Man ... that may reduce all their Wills ... unto one Will ....' When they do this, each member promises to 'give up my Right of Governing my self, to this Man ....' The resulting leader becomes the sovereign power, and the others subjects. Thus, although the resulting leader may not look all that different from the divine kingship of James I, the source of his legitimacy is altogether different. Here, leadership is grounded in the covenant of the people.

John Locke begins from a similar premise, in the sense that the legitimacy of leadership and government is based upon the consent of the people, but his investigation of consent and the limits placed upon it yield quite a different model of leadership. Somewhat like Hobbes, Locke posits a state of nature and man's agreement to create a civil society for the purpose of preserving 'himself, his liberty, and his property.' By their consent, men agree to set rulers over themselves. Locke takes some care to explore the nature of that consent and to whom and in what manner it extends. There are some things to which this consent emphatically does not extend. For example, since the protection of property is the end of government, 'the supreme power cannot take from any man any part of his property without his own consent.' We see here, then, a similar grounding of government, not in religion, but in a sovereign people. However, contrary to the Levellers, the relationship between the followers and their leaders is much more complex. Under Locke, there are clear limitations upon government, but the people – by consent – agree not to upset the governing structure for other than weighty reasons.

The Scottish moral philosopher David Hume serves as our final selection in this section. He rejects both the religious basis for legitimacy and the consent argument. Regarding those who think 'the Deity is the ultimate author of all government,' Hume argues that it is irrational to assume that God ever entered so specifically into the affairs of each state and even more unlikely that one can decipher the divine will. Likewise, Hume takes social contract theorists to task for the view 'that all men are still born equal, and owe allegiance to no prince or government, unless bound by the obligation and sanction of a *promise*.' Even a superficial look at the realities of the world gives the lie to such assertions, Hume says, and social contract thinking also engages in a circularity of argument. Hume is more pragmatic. He proposes that the foundations of government are 'the general interests or necessities of society' and concludes that 'new discoveries are not to be expected in these matters.'

We see, then, how key intellectuals sought, in the heat of events, to articulate some form of legitimation for government and leadership. Bundled within such arguments – in some more obviously than others – are profound implications for the role of participants in such polities. Our last two sections of this volume take up the notion of followers and the options they face when leadership goes bad.

The Status of Followers

Although the focus of much of the intellectual energy devoted to leadership was the leader, there were important acknowledgements of the key role that followers might play. The selections in this section are representative samples of commentators acknowledging the importance of followers.

For those unfamiliar with the entire corpus of his writings, Niccolo Machiavelli might seem an unusual choice to demonstrate the importance of followers. Yet, quite contrary to *The Prince*, his *Discourses on Livy* does exactly that. In the chosen passage, Machiavelli disagrees with those who fear the passions of the people. To the contrary, Machiavelli argues, 'I say that the people are more prudent and stable, and have better judgment than a prince ....' Indeed, according to Machiavelli, 'The voice of a people is the voice of God ....' Now, it must be said that Machiavelli advocates that the people should be well regulated by laws, but so too should a prince and, of the two, the people are definitely more trustworthy. It is not unimportant that Machiavelli, in his *Discourses*, addresses leadership in republics. Nevertheless, his is a strong early statement of the value of followers in the leadership equation.

Taking a somewhat different tack on the role of followers is Georg Wilhelm Friedrich Hegel. In this selection Hegel develops his famous master–slave dialectic in the context of a dense discussion of the notion of self-consciousness. In the beginning, the master has power and independence: 'The master relates himself to the bondsman mediately through independent existence, for that is precisely what keeps the bondsman in thrall; it is his chain, from which he could not in the struggle get away, and for that reason he proves himself dependent, shows that his independence consists in being a thing.' But the master comes to see that 'just where [he] has effectively achieved lordship, he really finds that something has come about quite different from an independent consciousness. It is not an independent, but rather a dependent consciousness that he has achieved.' In the end, the slave gets power and independence: 'By serving he cancels in every particular moment his dependence on and attachment to natural existence, and by his work removes this existence away.' Hegel thus provides us with an important piece for rethinking the central historical paradigm for the relationship between leaders and followers.

Yet another important statement is that by Mary Wollstonecraft, writing in the late eighteenth century. The chosen selection from her *A Vindication of the Rights of Woman* makes the argument that women and men should be treated as full moral equals. All human beings are endowed with reason, Wollstonecraft argues, but women are not permitted to develop theirs. Instead, women are brought up to rely upon emotion and feeling. Women have 'acquired all the follies and vices of civilization, and missed the useful fruit.' They should instead 'acquire the noble privilege of reason, [and] the power of discerning good from evil.' By so empowering 'one half of the human race,' Wollstonecraft concludes, mankind can better achieve morality and virtue and 'render the present state more complete.' Thereby could be achieved a 'true civilization' in which leaders and followers (including men and women) are treated as equals.

The hopeful note of Wollstonecraft finds its counterpart in the hurly-burly of the political arena in the form of Elizabeth Cady Stanton's 'Address to the American Equal Rights Association.' Stanton's address is an important (and representative) example of the nineteenth-century women's movement. In it, Stanton couches her call for women's suffrage in an appeal for universal suffrage. Both sexes can benefit from mutual interaction with the other. In addition to their potential role in the public realm, women can play a central leadership role in the private sphere as well. Stanton views the danger to society as not the threat of a dictator but the 'corruption of the people.' Women are the mothers and educators of the race, and, accordingly, play a crucial role in combating this. Thus, providing women with the proper respect will increase their ability to be leaders in both public and private life.

If Stanton calls for reform in the form of the empowerment of women, Ralph Waldo Emerson looks at what it takes to be a reformer. Emerson says it is the duty of every man (every follower) to call the institutions of society to account. These institutions, rather than being grounded in evil, must be based upon truth and justice. This can be achieved by individual efforts on the part of followers. The true reformer will try to avoid any activity that lends support to a corrupt system. One should therefore return to minimalism: live simply and, to the extent possible, consume only what one creates through manual labor. Moreover, reformers should pay particular attention to the plight of the poor. These efforts at reform must, in turn, be guided by noble principles. An individual should pursue knowledge and virtue, but the noblest principle of all is love.

In our final selection, John Dewey looks to the role of education in the creation of effective citizens of a democracy. At the most obvious level, 'a government resting upon popular suffrage cannot be successful unless those who elect and who obey their governors are educated.' Yet on another, more sophisticated plane, Dewey argues that education performs a social function, the nature of which depends upon the aims of the group served. In a democracy, which is characterized by the recognition of mutual interests and free interaction among groups, education must facilitate interaction and the diversity of views. Education must not serve class interests but must equip all for success. The result of successful education in a democracy will be the freeing of individual capacity and the utilization of that capacity toward binding people together in cooperative pursuits directed toward social aims.

This section has traced thinking about followers from the acknowledgement of their value in Machiavelli; through Hegel's dialectical overturning of the expected role of leaders and followers; to the possibilities for and reality of reform in the persons of Wollstonecraft, Stanton, and Emerson; and finally to Dewey's explication of the role education plays in creating effective followers. These selections, taken together, demonstrate the potential power of followers in the leadership relation. The final section turns to some important examples of how one might mount challenges to authority, always an important option in a healthy leadership climate.

Challenges to Authority

As we have seen in the preceding two sections, the concept of leadership is often hedged in by issues of authority. This does not preclude the possibility that authority itself must sometimes come into question. This is the explicit focus of our final section. The context, predictably, is upon leadership in the public, or political, sector. Each of the selections in this segment represents classic modes of challenge. Some, as we shall see, set forth theoretical justifications for resistance to authority; some suggest tactics of resistance; while still others represent calls from those actually oppressed. It is important to understand that those engaged in challenges to authority are themselves engaged in a form of leadership.

The first selection, by the French Huguenot Philippe Duplessis-Mornay, articulates a theory of resistance grounded in the contract theory of leadership and government (see the previous discussion of Locke). Duplessis-Mornay, writing in opposition to the oppression of the Huguenots by the French kings, does not oppose monarchy *per se* but suggests that even kings are constrained in their actions. This is due to a covenant entered into in the distant past between the king and the people. According to this compact, the monarch agrees to rule justly, and the people agree to follow him if he does so. Under this theory, if the leader does not rule justly, there is an obligation to resist. If the people do not resist, Duplessis-Mornay states, 'wee may justly be accounted breakers of the Lawes, betrayers of our Countrey, and contemnors of Religion.'

If Duplessis-Mornay believes that resistance to authority could be justified by breach of an original compact, Karl Marx and Frederick Engels think it a necessary outcome of historical forces (although they urge workers to hasten the process by joining the cause). In the *Manifesto of the Communist Party*, Marx and Engels lay out the doctrine of historical materialism and depict the sweep of history as a series of dialectical relations between various classes. In the current epoch (the 1840s), the bourgeoisie oppresses the proletarians, and the only resolution is through revolution. This, Marx and Engels say, is inevitable. 'But not only has the bourgeoisie forged the weapons that bring death to itself; it has also called into existence the men who are to wield those weapons – the modern working-class – the proletarians.' The result – after a period of transition – will be an entire new relation of equality and a utopian society wherein 'we shall have an association, in which the free development of each is the condition for the free development of all.' In their peroration, the call is to action: 'The proletarians have nothing to lose but their chains. They have a world to win. Working men of all countries unite!' Although the political applications of Marxism have met with a certain discredit, Marx and Engels's indictment of capitalist society and the relations between superior and subordinate continues to motivate resistance to authority the world over.

David Walker gives another justification for resistance in his 1829 *Appeal* against slavery. Walker, a free black man, draws upon Christian biblical texts to argue that leaders and systems of government that are unjust stand at God's judgment. The time for 'repentance' is now. Although Walker stops short of advocating direct action, many viewed this as a call for slave insurrection. Be that as it may, it is certainly a call for justice and transformation in the face of unjust leadership. History is replete with such moral calls for reformed leadership. Whether joined by action or not, such appeals are often powerful catalysts for resistance to authority.

Henry David Thoreau joins a moral stance with specific resistance tactics in his famous essay *Civil Disobedience*. Thoreau disagrees with the policies of the national government during the Mexican War and its stance toward slavery. His uncompromising call to stand up to unjust governments and leadership and to be willing to accept the punishment for such heroic action has inspired resistance to injustice throughout the world ever since – from Martin Luther King, Jr., in the American civil rights movement to Mohandas Gandhi in his campaign against British imperialism.

In our final selection, we trace a more subtle, and perhaps more lasting, mode of resistance to unjust authority. W.E.B. Du Bois, a black American activist writing at the turn of the twentieth century, had ample evidence of the unjustness of the dominant white treatment of his race. In this selection from *The Souls of Black Folk*, Du Bois advocates the educated leadership of a select group of African Americans as a means of resistance and overall transformation of the conditions and reality of African Americans. Through their actions, the entire race could be lifted from its oppressed state.

Taken together, the selections in this section set out a powerful tradition of resistance to unjust authority in our Western heritage. All are classics; many continue to inspire and motivate marginalized peoples the world over. In this sense, this set of readings is a fitting conclusion to our collection. Beginning with an exploration of the moral ends of leadership, continuing with models of ideal leadership, and concluding with several sections devoted to key leadership themes, this volume seeks to assemble in one place some of the greatest writings devoted to leadership in Western history. Of course this collection is designed to be a reference source for those interested in understanding more about the phenomenon of leadership. But the editors hope that this understanding will also serve as a call to action to those who have the capability – and who recognize the obligation – to make this world a better place. These readings suggest that the capability and the obligation are far more widely dispersed than is usually assumed.

Part I
The Moral Purpose of Leadership

1. The Republic*

Plato

Chapter III (I. 336 B–347 E)
Thrasymachus: Justice as the Interest of the Stronger

Socrates has opposed to the popular conception of justice one of his own deepest convictions. Polemarchus' ready acceptance of this provokes a violent protest from Thrasymachus, who represents the doctrine that might is right in an extreme form. He holds that justice or right is nothing but the name given by the men actually holding power in any state to any actions they enjoin by law upon their subjects; and that all their laws are framed to promote their own personal or class interests. 'Just' accordingly means what is for the interest of the stronger, ruling party. Right and wrong have no other meaning at all. This is not a theory of social contract: it is not suggested that the subject has ever made a bargain with the ruler, sacrificing some of his liberty to gain the benefits of a social order. The ruler imposes his 'rights' by sheer force. The perfect example of such a ruler is the despot (the Greek 'tyrant'), whose position Thrasymachus regards as supremely enviable. He is precisely the man who has the will and the power to 'do good to himself and his friends and to harm his enemies.'

The discussion begins by clearing up the ambiguities of Thrasymachus' formula. The word translated 'stronger' commonly means also 'superior' or 'better'; but 'better' has no moral sense for Thrasymachus, who does not recognize the existence of morality. The superiority of the stronger lies in the skill and determination which enable them to seize and hold power. 'Interest,' again, means the personal satisfaction and aggrandizement of the ruling individuals.

* Most scholars believe Plato wrote *The Republic* in stages sometime between 387 and 360 BCE. This particular selection was taken from Plato, *The Republic of Plato*, Book I, Chapter III, translated with introduction and notes by Francis MacDonald Cornford, 1941, reprint (New York: Oxford University Press, 1962), 14–29.

All this time Thrasymachus had been trying more than once to break in upon our conversation; but his neighbours had restrained him, wishing to hear the argument to the end. In the pause after my last words he could keep quiet no longer; but gathering himself up like a wild beast he sprang at us as if he would tear us in pieces. Polemarchus and I were frightened out of our wits, when he burst out to the whole company:

What is the matter with you two, Socrates? Why do you go on in this imbecile way, politely deferring to each other's nonsense? If you really want to know what justice means, stop asking questions and scoring off the answers you get. You know very well it is easier to ask questions than to answer them. Answer yourself, and tell us what you think justice means. I won't have you telling us it is the same as what is obligatory or useful or advantageous or profitable or expedient; I want a clear and precise statement; I won't put up with that sort of verbiage.

I was amazed by this onslaught and looked at him in terror. If I had not seen this wolf before he saw me, I really believe I should have been struck dumb;[1] but fortunately I had looked at him earlier, when he was beginning to get exasperated with our argument; so I was able to reply, though rather tremulously:

Don't be hard on us, Thrasymachus. If Polemarchus and I have gone astray in our search, you may be quite sure the mistake was not intentional. If we had been looking for a piece of gold, we should never have deliberately allowed politeness to spoil our chance of finding it; and now when we are looking for justice, a thing much more precious than gold, you cannot imagine we should defer to each other in that foolish way and not do our best to bring it to light. You must believe we are in earnest, my friend; but I am afraid the task is beyond our powers, and we might expect a man of your ability to pity us instead of being so severe.

Thrasymachus replied with a burst of sardonic laughter.

Good Lord, he said; Socrates at his old trick of shamming ignorance! I knew it; I told the others you would refuse to commit yourself and do anything sooner than answer a question.

Yes, Thrasymachus, I replied; because you are clever enough to know that if you asked someone what are the factors of the number twelve, and at the same time warned him: 'Look here, you are not to tell me that 12 is twice 6, or 3 times 4, or 6 times 2, or 4 times 3; I won't put up with any such nonsense' — you must surely see that no one would answer a question put like that. He would say: 'What do you mean, Thrasymachus? Am I forbidden to give any of these answers, even if one happens to be right? Do you want me to give a wrong one?' What would you say to that?

Humph! said he. As if that were a fair analogy!

I don't see why it is not, said I; but in any case, do you suppose our barring a certain answer would prevent the man from giving it, if he thought it was the truth?

Do you mean that you are going to give me one of those answers I barred?

I should not be surprised, if it seemed to me true, on reflection.

And what if I give you another definition of justice, better than any of those? What penalty are you prepared to pay?[2]

The penalty deserved by ignorance, which must surely be to receive instruction from the wise. So I would suggest that as a suitable punishment.

I like your notion of a penalty! he said; but you must pay the costs as well.

I will, when I have any money.

That will be all right, said Glaucon; we will all subscribe for Socrates. So let us have your definition, Thrasymachus.

Oh yes, he said; so that Socrates may play the old game of questioning and refuting someone else, instead of giving an answer himself!

But really, I protested, what can you expect from a man who does not know the answer or profess to know it, and, besides that, has been forbidden by no mean authority to put forward any notions he may have? Surely the definition should naturally come from you, who say you do know the answer and can tell it us. Please do not disappoint us. I should take it as a kindness, and I hope you will not be chary of giving Glaucon and the rest of us the advantage of your instruction.

Glaucon and the others added their entreaties to mine. Thrasymachus was evidently longing to win credit, for he was sure he had an admirable answer ready, though he made a show of insisting that I should be the one to reply. In the end he gave way and exclaimed:

So this is what Socrates' wisdom comes to! He refuses to teach, and goes about learning from others without offering so much as thanks in return.

I do learn from others, Thrasymachus; that is quite true; but you are wrong to call me ungrateful. I give in return all I can — praise; for I have no money. And how ready I am to applaud any idea that seems to me sound, you will see in a moment, when you have stated your own; for I am sure that will be sound.

Listen then, Thrasymachus began. What I say is that 'just' or 'right' means nothing but what is to the interest of the stronger party. Well, where is your applause? You don't mean to give it me.

I will, as soon as I understand, I said. I don't see yet what you mean by right being the interest of the stronger party. For instance, Polydamas, the athlete, is stronger than we are, and it is to his interest to eat beef for the sake of his muscles; but surely you don't mean that the same diet would be good for weaker men and therefore be right for us?

You are trying to be funny, Socrates. It's a low trick to take my words in the sense you think will be most damaging.

No, no, I protested; but you must explain.

Don't you know, then, that a state may be ruled by a despot, or a democracy, or an aristocracy?

Of course.

And that the ruling element is always the strongest?

Yes.

Well then, in every case the laws are made by the ruling party in its own interest; a democracy makes democratic laws, a despot autocratic ones, and so on. By making these laws they define as 'right' for their subjects whatever is for their own interest, and they call anyone who breaks them a 'wrongdoer' and punish him accordingly. That is what I mean: in all states alike 'right' has the same meaning, namely what is for the interest of

↑
Thrasymachus

the party established in power, and that is the strongest. So the sound conclusion is that what is 'right' is the same everywhere: the interest of the stronger party.

Now I see what you mean, said I; whether it is true or not, I must try to make out. When you define right in terms of interest, you are yourself giving one of those answers you forbade to me; though, to be sure, you add 'to the stronger party.'

An insignificant addition, perhaps!

Its importance is not clear yet; what is clear is that we must find out whether your definition is true. I agree myself that right is in a sense a matter of interest; but when you add 'to the stronger party,' I don't know about that. I must consider.

Go ahead, then.

I will. Tell me this. No doubt you also think it is right to obey the men in power?

I do.

Are they infallible in every type of state, or can they sometimes make a mistake?

Of course they can make a mistake.

In framing laws, then, they may do their work well or badly?

No doubt.

Well, that is to say, when the laws they make are to their own interest; badly, when they are not?

Yes.

But the subjects are to obey any law they lay down, and they will then be doing right?

Of course.

If so, by your account, it will be right to do what is not to the interest of the stronger party, as well as what is so.

What's that you are saying?

Just what you said, I believe; but let us look again. Haven't you admitted that the rulers, when they enjoin certain acts on their subjects, sometimes mistake their own best interests, and at the same time that it is right for the subjects to obey, whatever they may enjoin?

Yes, I suppose so.

Well, that amounts to admitting that it is right to do what is not to the interest of the rulers or the stronger party. They may unwittingly enjoin what is to their own disadvantage; and you say it is right for the others to do as they are told. In that case, their duty must be the opposite of what you said, because the weaker will have been ordered to do what is against the interest of the stronger. You with your intelligence must see how that follows.

Yes, Socrates, said Polemarchus, that is undeniable.

No doubt, Cleitophon broke in, if you are to be a witness on Socrates' side.

No witness is needed, replied Polemarchus; Thrasymachus himself admits that rulers sometimes ordain acts that are to their own disadvantage, and that it is the subjects' duty to do them.

That is because Thrasymachus said it was right to do what you are told by the men in power.

Yes, but he also said that what is to the interest of the stronger party is right; and, after making both these assertions, he admitted that the stronger sometimes command the weaker subjects to act against their interests. From all which it follows that what is in the stronger's interest is no more right than what is not.

No, said Cleitophon; he meant whatever the stronger *believes* to be in his own interest. That is what the subject must do, and what Thrasymachus meant to define as right.

That was not what he said, rejoined Polemarchus.

No matter, Polemarchus, said I; if Thrasymachus says so now, let us take him in that sense. Now, Thrasymachus, tell me, was that what you intended to say — that right means what the stronger thinks is to his interest, whether it really is so or not?

Most certainly not, he replied. Do you suppose I should speak of a man as 'stronger' or 'superior' at the very moment when he is making a mistake?

I did think you said as much when you admitted that rulers are not always infallible.

That is because you are a quibbler, Socrates. Would you say a man deserves to be called a physician at the moment when he makes a mistake in treating his patient and just in respect of that mistake; or a mathematician, when be does a sum wrong and just in so far as he gets a wrong result? Of course we do commonly speak of a physician or a mathematician or a scholar having made a mistake; but really none of these, I should say, is ever mistaken, in so far as he is worthy of the name we give him. So strictly speaking — and you are all for being precise — no one who practises a craft makes mistakes. A man is mistaken when his knowledge fails him; and at that moment he is no craftsman. And what is true of craftsmanship or any sort of skill is true of the ruler: he is never mistaken so long as he is acting as a ruler; though anyone might speak of a ruler making a mistake, just as he might of a physician. You must understand that I was talking in that loose way when I answered your question just now; but the precise statement is this. The ruler, in so far as he is acting as a ruler, makes no mistakes and consequently enjoins what is best for himself; and that is what the subject is to do. So, as I said at first, 'right' means doing what is to the interest of the stronger.

Very well, Thrasymachus, said I. So you think I am quibbling?

I am sure you are.

You believe my questions were maliciously designed to damage your position?

I know it. But you will gain nothing by that. You cannot outwit me by cunning, and you are not the man to crush me in the open.

Bless your soul, I answered, I should not think of trying. But, to prevent any more misunderstanding, when you speak of that ruler or stronger party whose interest the weaker ought to serve, please make it clear whether you are using the words in the ordinary way or in that strict sense you have just defined.

I mean a ruler in the strictest possible sense. Now quibble away and be as malicious as you can. I want no mercy. But you are no match for me.

Do you think me mad enough to beard a lion or try to outwit a Thrasymachus?

You did try just now, he retorted, but it wasn't a success.

[*Thrasymachus has already shifted his ground. At first 'the stronger' meant only the men ruling by superior force; but now their superiority must include the knowledge and ability needed to govern without making mistakes. This knowledge and ability constitute an art of government, comparable to other useful arts or crafts requiring special skill. The ruler in his capacity as ruler, or the craftsman* qua *craftsman, can also be spoken of as the craft personified, since a craft exists only in the man who embodies it, and we are considering the man only as the embodiment of this special capacity, neglecting all personal characteristics and any other capacities he may chance to have. When Socrates talks of the art or craft in this abstract way as having an interest of its own, he means the same thing as if he spoke of the interest of the craftsman* qua *craftsman. Granted that there is, as Thrasymachus suggested, an art of government exercised by a ruler who,* qua *ruler, is infallible and so in the full sense 'superior,' the question now is, what his interest should be, on the analogy of other crafts.*]

Enough of this, said I. Now tell me about the physician in that strict sense you spoke of: is it his business to earn money or to treat his patients? Remember, I mean your physician who is worthy of the name.

To treat his patients.

And what of the ship's captain in the true sense? Is he a mere seaman or the commander of the crew?

The commander.

Yes, we shall not speak of him as a seaman just because he is on board a ship. That is not the point. He is called captain because of his skill and authority over the crew.

Quite true.

And each of these people has some special interest?[3]

No doubt.

And the craft in question exists for the very purpose of discovering that interest and providing for it?

Yes.

Can it equally be said of any craft that it has an interest, other than its own greatest possible perfection?

What do you mean by that?

Here is an illustration. If you ask me whether it is sufficient for the human body just to be itself, with no need of help from without, I should say, Certainly not; it has weaknesses and defects, and its condition is not all that it might be. That is precisely why the art of medicine was invented: it was designed to help the body and provide for its interests. Would not that be true?

It would.

But now take the art of medicine itself. Has that any defects or weaknesses? Does any art stand in need of some further perfection, as the eye would be imperfect without the power of vision or the ear without hearing, so that in their case an art is required that will study their interests and provide for their carrying out those functions? Has the art itself any corresponding need of some further art to remedy its defects and look after its interests; and will that further art require yet another, and so on for ever? Or will every art look after its own interests? Or, finally, is it not true that no art needs to have its weaknesses remedied or its interests studied either by another art or by itself, because no art has in itself any weakness or fault, and the only interest it is required to serve is that of its subject-matter? In itself, an art is sound and flawless, so long as it is entirely true to its own nature as an art in the strictest sense — and it is the strict sense that I want you to keep in view. Is not that true?

So it appears.

Then, said I, the art of medicine does not study its own interest, but the needs of the body, just as a groom shows his skill by caring for horses, not for the art of grooming. And so every art seeks, not its own advantage — for it has no deficiencies — but the interest of the subject on which it is exercised.

It appears so.

But surely, Thrasymachus, every art has authority and superior power over its subject.

To this he agreed, though very reluctantly.

So far as arts are concerned, then, no art ever studies or enjoins the interest of the superior or stronger party, but always that of the weaker over which it has authority.

Thrasymachus assented to this at last, though he tried to put up a fight. I then went on:

So the physician, as such, studies only the patient's interest, not his own. For as we agreed, the business of the physician, in the strict sense, is not to make money for himself, but to exercise his power over the patient's body; and the ship's captain, again, considered strictly as no mere sailor, but in command of the crew, will study and enjoin the interest of his subordinates, not his own.

He agreed reluctantly.

And so with government of any kind: no ruler, in so far as he is acting as ruler, will study or enjoin what is for his own interest. All that he says and does will be said and done with a view to what is good and proper for the subject for whom he practises his art.

[*Thrasymachus can hardly challenge this last argument, based as it is on his own 'precise' distinction of the ruler acting in his special capacity with knowledge and ability like the craftsman's and impeccable. Accordingly he takes refuge in an appeal to facts. The ruler, from the Homeric king onwards, had been called the shepherd of the people. Thrasymachus truly remarks that these shepherds have commonly been less concerned with the good of their flock than with shearing and butchering them for their own profit and aggrandizement. This behaviour is called 'injustice' because it means getting more than one's fair share; but the entirely selfish autocrat who practises it on a grand scale is envied and admired; and Thrasymachus himself regards him as the happiest of men. Justice, fairness, honesty, he concludes, never pay; the life of injustice is always more profitable.*

Socrates leaves this more general proposition to be challenged in the next chapter. Here he is still concerned with the art of government. He takes up the analogy of the shepherd and applies once more Thrasymachus' own distinction of 'capacities.' The shepherd qua *shepherd cares for his flock; he receives wages in a different capacity,* qua *wage-earner. The fact that the rulers of mankind expect to be rewarded shows that the proper task of governing is commonly regarded as an irksome and unprofitable business.*]

At this point, when everyone could see that Thrasymachus' definition of justice had been turned inside out, instead of making any reply, he said:

Socrates, have you a nurse?

Why do you ask such a question as that? I said. Wouldn't it be better to answer mine?

Because she lets you go about sniffling like a child whose nose wants wiping. She hasn't even taught you to know a shepherd when you see one, or his sheep either.

What makes you say that?

Why, you imagine that a herdsman studies the interests of his flocks or cattle, tending and fattening them up with some other end in view than his master's profit or his own; and so you don't see that, in politics, the genuine ruler regards his subjects exactly like sheep, and thinks of nothing else, night and day, but the good he can get out of them for himself. You are so far out in your notions of right and wrong, justice and injustice, as not to know that 'right' actually means what is good for someone else, and to be 'just' means serving the interest of the stronger who rules, at the cost of the subject who obeys; whereas injustice is just the reverse, asserting its authority over those innocents who are called just, so that they minister solely to their master's advantage and happiness, and not in the least degree to their own. Innocent as you are yourself, Socrates, you must see that a just man always has the worst of it. Take a private business: when a partnership is wound up, you will never find that the more honest of two partners comes off with the larger share; and in their relations to the state, when there are taxes to be paid, the honest man will pay more than the other on the same amount of property; or if there is money to be distributed, the dishonest will get it all. When either of them hold some public office, even if the just man loses in no other way, his private affairs at any rate will suffer from neglect, while his principles will not allow him to help himself from the public funds; not to mention the offence he will give to his friends and relations by refusing to sacrifice those principles to do them a good turn. Injustice has all the opposite advantages. I am speaking of the type I described just now, the man who can get the better of other people on a large scale: you must fix your eye on him, if you want to judge how much it is to one's own interest not to be just. You can see that best in the most consummate form of injustice, which rewards wrongdoing with supreme welfare and happiness and reduces its victims, if they won't retaliate in kind, to misery. That form is despotism, which uses force or fraud to plunder the goods of others, public or private, sacred or profane, and to do it in a wholesale way. If you are caught committing any one of these crimes on a small scale, you are punished and disgraced; they call it sacrilege, kidnapping, burglary, theft and brigandage. But if, besides taking their property, you turn all your countrymen into slaves, you will hear no more of those ugly names; your countrymen themselves will call you the happiest of men and bless your name, and so will everyone who hears of such a complete triumph of injustice; for when people denounce injustice, it is because they are afraid of suffering wrong, not of doing it. So true is it, Socrates, that injustice, on a grand enough scale, is superior to justice in strength and freedom and autocratic power; and 'right,' as I said at first, means simply what serves the interest of the stronger party; 'wrong' means what is for the interest and profit of oneself.

Having deluged our ears with this torrent of words, as the man at the baths might empty a bucket over one's head, Thrasymachus meant to take himself off; but the company obliged him to stay and defend his position. I was specially urgent in my entreaties.

My good Thrasymachus, said I, do you propose to fling a doctrine like that at our heads and then go away without explaining it properly or letting us point out to you whether it is true or not? Is it so small a matter in your eyes to determine the whole course of conduct which every one of us must follow to get the best out of life?

Don't I realize it is a serious matter? he retorted.

Apparently not, said I; or else you have no consideration for us, and do not care whether we shall lead better or worse lives for being ignorant of this truth you profess to know. Do take the trouble to let us into your secret; if you treat us handsomely, you may be sure it will be a good investment; there are so many of us to show our gratitude. I will make no secret of my own conviction, which is that injustice is not more profitable than justice, even when left free to work its will unchecked. No; let your unjust man have full power to do wrong, whether by successful violence or by escaping detection; all the same he will not convince me that he will gain more than he would by being just. There may be others here who feel as I do, and set justice above injustice. It is for you to convince us that we are not well advised.

How can I? he replied. If you are not convinced by what I have just said, what more can I do for you? Do you want to be fed with my ideas out of a spoon?

God forbid! I exclaimed; not that. But I do want you to stand by your own words; or, if you shift your ground, shift it openly and stop trying to hoodwink us as you are doing now. You see, Thrasymachus, to go back to your earlier argument, in speaking of the shepherd you did not think it necessary to keep to that strict sense you laid down when you defined the genuine physician. You represent him, in his character of shepherd, as feeding up his flock, not for their own sake but for the table or the market, as if he were out to make money as a caterer or a cattle-dealer, rather than a shepherd. Surely the sole concern of the shepherd's art is to do the best for the charges put under its care; its own best interest is sufficiently provided for, so long as it does not fall short of all that shepherding should imply. On that principle it followed, I thought, that any kind of authority, in the state or in private life, must, in its character of authority, consider solely what is best for those under its care. Now what is your opinion? Do you think that the men who govern states — I mean rulers in the strict sense — have no reluctance to hold office?

I don't think so, he replied; I know it.

Well, but haven't you noticed, Thrasymachus, that in other positions of authority no one is willing to act unless he is paid wages, which he demands on the assumption that all the benefit of his action will go to his charges? Tell me: Don't we always distinguish one form of skill from another by its power to effect some particular result? Do say what you really think, so that we may get on.

Yes, that is the distinction.

And also each brings us some benefit that is peculiar to it: medicine gives health, for example; the art of navigation, safety at sea; and so on.

Yes.

And wage-earning brings us wages; that is its distinctive product. Now, speaking with that precision which you proposed, you would not say that the art of navigation is the same as the art of medicine, merely on the ground that a ship's captain regained his health on a voyage, because the sea air was good for him. No more would you identify the practice of medicine with wage-earning because a man may keep his health while earning wages, or a physician attending a case may receive a fee.

No.

And, since we agreed that the benefit obtained by each form of skill is peculiar to it, any common benefit enjoyed alike by all these practitioners must come from some further practice common to them all?

It would seem so.

Yes, we must say that if they all earn wages, they get that benefit in so far as they are engaged in wage-earning as well as in practising their several arts.

He agreed reluctantly.

This benefit, then — the receipt of wages — does not come to a man from his special art. If we are to speak strictly, the physician, as such, produces health; the builder, a house; and then each, in his further capacity of wage-earner, gets his pay. Thus every art has its own function and benefits its proper subject. But suppose the practitioner is not paid; does he then get any benefit from his art?

Clearly not.

And is he doing no good to anyone either, when he works for nothing?

No, I suppose he does some good.

Well then, Thrasymachus, it is now clear that no form of skill or authority provides for its own benefit. As we were saying some time ago, it always studies and prescribes what is good for its subject — the interest of the weaker party, not of the stronger. And that, my friend, is why I said that no one is willing to be in a position of authority and undertake to set straight other men's troubles, without demanding to be paid; because, if he is to do his work well, he will never, in his capacity of ruler, do, or command others to do, what is best for himself, but only what is best for the subject. For that reason, if he is to consent, he must have his recompense, in the shape of money or honour, or of punishment in case of refusal.

[margin note: unless wages are involved]

What do you mean, Socrates? asked Glaucon. I recognize two of your three kinds of reward; but I don't understand what you mean by speaking of punishment as a recompense.

Then you don't understand the recompense required by the best type of men, or their motive for accepting authority when they do consent. You surely know that a passion for honours or for money is rightly regarded as something to be ashamed of.

Yes, I do.

For that reason, I said, good men are unwilling to rule, either for money's sake or for honour. They have no wish to be called mercenary for demanding to be paid, or thieves for making a secret profit out of their office; nor yet will honours tempt them, for they are not ambitious. So they must be forced to consent under threat of penalty; that may be why a readiness to accept power under no such constraint is thought discreditable. And the heaviest penalty for declining to rule is to be ruled by someone inferior to yourself. That is the fear, I believe, that makes decent people accept power; and when they do so, they face the prospect of authority with no idea that they are coming into the enjoyment of a comfortable berth; it is forced upon them because they can find no one better than themselves, or even as good, to be entrusted with power. If there could ever be a society of perfect men, there might well be as much competition to evade office as there now is to gain it; and it would then be clearly seen that the genuine ruler's nature is to seek only the advantage of the subject, with the consequence that any man of understanding would sooner have another to do the best for him than be at the pains to do the best for that other himself. On this point, then, I entirely disagree with Thrasymachus' doctrine that right means what is to the interest of the stronger.

Notes

[1] A popular superstition, that if a wolf sees you first, you become dumb.

[2] In certain lawsuits the defendant, if found guilty, was allowed to propose a penalty alternative to that demanded by the prosecution. The judges then decided which should be inflicted. The 'costs' here means the fee which the sophist, unlike Socrates, expected from his pupils.

[3] All the persons mentioned have some interest. The craftsman *qua* craftsman has an interest in doing his work as well as possible, which is the same thing as serving the interest of the subjects on whom his craft is exercised; and the subjects have their interest, which the craftsman is there to promote.

2. Politics*

Aristotle

Chapter IX (vv. 1280a–1281a)

Let us first determine what are the proper limits of an oligarchy and a democracy, and
what is just in each of these states; for all men have some natural inclination to justice;
but they proceed therein only to a certain degree; nor can they universally point out what
is absolutely just; as, for instance, what is equal appears just, and is so; but not to all; only
among those who are equals: and what is unequal appears just, and is so; but not to all,
only amongst those who are unequals; which circumstance some people neglect, and
therefore judge ill; the reason for which is, they judge for themselves, and every one
almost is the worst judge in his own cause. Since then justice has reference to persons, the
same distinctions must be made with respect to persons which are made with respect to
things, in the manner that I have already described in my *Ethics*.

As to the equality of the things, these they agree in; but their dispute is concerning the
equality of the persons, and chiefly for the reason above assigned; because they judge ill
in their own cause; and also because each party thinks, that if they admit what is right in
some particulars, they have done justice on the whole: thus, for instance, if some persons
are unequal in riches, they suppose them unequal in the whole; or, on the contrary, if they
are equal in liberty, they suppose them equal in the whole: but what is absolutely just they
omit; for if civil society was founded for the sake of preserving and increasing property,
every one's right in the city would be equal to his fortune; and then the reasoning of those
who insist upon an oligarchy would be valid; for it would not be right that he who
contributed one mina should have an equal share in the hundred along with him who
brought in all the rest, either of the original money or what was afterwards acquired.

Nor was civil society founded merely to preserve the lives of its members; but that they
might live well: for otherwise a state might be composed of slaves, or the animal creation:

* Aristotle wrote the *Politics* circa 335–322 BCE. This particular selection was taken from
Aristotle, *A Treatise on Government*, Book III, Chapters IX–XIII, edited by Ernest Rhys, translated
by William Ellis, with an introduction by A.D. Lindsay (London: J.M. Dent & Sons, Ltd, 1900),
81–94.

but this is not so; for these have no share in the happiness of it; nor do they live after their own choice; nor is it an alliance mutually to defend each other from injuries, or for a commercial intercourse: for then the Tyrrhenians and Carthaginians, and all other nations between whom treaties of commerce subsist, would be citizens of one city; for they have articles to regulate their exports and imports, and engagements for mutual protection, and alliances for mutual defence; but yet they have not all the same magistrates established among them, but they are different among the different people; nor does the one take any care, that the morals of the other should be as they ought, or that none of those who have entered into the common agreements should be unjust, or in any degree vicious, only that they do not injure any member of the confederacy. But whosoever endeavours to establish wholesome laws in a state, attends to the virtues and the vices of each individual who composes it; from whence it is evident, that the first care of him who would found a city, truly deserving that name, and not nominally so, must be to have his citizens virtuous; for otherwise it is merely an alliance for self-defence; differing from those of the same cast which are made between different people only in place: for law is an agreement and a pledge, as the sophist Lycophron says, between the citizens of their intending to do justice to each other, though not sufficient to make all the citizens just and good: and that this is fact is evident, for could any one bring different places together, as, for instance, enclose Megara and Corinth in a wall, yet they would not be one city, not even if the inhabitants intermarried with each other, though this inter-community contributes much to make a place one city. Besides, could we suppose a set of people to live separate from each other, but within such a distance as would admit of an intercourse, and that there were laws subsisting between each party, to prevent their injuring one another in their mutual dealings, supposing one a carpenter, another a husbandman, shoemaker, and the like, and that their numbers were ten thousand, still all that they would have together in common would be a tariff for trade, or an alliance for mutual defence, but not the same city. And why? not because their mutual intercourse is not near enough, for even if persons so situated should come to one place, and every one should live in his own house as in his native city, and there should be alliances subsisting between each party to mutually assist and prevent any injury being done to the other, still they would not be admitted to be a city by those who think correctly, if they preserved the same customs when they were together as when they were separate.

It is evident, then, that a city is not a community of place; nor established for the sake of mutual safety or traffic with each other; but that these things are the necessary consequences of a city, although they may all exist where there is no city: but a city is a society of people joining together with their families and their children to live agreeably for the sake of having their lives as happy and as independent as possible: and for this purpose it is necessary that they should live in one place and intermarry with each other: hence in all cities there are family-meetings, clubs, sacrifices, and public entertainments to promote friendship; for a love of sociability is friendship itself; so that the end then for which a city is established is, that the inhabitants of it may live happy, and these things are conducive to that end: for it is a community of families and villages for the sake of a perfect independent life; that is, as we have already said, for the sake of living well and happily. It is not therefore founded for the purpose of men's merely living together, but for their living as men ought; for which reason those who contribute most to this end deserve to have greater power in the city than those who are their equals in family and freedom, but their inferiors in civil virtue, or those who excel them in wealth but are below them in worth. It is evident from what has been said, that in all disputes upon government each party says something that is just.

Chapter X (v. 1281a)

It may also be a doubt where the supreme power ought to be lodged. Shall it be with the majority, or the wealthy, with a number of proper persons, or one better than the rest, or with a tyrant? But whichever of these we prefer some difficulty will arise. For what? shall the poor have it because they are the majority? they may then divide among themselves what belongs to the rich: nor is this unjust; because truly it has been so judged by the supreme power. But what avails it to point out what is the height of injustice if this is not? Again, if the many seize into their own hands everything which belongs to the few, it is evident that the city will be at an end. But virtue will never destroy what is virtuous; nor can what is right be the ruin of the state: therefore such a law can never be right, nor can the acts of a tyrant ever be wrong, for of necessity they must all be just; for he, from his unlimited power, compels every one to obey his command, as the multitude oppress the rich. Is it right then that the rich, the few, should have the supreme power? and what if they be guilty of the same rapine and plunder the possessions of the majority, that will be as right as the other: but that all things of this sort are wrong and unjust is evident. Well then, these of the better sort shall have it: but must not then all the other citizens live unhonoured, without sharing the offices of the city; for the offices of a city are its honours, and if one set of men are always in power, it is evident that the rest must be without honour. Well then, let it be with one person of all others the fittest for it: but by this means the power will be still more contracted, and a greater number than before continue unhonoured. But some one may say, that it is wrong to let man have the supreme power and not the law, as his soul is subject to so many passions. But if this law appoints an aristocracy, or a democracy, how will it help us in our present doubts? for those things will happen which we have already mentioned.

Chapter XI (vv. 1281a–1282b)

Other particulars we will consider separately; but it seems proper to prove, that the supreme power ought to be lodged with the many, rather than with those of the better sort, who are few; and also to explain what doubts (and probably just ones) may arise: now, though not one individual of the many may himself be fit for the supreme power, yet when these many are joined together, it does not follow but they may be better qualified for it than those; and this not separately, but as a collective body; as the public suppers exceed those which are given at one person's private expense: for, as they are many, each person brings in his share of virtue and wisdom; and thus, coming together, they are like one man made up of a multitude, with many feet, many hands, and many intelligences: thus is it with respect to the manners and understandings of the multitude taken together; for which reason the public are the best judges of music and poetry; for some understand one part, some another, and all collectively the whole; and in this particular men of consequence differ from each of the many; as they say those who are beautiful do from those who are not so, and as fine pictures excel any natural objects, by collecting the several beautiful parts which were dispersed among different originals into one, although the separate parts, as the eye or any other, might be handsomer than in the picture.

But if this distinction is to be made between every people and every general assembly, and some few men of consequence, it may be doubtful whether it is true; nay, it is clear enough that, with respect to a few, it is not; since the same conclusion might be applied even to brutes: and indeed wherein do some men differ from brutes? Not but that nothing prevents what I have said being true of the people in some states. The doubt then which we have lately proposed, with all its consequences, may be settled in this manner; it is necessary that the freemen who compose the bulk of the people should have absolute power in some things; but as they are neither men of property, nor act uniformly upon principles of virtue, it is not safe to trust them with the first offices in the state, both on account of their iniquity and their ignorance; from the one of which they will do what is wrong, from the other they will mistake: and yet it is dangerous to allow them no power or share in the government; for when there are many poor people who are incapable of acquiring the honours of their country, the state must necessarily have many enemies in it; let them then be permitted to vote in the public assemblies and to determine causes; for which reason Socrates, and some other legislators, gave them the power of electing the officers of the state, and also of inquiring into their conduct when they came out of office, and only prevented their being magistrates by themselves; for the multitude when they are collected together have all of them sufficient understanding for these purposes, and, mixing among those of higher rank, are serviceable to the city, as some things, which alone are improper for food, when mixed with others make the whole more wholesome than a few of them would be.

But there is a difficulty attending this form of government, for it seems, that the person who himself was capable of curing any one who was then sick, must be the best judge whom to employ as a physician; but such a one must be himself a physician; and the same holds true in every other practice and art: and as a physician ought to give an account of his practice to a physician, so ought it to be in other arts: those whose business is physic may be divided into three sorts, the first of these is he who makes up the medicines; the second prescribes, and is to the other as the architect is to the mason; the third is he who understands the science, but never practises it: now these three distinctions may be found in those who understand all other arts; nor have we less opinion of their judgment who are only instructed in the principles of the art than of those who practise it: and with respect to elections the same method of proceeding seems right; for to elect a proper person in any science is the business of those who are skilful therein; as in geometry, of geometricians; in steering, of steersmen: but if some individuals should know something of particular arts and works, they do not know more than the professors of them: so that even upon this principle neither the election of magistrates, nor the censure of their conduct, should be entrusted to the many.

But probably all that has been here said may not be right; for, to resume the argument I lately used, if the people are not very brutal indeed, although we allow that each

individual knows less of these affairs than those who have given particular attention to
them, yet when they come together they will know them better, or at least not worse;
besides, in some particular arts it is not the workman only who is the best judge; namely,
in those the works of which are understood by those who do not profess them: thus he
who builds a house is not the only judge of it, for the master of the family who inhabits it
is a better; thus also a steersman is a better judge of a tiller than he who made it; and he
who gives an entertainment than the cook. What has been said seems a sufficient solution
of this difficulty; but there is another that follows: for it seems absurd that the power of
the state should be lodged with those who are but of indifferent morals, instead of those
who are of excellent characters. Now the power of election and censure are of the utmost
consequence, and this, as has been said, in some states they entrust to the people; for the
general assembly is the supreme court of all, and they have a voice in this, and deliberate
in all public affairs, and try all causes, without any objection to the meanness of their
circumstances, and at any age: but their treasurers, generals, and other great officers of
state are taken from men of great fortune and worth. This difficulty also may be solved
upon the same principle; and here too they may be right, for the power is not in the man
who is member of the assembly, or council, but the assembly itself, and the council, and
the people, of which each individual of the whole community are the parts, I mean as
senator, adviser, or judge; for which reason it is very right, that the many should have the
greatest powers their own hands; for the people, the council, and the judges are composed
of them, and the property of all these collectively is more than the property of any person,
or a few who fill the great offices of the state: and thus I determine these points.

The first question that we stated shows plainly, that the supreme power should be
lodged in laws duly made, and that the magistrate or magistrates, either one or more,
should be authorised to determine those cases which the laws cannot particularly speak
to, as it is impossible for them, in general language, to explain themselves upon
everything that may arise: but what these laws are which are established upon the best
foundations has not been yet explained, but still remains a matter of some question: but
the laws of every state will necessarily be like every state, either trifling or excellent, just
or unjust; for it is evident, that the laws must be framed correspondent to the constitution
of the government; and, if so, it is plain, that a well-formed government will have good
laws, a bad one, bad ones.

Chapter XII (vv. 1282b–1283a)

Since in every art and science the end aimed at is always good, so particularly in this,
which is the most excellent of all, the founding of civil society, the good wherein aimed
at is justice; for it is this which is for the benefit of all. Now, it is the common opinion,
that justice is a certain equality; and in this point all the philosophers are agreed when
they treat of morals: for they say what is just, and to whom; and that equals ought to
receive equal: but we should know how we are to determine what things are equal and
what unequal; and in this there is some difficulty, which calls for the philosophy of the
politician. Some persons will probably say, that the employments of the state ought to be
given according to every particular excellence of each citizen, if there is no other

difference between them and the rest of the community, but they are in every respect else alike: for justice attributes different things to persons differing from each other in their character, according to their respective merits. But if this is admitted to be true, complexion, or height, or any such advantage will be a claim for a greater share of the public rights. But that this is evidently absurd is clear from other arts and sciences; for with respect to musicians who play on the flute together, the best flute is not given to him who is of the best family, for he will play never the better for that, but the best instrument ought to be given to him who is the best artist. *doesn't want gov. to be based on blood, but on merit.*

oligarchy?

If what is now said does not make this clear, we will explain it still further: if there should be any one, a very excellent player on the flute, but very deficient in family and beauty, though each of them are more valuable endowments than a skill in music, and excel this art in a higher degree than that player excels others, yet the best flutes ought to be given to him; for the superiority in beauty and fortune should have a reference to the business in hand; but these have none. Moreover, according to this reasoning, every possible excellence might come in comparison with every other; for if bodily strength might dispute the point with riches or liberty, even any bodily strength might do it; so that if one person excelled in size more than another did in virtue, and his size was to qualify him to take place of the other's virtue, everything must then admit of a comparison with each other; for if such a size is greater than virtue by so much, it is evident another must be equal to it: but, since this is impossible, it is plain that it would be contrary to common sense to dispute a right to any office in the state from every superiority whatsoever: for if one person is slow and the other swift, neither is the one better qualified nor the other worse on that account, though in the gymnastic races a difference in these particulars would gain the prize; but a pretension to the offices of the state should be founded on a superiority in those qualifications which are useful to it: for which reason those of family, independency, and fortune, with great propriety, contend with each other for them; for these are the fit persons to fill them: for a city can no more consist of all poor men than it can of all slaves. But if such persons are requisite, it is evident that those also who are just and valiant are equally so; for without justice and valour no state can be supported, the former being necessary for its existence, the latter for its happiness.

Chapter XIII (vv. 1283a–1284b)

It seems, then, requisite for the establishment of a state, that all, or at least many of these particulars should be well canvassed and inquired into; and that virtue and education may most justly claim the right of being considered as the necessary means of making the citizens happy, as we have already said. As those who are equal in one particular are not therefore equal in all, and those who are unequal in one particular are not therefore unequal in all, it follows that all those governments which are established upon a principle which supposes they are, are erroneous.

We have already said, that all the members of the community will dispute with each other for the offices of the state; and in some particulars justly, but not so in general; the rich, for instance, because they have the greatest landed property, and the ultimate right to the soil is vested in the community; and also because their fidelity is in general most to be

against monarchy

depended on. The freemen and men of family will dispute the point with each other, as nearly on an equality; for these latter have a right to a higher regard as citizens than obscure persons, for honourable descent is everywhere of great esteem: nor is it an improper conclusion, that the descendants of men of worth will be men of worth themselves; for noble birth is the fountain of virtue to men of family: for the same reason also we justly say, that virtue has a right to put in her pretensions. Justice, for instance, is a virtue, and so necessary to society, that all others must yield her the precedence.

Let us now see what the many have to urge on their side against the few; and they may say, that if, when collectively taken, they are compared with them, they are stronger, richer, and better than they are. But should it ever happen that all these should inhabit the same city, I mean the good, the rich, the noble, as well as the many, such as usually make up the community, I ask, will there then be any reason to dispute concerning who shall govern, or will there not? for in every community which we have mentioned there is no dispute where the supreme power should be placed; for as these differ from each other, so do those in whom that is placed; for in one state the rich enjoy it, in others the meritorious, and thus each according to their separate manners. Let us however consider what is to be done when all these happen at the same time to inhabit the same city. If the virtuous should be very few in number, how then shall we act? shall we prefer the virtuous on account of their abilities, if they are capable of governing the city? or should they be so many as almost entirely to compose the state?

There is also a doubt concerning the pretensions of all those who claim the honours of government: for those who found them either on fortune or family have nothing which they can justly say in their defence; since it is evident upon their principle, that if any one person can be found richer than all the rest, the right of governing all these will be justly vested in this one person. In the same manner, one man who is of the best family will claim it from those who dispute the point upon family merit: and probably in an aristocracy the same dispute might arise on the score of virtue, if there is one man better than all the other men of worth who are in the same community; it seems just, by the same reasoning, that he should enjoy the supreme power. And upon this principle also, while the many suppose they ought to have the supreme command, as being more powerful than the few, if one or more than one, though a small number, should be found stronger than themselves, these ought rather to have it than they.

All these things seem to make it plain, that none of these principles are justly founded on which these persons would establish their right to the supreme power; and that all men whatsoever ought to obey them: for with respect to those who claim it as due to their virtue or their fortune, they might have justly some objection to make; for nothing hinders but that it may sometimes happen, that the many may be better or richer than the few, not as individuals, but in their collective capacity.

As to the doubt which some persons have proposed and objected, we may answer it in this manner; it is this, whether a legislator, who would establish the most perfect system of laws, should calculate them for the use of the better part of the citizens, or the many, in the circumstances we have already mentioned? The rectitude of anything consists in its equality; that therefore which is equally right will be advantageous to the whole state, and to every member of it in common.

Now, in general, a citizen is one who both shares in the government and also in his turn submits to be governed; their condition, it is true, is different in different states: the best is that in which a man is enabled to choose and to persevere in a course of virtue during his whole life, both in his public and private state. But should there be one person, or a very few, eminent for an uncommon degree of virtue, though not enough to make up a civil state, so that the virtue of the many, or their political abilities, should be too inferior to come in comparison with theirs, if more than one; or if but one, with his only; such are not to be considered as part of the city; for it would be doing them injustice to rate them on a level with those who are so far their inferiors in virtue and political abilities, that they appear to them like a god amongst men. From whence it is evident, that a system of laws must be calculated for those who are equal to each other in nature and power. Such men, therefore, are not the object of law; for they are themselves a law: and it would be ridiculous in any one to endeavour to include them in the penalties of a law: for probably they might say what Antisthenes tells us the lions did to the hares when they demanded to be admitted to an equal share with them in the government. And it is on this account that democratic states have established the ostracism; for an equality seems the principal object of their government. For which reason they compel all those who are very eminent for their power, their fortune, their friendships, or any other cause which may give them too great weight in the government, to submit to the ostracism, and leave the city for a stated time; as the fabulous histories relate the Argonauts served Hercules, for they refused to take him with them in the ship *Argo* on account of his superior valour. For which reason those who hate a tyranny and find fault with the advice which Periander gave to Thrasybulus, must not think there was nothing to be said in its defence; for the story goes, that Periander said nothing to the messenger in answer to the business he was consulted about, but striking off those ears of corn which were higher than the rest, reduced the whole crop to a level; so that the messenger, without knowing the cause of what was done, related the fact to Thrasybulus, who understood by it that he must take off all the principal men in the city. Nor is this serviceable to tyrants only; nor is it tyrants only who do it; for the same thing is practised both in oligarchies and democracies; for the ostracism has in a manner nearly the same power, by restraining and banishing those who are too great; and what is done in one city is done also by those who have the supreme power in separate states; as the Athenians with respect to the Samians, the Chians, and the Lesbians; for when they suddenly acquired the superiority over all Greece, they brought the other states into subjection, contrary to the treaties which subsisted between them. The King of Persia also very often reduces the Medes and Babylonians when they assume upon their former power: and this is a principle which all governments whatsoever keep in their eye; even those which are best administered, as well as those which are not, do it; these for the sake of private utility, the others for the public good.

The same thing is to be perceived in the other arts and sciences; for a painter would not represent an animal with a foot disproportionally large, though he had drawn it remarkably beautiful; nor would the shipwright make the prow or any other part of the vessel larger than it ought to be; nor will the master of the band permit any who sings louder and better than the rest to sing in concert with them. There is therefore no reason that a monarch should not act in agreement with free states, to support his own power, if they do the same thing for the benefit of their respective communities; upon which account when there is any acknowledged difference in the power of the citizens, the reason upon which the ostracism is founded will be politically just; but it is better for the legislator so to establish his state at the beginning as not to want this remedy: but if in course of time such an inconvenience should arise, to endeavour to amend it by some such correction. Not that this was the use it was put to: for many did not regard the benefit of their respective communities, but made the ostracism a weapon in the hand of sedition.

It is evident, then, that in corrupt governments it is partly just and useful to the individual, though probably it is as clear that it is not entirely just: for in a well-governed state there may be great doubts about the use of it, not on account of the pre-eminence which one may have in strength, riches, or connection: but when the pre-eminence is virtue, what then is to be done? for it seems not right to turn out and banish such a one; neither does it seem right to govern him, for that would be like desiring to share the power with Jupiter and to govern him: nothing then remains but what indeed seems natural, and that is for all persons quietly to submit to the government of those who are thus eminently virtuous, and let them be perpetually kings in the separate states.

3. The Social Contract*

Jean-Jacques Rousseau

Book I.

I wish to discover whether, in the existing social order, there may not be some rule of safe and legitimate administration, taking men as they are, and laws as they might be. I shall try to ally, in this research, that which the law permits with that which interest prescribes, so that justice and utility may not be divided.

I enter upon this discussion without proving the importance of the subject. I shall be asked if I am a prince or a legislator, that I write about politics. I shall answer, No, — and that for this reason I write about politics. If I were a prince or a legislator, I should not lose time in telling what ought to be done; I should do it or be silent.

Born citizen of a free state[1] and member of the sovereign people, however feeble the influence of my voice in public affairs, the right to vote upon them imposes upon me the duty of instructing myself. Whenever I meditate upon governments I am happy to find in my investigations new reasons for loving that of my own country.

Chapter I.
Subject of the First Book.

Man is born free, and he is everywhere in chains. A man believes himself the master of others, but is for all that more a slave than they. How is this brought about? I do not know. What could make it legitimate? I think I can answer this question.

If I considered force alone and the effects derived from it, I should say: As long as a

---

* *The Social Contract* was originally published in 1762. This particular selection was taken from Rousseau, *The Social Contract or the Principles of Political Rights*, Book I, Chapters I–IX, translated by Rose M. Harrington, with introduction and notes by Edward L. Walter (New York: G.P. Putnam's Sons, 1893), 1–33.

people is compelled to obey and obeys, it does well; as soon as it can shake off the yoke, and shakes it off, it does better: for, recovering its liberty by the same right by which it was taken away, either a people is justified in recovering its liberty, or there was no justification in taking it away.

Social order is a sacred right which serves as a basis for all others. But this right does not come from nature; it is founded upon conventions. We must know what these conventions are; but before reaching that point I must establish what I have just asserted.

Chapter II.
The First Societies.

The most ancient of all societies, and the only natural one, is that of the family; yet children remain dependent upon the father only as long as they have need of him for self-preservation. As soon as this need ceases, the natural bond is dissolved. The children, exempt from the obedience which they owed to the father; the father, exempt from the care which he owed to his children, become equally independent. If they remain united it is no longer naturally, it is voluntarily; and the family itself is maintained only by agreement.

This common liberty is a consequence of the nature of man. His first law is that of self-preservation, his first cares are those which he owes to himself; and as soon as he has reached years of discretion, he alone being judge of the means necessary for his preservation, becomes thereby his own master.

The family is, then, if you will, the first model of political societies: the chief is the father, the people are the children; and all being born equal and free, alienate their liberty only for their benefit. All the difference is that, in the family, the love of the father for his children pays him for his care of them, and in the state the pleasure of commanding makes up for the love which the chief has not for his people.

Grotius[2] denies that all human power is established in favor of those who are governed: he cites slavery as an example. His most ordinary mode of reasoning is to establish right by fact.[3] A method might be employed which would be more logical, but not more favorable to tyrants.

It is doubtful then, according to Grotius, whether mankind belongs to a hundred men, or the hundred men belong to mankind; and he seems throughout his book to lean to the first opinion; it is also Hobbes'[4] opinion. So here is the human species divided into herds, each having a chief, who guards only to devour it.

As a herdsman is of a nature superior to his herd, the pastors of men, who are their chiefs, are also of a nature superior to their people. The Emperor Caligula[5] reasoned thus, according to Philo,[6] concluding from this analogy that kings are gods, or that the people are brutes.

The reasoning of Caligula amounts to that of Hobbes and Grotius. Aristotle said before any of them that men were not naturally equal, but that some were born for slavery, and others for domination.

Aristotle[7] was right, but he took the effect for the cause. Every man, born in slavery, is born for slavery, nothing is more certain. Slaves lose all in their chains, even the desire to leave them; they love servitude as the companions of Ulysses[8] loved brutishness. If then, there are slaves by nature, it is because there have been slaves contrary to nature. Force made the first slaves, their cowardice perpetuated them.

I have said nothing of King Adam, nor of Emperor Noah, father of three great monarchs who shared the universe, as did the children of Saturn, whom some think they recognize in them.[9] I hope, I shall receive credit for this moderation, for descending directly from one of these princes, and perhaps from the elder branch, how do I know whether, by the verification of titles, I should not find myself the legitimate king of mankind? However that may be, it cannot be denied that Adam was sovereign of the world, as Robinson of his island, as long as he was the only inhabitant, and what was convenient in this empire was that the monarch, safe upon his throne, had neither rebellion, nor war, nor conspirators to fear.

Chapter III.
The Right of the Strongest. Force

The strongest is never strong enough to be always master, unless he transforms his strength into right, and obedience to duty. Machiavelli is wrong

From this comes the right of the strongest; a right taken ironically in appearance, and established really in principle. Strength is physical power; I do not see what moral force could result from its action. To yield to force is an act of necessity, not of will; it is at the most an act of prudence. In what sense could it be a duty?

Let us for a moment grant this pretended right. I say that there would result from it only an inexplicable muddle; for as soon as it is strength that makes right, the effect changes with the cause: any force which overcomes first succeeds to the right. As soon as disobedience can be practised with impunity, it can be practised legitimately; and as the strongest is always right, it is only necessary to arrange always to be strongest. Now, what is a right which perishes when strength ceases? If obedience must be rendered to strength, it is not necessary to obey from duty; and if obedience is not exacted, it is not necessary to obey. It may be seen then that the word *right* adds nothing to strength; it has no significance here.

Obey them that have the rule over you. If that means, yield to force, the precept is good, but superfluous: I answer for its never being violated.

All power comes from God, I acknowledge it; but all sickness comes from Him too: does that mean that it is forbidden to call a physician? If a brigand surprises me in a wood, I am forced to give him my purse; but if I could conceal it, am I in conscience bound to give it up? For the pistol which he carries in his hand is a power.

Let us agree, then, that strength does not make right, and that obedience only to legitimate power is obligatory. So my original question comes up again.

Chapter IV.
Slavery.[10]

Since no man has natural authority over his kind, and since strength does not make right, there remains only agreement for the basis of all legitimate authority among men.

If one individual, said Grotius, can alienate his liberty and make himself the slave of a master, why cannot a whole people alienate its liberty, and make itself subject to a king? There are many words there which require explanation, but let us take the word *alienate*. To alienate is to give or sell. Now a man who makes himself the slave of another does not give himself, he sells himself, at the least for his subsistence; but a people, — why should it sell itself? A king is far from furnishing his subjects their subsistence, he draws his from them; and, according to Rabelais,[11] a king does not live upon little. Subjects, then, give their persons on condition that their goods shall be taken also. I do not see what they have left to preserve.

It will be said that the despot assures his subjects civil tranquillity; so be it; but what do they gain by it, if the wars which his ambition brings upon them, if his insatiable avidity, if the vexations of his ministry, despoil them more than their own dissensions? What do they gain by it, if this tranquillity is itself but a misfortune? Tranquillity of life can also be found in a prison; is that enough to bring contentment?

The Greeks shut up in the Cyclops'[12] cave lived there tranquilly, waiting their turn to be devoured.

To say that a man gives himself gratuitously is to say something absurd and inconceivable; such an act is illegitimate and null, for the reason alone that he who has done it is not in his right mind. To say the same thing of a whole people is to suppose a people of madmen, — madness does not make right.

If each man could alienate himself he could not alienate his children, they are born men and free; their liberty belongs to them, no one else has a right to dispose of it. Before they have reached years of discretion the father can, in their name, stipulate conditions for their preservation, for their welfare, but cannot give them away irrevocably and without condition, for such a gift is contrary to the ends of nature, and exceeds the rights of paternity. It would be necessary, then, in order that an arbitrary government be legitimate, that in each generation the people be at liberty to admit or reject it, but then the government would no longer be arbitrary.

To renounce liberty is to renounce the quality of manhood, the rights of humanity, and even its duties. There is no possible compensation for him who renounces everything. Such a renunciation is incompatible with the nature of man; and it takes all moral force from his actions to take away all liberty from his will. Finally, it is a vain and contradictory agreement to stipulate absolute authority on one side and obedience without limit on the other. Is it not clear that there is no obligation towards one from whom you have the right to demand everything? And does not this one condition without equivalent or exchange involve the nullity of the act? For what right would a slave have against me, since all that he has belongs to me, and his right being mine, to talk of my right against myself is absurd.

Grotius and others find in war another origin of the pretended right of slavery. The conqueror having, according to them, the right to kill the conquered, the latter can buy back his life at the expense of his liberty; an agreement the more legitimate as it turns to the profit of both.

But it is clear that this pretended right to kill the conquered, results in no way from the state of war. From the fact alone, that men, living in their primitive independence, have not among themselves relations sufficiently permanent to constitute either the state of peace or the state of war, they are not naturally enemies. It is the relation of things and not of men that constitutes war; and as it is impossible for war to arise from simple personal relations, but only from property relations, private war or war between man and man can exist neither in the state of nature where there is no permanent property, nor in the social state, where all is under the authority of the laws.

Single combats, duels, and encounters are acts which do not constitute a state of war; and in regard to private wars, authorized by the *Establishments*[13] of Louis IX., King of France, and suspended by the Peace of God,[14] they are abuses of feudal government — an absurd system, if ever there was one, contrary to the principles of natural right and of all good polity.

War, then, is not a relation between man and man, but a relation between state and state, in which individuals are enemies only by accident, not as men, nor even as citizens,[15] but as soldiers; not as members of the country, but as its defenders. Finally, each state can have only other states, not men, for enemies, because between things of such different natures no real relation can be fixed.

This principle conforms to the maxims established in all times and by the constant practice of all civilized nations. Declarations of war are less notifications to the powers than to their subjects. The foreigner, whether he be king or individual or people, who steals, kills, or confines subjects, without declaring war to the Prince, is not an enemy, but a brigand. Even in open war a just prince seizes, perhaps, anything that belongs to the public, but he respects the person and property of individuals; he respects rights upon which his own are founded. The object of war being the destruction of the enemies of the state, the conqueror has the right to kill its defenders as long as they bear arms; but as soon as they yield their arms and give themselves up, they become men simply, and the conqueror has no further right over their lives. Sometimes a state may be killed, without killing a single one of its members: war gives no rights which are not necessary to its object. These principles are not those of Grotius; they are not founded upon the authority of poets; but they are derived from the nature of things, and are founded upon reason.

In regard to the right of conquest it has no foundation except the law of the strongest. If war does not give to the victor the right to massacre the vanquished people, this right which they have not cannot be the foundation of one to enslave them. The victor has not the right to kill the enemy except when he cannot enslave him; the right to enslave does not come, then, from the right to kill; it is then an unjust exchange to make him buy with his liberty his life, over which no one has any right. In establishing the right of life and death upon that of slavery, and the right of slavery upon the right of life and death, is it not clear that we reason in a circle?

In supposing even this terrible right to kill everybody, I say that a slave made in war, or a conquered people, has no obligations with regard to his master, except to obey him as long as he is forced to do it. In taking an equivalent for his life the victor has not spared it;

instead of killing him without profit, he has killed him profitably. He is far from having acquired any authority over him except that of force; the state of war exists between them as before; their relation itself is the effect of it, and the exercise of the right of war supposes no treaty of peace. They have made an agreement, — so be it; but this agreement far from destroying the state of war, supposes its continuity.

Thus, from whatever direction the subject is regarded, the right of slavery is null; not only because it is illegitimate, but because it is absurd and signifies nothing. The words slave and right are contradictory — they mutually exclude each other. Whether from man to man, or from man to a people, this discourse will always be alike senseless: "I make an agreement with you, entirely at your expense and to my profit, which I will observe as long as I please, and which you will observe as long as it pleases me."

Chapter V.
Returning to the First Agreement. *the social contract*

Should I accord all that I have refuted up to this time, the abettors of despotism would be no further advanced. There will always be a great difference between subduing a multitude and governing a society.

If scattered individuals are successively enslaved by a single man, in whatever number it may be, I see in it only a master and slaves, I do not see a people and its chief: it is, if you will, an aggregation but not an association; there is neither public property nor political body. This man, had he enslaved half the world would still be but an individual; his interest, separated from that of others, is always a private interest. Should this man die, his empire would remain after him, scattered and without union, as an oak dissolves and falls in a heap of cinders after having been consumed by fire.

"A people," says Grotius, "can give itself to a king." According to Grotius, a people is a people before giving itself to a king. This gift is a civil act, it supposes public deliberation. Before examining, then, the act by which a people chooses a king, it would be well to examine the act by which a people becomes a people; for this act, necessarily preceding the other, is the true foundation of society.

In fact, if there were no previous agreement, where would be — unless the election were unanimous — the obligation of the minority to submit to the majority? and how would a hundred who desire a master have the right to vote for ten who do not desire it? The law of plurality of suffrages is itself established by agreement, and supposes unanimity at least in the beginning.

Chapter VI.
The Social Compact.[16]

I suppose man arrived at a point where obstacles, which prejudice his preservation in the state of nature, outweigh, by their resistance, the force which each individual can employ to maintain himself in this condition. Then the primitive state can no longer exist; and mankind would perish did it not change its way of life.

Now, as men cannot engender new forces, but can only unite and direct those which exist, they have no other means of preservation than to form by aggregation a sum of forces which could prevail against resistance, and to put them in play by a single motive and make them act in concert.

This sum of forces can be established only by the concurrence of many; but the strength and liberty of each man being the primary instruments of his preservation, how can he pledge them without injury to himself and without neglecting the care which he owes to himself? This difficulty as related to my subject may be stated as follows:

"To find a form of association which shall defend and protect with the public force the person and property of each associate, and by means of which each, uniting with all, shall obey however only himself, and remain as free as before." Such is the fundamental problem of which the *Social Contract* gives the solution.

The clauses of this contract are so determined by the nature of the act, that the least modification would render them vain and of no effect; so that, although they may, perhaps, never have been formally enunciated, they are everywhere the same, everywhere tacitly admitted and recognized until, the social compact being violated, each enters again into his first rights and resumes his natural liberty, — thereby losing the conventional liberty for which he renounced it.

These clauses, clearly understood, may be reduced to one: that is, the total alienation of each associate with all his rights to the entire community, — for, first, each giving himself entirely, the condition is the same for all; and the conditions being the same for all, no one has an interest in making it onerous for the others.

Further, the alienation being without reserve, the union is as complete as it can be, and no associate has anything to claim: for, if some rights remained to individuals, as there would be no common superior who could decide between them and the public, each, being in some points his own judge, would soon profess to be so in everything; the state of nature would subsist, and the association would necessarily become tyrannical and useless. *no one (one person)* ←*you are empowering the community, not a ruler*

Finally, each giving himself to all, gives himself to none; and as there is not an associate over whom he does not acquire the same right as is ceded, an equivalent is gained for all that is lost, and more force to keep what he has.

If, then, we remove from the social contract all that is not of its essence, it will be reduced to the following terms: "Each of us gives in common his person and all his force under the supreme direction of the general will; and we receive each member as an indivisible part of the whole."

Immediately, instead of the individual person of each contracting party, this act of association produces a moral and collective body, composed of as many members as the assembly has votes, which receives from this same act its unity, — its common being, its life and its will. This public personage, thus formed by the union of all the others, formerly took the name of city, and now takes that of republic or body politic. This is called the *state* by its members when it is passive; the *sovereign* when it is active; and a *power* when comparing it to its equals. With regard to the associates, they take collectively the name *people*, and call themselves individually *citizens*, as participating in the sovereign authority, and *subjects*, as submitted to the laws of the state. But these terms are often confounded and are taken one for the other. It is enough to know how to distinguish them when they are employed with all precision.

Chapter VII.
The Sovereign. (the people)

We see by this formula that the act of association includes a reciprocal engagement between the public and individuals, and that each individual contracting, so to speak, with himself, finds himself engaged under a double relation: *i.e.*, as member of the sovereign to the individuals, and as member of the state to the sovereign. But the maxim of civil law, that no one is bound by engagements made with himself, cannot be applied here, for there is a great difference between an obligation to one's self and to a whole, of which the individual forms a part.

It should be observed, too, that public deliberation, — which may bind all subjects to the sovereign, on account of the two different relations under which each of them is considered, — cannot for the contrary reason bind the sovereign towards himself, and that consequently it is against the nature of the body politic that the sovereign impose upon himself a law which he cannot infringe. Being unable to consider himself except under the one relation, he is then in the position of an individual contracting with himself; whereby it is evident that there is not and cannot be any sort of obligatory fundamental law for the body of the people, not even the social contract. This does not mean that the body cannot engage itself perfectly towards others, in that which is not derogatory to this contract; for with regard to the foreigner, he becomes a simple being, an individual.

But the body politic or the sovereign, deriving its existence only from the sanctity of the contract, can never bind itself even towards others, to anything which is derogatory to this first act, — as to alienate some part of itself, or to submit to another sovereign. To violate the act by which it exists would be self-annihilation; and that which is nothing produces nothing.

As soon as this multitude is thus united into a body, one of the members cannot be injured without attacking the body, and still less can the body be injured without the members feeling its effects. Thus duty and interest alike oblige the two contracting parties to mutually aid each other; and the same men should seek to unite under this double relation, all the advantages which may be derived from it.

Now the sovereign, being formed only of the individuals comprising it, neither has nor could have interests contrary to theirs; consequently the sovereign power has no need of guaranty towards the subjects, for it is impossible for the body to seek to injure all its members; and it will be seen hereafter that it can injure no one in particular.

The sovereign by the fact alone that it is, is always what it must be.

But this is not true of subjects towards a sovereign, to whom in spite of common interests, nothing binds them to their engagements unless means are taken to assure their fidelity. In fact each individual can, as man, have an individual will contrary to or different from the general will which he has as a citizen: his individual interest may speak quite differently from the common interest; his absolute and naturally independent existence may make him consider what he owes to the common cause as a gratuitous contribution, the loss of which would be less injurious to others than the payment of it would be onerous to him; and regarding the moral entity which constitutes the state as a legal fiction, because it is not a man, he would like to enjoy the rights of a citizen, without being willing to fulfil the duties of a subject; an injustice, the progress of which would cause the ruin of the body politic.

Punishment for going against social contract

In order then that the social compact may not be an idle formula, it includes tacitly this engagement, which alone can give force to the others, that whoever shall refuse to obey the general will, shall be compelled to it by the whole body, which signifies nothing if not that he will be forced to be free; for it is this condition which, giving each citizen to the country, guarantees him from all personal dependence, a condition which forms the device and working of the political machine, and alone renders civil engagements legitimate, which without that would be absurd, tyrannical, and subject to great abuse.

Chapter VIII.
The Civil State.

The passage from the state of nature to the civil state produces in man a very remarkable change, by substituting in his conduct justice for interest, and giving to his actions a moral force which they lacked before. Then only does the voice of duty succeed to physical impulse, and law to appetite, and man who until then had thought only of himself, sees himself forced to act upon other principles, and to consult his reason before listening to his desires. Although he deprives himself in this state of several advantages which he holds from nature, he gains other advantages so great — his faculties exercise and develop, his ideas expand, his sentiments become ennobled, his whole spirit is elevated to such a point that, if the abuse of this new condition did not often degrade him below that from which he came, he ought to bless without ceasing the happy moment which took him from it forever, and which has made of a dull, stupid animal, an intelligent being — a man.

Let us reduce all this account to terms which may be easily compared: What man loses by the social contract is his natural liberty and an unlimited right to anything that tempts him, which he can obtain; what he gains is civil liberty and the ownership of all that he possesses. Not to be deceived in these compensations, we must distinguish the natural liberty, which has no limits but the strength of the individual, from civil liberty, which is limited by the general will; and possession, which is only the effect of the force or right of the first occupant, from the ownership which is founded only upon a positive title.

After what precedes, there ought to be added to the credit side of the civil state, that of moral liberty, which alone renders man master of himself; for the impulse of one appetite is slavery, and obedience to self-prescribed law is liberty. But I have already said too much about this. The philosophical meaning of the word liberty is not a part of my subject here.

Ignorance of the law is not an excuse

Chapter IX.
Realty. property & possessions

[margin handwriting: right of 1st occupant = native]

Each member of the community gives himself to it, as soon as it is formed, such as he then is, himself and all his force of which his property forms a part. It is not that, by this act, the possession changes its nature in changing hands, and becomes property in the hands of the sovereign; but as the strength of the city is incomparably greater than that of an individual, the public possession is also, in fact stronger and more irrevocable, without being more legitimate, at least as regards foreigners; for the state, in regard to its members, is master of all their property by the social contract, which, in the state, serves as the basis of all rights, but the state is not master with regard to other powers, except by the right of the first occupant which it holds from individuals.

The right of the first occupant, although more real than that of the strongest, does not become a true right until after the establishment of that of ownership. Every man has naturally a right to everything that is necessary to him; but the positive act which makes him proprietor of certain property excludes him from the rest. His part being taken he must limit himself to it, and has no further right to the community.

This is why the right of the first occupant, — so weak in a state of nature, — is respected by every man in civil life. Under this law, that which belongs to others is less respected than that which is not one's own. *[margin handwriting: taking the side of the colonizer]*

In general, to authorize the right of the first occupant upon any territory, the following conditions are necessary: first, that the land shall never have been occupied; second, that only such a quantity be occupied as will be necessary for subsistence; third, that it be taken possession of not by an empty ceremony but by labor and cultivation, — the only sign of ownership which, in default of legal title, should be respected by others.

In fact, in according to necessity and labor the right of the first occupant, is it not going as far as would be justifiable? Can the limits of this right be defined? Would it suffice to set foot upon common territory, and to profess immediately to be its master? Would it be enough to have the force to remove other people for a moment, in order to take from them the right ever to return? How can a man or a people seize upon an immense territory, and deprive all the rest of mankind of it, otherwise than by punishable usurpation, for they take from other men the dwelling-place and food which nature gives them in common?

When Nunez Balboa[17] took, upon the shore, possession of the South Seas and all South America, in the name of the Crown of Castile, was that enough to dispossess all the inhabitants, and to exclude from it all the princes of the world? Upon such a footing these ceremonies multiplied uselessly; and the Catholic king had only suddenly to take possession of the whole universe, cutting off only from his empire what had previously been possessed by other princes.

It may be conceived how the lands of individuals united and contiguous become public territory, and how the right of sovereignty, extending from the subjects to the lands which they occupy, becomes at the same time real and personal; which places the possessors in a state of greater dependence, and makes of their force itself a guaranty of their fidelity; an advantage which seems not to have been appreciated by monarchs of former times, who called themselves kings of the Persians, of the Scythians, of the Macedonians, seeming to regard themselves as chiefs of men rather than masters of the country. Those of to-day call themselves more clearly kings[18] of France, Spain, England. In thus holding the territory, they are quite sure of holding the inhabitants.

What is singular in this alienation is that, far from despoiling the individual in accepting his property, the community assures him of its legitimate possession; it changes usurpation into a veritable right, and enjoyment into ownership.

The owners now being considered as depositories of the public property, their rights being respected by all the members of the state and maintained with all their force against the stranger, — by a transfer which is advantageous to the public and more so to themselves, they have, so to speak, acquired all that they have given: a paradox easily explained by the distinction of rights which the sovereign and the proprietor have over the same property, as will be seen later.

It might happen, too, that men began to unite together before possessing anything, and that taking possession of a territory sufficient for all, they enjoy it in common, or divide it among themselves either equally or in the proportions established by the sovereign. In whatever way the acquisition is made, the right which each individual has over his own property is subordinate to the right which the community has over all; without this there would be neither solidity in the social tie, nor real force in the exercise of sovereignty.

I will finish this chapter and this book by a statement, which must serve as the basis of all social systems; it is that, instead of destroying natural equality, the fundamental compact substitutes, on the contrary, a moral and legitimate equality for that which nature may have given of physical inequality among men; and while they may be unequal in strength or genius, they become equal by agreement and right.[19]

Notes

[1] Born in Geneva in 1712; lost his rights as citizen when he embraced the Roman Catholic faith in 1728; restored to his rights as citizen when he returned to the Protestant faith in 1754. — ED.

[2] Hugo de Groot, better known by the Latinized form of the name, Grotius, Dutch statesman, jurist, and theologian, born 1583, died 1645. His treatise, *De Jure Belli et Pacis*, is usually considered the foundation of modern international law. — ED.

[3] "Learned researches upon public rights are often only the history of ancient abuses; and it is lost labor to take the trouble to study them too much." (*Traité des Intérêts de la France avec ses Voisins*, par M. Le Marquis d'Argenson, imprimé chez Rey, à Amsterdam.) This is exactly what Grotius does.

[4] Thomas Hobbes of Malmesbury, celebrated English philosopher, the ablest defender in his day of absolute governments, born 1588, died 1679. — ED.

[5] Caligula, Emperor of Rome from A.D. 37 to 41, born 12. — ED.

[6] Philo, called Judæus, a native of Alexandria, born about 20 B.C. He came to Rome to intercede with Caligula for his fellow Jews in 40 A.D. He left voluminous writings on philosophical subjects. — ED.

[7] Aristotle, the celebrated Greek philosopher and preceptor of Alexander, born B.C. 384, died 322. — ED.

[8] See *Odyssey*, X.–XII. — ED.

[9] See Locke's *Treatise on Government*, Book I., Chapter XI. — ED.

[10] Compare Locke, II., 4. — ED.

[11] François Rabelais, French writer, born in the latter half of the fifteenth century, died about 1550. For the allusion in the text, see Book I. of his celebrated romance, Chapters VII. and VIII., the provision made for the child Gargantua. — ED.

[12] See *Odyssey*, IX. — ED.

[13] The *Éstablissements* of Louis IX., born in 1215, King of France from 1226 to 1270, is the collection of the legislative measures passed by the king during his long reign. It is only by implication that Louis can be said to have authorized private wars. By instituting in 1245 *le Quarantaine du Roi*, establishing a truce of forty days between the families of the offender and the offended, counting from the day of the offence, he may be said to have impliedly authorized them at other times. But in 1257 he prohibited all private wars on the lands subject to him, and in 1260 he forbade also the trial by combat. — ED.

[14] The Peace of God, proclaimed by the council of bishops of Gaul in 1035; in 1041, the Truce of God, proclaimed by the same bishops, commanding peace for all Christians between Wednesday evening and Monday morning. — ED.

[15] The Romans, who understood and respected the rights of war more than any other nation of the world, carried their scruples in this regard so far that a citizen was not permitted to serve as a volunteer, without engaging expressly against the enemy, and by name against a certain enemy. A legion, in which the younger Cato [See Cicero, *De Officiis*, I., II, 36.–ED.] took his first lessons in arms under Popilius, having been re-formed, Cato, the elder, wrote to Popilius that, if he wished his son to continue to serve under him, he must have him take a new military oath, because, the first being annulled, he could no longer bear arms against the enemy. The same Cato wrote to his son, to take care not to present himself in the combat until he had taken the new oath. I know that I may be met with the siege of Clusium [See Livy, V., 35–37. — ED.] and other special facts, but I cite laws and usages. The Romans are the people who have least frequently violated their laws, and are the only nation whose laws have been so good.

[16] Compare Hobbes, *Leviathan*, Chaps. XVII. and XVIII.; Locke, *Treatise*, II., 7 and 8. — ED.

[17] Vasco Nunez de Balboa, born 1475, died 1517. Spanish adventurer, discovered the Pacific Ocean from a mountain in the Isthmus of Panama in September, 1513. — ED.

[18] The ruler of the present German Empire is entitled, by express agreement among the German states, Deutscher Kaiser, and not Kaiser Deutschlands. — ED.

[19] Under bad governments this equality is only apparent and illusory; it serves only to maintain the poor in his misery and the rich in his usurpation. In fact laws are always useful to those who possess, and injurious to those who have nothing; from which it follows that the social state is advantageous to man only when he has some property, and that no one has too much.

4. An Answer to the Question: 'What is Enlightenment?'[*][1]

Immanuel Kant

Enlightenment is man's emergence from his self-incurred immaturity. Immaturity is the inability to use one's own understanding without the guidance of another. This immaturity is *self-incurred* if its cause is not lack of understanding, but lack of resolution and courage to use it without the guidance of another. The motto of enlightenment is therefore: *Sapere aude!*[2] Have courage to use your *own* understanding!

Laziness and cowardice are the reasons why such a large proportion of men, even when nature has long emancipated them from alien guidance (*naturaliter maiorennes*),[3] nevertheless gladly remain immature for life. For the same reasons, it is all too easy for others to set themselves up as their guardians. It is so convenient to be immature! If I have a book to have understanding in place of me, a spiritual adviser to have a conscience for me, a doctor to judge my diet for me, and so on, I need not make any efforts at all. I need not think, so long as I can pay; others will soon enough take the tiresome job over for me. The guardians who have kindly taken upon themselves the work of supervision will soon see to it that by far the largest part of mankind (including the entire fair sex) should consider the step forward to maturity not only as difficult but also as highly dangerous. Having first infatuated their domesticated animals, and carefully prevented the docile creatures from daring to take a single step without the leading-strings to which

[*] This essay was originally published in 1784. This particular translation of the essay was taken from Kant, 'An Answer to the Question: "What is Enlightenment?"' in *Kant's Political Writings*, edited by Hans Reiss and translated by H.B. Nisbet (Cambridge: Cambridge University Press, 1970), 54–60, 192-193.

they are tied, they next show them the danger which threatens them if they try to walk unaided. Now this danger is not in fact so very great, for they would certainly learn to walk eventually after a few falls. But an example of this kind is intimidating, and usually frightens them off from further attempts.

Thus it is difficult for each separate individual to work his way out of the immaturity which has become almost second nature to him. He has even grown fond of it and is really incapable for the time being of using his own understanding, because he was never allowed to make the attempt. Dogmas and formulas, those mechanical instruments for rational use (or rather misuse) of his natural endowments, are the ball and chain of his permanent immaturity. And if anyone did throw them off, he would still be uncertain about jumping over even the narrowest of trenches, for he would be unaccustomed to free movement of this kind. Thus only a few, by cultivating their own minds, have succeeded in freeing themselves from immaturity and in continuing boldly on their way.

There is more chance of an entire public enlightening itself. This is indeed almost inevitable, if only the public concerned is left in freedom. For there will always be a few who think for themselves, even among those appointed as guardians of the common mass. Such guardians, once they have themselves thrown off the yoke of immaturity, will disseminate the spirit of rational respect for personal value and for the duty of all men to think for themselves. The remarkable thing about this is that if the public, which was previously put under this yoke by the guardians, is suitably stirred up by some of the latter who are incapable of enlightenment, it may subsequently compel the guardians themselves to remain under the yoke. For it is very harmful to propagate prejudices, because they finally avenge themselves on the very people who first encouraged them (or whose predecessors did so). Thus a public can only achieve enlightenment slowly. A revolution may well put an end to autocratic despotism and to rapacious or power-seeking oppression, but it will never produce a true reform in ways of thinking. Instead, new prejudices, like the ones they replaced, will serve as a leash to control the great unthinking mass.

For enlightenment of this kind, all that is needed is *freedom*. And the freedom in question is the most innocuous form of all — freedom to make *public use* of one's reason in all matters. But I hear on all sides the cry: *Don't argue!* The officer says: Don't argue, get on parade! The tax official: Don't argue, pay! The clergyman: Don't argue, believe! (Only one ruler in the world says: *Argue* as much as you like and about whatever you like, *but obey!*)[4] All this means restrictions on freedom everywhere. But which sort of restriction prevents enlightenment, and which, instead of hindering it, can actually promote it? I reply: The *public* use of man's reason must always be free, and it alone can bring about enlightenment among men; the *private use* of reason may quite often be very narrowly restricted, however, without undue hindrance to the progress of enlightenment. But by the public use of one's own reason I mean that use which anyone may make of it *as a man of learning* addressing the entire *reading public*. What I term the private use of reason is that which a person may make of it in a particular *civil* post or office with which he is entrusted.

Now in some affairs which affect the interests of the commonwealth, we require a certain mechanism whereby some members of the commonwealth must behave purely passively, so that they may, by an artificial common agreement, be employed by the

[handwritten margin note: religion - restriction on freedom]

government for public ends (or at least deterred from vitiating them). It is, of course, impermissible to argue in such cases; obedience is imperative. But in so far as this or that individual who acts as part of the machine also considers himself as a member of a complete commonwealth or even of cosmopolitan society, and thence as a man of learning who may through his writings address a public in the truest sense of the word, he may indeed argue without harming the affairs in which he is employed for some of the time in a passive capacity. Thus it would be very harmful if an officer receiving an order from his superiors were to quibble openly, while on duty, about the appropriateness or usefulness of the order in question. He must simply obey. But he cannot reasonably be banned from making observations as a man of learning on the errors in the military service, and from submitting these to his public for judgement. The citizen cannot refuse to pay the taxes imposed upon him; presumptuous criticisms of such taxes, where someone is called upon to pay them, may be punished as an outrage which could lead to general insubordination. Nonetheless, the same citizen does not contravene his civil obligations if, as a learned individual, he publicly voices his thoughts on the impropriety or even injustice of such fiscal measures. In the same way, a clergyman is bound to instruct his pupils and his congregation in accordance with the doctrines of the church he serves, for he was employed by it on that condition. But as a scholar, he is completely free as well as obliged to impart to the public all his carefully considered, well-intentioned thoughts on the mistaken aspects of those doctrines, and to offer suggestions for a better arrangement of religious and ecclesiastical affairs. And there is nothing in this which need trouble the conscience. For what he teaches in pursuit of his duties as an active servant of the church is presented by him as something which he is not empowered to teach at his own discretion, but which he is employed to expound in a prescribed manner and in someone else's name. He will say: Our church teaches this or that, and these are the arguments it uses. He then extracts as much practical value as possible for his congregation from precepts to which he would not himself subscribe with full conviction, but which he can nevertheless undertake to expound, since it is not in fact wholly impossible that they may contain truth. At all events, nothing opposed to the essence of religion is present in such doctrines. For if the clergyman thought he could find anything of this sort in them, he would not be able to carry out his official duties in good conscience, and would have to resign. Thus the use which someone employed as a teacher makes of his reason in the presence of his congregation is purely *private*, since a congregation, however large it is, is never any more than a domestic gathering. In view of this, he is not and cannot be free as a priest, since he is acting on a commission imposed from outside. Conversely, as a scholar addressing the real public (i.e. the world at large) through his writings, the clergyman making *public use* of his reason enjoys unlimited freedom to use his own reason and to speak in his own person. For to maintain that the guardians of the people in spiritual matters should themselves be immature, is an absurdity which amounts to making absurdities permanent.

But should not a society of clergymen, for example an ecclesiastical synod or a venerable presbytery (as the Dutch call it), be entitled to commit itself by oath to a certain unalterable set of doctrines, in order to secure for all time a constant guardianship over each of its members, and through them over the people? I reply that this is quite impossible. A contract of this kind, concluded with a view to preventing all further enlightenment of mankind for ever, is absolutely null and void, even if it is ratified by the supreme power, by Imperial Diets and the most solemn peace treaties. One age cannot enter into an alliance on oath to put the next age in a position where it would be impossible for it to extend and correct its knowledge, particularly on such important matters, or to make any progress whatsoever in enlightenment. This would be a crime against human nature, whose original destiny lies precisely in such progress. Later generations are thus perfectly entitled to dismiss these agreements as unauthorised and criminal. To test whether any particular measure can be agreed upon as a law for a people, we need only ask whether a people could well impose such a law upon itself. This might well be possible for a specified short period as a means of introducing a certain order, pending, as it were, a better solution. This would also mean that each citizen, particularly the clergyman, would be given a free hand as a scholar to comment publicly, i.e. in his writings, on the inadequacies of current institutions. Meanwhile, the newly established order would continue to exist, until public insight into the nature of such matters had progressed and proved itself to the point where, by general consent (if not unanimously), a proposal could be submitted to the crown. This would seek to protect the congregations who had, for instance, agreed to alter their religious establishment in accordance with their own notions of what higher insight is, but it would not try to obstruct those who wanted to let things remain as before. But it is absolutely impermissible to agree, even for a single lifetime, to a permanent religious constitution which no-one might publicly question. For this would virtually nullify a phase in man's upward progress, thus making it fruitless and even detrimental to subsequent generations. A man may for his own person, and even then only for a limited period, postpone enlightening himself in matters he ought to know about. But to renounce such enlightenment completely, whether for his own person or even more so for later generations, means violating and trampling underfoot the sacred rights of mankind. But something which a people may not even impose upon itself can still less be imposed on it by a monarch; for his legislative authority depends precisely upon his uniting the collective will of the people in his own. So long as he sees to it that all true or imagined improvements are compatible with the civil order, he can otherwise leave his subjects to do whatever they find necessary for their salvation, which is none of his business. But it is his business to stop anyone forcibly hindering others from working as best they can to define and promote their salvation. It indeed detracts from his majesty if he interferes in these affairs by subjecting the writings in which his subjects attempt to clarify their religious ideas to governmental supervision. This applies if he does so acting upon his own exalted opinions — in which case he exposes himself to the reproach: *Caesar non est supra Grammaticos*[5] — but much more so if he demeans his high authority so far as to support the spiritual despotism of a few tyrants within his state against the rest of his subjects.

If it is now asked whether we at present live in an *enlightened* age, the answer is: No, but we do live in an age of *enlightenment*. As things are at present, we still have a long way to go before men as a whole can be in a position (or can even be put into a position) of using their own understanding confidently and well in religious matters, without outside guidance. But we do have distinct indications that the way is now being cleared for them to work freely in this direction, and that the obstacles to universal enlightenment, to man's emergence from his self-incurred immaturity, are gradually becoming fewer. In this respect our age is the age of enlightenment, the century of *Frederick.*[6]

A prince who does not regard it as beneath him to say that he considers it his duty, in religious matters, not to prescribe anything to his people, but to allow them complete freedom, a prince who thus even declines to accept the presumptuous title of *tolerant*, is himself enlightened. He deserves to be praised by a grateful present and posterity as the man who first liberated mankind from immaturity (as far as government is concerned), and who left all men free to use their own reason in all matters of conscience. Under his rule, ecclesiastical dignitaries, notwithstanding their official duties, may in their capacity as scholars freely and publicly submit to the judgement of the world their verdicts and opinions, even if these deviate here and there from orthodox doctrine. This applies even more to all others who are not restricted by any official duties. This spirit of freedom is also spreading abroad, even where it has to struggle with outward obstacles imposed by governments which misunderstand their own function. For such governments can now witness a shining example of how freedom may exist without in the least jeopardising public concord and the unity of the commonwealth. Men will of their own accord gradually work their way out of barbarism so long as artificial measures are not deliberately adopted to keep them in it.

I have portrayed *matters of religion* as the focal point of enlightenment, i.e. of man's emergence from his self-incurred immaturity. This is firstly because our rulers have no interest in assuming the role of guardians over their subjects so far as the arts and sciences are concerned, and secondly, because religious immaturity is the most pernicious and dishonourable variety of all. But the attitude of mind of a head of state who favours freedom in the arts and sciences extends even further, for he realises that there is no danger even to his *legislation* if he allows his subjects to make *public* use of their own reason and to put before the public their thoughts on better ways of drawing up laws, even if this entails forthright criticism of the current legislation. We have before us a brilliant example of this kind, in which no monarch has yet surpassed the one to whom we now pay tribute.

But only a ruler who is himself enlightened and has no fear of phantoms, yet who likewise has at hand a well-disciplined and numerous army to guarantee public security, may say what no republic would dare to say: *Argue as much as you like and about whatever you like, but obey!* This reveals to us a strange and unexpected pattern in human affairs (such as we shall always find if we consider them in the widest sense, in which nearly everything is paradoxical). A high degree of civil freedom seems advantageous to a people's *intellectual* freedom, yet it also sets up insuperable barriers to it. Conversely, a lesser degree of civil freedom gives intellectual freedom enough room to expand to its fullest extent. Thus once the germ on which nature has lavished most care — man's inclination and duty to *think freely* — has developed within this hard shell, it gradually reacts upon the mentality of the people, who thus gradually become increasingly able to *act freely*. Eventually, it even influences the principles of governments, which find that they can themselves profit by treating man, who is *more than a machine*,[7] in a manner appropriate to his dignity.*

Königsberg in Prussia, 30th September, 1784.

*I read today on the 30th September in Büsching's[8] *Wöchentliche Nachrichten* of 13th September a notice concerning this month's *Berlinische Monatsschrift*. The notice mentions Mendelssohn's[9] answer to the same question as that which I have answered. I have not yet seen this journal, otherwise I should have held back the above reflections. I let them stand only as a means of finding out by comparison how far the thoughts of two individuals may coincide by chance.

Notes

[1] *Beantwortung der Frage: Was ist Aufklärung?*, AA VIII, 33–42. First published in *Berlinische Monatsschrift*, IV (12 December 1784), 481–94. There is a reference in the original edition of the *Berlinische Monatsschrift* to p. 516 of the number of that journal published on 5 December 1783. This reference is to an essay by the Rev. Zöllner, 'Is it advisable to sanction marriage through religion?'. The relevant passage reads (in translation): '*What is Enlightenment?* The question, which is almost as important as the question *What is truth?*, should be answered before one begins to enlighten others. And yet I have never found it answered anywhere.'

[2] Literal translation: 'Dare to be wise'. Horace, *Epodes* 1, 2, 40. Cf. Elizabeth M. Wilkinson and L. A. Willoughby (eds. and trs.), Friedrich Schiller, *On the Aesthetic Education of Man* (Oxford, 1967), LXXIV ff.; cf. also Franco Venturi, 'Was ist Aufklärung? Sapere Aude!', *Rivista Storica Italiana*, Lxxi (1959), 119 ff. Venturi traces the use made of this quotation from Horace throughout the centuries.

[3] 'Those who have come of age by virtue of nature.'

[4] The allusion is to Frederick II (the Great), King of Prussia (1740–86).

[5] 'Caesar is not above the grammarians.'

[6] Kant here refers, of course, to Frederick the Great.

[7] This allusion amounts to a repudiation of Julien Offray de Lamettrie's (1709–51) materialism as expressed in *L'Homme Machine* (1748).

[8] Anton Friedrich Büsching (1724–93), professor in the University of Göttingen, theologian and leading geographer of the day, editor of *Wöchentliche Nachrichten von neuen Landkarten, geographischen, statistischen und historischen Büchern*. Kant's reference is to XII, 1784 (Berlin, 1785), 291.

[9] Moses Mendelssohn (1729–86), a leading philosopher of the German Enlightenment. The reference is to Mendelssohn's essay 'Über die Frage: was heisst Aufklärung?' ('On the question: what is Enlightenment?'), *Berlinische Monatsschrift*, IV (9 September 1784), 193–200.

5.   The Federalist*

James Madison

If we cannot avoid faction without sacrificing
liberty, we must control it's effects. What does
madison propose? Has the solution he proposed
worked out? Why not?

Number X.
The Same Subject Continued.

Among the numerous advantages promised by a well constructed union, none deserves to be more accurately developed than its tendency to break and control the violence of faction. The friend of popular governments, never finds himself so much alarmed for their character and fate, as when he contemplates their propensity to this dangerous vice. He will not fail, therefore, to set a due value on any plan which, without violating the principles to which he is attached, provides a proper cure for it. The instability, injustice, and confusion, introduced into the public councils, have in truth, been the mortal diseases under which popular governments have everywhere perished; as they continue to be the favorite and fruitful topics from which the adversaries to liberty derive their most specious declamations. The valuable improvements made by the American constitutions on the popular models, both ancient and modern, cannot certainly be too much admired; but it would be an unwarrantable partiality, to contend that they have as effectually obviated the danger on this side, as was wished and expected. Complaints are everywhere heard from our most considerate and virtuous citizens, equally the friends of public and private faith, and of public and personal liberty, that our governments are too unstable; that the public good is disregarded in the conflicts of rival parties; and that measures are too often decided, not according to the rules of justice, and the rights of the minor party, but by the superior force of an interested and overbearing majority. However anxiously we may wish that these complaints had no foundation, the evidence of known facts will not permit us to deny that they are in some degree true. It will be found, indeed, on a candid review of our situation, that some of the distresses under which we labor, have

* The essays which later comprised *The Federalist* were published individually in newspapers from October 1787 to August 1788; 'The Federalist Number X' first appeared in a newspaper in November 1787. The essay printed here came from Madison, 'Number X,' in *The Federalist on the New Constitution*, by Alexander Hamilton, James Madison, and John Jay (Hallowell, ME: Masters, Smith & Co., 1857), 42–48.

been erroneously charged on the operation of our governments; but it will be found, at the same time, that other causes will not alone account for many of our heaviest misfortunes; and, particularly, for that prevailing and increasing distrust of public engagements, and alarm for private rights, which are echoed from one end of the continent to the other. These must be chiefly, if not wholly, effects of the unsteadiness and injustice, with which a factious spirit has tainted our public administrations.

By a faction, I understand a number of citizens, whether amounting to a majority or minority of the whole, who are united and actuated by some common impulse of passion, or of interest, adverse to the rights of other citizens, or to the permanent and aggregate interests of the community.

There are two methods of curing the mischiefs of faction: The one, by removing its causes; the other, by controlling its effects.

There are again two methods of removing the causes of faction: The one, by destroying the liberty which is essential to its existence; the other, by giving to every citizen the same opinions, the same passions, and the same interests.

It could never be more truly said, than of the first remedy, that it was worse than the disease. Liberty is to faction, what air is to fire, an aliment without which it instantly expires. But it could not be a less folly to abolish liberty, which is essential to political life, because it nourishes faction, than it would be to wish the annihilation of air, which is essential to animal life, because it imparts to fire its destructive agency.

The second expedient is as impracticable, as the first would be unwise. As long as the reason of man continues fallible, and he is at liberty to exercise it, different opinions will be formed. As long as the connection subsists between his reason and his self-love, his opinions and his passions will have a reciprocal influence on each other; and the former will be objects to which the latter will attach themselves. The diversity in the faculties of men, from which the rights of property originate, is not less an insuperable obstacle to an uniformity of interests. The protection of these faculties is the first object of government. From the protection of different and unequal faculties of acquiring property, the possession of different degrees and kinds of property immediately results; and from the influence of these on the sentiments and views of the respective proprietors, ensues a division of the society into different interests and parties.

The latent causes of faction are thus sown in the nature of man; and we see them everywhere brought into different degrees of activity, according to the different circumstances of civil society. A zeal for different opinions concerning religion, concerning government, and many other points, as well of speculation as of practice; an attachment to different leaders, ambitiously contending for preeminence and power; or to persons of other descriptions, whose fortunes have been interesting to the human passions, have, in turn, divided mankind into parties, inflamed them with mutual animosity, and rendered them much more disposed to vex and oppress each other, than to coöperate for their common good. So strong is this propensity of mankind, to fall into mutual animosities, that where no substantial occasion presents itself, the most frivolous and fanciful distinctions have been sufficient to kindle their unfriendly passions, and excite their most violent conflicts. But the most common and durable source of factions, has been the various and unequal distribution of property. Those who hold, and those who are without property, have ever formed distinct interests in society. Those who are creditors, and those who are debtors, fall under a like discrimination. A landed interest, a manufacturing interest, a mercantile interest, a moneyed interest, with many lesser interests, grow up of necessity in civilized nations and divide them into different classes, actuated by different sentiments and views. The regulation of these various and interfering interests forms the principal task of modern legislation, and involves the spirit of party and faction in the necessary and ordinary operations of the government.

No man is allowed to be a judge in his own cause; because his interest will certainly bias his judgment, and, not improbably, corrupt his integrity. With equal, nay with greater reason, a body of men are unfit to be both judges and parties at the same time; yet what are many of the most important acts of legislation but so many judicial determinations, not indeed concerning the rights of single persons, but concerning the rights of large bodies of citizens? and what are the different classes of legislators, but advocates and parties to the causes which they determine? Is a law proposed concerning private debts? It is a question to which the creditors are parties on one side, and the debtors on the other. Justice ought to hold the balance between them. Yet the parties are, and must be, themselves the judges; and the most numerous party, or, in other words, the most powerful faction must be expected to prevail. Shall domestic manufactures be encouraged, and in what degree by restrictions on foreign manufactures? are questions which would be differently decided by the landed and the manufacturing classes; and probably by neither with a sole regard to justice and the public good. The apportionment of taxes on the various descriptions of property, is an act which seems to require the most exact impartiality; yet there is, perhaps, no legislative act in which greater opportunity and temptation are given to a predominant party, to trample on the rules of justice. Every shilling, with which they overburden the inferior number, is a shilling saved to their own pockets.

It is in vain to say, that enlightened statesmen will be able to adjust these clashing interests, and render them all subservient to the public good. Enlightened statesmen will not always be at the helm: nor in many cases, can such an adjustment be made at all, without taking into view indirect and remote considerations, which will rarely prevail over the immediate interest which one party may find in disregarding the rights of another, or the good of the whole.

The inference to which we are brought is, that the *causes* of faction cannot be removed; and that relief is only to be sought in the means of controlling its *effects*.

If a faction consists of less than a majority, relief is supplied by the republican principle, which enables the majority to defeat its sinister views, by regular vote. It may clog the administration, it may convulse the society; but it will be unable to execute and mask its violence under the forms of the constitution. When a majority is included in a faction, the form of popular government, on the other hand, enables it to sacrifice to its ruling passion or interest, both the public good and the rights of other citizens. To secure the public good, and private rights, against the danger of such a faction, and at the same time to preserve the spirit and the form of popular government, is then the great object to which our inquiries are directed. Let me add, that it is the great desideratum, by which alone this form of government can be rescued from the opprobrium under which it has so long labored, and be recommended to the esteem and adoption of mankind.

By what means is this object attainable? Evidently by one of two only. Either the existence of the same passion or interest in a majority, at the same time, must be prevented; or the majority, having such coëxistent passions or interest, must be rendered, by their number and local situation, unable to concert and carry into effect schemes of oppression. If the impulse and the opportunity be suffered to coincide, we well know, that neither moral nor religious motives can be relied on as an adequate control. They are not found to be such on the injustice and violence of individuals, and lose their efficacy in proportion to the number combined together; that is, in proportion as their efficacy becomes needful.

From this view of the subject, it may be concluded, that a pure democracy, by which I mean a society consisting of a small number of citizens, who assemble and administer the government in person, can admit of no cure from the mischiefs of faction. A common passion or interest will, in almost every case be felt by a majority of the whole; a communication and concert, results from the form of government itself; and there is nothing to check the inducements to sacrifice the weaker party, or an obnoxious individual. Hence it is, that such democracies have ever been spectacles of turbulence and contention; have ever been found incompatible with personal security, or the rights of property; and have in general, been as short in their lives, as they have been violent in their deaths. Theoretic politicians, who have patronized this species of government, have erroneously supposed, that by reducing mankind to a perfect equality in their political rights, they would, at the same time, be perfectly equalized and assimilated in their possessions, their opinions, and their passions.

A republic, by which I mean a government in which the scheme of representation takes place, opens a different prospect, and promises the cure for which we are seeking. Let us examine the points in which it varies from a pure democracy, and we shall comprehend both the nature of the cure and the efficacy which it must derive from the union.

The two great points of difference, between a democracy and a republic, are, first, the delegation of the government, in the latter to a small number of citizens elected by the rest; secondly, the greater number of citizens, and greater sphere of country, over which the latter may be extended.

The effect of the first difference is, on the one hand, to refine and enlarge the public views, by passing them through the medium of a chosen body of citizens, whose wisdom may best discern the true interest of their country, and whose patriotism and love of justice, will be least likely to sacrifice it to temporary or partial considerations. Under such a regulation, it may well happen, that the public voice, pronounced by the representatives of the people, will be more consonant to the public good than if pronounced by the people themselves, convened for the purpose. On the other hand the effect may be inverted. Men of factious tempers, of local prejudices, or of sinister designs, may by intrigue, by corruption, or by other means first obtain the suffrages, and then betray the interests of the people. The question resulting is, whether small or extensive republics are most favorable to the election of proper guardians of the public weal; and it is clearly decided in favor of the latter by two obvious considerations.

In the first place, it is to be remarked, that however small the republic may be, the representatives must be raised to a certain number, in order to guard against the cabals of a few; and that however large it may be, they must be limited to a certain number, in order to guard against the confusion of a multitude. Hence, the number of representatives in the two cases not being in proportion to that of the constituents, and being proportionally greatest in the small republic, it follows, that if the proportion of fit characters be not less in the large than in the small republic, the former will present a greater option, and consequently a greater probability of a fit choice.

In the next place, as each representative will be chosen by a greater number of citizens in the large than in the small republic, it will be more difficult for unworthy candidates to practice with success the vicious arts, by which elections are too often carried; and the suffrages of the people being more free, will be more likely to centre in men who possess the most attractive merit, and the most diffusive and established characters.

It must be confessed, that in this, as in most other cases, there is a mean, on both sides of which inconveniences will be found to lie. By enlarging too much the number of electors, you render the representative too little acquainted with all their local circumstances and lesser interests; as by reducing it too much, you render him unduly attached to these, and too little fit to comprehend and pursue great and national objects. The federal constitution forms a happy combination in this respect; the great and aggregate interests being referred to the national, the local and particular to the state legislatures.

The other point of difference is, the greater number of citizens and extent of territory, which may be brought within the compass of republican, than of democratic government; and it is this circumstance principally which renders factious combinations less to be dreaded in the former, than in the latter. The smaller the society, the fewer probably will be the distinct parties and interests composing it; the fewer the distinct parties and interests, the more frequently will a majority be found of the same party; and the smaller the number of individuals composing a majority, and the smaller the compass within which they are placed, the more easily will they concert and execute their plans of oppression. Extend the sphere, and you take in a greater variety of parties and interests; you make it less probable that a majority of the whole will have a common motive to invade the rights of other citizens, or if such a common motive exists, it will be more difficult for all who feel it to discover their own strength, and to act in unison with each other. Besides other impediments, it may be remarked, that where there is a consciousness of unjust or dishonorable purposes, communication is always checked by distrust, in proportion to the number whose concurrence is necessary.

Hence, it clearly appears, that the same advantage, which a republic has over a democracy, in controlling the effects of faction, is enjoyed by a large over a small republic — is enjoyed by the union over the states composing it. Does this advantage consist in the substitution of representatives, whose enlightened views and virtuous sentiments render them superior to local prejudices, and to schemes of injustice? It will not be denied, that the representation of the union will be most likely to possess these requisite endowments. Does it consist in the greater security afforded by a greater variety of parties, against the event of any one party being able to outnumber and oppress the rest? In an equal degree does the increased variety of parties, comprised within the union, increase this security. Does it, in fine, consist in the greater obstacles opposed to the concert and accomplishment of the secret wishes of an unjust and interested majority? Here, again, the extent of the union gives it the most palpable advantage.

The influence of factious leaders may kindle a flame within their particular states, but will be unable to spread a general conflagration through the other states: a religious sect may degenerate into a political faction in a part of the confederacy; but the variety of sects dispersed over the entire face of it, must secure the national councils against any danger from that source: a rage for paper money, for an abolition of debts, for an equal division of property, or for any other improper or wicked project, will be less apt to pervade the whole body of the union than a particular member of it; in the same proportion as such a malady is more likely to taint a particular county or district, than an entire state.

In the extent and proper structure of the union, therefore, we behold a republican remedy for the diseases most incident to republican government. And according to the degree of pleasure and pride we feel in being republicans, ought to be our zeal in cherishing the spirit; and supporting the character of federalists.

PUBLIUS.

bad conscience began with transition from nomadic
to permanent settlements (had to rely on conscious mind)
-transition was violent → leads to tyranny
★ no social contract Among
- as tribe becomes more powerful, more debt is owed to ancestors
┌ Christian God = guilty indebtedness
└ Greek gods celebrate animal instincts to ward off bad conscience
↳ God becomes man (Jesus) + we kill him which increases our guilt

6. The Genealogy of Morals*

Friedrich Nietzsche

our morals came from guilt/gratitude

nomads could no longer harm others, roam free, + obey instincts have to turn power in ward leading to slave morality + bad conscience

Second Essay *+ frustrated because humans are not strong enough to win the struggle*

17. *bad conscience = freedom forced back*
rulers impose their will + you feel gracious toward them for your success

It is primarily involved in this hypothesis of the origin of the bad conscience, that that alteration was no gradual and no voluntary alteration, and that it did not manifest itself as an organic adaptation to new conditions, but as a break, a jump, a necessity, an inevitable fate, against which there was no resistance and never a spark of resentment. And secondarily, that the fitting of a hitherto unchecked and amorphous population into a fixed form, starting as it had done in an act of violence, could only be accomplished by acts of violence and nothing else — that the oldest "State" appeared consequently as a ghastly tyranny, a grinding ruthless piece of machinery, which went on working, till this raw material of a semi-animal populace was not only thoroughly kneaded and elastic, but also *moulded.* I used the word "State"; my meaning is self-evident, namely, a herd of blonde beasts of prey, a race of conquerors and masters, which with all its warlike organisation and all its organising power pounces with its terrible claws on a population, in numbers possibly tremendously superior, but as yet formless, as yet nomad. Such is the origin of the "State." That fantastic theory that makes it begin with a contract is, I think, disposed of. He who can command, he who is a master by "nature," he who comes on the scene forceful in deed and gesture — what has he to do with contracts? Such beings defy calculation, they come like fate, without cause, reason, notice, excuse, they are there as the lightning is there, too terrible, too sudden, too convincing, too "different," to be personally even hated. Their work is an instinctive creating and impressing of forms, they are the most involuntary, unconscious artists that there are: — their appearance produces instantaneously a scheme of sovereignty which is *live,* in which the functions are partitioned and apportioned, in which above all no part is received or finds a place, until

tyranny molds people

birth of patriarchy

---

* *The Genealogy of Morals* was first published in 1887. This particular translation was taken from Nietzsche, *The Genealogy of Morals*, Second Essay, Sections 17–25, translated by Horace B. Samuel (New York: Modern Library, 1918), 78–93.

pregnant with a "meaning" in regard to the whole. They are ignorant of the meaning of guilt, responsibility, consideration, are these born organisers; in them predominates that terrible artist-egoism, that gleams like brass, and that knows itself justified to all eternity, in its work, even as a mother in her child. It is not in *them* that there grew the bad conscience, that is elementary — but it would not have grown *without them*, repulsive growth as it was, it would be missing, had not a tremendous quantity of freedom been expelled from the world by the stress of their hammer-strokes, their artist violence, or been at any rate made invisible and, as it were, *latent*. This *instinct of freedom* forced into being latent — it is already clear — this instinct of freedom forced back, trodden back, imprisoned within itself, and finally only able to find vent and relief in itself; this, only this, is the beginning of the "bad conscience."

18. Will to power

Beware of thinking lightly of this phenomenon, by reason of its initial painful ugliness. At bottom it is the same active force which is at work on a more grandiose scale in those potent artists and organisers, and builds states, where here, internally, on a smaller and pettier scale and with a retrogressive tendency, makes itself a bad conscience in the "labyrinth of the breast," to use Goethe's phrase, and which builds negative ideals; it is, I repeat, that identical *instinct of freedom* (to use my own language, the will to power): only the material, on which this force with all its constructive and tyrannous nature is let loose, is here man himself, his whole old animal self — and *not* as in the case of that more grandiose and sensational phenomenon, the *other* man, *other* men. This secret self-tyranny, this cruelty of the artist, this delight in giving a form to one's self as a piece of difficult, refractory, and suffering material, in burning in a will, a critique, a contradiction, a contempt, a negation; this sinister and ghastly labour of love on the part of a soul, whose will is cloven in two within itself, which makes itself suffer from delight in the infliction of suffering; this wholly *active* bad conscience has finally (as one already anticipates) — true fountainhead as it is of idealism and imagination — produced an abundance of novel and amazing beauty and affirmation, and perhaps has really been the first to give birth to beauty at all. What would beauty be, forsooth, if its contradiction had not first been presented to consciousness, if the ugly had not first said to itself, "I am ugly"? At any rate, after this hint the problem of how far idealism and beauty can be traced in such opposite ideas as "*selflessness*," *self-denial*, *self-sacrifice*, becomes less problematical; and indubitably in future we shall certainly know the real and original character of the *delight* experienced by the self-less, the self-denying, the self-sacrificing: this delight is a phase of cruelty. — So much provisionally for the origin of "altruism" as a *moral* value, and the marking out the ground from which this value has grown: it is only the bad conscience, only the will for self-abuse, that provides the necessary conditions for the existence of altruism as a *value*.

19. Ancestors are Gods

Undoubtedly the bad conscience is an illness, but an illness as pregnancy is an illness. If we search out the conditions under which this illness reaches its most terrible and sublime zenith, we shall see what really first brought about its entry into the world. But to do this we must take a long breath, and we must first of all go back once again to an earlier point of view. The relation at civil law of the ower to his creditor (which has already been discussed in detail), has been interpreted once again (and indeed in a manner which historically is exceedingly remarkable and suspicious) into a relationship, which is perhaps more incomprehensible to us moderns than to any other era; that is, into the relationship of the *existing* generation to its *ancestors*. Within the original tribal association — we are talking of primitive times — each living generation recognises a legal obligation towards the earlier generation, and particularly towards the earliest, which founded the family (and this is something much more than a mere sentimental obligation, the existence of which, during the longest period of man's history, is by no means indisputable). There prevails in them the conviction that it is only thanks to sacrifices and efforts of their ancestors, that the race *persists* at all — and that this has to be *paid back* to them by sacrifices and services. Thus is recognized the *owing* of a debt, which accumulates continually by reason of these ancestors never ceasing in their subsequent life as potent spirits to secure by their power new privileges and advantages to the race. Gratis, perchance? But there is no gratis for that raw and "mean-souled" age. What return can be made? — Sacrifice (at first, nourishment, in its crudest sense), festivals, temples, tributes of veneration, above all, obedience — since all customs are, *quâ* works of the ancestors, equally their precepts and commands — are the ancestors ever given enough? This suspicion remains and grows: from time to time it extorts a great wholesale ransom, something monstrous in the way of repayment of the creditor (the notorious sacrifice of the first-born, for example, blood, human blood in any case). The *fear* of ancestors and their power, the consciousness of owing debts to them, necessarily increases, according to this kind of logic, in the exact proportion that the race itself increases, that the race itself becomes more victorious, more independent, more honoured, more feared. This, and not the contrary, is the fact. Each step towards race decay, all disastrous events, all symptoms of degeneration, of approaching disintegration, always *diminish* the fear of the founders' spirit, and whittle away the idea of his sagacity, providence, and potent presence. Conceive this crude kind of logic carried to its climax: it follows that the ancestors of the *most powerful* races must, through the growing fear that they exercise on the imaginations, grow themselves into monstrous dimensions, and become relegated to the gloom of a divine mystery that transcends imagination — the ancestor becomes at last necessarily transfigured into a *god*. Perhaps this is the very origin of the gods, that is, an origin from *fear*! And those who feel bound to add, "but from piety also," will have difficulty in maintaining this theory, with regard to the primeval and longest period of the human race. And, of course, this is even more the case as regards the *middle* period, the formative period of the aristocratic races — the aristocratic races which have given back with interest to their founders, the ancestors (heroes, gods), all those qualities which in the meanwhile have appeared in themselves, that is, the aristocratic qualities. We will later on glance again at the ennobling and promotion of the gods (which, of course, is totally distinct from their "sanctification"): let us now provisionally follow to its end the course of the whole of this development of the consciousness of "owing."

20. *we owe + are indebted to the diety*
— responsibility to pay back debt creates consciousness

According to the teaching of history, the consciousness of owing debts to the deity by no means came to an end with the decay of the clan organisation of society; just as mankind has inherited the ideas of "good" and "bad" from the race-nobility (together with its fundamental tendency towards establishing social distinctions), so with the heritage of the racial and tribal gods it has also inherited the incubus of debts as yet unpaid and the desire to discharge them. The transition is effected by those large populations of slaves and bondsmen, who, whether through compulsion or through submission and "mimicry," have accommodated themselves to the religion of their masters; through this channel these inherited tendencies inundate the world. The feeling of owing a debt to the deity has grown continuously for several centuries, always in the same proportion in which the idea of God and the consciousness of God have grown and become exalted among mankind. (The whole history of ethnic fights, victories, reconciliations, amalgamations, everything, in fact, which precedes the eventual classing of all the social elements in each great race-synthesis, are mirrored in the hotch-potch genealogy of their gods, in the legends of their fights, victories, and reconciliations. Progress towards universal empires invariably means progress towards universal deities; despotism, with its subjugation of the independent nobility, always paves the way for some system or other of monotheism.) The appearance of the Christian god, as the record god up to this time, has for that very reason brought equally into the world the record amount of guilt consciousness. Granted that we have gradually started on the *reverse* movement, there is no little probability in the deduction, based on the continuous decay in the belief in the Christian god, to the effect that there also already exists a considerable decay in the human consciousness of owing (ought); in fact, we cannot shut our eyes to the prospect of the complete and eventual triumph of atheism freeing mankind from all this feeling of obligation of their origin, their *causa prima*. Atheism and a kind of second innocence complement and supplement each other.

21. *man is not able to repay his debt → "eternal punishment"*

So much for my rough and preliminary sketch of the interrelation of the ideas "ought" (owe) and "duty" with the postulates of religion. I have intentionally shelved up to the present the actual moralisation of these ideas (their being pushed back into the conscience, or more precisely the interweaving of the *bad* conscience with the idea of God), and at the end of the last paragraph used language to the effect that this moralisation did not exist, and that consequently these ideas had necessarily come to an end, by reason of what had happened to their hypothesis, the credence in our "creditor," in God. The actual facts differ terribly from this theory. It is with the moralisation of the ideas "ought" and "duty," and with their being pushed back into the *bad* conscience, that comes the first actual attempt to *reverse* the direction of the development we have just described, or at any rate to arrest its evolution; it is just at this juncture that the very hope of an eventual redemption *has to* put itself once for all into the prison of pessimism, it is at this juncture that the eye *has to* recoil and rebound in despair from off an adamantine impossibility, it is at this juncture that the ideas "guilt" and "duty" have to turn backwards

— turn backwards against *whom*? There is no doubt about it; primarily against the "ower," in whom the bad conscience now establishes itself, eats, extends, and grows like a polypus throughout its length and breadth, all with such virulence, that at last, with the impossibility of paying the debt, there becomes conceived the idea of the impossibility of paying the penalty, the thought of its inexpiability (the idea of "eternal punishment") — finally, too, it turns against the "creditor," whether found in the *causa prima* of man, the origin of the human race, its sire, who henceforth becomes burdened with a curse ("Adam," "original sin," "determination of the will"), or in Nature from whose womb man springs, and on whom the responsibility for the principle of evil is now cast ("Diabolisation of Nature"), or in existence generally, on this logic an absolute *white elephant*, with which mankind is landed (the Nihilistic flight from life, the demand for Nothingness, or for the opposite of existence, for some other existence, Buddhism and the like) — till suddenly we stand before that paradoxical and awful expedient, through which a tortured humanity has found a temporary alleviation, that stroke of genius called Christianity: — God personally immolating himself for the debt of man, God paying himself personally out of a pound of his own flesh, God as the one being who can deliver man from what man had become unable to deliver himself — the creditor playing scapegoat for his debtor, from *love* (can you believe it?), from love of his debtor!...

22. *God + eternal punishment isn't real, man has the will to think of himself as punished*

The reader will already have conjectured what took place on the stage and *behind the scenes* of this drama. That will for self-torture, that inverted cruelty of the animal man, who, turned subjective and scared into introspection (encaged as he was in "the State," as part of his taming process), invented the bad conscience so as to hurt himself, after the *natural* outlet for this will to hurt, became blocked — in other words, this man of the bad conscience exploited the religious hypothesis so as to carry his martyrdom to the ghastliest pitch of agonised intensity. Owing something to *God*: this thought becomes his instrument of torture. He apprehends in God the most extreme antitheses that he can find to his own characteristic and ineradicable animal instincts, he himself gives a new interpretation to these animal instincts as being against what he "owes" to God (as enmity, rebellion, and revolt against the "Lord," the "Father," the "Sire," the "Beginning of the world"), he places himself between the horns of the dilemma, "God" and "Devil." Every negation which he is inclined to utter to himself, to the nature, naturalness, and reality of his being, he whips into an ejaculation of "yes," uttering it as something existing, living, efficient, as being God, as the holiness of God, the judgment of God, as the hangmanship of God, as transcendence, as eternity, as unending torment, as hell, as infinity of punishment and guilt. This is a kind of madness of the will in the sphere of psychological cruelty which is absolutely unparalleled: — man's *will* to find himself guilty and blameworthy to the point of inexpiability, his *will* to think of himself as punished, without the punishment ever being able to balance the guilt, his *will* to infect and to poison the fundamental basis of the universe with the problem of punishment and guilt, in order to cut off once and for all any escape out of this labyrinth of "fixed ideas," his will for rearing an ideal — that of the "holy God" — face to face with which he can have tangible proof of his own unworthiness. Alas for this mad melancholy beast man!

[handwritten margin note: No such thing as God → man made it up because we naturally want to punish ourselves]

What phantasies invade it, what paroxysms of perversity, hysterical senselessness, and *mental bestiality* break out immediately, at the very slightest check on its being the beast of action! All this is excessively interesting, but at the same time tainted with a black, gloomy, enervating melancholy, so that a forcible veto must be invoked against looking too long into these abysses. Here is *disease*, undubitably, the most ghastly disease that has as yet played havoc among men: and he who can still hear (but man turns now deaf ears to such sounds), how in this night of torment and nonsense there has rung out the cry of *love*, the cry of the most passionate ecstasy, of redemption in *love*, he turns away gripped by an invincible horror — in man there is so much that is ghastly — too long has the world been a mad-house.

23. Idea of God should be used for good not bad

Let this suffice once for all concerning the origin of the "holy God." The fact that *in itself* the conception of gods is not bound to lead necessarily to this degradation of the imagination (a temporary representation of whose vagaries we felt bound to give), the fact that there exist *nobler* methods of utilising the invention of gods than in this self-crucifixion and self-degradation of man, in which the last two thousand years of Europe have been past masters — these facts can fortunately be still perceived from every glance that we cast at the Grecian gods, these mirrors of noble and grandiose men, in which the *animal* in man felt itself deified, and did *not* devour itself in subjective frenzy. These Greeks long utilised their gods as simple buffers against "bad conscience" — so that they could continue to enjoy their freedom of soul: this, of course, is diametrically opposed to Christianity's theory of its god. They went *very far* on this principle, did these splendid and lion-hearted children; and there is no lesser authority than that of the Homeric Zeus for making them realise occasionally that they are taking life too casually. "Wonderful," says he on one occasion — it has to do with the case of Ægistheus, a *very* bad case indeed —

Gods can be blamed for evil rather than man.

"Wonderful how they grumble, the mortals against the immortals
Only from us, they presume, *comes evil*, but in their folly,
Fashion they, spite of fate, the doom of their own disaster."

Yet the reader will note and observe that this Olympian spectator and judge is far from being angry with them and thinking evil of them on this score. "How *foolish* they are," so thinks he of the misdeeds of mortals — and "folly," "imprudence," "a little brain disturbance," and nothing more, are what the Greeks, even of the strongest, bravest period, have admitted to be the ground of much that is evil and fatal. — Folly, *not* sin, do you understand?... But even this brain disturbance was a problem — "Come, how is it even possible? How could it have really got in brains like ours, the brains of men of aristocratic ancestry, of men of fortune, of men of good natural endowments, of men of the best society, of men of nobility and virtue?" This was the question that for century on century the aristocratic Greek put to himself when confronted with every (to him incomprehensible) outrage and sacrilege with which one of his peers had polluted himself. "It must be that a *god* had infatuated him," he would say at last, nodding his head. — This solution is *typical* of the Greeks,...accordingly the gods in those times subserved the functions of justifying man to a certain extent even in evil — in those days they took upon themselves not the punishment, but, what is *more noble*, the guilt.

24.

I conclude with three queries, as you will see. "Is an ideal actually set up here, or is one pulled down?" I am perhaps asked.... But have ye sufficiently asked yourselves how dear a payment has the setting up of *every* ideal in the world exacted? To achieve that consummation how much truth must always be traduced and misunderstood, how many lies must be sanctified, how much conscience has got to be disturbed, how many pounds of "God" have got to be sacrificed every time? To enable a sanctuary to be set up *a sanctuary has got to be destroyed*: that is a law — show me an instance where it has not been fulfilled!... We modern men, we inherit the immemorial tradition of vivisecting the conscience, and practising cruelty to our animal selves. That is the sphere of our most protracted training, perhaps of our artistic prowess, at any rate our dilettantism and our perverted taste. Man has for too long regarded his natural proclivities with an "evil eye," so that eventually they have become in his system affiliated to a bad conscience. A converse endeavour would be intrinsically feasible — but who is strong enough to attempt it? — namely, to affiliate to the "bad conscience" all those *unnatural* proclivities, all those transcendental aspirations, contrary to sense, instinct, nature, and animalism — in short, all past and present ideals, which are all ideals opposed to life, and traducing the world. To whom is one to turn nowadays with *such* hopes and pretensions? — It is just the *good* men that we should thus bring about our ears; and in addition, as stands to reason, the indolent, the hedgers, the vain, the hysterical, the tired.... What is more offensive or more thoroughly calculated to alienate, than giving any hint of the exalted severity with which we treat ourselves? And again how conciliatory, how full of love does all the world show itself towards us so soon as we do as all the world does, and "let ourselves go" like all the world. For such a consummation we need spirits of *different* calibre than seems really feasible in this age; spirits rendered potent through wars and victories, to whom conquest, adventure, danger, even pain, have become a need; for such a consummation we need habituation to sharp, rare air, to winter wanderings, to literal and metaphorical ice and mountains; we even need a kind of sublime malice, a supreme and most self-conscious insolence of knowledge, which is the appanage of great health; we need (to summarise the awful truth) just this *great health*!

Is this even feasible to-day?... But some day, in a stronger age than this rotting and introspective present, must he in sooth come to us, even the *redeemer* of great love and scorn, the creative spirit, rebounding by the impetus of his own force back again away from every transcendental plane and dimension, he whose solitude is misunderstanded of the people, as though it were a flight *from* reality; — while actually it is only his diving, burrowing, and penetrating *into* reality, so that when he comes again to the light he can at once bring about by these means the *redemption* of this reality; its redemption from the curse which the old ideal has laid upon it. This man of the future, who in this wise will redeem us from the old ideal, as he will from that ideal's necessary corollary of great

Attack on christianity, society, + law
Romantic idea is freedom (liberty)

nausea, will to nothingness, and Nihilism; this tocsin of noon and of the great verdict, which renders the will again free, who gives back to the world its goal and to man his hope, this Antichrist and Antinihilist, this conqueror of God and of Nothingness — *he must one day come.*

Übermench - Godless, need to rule
impose rule by will

25.

But what am I talking of? Enough! Enough? At this juncture I have only one proper course, silence: otherwise I trespass on a domain open alone to one who is younger than I, one stronger, more *"future"* than I — open alone to *Zarathustra, Zarathustra the godless.*

wants all of us to be ubermench (have to live in isolation)

- return to a natural state
without society, we need to be
independent + self sufficient
↓
no longer have to depend or
be indebted to ancestors

master race (ubermench)
master vs slave

not everyone wants ind.
⚹freedom
independent
enslavement (ubermench)
unhappy
guilty! debt to ancestors

- we created Gods that made us feel guilty

Greek Gods dont create guilt = amoral
christian God = moral

- we need to embrace amoral goods

have to become athiest
↓ ubermench

autonomy = utter self control, cant happen
if there is a God. guilt = unhappiness

Part II
Ideal Leadership

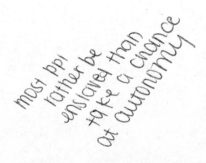

most ppl
rather be
enslaved than
take a chance
at autonomy

7. The Republic*

Plato

Chapter XVIII (V. 471 C–474 B)

The Paradox: Philosophers Must Be Kings

Challenged to show that the ideal state can exist, Socrates first claims that an ideal is none the worse for not being realizable on earth. The assertion that theory comes closer than practice to truth or reality is characteristically Platonic. The ideal state or man is the true state or man; for if men, who are in fact always imperfect, could reach perfection, they would only be realizing all that their nature aims at being and might conceivably be. Further, the realm of ideals is the real world, unchanging and eternal, which can be known by thought. The visible and tangible things commonly called real are only a realm of fleeting appearance, where the ideal is imperfectly manifested in various degrees of approximation. This contrast will be drawn in Chapter XIX.

An ideal has an indispensable value for practice, in that thought thereby gives to action its right aim. So, instead of proving that the ideal state or man can exist here, it is enough to discover the least change, within the bounds of possibility, that would bring the actual state nearest to the ideal. This change would be the union, in the same persons, of political power and the love of wisdom, so as to close the gulf, which had been growing wider since the age of Pericles, between the men of thought and the men of action. The corresponding change in the individual is the supremacy of the reason, the divine element in man, over the rest of our nature.

---

* Most scholars believe Plato wrote *The Republic* in stages sometime between 387 and 360 BCE. This particular selection was taken from Plato, *The Republic of Plato*, Books V and VI, Chapters XVIII, XX, XXI, and XXII, edited and translated by Francis MacDonald Cornford, 1941, reprint (New York: Oxford University Press, 1962), 175–179, 189–211.

But really, Socrates, Glaucon continued, if you are allowed to go on like this, I am afraid you will forget all about the question you thrust aside some time ago: whether a society so constituted can ever come into existence, and if so, how. No doubt, if it did exist, all manner of good things would come about. I can even add some that you have passed over. Men who acknowledged one another as fathers, sons, or brothers and always used those names among themselves would never desert one another; so they would fight with unequalled bravery. And if their womenfolk went out with them to war, either in the ranks or drawn up in the rear to intimidate the enemy and act as a reserve in case of need, I am sure all this would make them invincible. At home, too, I can see many advantages you have not mentioned. But, since I admit that our commonwealth would have all these merits and any number more, if once it came into existence, you need not describe it in further detail. All we have now to do is to convince ourselves that it can be brought into being and how.

This is a very sudden onslaught, said I; you have no mercy on my shilly-shallying. Perhaps you do not realize that, after I have barely escaped the first two waves,[1] the third, which you are now bringing down upon me, is the most formidable of all. When you have seen what it is like and heard my reply, you will be ready to excuse the very natural fears which made me shrink from putting forward such a paradox for discussion.

The more you talk like that, he said, the less we shall be willing to let you off from telling us how this constitution can come into existence; so you had better waste no more time.

Well, said I, let me begin by reminding you that what brought us to this point was our inquiry into the nature of justice and injustice.

True; but what of that?

Merely this: suppose we do find out what justice is,[2] are we going to demand that a man who is just shall have a character which exactly corresponds in every respect to the ideal of justice? Or shall we be satisfied if he comes as near to the ideal as possible and has in him a larger measure of that quality than the rest of the world?

That will satisfy me.

If so, when we set out to discover the essential nature of justice and injustice and what a perfectly just and a perfectly unjust man would be like, supposing them to exist, our purpose was to use them as ideal patterns: we were to observe the degree of happiness or unhappiness that each exhibited, and to draw the necessary inference that our own destiny would be like that of the one we most resembled. We did not set out to show that these ideals could exist in fact.

That is true.

Then suppose a painter had drawn an ideally beautiful figure complete to the last touch, would you think any the worse of him, if he could not show that a person as beautiful as that could exist?

No, I should not.

Well, we have been constructing in discourse the pattern of an ideal state. Is our theory any the worse, if we cannot prove it possible that a state so organized should be actually founded?

Surely not.

That, then, is the truth of the matter. But if, for your satisfaction, I am to do my best to

[Handwritten marginalia:]
strong family tie
1st: equality of women
2nd: free love abolish fam
3rd: creation of philosopher king
(w) 1 < okay or close or up perfectly
didn't think perfectly just or unjust existed
just an ideal

show under what conditions our ideal would have the best chance of being realized, I must ask you once more to admit that the same principle applies here. Can theory ever be fully realized in practice? Is it not in the nature of things that action should come less close to truth than thought? People may not think so; but do you agree or not?

I do.

Then you must not insist upon my showing that this construction we have traced in thought could be reproduced in fact down to the last detail. You must admit that we shall have found a way to meet your demand for realization, if we can discover how a state might be constituted in the closest accordance with our description. Will not that content you? It would be enough for me.

And for me too.

Then our next attempt, it seems, must be to point out what defect in the working of existing states prevents them from being so organized, and what is the least change that would effect a transformation into this type of government — a single change if possible, or perhaps two; at any rate let us make the changes as few and insignificant as may be.

By all means.

Well, there is one change which, as I believe we can show, would bring about this revolution — not a small change, certainly, nor an easy one, but possible.

What is it?

I have now to confront what we called the third and greatest wave. But I must state my paradox, even though the wave should break in laughter over my head and drown me in ignominy. Now mark what I am going to say.

Go on.

Unless either philosophers become kings in their countries or those who are now called kings and rulers come to be sufficiently inspired with a genuine desire for wisdom; unless, that is to say, political power and philosophy meet together, while the many natures who now go their several ways in the one or the other direction are forcibly debarred from doing so, there can be no rest from troubles, my dear Glaucon, for states, nor yet, as I believe, for all mankind; nor can this commonwealth which we have imagined ever till then see the light of day and grow to its full stature. This it was that I have so long hung back from saying; I knew what a paradox it would be, because it is hard to see that there is no other way of happiness either for the state or for the individual.

Socrates, exclaimed Glaucon, after delivering yourself of such a pronouncement as that, you must expect a whole multitude of by no means contemptible assailants to fling off their coats, snatch up the handiest weapon, and make a rush at you, breathing fire and slaughter. If you cannot find arguments to beat them off and make your escape, you will learn what it means to be the target of scorn and derision.

Well, it was you who got me into this trouble.

Yes, and a good thing too. However, I will not leave you in the lurch. You shall have my friendly encouragement for what it is worth; and perhaps you may find me more complaisant than some would be in answering your questions. With such backing you must try to convince the unbelievers.

I will, now that I have such a powerful ally....

Chapter XX (VI. 484 A–487 A)
The Philosopher's Fitness to Rule

The above definition of the philosopher might suggest an unpractical head-in-air, unfit to control life in the state. But the qualities most valuable in a ruler will follow naturally from the master passion for truth in a nature of the type described earlier (Chap. X), when it is perfected by time and education.

So at last, Glaucon, after this long and weary way, we have come to see who are the philosophers and who are not.

I doubt if the way could have been shortened.

Apparently not. I think, however, that we might have gained a still clearer view, if this had been the only topic to be discussed; but there are so many others awaiting us, if we mean to discover in what ways the just life is better than the unjust.

Which are we to take up now?

Surely the one that follows next in order. Since the philosophers are those who can apprehend the eternal and unchanging, while those who cannot do so, but are lost in the mazes of multiplicity and change, are not philosophers, which of the two ought to be in control of a state?

I wonder what would be a reasonable solution.

To establish as Guardians whichever of the two appear competent to guard the laws and ways of life in society.

True.

Well, there can be no question whether a guardian who is to keep watch over anything needs to be keen-sighted or blind. And is not blindness precisely the condition of men who are entirely cut off from knowledge of any reality, and have in their soul no clear pattern of perfect truth, which they might study in every detail and constantly refer to, as a painter looks at his model, before they proceed to embody notions of justice, honour, and goodness in earthly institutions or, in their character of Guardians, to preserve such institutions as already exist?

Certainly such a condition is very like blindness.

Shall we, then, make such as these our Guardians in preference to men who, besides their knowledge of realities, are in no way inferior to them in experience and in every excellence of character?

It would be absurd not to choose the philosophers, whose knowledge is perhaps their greatest point of superiority, provided they do not lack those other qualifications.

What we have to explain, then, is how those qualifications can be combined in the same persons with philosophy.

Certainly.

The first thing, as we said at the outset, is to get a clear view of their inborn disposition.[3] When we are satisfied on that head, I think we shall agree that such a combination of qualities is possible and that we need look no further for men fit to be in control of a commonwealth. One trait of the philosophic nature we may take as already granted: a constant passion for any knowledge that will reveal to them something of that reality which endures for ever and is not always passing into and out of existence. And, we may add, their desire is to know the whole of that reality; they will not willingly renounce any part of it as relatively small and insignificant, as we said before when we compared them to the lover and to the man who covets honour.

True.

Is there not another trait which the nature we are seeking cannot fail to possess — truthfulness, a love of truth and a hatred of falsehood that will not tolerate untruth in any form?

Yes, it is natural to expect that.

It is not merely natural, but entirely necessary that an instinctive passion for any object should extend to all that is closely akin to it; and there is nothing more closely akin to wisdom than truth. So the same nature cannot love wisdom and falsehood; the genuine lover of knowledge cannot fail, from his youth up, to strive after the whole of truth.

I perfectly agree.

Now we surely know that when a man's desires set strongly in one direction, in every other channel they flow more feebly, like a stream diverted into another bed. So when the current has set towards knowledge and all that goes with it, desire will abandon those pleasures of which the body is the instrument and be concerned only with the pleasure which the soul enjoys independently — if, that is to say, the love of wisdom is more than a mere pretence. Accordingly, such a one will be temperate and no lover of money; for he will be the last person to care about the things for the sake of which money is eagerly sought and lavishly spent.

That is true.

Again, in seeking to distinguish the philosophic nature, you must not overlook the least touch of meanness. Nothing could be more contrary than pettiness to a mind constantly bent on grasping the whole of things, both divine and human.

Quite true.

And do you suppose that one who is so high-minded and whose thought can contemplate all time and all existence will count this life of man a matter of much concern?

No, he could not.

So for such a man death will have no terrors.

None.

A mean and cowardly nature, then, can have no part in the genuine pursuit of wisdom.

I think not.

And if a man is temperate and free from the love of money, meanness, pretentiousness, and cowardice, he will not be hard to deal with or dishonest. So, as another indication of the philosophic temper, you will observe whether, from youth up, he is fair-minded, gentle, and sociable.

Certainly.

Also you will not fail to notice whether he is quick or slow to learn. No one can be expected to take a reasonable delight in a task in which much painful effort makes little headway. And if he cannot retain what he learns, his forgetfulness will leave no room in his head for knowledge; and so, having all his toil for nothing, he can only end by hating

(margin note: Good memory)

himself as well as his fruitless occupation. We must not, then, count a forgetful mind as competent to pursue wisdom; we must require a good memory.

By all means.

Further, there is in some natures a crudity and awkwardness that can only tend to a lack of measure and proportion; and there is a close affinity between proportion and truth. Hence, besides our other requirements, we shall look for a mind endowed with measure and grace, which will be instinctively drawn to see every reality in its true light.

Yes.

Well then, now that we have enumerated the qualities of a mind destined to take its full part in the apprehension of reality, have you any doubt about their being indispensable and all necessarily going together?

None whatever.

(margin note: important characteristics)

Then have you any fault to find with a pursuit which none can worthily follow who is not by nature quick to learn and to remember, magnanimous and gracious, the friend and kinsman of truth, justice, courage, temperance?

No; Momus[4] himself could find no flaw in it.

Well then, when time and education have brought such characters as these to maturity, would you entrust the care of your commonwealth to anyone else?

Chapter XXI (VI. 487 B–497 A)
Why the Philosophic Nature Is Useless or Corrupted in Existing Society

(margin note: solution/problem #2, issues/difficulties)

Adeimantus objects that the above description of the man of thought as gifted with all the qualities of a ruler is only an ideal. In actual fact the better sort of philosophers prove useless to the state, and others who have the natural gifts are demoralized.

Socrates replies: The better sort are useless because a democratic state has no use for men like Socrates and his companions (including Plato); and the corruption of promising natures, like Alcibiades, is ultimately the fault of the public itself.

(margin note: Sophist)

Socrates was accused at his trial of having 'demoralized the young men' of the upper class, who were concerned in anti-democratic movements during the Peloponnesian War. He was confused in the public mind with the Sophists, and both were thought to have undermined traditional morality and loyalty to the constitution. The Sophists were travelling teachers, who met a growing need for advanced education by lecturing in private houses to young men rich enough to pay their fees. Socrates never taught in private or took fees; he conversed publicly with all comers. The name 'Sophist' had originally meant an expert in any art or a man of special sagacity in practical life or in speculation. But in Plato it has acquired some of the modern meaning and stands for a tendency antagonistic to the Socratic philosophy. The Gorgias defines rhetoric, which many of the Sophists taught, as the art of influencing public assemblies without any real knowledge of right and wrong. The Sophist lives wholly in the world of appearances; he only echoes the conventional notions of the public and teaches the ambitious young how to get on in life by flattering and cajoling the Great Beast. The extreme consequences of such teaching are expressed in Thrasymachus' view of life.

So the disinterested pursuit of truth is abandoned by those promising natures which corrupting influences have diverted to seek power by flattery. Philosophy falls a prey to unworthy aspirants. (It is not known what sort of persons are typified by the 'bald-headed tinker' at 495 e, p. 68.) The faithful few, like Socrates and Plato himself, must stand aside, powerless to help society, and can only save their own souls.

Here Adeimantus interposed: No one could deny all that, Socrates; but, whenever you talk in this way, your hearers feel a certain misgiving: they think that, because they are inexperienced in your method of question and answer, at each question the reasoning leads them a little farther astray, until at last these slight divergences amount to a serious error and they find themselves contradicting their original position. Just as in draughts the less skilful player is finally hemmed into a corner where he cannot make a move, so in this game where words take the place of counters they feel they are being cornered and reduced to silence, but that does not really prove them in the wrong. I say this with an eye to the present situation. Anyone might say now that at each question you ask there is no contradicting you, but that nevertheless, as a matter of plain fact, the votaries of philosophy, when they carry on the study too long, instead of taking it up in youth as a part of general culture and then dropping it, almost always become decidedly queer, not to say utterly worthless; while even the most respectable are so far the worse for this pursuit you are praising as to become useless to society.

Well, I replied, do you think that charge is untrue?

I do not know, he answered; I should like to hear your opinion.

You shall; I think it is true.

Then how can it be right to say that there will be no rest from trouble until states are ruled by these philosophers whom we are now admitting to be of no use to them?

That is a question which needs to be answered by means of a parable.

Whereas you, of course, never talk in parables!

Ah, said I, mocking me, are you? after forcing upon me a thesis that is so hard to prove. But never mind; listen to my parable, and you will see once more what an effort it costs me to scrape one together. The better sort of philosophers are placed in such a cruel position in relation to their country that there is no one thing in nature to be compared to it; I can plead their cause only by collecting materials for my parable from more than one quarter,[5] like an artist drawing a goat-stag or other such composite monster.

Imagine this state of affairs on board a ship or a number of ships. The master is bigger and burlier than any of the crew, but a little deaf and short-sighted and no less deficient in seamanship. The sailors are quarrelling over the control of the helm; each thinks he ought to be steering the vessel, though he has never learnt navigation and cannot point to any teacher under whom he has served his apprenticeship; what is more, they assert that navigation is a thing that cannot be taught at all, and are ready to tear in pieces anyone who says it can. Meanwhile they besiege the master himself, begging him urgently to trust them with the helm; and sometimes, when others have been more successful in gaining his ear, they kill them or throw them overboard, and, after somehow stupefying the worthy master with strong drink or an opiate, take control of the ship, make free with its stores, and turn the voyage, as might be expected of such a crew, into a drunken carousal. Besides all this, they cry up as a skilled navigator and master of seamanship anyone clever enough to lend a hand in persuading or forcing the master to set them in command. Every other kind of man they condemn as useless. They do not understand that the genuine navigator can only make himself fit to command a ship by studying the seasons of the year, sky, stars, and winds, and all that belongs to his craft; and they have no idea that, along with the science of navigation, it is possible for him to gain, by instruction or practice, the skill to keep control of the helm whether some of them like it or not. If a ship were managed in that way, would not those on board be likely to call the expert in navigation a mere star-gazer, who spent his time in idle talk and was useless to them?

They would indeed.

I think you understand what I mean and do not need to have my parable interpreted in order to see how it illustrates the attitude of existing states towards the true philosopher.

Quite so.

Use it, then, to enlighten that critic whom you spoke of as astonished that philosophers are not held in honour by their country. You may try, in the first place, to convince him that it would be far more astonishing if they were; and you may tell him further that he is right in calling the best sort of philosophers useless to the public; but for that he must rather blame those who make no use of them. It is not in the natural course of things for the pilot to beg the crew to take his orders, any more than for the wise to wait on the doorsteps of the rich; the author of that epigram[6] was mistaken. What is natural is that the sick man, whether rich or poor, should wait at the door of the physician, and that all who need to be governed should seek out the man who can govern them; it is not for him to beg them to accept his rule, if there is really any help in him. But our present rulers may fairly be compared to the sailors in our parable, and the useless visionaries, as the politicians call them, to the real masters of navigation.

Quite true.

Under these conditions, the noblest of pursuits can hardly be thought much of by men whose own way of life runs counter to it. But by far the most formidable reproach is brought upon philosophy by those professed followers whom your critic no doubt had in mind when he denounced almost all of its votaries as utterly worthless and the best of them as of no use. I admitted the truth of that, did I not?

Yes.

Well, we have explained why the better sort are of no use. Shall we now go on to the question why the majority cannot fail to be worthless, and try to show, if we can, that here again the fault does not lie with philosophy?

Yes, by all means.

Before we begin the discussion, let us recall the point from which we started in describing the inborn disposition required for the making of a noble character. The leading characteristic, if you remember, was truth, which he must always and everywhere follow or else be an impostor with no part in true philosophy. This was one point where the current estimate of the philosopher is very much against us.

It is.

But might we not fairly plead in defence our account of the true lover of knowledge as one born to strive towards reality, who cannot linger among that multiplicity of things which men believe to be real, but holds on his way with a passion that will not faint or fail until he has laid hold upon the essential nature of each thing with that part of his soul which can apprehend reality because of its affinity therewith; and when he has by that means approached real being and entered into union with it, the offspring of this marriage is intelligence and truth; so that at last, having found knowledge and true life and nourishment, he is at rest from his travail?

No defence could be fairer.

Well then, such a one cannot but hate falsehood and love the truth; and when truth takes the lead, we may look to find in its train, not a whole company of defects, but a sound character, in which temperance attends on justice. Nor is there any need to prove once more that a whole array of other qualities must go with the philosophic nature: you will remember how it entailed courage, magnanimity, quickness to learn, and a good memory. Then you objected that, though everyone must assent to all this, yet, if he turned his attention from theory to fact, he would find the actual persons in question to be some of them useless, and most of them having every possible fault. Looking for the grounds of this reproach, we are now inquiring why the majority have these defects; and it was with a view to this problem that we have defined once more the qualities which the genuinely philosophic nature cannot fail to possess.

That is so.

Next then, we must study the influences that corrupt this nature and in many cases completely ruin it, though some few escape, who, as you remark, are said to be of no use, but not altogether worthless. Then we will consider the quality of those counterfeit natures which take to a pursuit too high and too good for them and by their manifold delinquencies have fastened upon philosophy, all the world over, the reputation you spoke of.

What are these corrupting influences?

I will describe them as well as I can. Everyone, I think, would agree that a nature with all the qualities we required to make the perfect philosopher is a rare growth, seldom seen among men.

Extremely rare.

Consider, then, how many grave dangers threaten to destroy these few. Strangest of all, every one of those qualities which we approved — courage, temperance, and all the rest — tends to ruin its possessor and to wrest his mind away from philosophy.

That does sound strange.

And, besides this, all the good things of life, as they are called, corrupt and distract the soul: beauty, wealth, strength, powerful connexions, and so forth — you know the sort of thing I mean.

Yes, but I should like you to explain in more detail.

The matter will be clear enough, and what I have just said will not seem so strange, when you have grasped the underlying principle. We know it to be true of any seed or growing thing, whether plant or animal, that if it fails to find its proper nourishment or climate or soil, then the more vigorous it is, the more it will lack the qualities it should possess. Evil is a worse enemy to the good than to the indifferent; so it is natural that bad conditions of nurture should be peculiarly uncongenial to the finest nature and that it should come off worse under them than natures of an insignificant order.

That is so.

Is not the same principle true of the mind, Adeimantus: if their early training is bad, the most gifted turn out the worst. Great crimes and unalloyed wickedness are the outcome of a nature full of generous promise, ruined by bad upbringing; no great harm, or great good either, will ever come of a slight or feeble disposition.

That is true.

So is it, then, with this temperament we have postulated for the philosopher: given the right instruction, it must grow to the full flower of excellence; but if the plant is sown and reared in the wrong soil, it will develop every contrary defect, unless saved by some miracle. Or do you hold the popular belief that, here and there, certain young men are demoralized by the private instructions of some individual sophist? Does that sort of influence amount to much? Is not the public itself the greatest of all sophists, training up young and old, men and women alike, into the most accomplished specimens of the character it desires to produce?

When does that happen?

Whenever the populace crowds together at any public gathering, in the Assembly, the law-courts, the theatre, or the camp, and sits there clamouring its approval or disapproval, both alike excessive, of whatever is being said or done; booing and clapping till the rocks ring and the whole place redoubles the noise of their applause and outcries. In such a scene what do you suppose will be a young man's state of mind? What sort of private instruction will have given him the strength to hold out against the force of such a torrent, or will save him from being swept away down the stream, until he accepts all their notions of right and wrong, does as they do, and comes to be just such a man as they are?

Yes, Socrates, such influence must be irresistible.

And I have said nothing of the most powerful engines of persuasion which the masters in this school of wisdom bring to bear when words have no effect. As you know, they punish the recalcitrant with disfranchisement, fines, and death.

They do.

How could the private teaching of any individual sophist avail in counteracting theirs? It would be great folly even to try; for no instruction aiming at an ideal contrary to the training they give has ever produced, or ever will produce, a different type of character — on the level, that is to say, of common humanity: one must always make an exception of the superhuman; and you may be sure that, in the present state of society, any character that escapes and comes to good can only have been saved by some miraculous interposition.[7]

I quite agree.

Then I hope you will also agree to this. Every one of these individuals who make a living by teaching in private and whom the public are pleased to call sophists and to regard as their rivals, is teaching nothing else than the opinions and beliefs expressed by the public itself when it meets on any occasion; and that is what he calls wisdom. It is as if the keeper of some huge and powerful creature should make a study of its moods and *essence?*

desires, how it may best be approached and handled, when it is most savage or gentle and what makes it so, the meaning of its various cries and the tones of voice that will soothe or provoke its anger; and, having mastered all this by long familiarity, should call it wisdom, reduce it to a system, and set up a school. Not in the least knowing which of these humours and desires is good or bad, right or wrong, he will fit all these terms to the fancies of the great beast and call what it enjoys good and what vexes it bad. He has no other account to give of their meaning; for him any action will be 'just' and 'right' that is done under necessity,[8] since he is too blind to tell how great is the real difference between what must be and what ought to be. It would be a queer sort of education that such a person could offer, would it not?

It would indeed.

And is there anything to choose between him and one who thinks it is wisdom to have studied the moods and tastes of the assembled multitude, either in painting and music or in politics? Certainly, no one can go into such mixed company and submit to their judgement a poem or a work of art or some service he would render to the state, thus going out of his way to make the public his masters, without falling under the fatal necessity to give them whatever they like and do whatever they approve; but have you ever heard any argument which was not beneath contempt to show that what they admire is really beautiful or what they approve really good?

No; and I do not expect to hear one.

Now, with all this in mind, recall that distinction we drew earlier, between Beauty itself and the multiplicity of beautiful things. Is it conceivable that the multitude should ever believe in the existence of any real essence, as distinct from its many manifestations, or listen to anyone who asserts such a reality?

Assuredly not.

If that is so, the multitude can never be philosophical. Accordingly it is bound to *multitude ≠ philosophical* disapprove of all who pursue wisdom; and so also, of course, are those individuals who associate with the mob and set their hearts on pleasing it.

That is clear.

What hope can you see, then, that a philosophic nature should be saved to persevere in *slip #4* the pursuit until the goal is reached? Remember how we agreed that the born philosopher ← *corrupted* will be distinguished by quickness of understanding, good memory, courage, and *others any* generosity. With such gifts, already as a boy he will stand out above all his companions, *want to* especially if his person be a match for his mind; and when he grows older, his friends and ← *him* his fellow citizens will no doubt want to make use of him for their own purposes. They will fawn upon him with their entreaties and promises of advancement, flattering beforehand the power that will some day be his.

Yes, that happens often enough.

What will become of a youth so circumstanced, above all if he belongs to a great *flattery =* country and is conspicuous there for his birth and wealth, as well as for a tall and *bad for* handsome person? Will he not be filled with unbounded ambition, believing himself well *philosopher* able to manage the affairs of all the world, at home and abroad, and there upon give *king* himself airs and be puffed up with senseless self-conceit?[9]

No doubt.

If someone tells Phil. king he looks a house)

Now suppose that while this frame of mind is gaining upon him, someone should come and quietly tell him the truth, that there is no sense in him and that the only way to get the understanding he needs is to work for it like a slave: will he find it easy to listen, surrounded by all these evil influences?

Certainly not.

Perhaps, however, because there is something in a fine nature that responds to the voice of reason, he might be sensitive to the force which would draw him towards philosophy and begin to yield. But then those friends of his will see that they are in danger of losing one who might do so much for their party. Sooner than let him be won over, there is no engine of force or persuasion, from private intrigue to prosecution in the courts, that they will not bring to bear either upon him or upon his counsellor. How can he ever become a lover of wisdom?

He never will.

good qualities, but w/a bad upbringing lead to his downfall

You see, then, I was not wrong in saying that, in a way, the very qualities which make up the philosopher's nature may, with a bad upbringing, be the cause of his falling away, no less than wealth and all other so-called advantages.

Yes, you were right.

These, then, are the dangers which threaten the noblest natures, rare enough in any case, and spoil them for the highest of all pursuits. And among men of this type will be found those who do the greatest harm or, if the current should chance to set the other way, the greatest good, to society and to individuals; whereas no great good or harm will come to either from a little mind.

Quite true.

So Philosophy is left forlorn, like a maiden deserted by her nearest kin; and while these apostates take to a life that is no true life for them, she, bereft of her natural protectors, is dishonoured by unworthy interlopers, who fasten on her the reproach you have repeated, that some who have to do with her are worthless and most of them deserve heavy punishment.

That is what people say.

"wannabes"

Naturally enough; when any poor creature who has proved his cleverness in some mechanical craft, sees here an opening for a pretentious display of high-sounding words and is glad to break out of the prison of his paltry trade and take sanctuary in the shrine of philosophy. For as compared with other occupations, philosophy, even in its present case, still enjoys a higher prestige, enough to attract a multitude of stunted natures, whose souls a life of drudgery has warped and maimed no less surely than their sedentary crafts have disfigured their bodies. For all the world they are like some little bald-headed tinker, who, having come into some money, has just got out of prison, had a good wash at the baths, and dressed himself up in a new coat as a bridegroom, ready to marry his master's daughter, who has been left poor and friendless. Could the issue of such a match ever be anything but pitiful base-born creatures? And, by the same token, what sort of ideas and opinions will be begotten of the misalliance of Philosophy with men incapable of culture? Not any true-born child of wisdom; the only right name for them will be sophistry.

Quite true.

So, Adeimantus, the remnant who are worthy to consort with Philosophy will be small

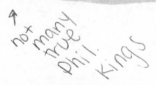

not many true Phil. Kings

indeed: perhaps some noble and well-nurtured character, saved by exile from those influences which would have impaired his natural impulse to be constant in her service; or it may be a great mind born in a petty state whose affairs are beneath its notice; and, possibly, a gifted few who have turned to philosophy from some other calling which they rightly disdain. Some, again, might be held back like our friend Theages, who, with every temptation to abandon study for a public life, has been restrained by ill health.[10] Of my own case there is little need to speak; the warning of the divine sign, I dare say, has come to few men, if any, before me.[11] One who has joined this small company and tasted the happiness that is their portion; who has watched the frenzy of the multitude and seen that there is no soundness in the conduct of public life, nowhere an ally at whose side a champion of justice could hope to escape destruction; but that, like a man fallen among wild beasts, if he should refuse to take part in their misdeeds and could not hold out alone against the fury of all, he would be destined, before he could be of any service to his country or his friends, to perish, having done no good to himself or to anyone else — one who has weighed all this keeps quiet and goes his own way, like the traveller who takes shelter under a wall from a driving storm of dust and hail; and seeing lawlessness spreading on all sides, is content if he can keep his hands clean from iniquity while this life lasts, and when the end comes take his departure, with good hopes, in serenity and peace.[12]

Surely, said Adeimantus, that would be no small achievement. Yes; but far less than he might achieve, if his lot were cast in a society congenial to his nature, where he could grow to his full height and save his country as well as himself.

Chapter XXII (vi. 497 a–502 c)
A Philosophic Ruler Is Not an Impossibility

The pessimism of the last chapter is now redeemed by a ray of hope. The public might be reconciled to the rule of a philosopher, if we could make them see what the love of wisdom means and produce even a single man capable of remoulding human character after the pattern which he alone can know.

Plato alludes to hopes, perhaps conceived on his first visit to southern Italy and Syracuse (388/7 B.C.), of a reform of society from above by an enlightened despot or by some philosophic statesman trained at the Academy. But the philosopher king will not be like the ordinary absolute ruler, free 'to do whatever he likes.' On the contrary, he is compared to an artist working with constant reference to an unchanging model, which irrevocably determines the outline and basic principles of his work.

Well then, I went on, enough has been said about the prejudice against philosophy, why it exists and how unfair it is, unless you have anything to add.

No, nothing on that head. But is there any existing form of society that you would call congenial to philosophy?

Not one. That is precisely my complaint: no existing constitution is worthy of the philosophic nature; that is why it is perverted and loses its character. As a foreign seed sown in a different soil yields to the new influence and degenerates into the local variety, so this nature cannot now keep its proper virtue, but falls away and takes on an alien character. If it can ever find the ideal form of society, as perfect as itself, then we shall see that it is in reality something divine, while all other natures and ways of life are merely human. No doubt you will ask me next what this ideal society is.

You are mistaken, he replied; I was going to ask whether you meant the commonwealth we have been founding.

Yes, in all points but one: our state must always contain some authority which will hold to the same idea of its constitution that you had before you in framing its laws. We did, in fact, speak of that point before, but not clearly enough; you frightened me with your objections, which have shown that the explanation is a long and difficult matter; and the hardest part is still to come.

What is that?

The question how a state can take in hand the pursuit of philosophy without disaster; for all great attempts are hazardous, and the proverb is only too true, that what is worth while is never easy.

All the same, this point must be cleared up to complete your account.

If I fail, it will not be for want of goodwill; 'yourself shall see me do my uttermost.'[13] In proof of which I shall at once be rash enough to remark that the state should deal with this pursuit, not as it does now, but in just the opposite way. As things are, those who take it up at all are only just out of their childhood. In the interval before they set up house and begin to earn their living, they are introduced to the hardest part — by which I mean abstract discussions — and then, when they have done with that, their philosophic education is supposed to be complete. Later, they think they have done much if they accept an invitation to listen to such a discussion, which is, in their eyes, to be taken as a pastime; and as age draws on, in all but a very few the light is quenched more effectually than the sun of Heraclitus,[14] inasmuch as it is never rekindled.

And what would be the right plan?

Just the opposite. Boys and youths should be given a liberal education suitable to their age; and, while growing up to manhood, they should take care to make their bodies into good instruments for the service of philosophy. As the years go on in which the mind begins to reach maturity, intellectual training should be intensified. Finally, when strength fails and they are past civil and military duties, let them range at will, free from all serious business but philosophy; for theirs is to be a life of happiness, crowned after death with a fitting destiny in the other world.

You really do seem to be doing your uttermost, Socrates. But I fancy most of your hearers will be even more in earnest on the other side. They are not at all likely to agree; least of all Thrasymachus.

Don't try to make a quarrel between Thrasymachus and me, when we have just become friends — not that we were enemies before. You and I will spare no effort until we convince him and the rest of the company, or at least take them some way with us, against the day when they may find themselves once more engaged in discussions like ours in some future incarnation.

Rather a distant prospect!

No more than a moment in the whole course of time. However, it is no wonder that most people have no faith in our proposals, for they have never seen our words come true in fact. They have heard plenty of eloquence, not like our own unstudied discourse, but full of balanced phrases and artfully matched antitheses;[15] but a man with a character so finely balanced as to be a match for the ideal of virtue in word and deed, ruling in a society as perfect as himself — that they have never yet seen in a single instance.

They have not.

Nor yet have they cared to listen seriously to frank discussion of the nobler sort that is entirely bent on knowing the truth for its own sake and leaves severely alone those tricks of special pleading in the law-court or the lecture-room which aim only at influencing opinion or winning a case.

Quite true.

These, then, were the obstacles I foresaw when, in spite of my fears, truth compelled me to declare that there will never be a perfect state or constitution, nor yet a perfect man, until some happy circumstance compels these few philosophers who have escaped corruption but are now called useless, to take charge, whether they like it or not, of a state which will submit to their authority; or else until kings and rulers or their sons are divinely inspired with a genuine passion for true philosophy. If either alternative or both were impossible, we might justly be laughed at as idle dreamers; but, as I maintain, there is no ground for saying so. Accordingly, if ever in the infinity of time, past or future, or even to-day in some foreign region far beyond our horizon, men of the highest gifts for philosophy are constrained to take charge of a commonwealth, we are ready to maintain that, then and there, the constitution we have described has been realized, or will be realized when once the philosophic muse becomes mistress of a state. For that might happen. Our plan is difficult — we have admitted as much — but not impossible.

I agree to that.

But the public, you are going to say, think otherwise?

Perhaps.

My dear Adeimantus, you must not condemn the public so sweepingly; they will change their opinion, if you avoid controversy and try gently to remove their prejudice against the love of learning. Repeat our description of the philosopher's nature and of his pursuits, and they will see that you do not mean the sort of person they imagine. It is only ill-temper and malice in oneself that call out those qualities in others who are not that way inclined; and I will anticipate you by declaring that, in my belief, the public with a few exceptions is not of such an unyielding temper.

Yes, I agree with you there.

Will you also agree that, if it is ill-disposed towards philosophy, the blame must fall on that noisy crew of interlopers who are always bandying abuse and spiteful personalities — the last thing of which a philosopher can be guilty? For surely, Adeimantus, a man whose thoughts are fixed on true reality has no leisure to look downwards on the affairs of men, to take part in their quarrels, and to catch the infection of their jealousies and hates. He contemplates a world of unchanging and harmonious order, where reason governs and nothing can do or suffer wrong; and, like one who imitates an admired companion, he cannot fail to fashion himself in its likeness. So the philosopher, in constant companionship with the divine order of the world, will reproduce that order in his soul and, so far as man may, become godlike; though here, as everywhere, there will be scope for detraction.

Quite true.

Suppose, then, he should find himself compelled to mould other characters besides his own and to shape the pattern of public and private life into conformity with his vision of the ideal, he will not lack the skill to produce such counterparts of temperance, justice, and all the virtues as can exist in the ordinary man. And the public, when they see that we have described him truly, will be reconciled to the philosopher and no longer disbelieve our assertion that happiness can only come to a state when its lineaments are traced by an artist working after the divine pattern.

Yes, they will be reconciled when once they understand. But how will this artist set to work?

He will take society and human character as his canvas, and begin by scraping it clean. That is no easy matter; but, as you know, unlike other reformers, he will not consent to take in hand either an individual or a state or to draft laws, until he is given a clean surface to work on or has cleansed it himself.[16]

Quite rightly.

Next, he will sketch in the outline of the constitution. Then, as the work goes on, he will frequently refer to his model, the ideals of justice, goodness, temperance, and the rest, and compare with them the copy of those qualities which he is trying to create in human society. Combining the various elements of social life as a painter mixes his colours, he will reproduce the complexion of true humanity, guided by that divine pattern whose likeness Homer saw in the men he called godlike. He will rub out and paint in again this or that feature, until he has produced, so far as may be, a type of human character that heaven can approve.

No picture could be more beautiful than that.

Are we now making any impression on those assailants who, you said, would fall upon us so furiously when we spoke in praise of the philosopher and proposed to give him control of the state? Will they be calmer now that we have told them we mean an artist who will use his skill in this way to design a constitution?

They ought to be, if they have any sense.

Yes, for what ground is left for dispute? It would be absurd to deny that a philosopher is a lover of truth and reality; or that his nature, as we have described it, is allied to perfection; or again, that given the right training, no other will be so completely good and enlightened. They will hardly give the preference to those impostors whom we have ruled out.

Surely not.

So they will no longer be angry with us for saying that, until philosophers hold power, neither states nor individuals will have rest from trouble, and the commonwealth we have imagined will never be realized.

Less angry perhaps.

I suggest that, if we go farther and assume them to be completely pacified and convinced, then, perhaps, they might agree with us for very shame.

Certainly they might.

Granted, then, that they are convinced so far, no one will dispute our other point, that kings and hereditary rulers might have sons with a philosophic nature, and these might conceivably escape corruption. It would be hard to save them, we admit; but can anyone say that, in the whole course of time, not a single one could be saved?

Surely not.

Well, one would be enough to effect all this reform that now seems so incredible, if he had subjects disposed to obey; for it is surely not impossible that they should consent to carry out our laws and customs when laid down by a ruler.[17] It would be no miracle if others should think as we do; and we have, I believe, sufficiently shown that our plan, if practicable, is the best. So, to conclude: our institutions would be the best, if they could be realized, and to realize them, though hard, is not impossible.

Yes, that is the conclusion.

Notes

[1] The equality of women (Chap. XV) and the abolition of the family (Chap. XVI). The wave metaphor was introduced at 457 B.

[2] Justice, as a 'civic' virtue, has been defined in Chaps. XII and XIV; but the wise man's virtue, based on knowledge, has still to be described.

[3] The subject of the present chapter. Chapter XXIII explains why the other qualifications, of experience and character, are too often lacking.

[4] The spirit of faultfinding, one of the children of Night in Hesiod's *Theogony*.

[5] Perhaps this alludes to comedies, such as Aristophanes' *Knights*, which represented the burly Demos with the shameless politicians competing for his favour, and the *Clouds*, in which Socrates had been shown as a star-gazing head-in-air. In Plato's parable the master of the ship is the sovereign people, Demos, and the crew are the politicians or demagogues, who have no idea that a ruler needs any moral or intellectual training.

[6] Simonides was asked by Hiero's queen whether it was better to be wise (a man of genius) or rich. He replied: Rich; for the wise are to be found at the court of the rich.

[7] This speech has been variously interpreted. Adam explains: 'Cities are either actual or ideal. In the ideal city, education does not produce a type of character which conflicts with public opinion, because public opinion is itself formed by education. In actual cities, education must conform to the same standard if it is to exist at all.' As things are, Plato accounts for the occasional appearance of a good statesman by suggesting (sometimes ironically) that, like poets and prophets, they are inspired by a sort of irrational genius or 'divine' afflatus.

[8] From Socrates' next speech it appears that the necessity of conforming to the Beast's humours is meant.

[9] The description fits Alcibiades, for whose disastrous career Socrates was held responsible by his enemies. In the dialogue *Alcibiades I*, Socrates takes him to task for his senseless conceit and ambition, and in the *Symposium* Alcibiades himself describes his admiration for Socrates' character and the wisdom of his advice. At the same time Plato may well be thinking also of his own youth, distracted between the influence of Socrates and the importunities of his political friends.

[10] The text here has the phrase 'the bridle of Theages,' which became proverbial.

[11] One of those supernatural intimations which came to Socrates had forbidden him to take more than the necessary part in public life. At *Apology* 31 D Socrates says: 'It is this sign which opposes my taking part in politics. And well for me that it does so; for you may be sure that, if I had, I should have perished long ago and done no good to you or to myself.'

[12] This last sentence alludes to the position of Plato himself, after he had renounced his early hopes of a political career and withdrawn to his task of training philosophic statesmen in the Academy.

[13] The iambic rhythm and the word παρών, otherwise hard to account for, suggest a quotation from tragedy. *Rep.* 533 A, *Symp.* 210 A, and *Meno* 77 A (all associated with the revelation of a mystery) may allude to the same context, which perhaps also included the words τὰ γὰρ δὴ μεγάλα πάντ' ἐπισφαλῆ (497 D).

[14] Heraclitus said 'there is a new sun every day,' since all things change and nothing remains the same.

[15] Refers to the political speeches and tracts of Isocrates, whose school for future statesmen was a rival of Plato's Academy, and who taught his pupils a very elegant style. Plato contrives to parody one of its artificial devices with a play upon words that defies translation.

[16] At 540 E, Plato proposes to rusticate the whole population above the age of ten. Contrast the piecemeal tinkering at reform satirized at 425 E.

[17] At *Laws* 709 E Plato again suggests the conjunction of a lawgiver with a young, intelligent, and self-controlled despot.

8. On the Government of Rulers[*]

Thomas Aquinas

Book I

Prologue

When I was pondering what I could offer that would be worthy of Your Royal Highness and suitable to my profession and office, it occurred to me that what I could best offer a king was to compose a book about the kingdom. In it, to the best of my ability, I would diligently bring to light the origin of the kingdom and what pertains to the office of king, according to the authority of divine scripture, the teaching of philosophers, and the examples given by those who praise rulers, relying for the beginning, progress, and consummation of this work on the aid of the one who is King of Kings and Lord of Lords; through whom kings reign: God, Great Lord, and Great King above all gods.[1]

---

[*]Although Ptolemy of Lucca (also known as Bartholomew of Lucca) was listed as the author of *On the Government of Rulers* (*De Regimine Principum*) during the Middle Ages, most scholars agree that the treatise was the work of at least two authors, with Thomas Aquinas (circa 1225–1274) generally being credited with writing Book I and the first half of Book II, while Ptolemy of Lucca (circa 1236–1327) almost certainly wrote the remainder of the treatise circa 1300. This particular selection comes from Ptolemy of Lucca, *On the Government of Rulers: De Regimine Principum*, Book I, Prologue and Chapters 1–4, translated and edited by James M. Blythe (Philadelphia: University of Pennsylvania Press, 1997), 60–70.

Chapter 1

Something must govern human beings who live together.

[1] To begin to fulfill my intention, I must explain how we should understand the title "king."

[2] There needs to be something that directs all things ordained to an end, which might be achieved in various ways, so that they might achieve the due end by a direct path. A ship, impelled by changing winds, moves in various directions, and it could not arrive at its destined end unless the industry of a pilot directed it to port. There is an end for human beings, to which their whole lives and actions are ordained, since they act through the intellect, which characteristically and manifestly works toward an end. Humans proceed in various ways toward their intended end, which the diversity of human endeavors and actions demonstrates, and so they need something directing them to their end. The light of reason is implanted naturally in all human beings, and it may direct them in their acts toward their end.

[3] If it were suitable for humans, like many other animals, to live alone, they would need nothing else to direct them to their end, and all would be kings to themselves under God, the highest king, in that they all would direct themselves in their acts through the divinely given light of reason. But, more than for any other animal, it is natural for human beings to be social and political animals,[2] living in a multitude, as natural necessity requires. Nature has prepared food for all other animals, hair to cover them, and defenses, such as teeth, horns, or claws, or at least speed for flight. But human beings were established with nothing of the sort prepared for them by nature. In place of all of these things reason was given to them, through which they could prepare all these things for themselves by the use of their hands.[3] One person acting alone is not enough to obtain a sufficient life, so it is natural for human beings to live in the society of many.

[4] Other animals also have natural diligence implanted in them by which they know what things are useful or harmful. For example, a sheep naturally judges a wolf to be an enemy. From this natural diligence some animals also recognize medicinal herbs and other necessities for their lives. But human beings have only a general cognition of the necessities of life, in that by reasoning from universal principles they can achieve a cognition of the individual things that are necessary for human life. It is not possible for individual human beings to attain all things of this sort through their own reason. It is therefore necessary for humans to live in a multitude, so that one might help another and different ones might be occupied in finding out different things. For example, one could study medicine, another something different, and still another something else.

[5] This is most clearly shown by the fact that it is characteristic of human beings to use speech, through which individuals can completely express their own concepts to others.[4] Other animals express their own passions to each other only in general, as when a dog shows anger by barking, or other animals display their own passions in various ways. Human beings are more communicative to each other than any other animal that seems to be gregarious, such as the crane, the ant, or the bee.[5] Considering this, Solomon says in Ecclesiastes: "It is better that there be two than one. For they have the advantage of their mutual society."[6]

[6] If, therefore, it is natural for human beings to live in the society of many, it is necessary that among human beings there be that through which the multitude may be governed. For if there were many persons and all individual persons provided only that which was suitable for themselves individually, the multitude would be broken up and dispersed unless there were something to take care of what pertained to the good of the multitude. Likewise, the body of a human or of any animal would dissipate unless there were some general governing strength in the body to attend to the common good of all the members. Considering this, Solomon says: "Where there is no governor, the people will be scattered."[7]

[7] This is rational, since that which is individual is not the same as that which is in common. They differ by their individual characteristics, but they are united by what they have in common. But different things have different causes. Therefore, it is necessary for there to be something which impels to the common good of the many beyond that which impels to the particular good. For this reason, one finds something governing all things ordained to one end.[8] In the physical universe the first body, namely the celestial body, governs the other bodies through the order of divine providence, and all bodies are governed by rational creatures.[9] In individual human beings the spirit governs the body, and among the parts of the spirit, the irascible and concupiscible are ruled by reason.[10] Likewise, among the members of the body one is principal, like the heart or head, and this moves all others.[11] Therefore, it is necessary that there be something that governs in every multitude.

Chapter 2

Distinctions among the various forms of lordship or government.

[1] In the case of certain things that are ordained to an end it is possible to proceed either rightly or not rightly. There is also both a right approach and one that is not right in the government of a multitude.[12] It is directed rightly when it is led to a suitable end, not rightly when it is led to a unsuitable end. But the end suitable for a multitude of the free is different than that for a multitude of servants, since the free exist for their own sake, while servants are servants for the sake of another.[13] If, therefore, the one governing ordains a multitude of the free to the common good of the multitude, the government will be right and just, as is suitable for the free. But if the government is ordained to the private good of the one governing, the government will be unjust and perverse.[14] The Lord threatens such rectors through Ezekiel, saying: "Woe to the shepherds who feed themselves," that is, those who seek their own profit, "should not the flocks be fed by the shepherds?"[15] Shepherds certainly ought to seek the good of the flock, and all rectors should seek the good of the multitude subject to them.

[2] Therefore, one alone who brings about an unjust government by seeking individual profit from the government, and not the good of the multitude subject to that rector, is called a tyrant. This name is derived from "fortitude,"[16] because a tyrant oppresses through might instead of governing through justice, which is why mighty ones were

[margin handwriting: oligarchy]

called tyrants among the ancients. But if more than one, although still a few, bring about an unjust government, it is called "oligarchy," that is, the rule of the few. This occurs when a few oppress the plebs for the sake of riches, and they only differ from a tyrant by their plurality. But if the many exercise an unjust government it is named "democracy," that is, hegemony of the people. This occurs when the plebeian people oppresses the rich through the might of the multitude. Then, the whole people will act as if it were a single tyrant.

[3] I must distinguish just governments in a similar way. If some multitude administers the government, it is called by the common name "polity"; for example, when a multitude of warriors exercises lordship in a city or province. But if a few virtuous ones administer a government of this kind, it is called "aristocracy," that is the best hegemony, or hegemony of the best, and for this reason the few are called "optimates."[17] But if one alone is involved with just government, that one is properly called "king." The Lord says through Ezekiel: "My servant David will be king over all, and there will be one shepherd of all of them."[18] This shows clearly that the very idea of king is one who presides, and that he should be a shepherd seeking the common good of the multitude and not his own profit. *[handwriting: responsibility of a king]*

[4] Since it is appropriate for human beings to live in a multitude, because as solitary individuals they are not self-sufficient with respect to the necessities of life, it follows that the more perfect the society of the multitude is, the more it will be self-sufficient with respect to the necessities of life. There is, no doubt, some sufficiency for life in one household living in one home–that which pertains to natural acts of nutrition, giving birth to offspring, and other things of this kind–and in one neighborhood with respect to the things pertaining to one craft. But in a city, which is the perfect community, there is sufficiency with respect to the necessities of life, and it is even more present in a province, since there is a necessity of fighting together and giving mutual aid against the enemy.[19]

[5] Therefore, one who governs the perfect community, that is a city or province, is called by the epithet "the king,"[20] but one who governs a home, is called "paterfamilias" and not king. Nevertheless, he is similar in some ways to a king, and for this reason kings are sometimes called fathers of their peoples.

[6] Therefore, it is clear from what I have said that a king is one who governs the multitude of one city or province for the common good. As Solomon says in Ecclesiastes: "The king commands all the land serving him."[21]

Chapter 3

It is more useful to the multitude of human beings living together to be governed by one than by many.

[1] Now that I have set out these introductory points, I must ask whether it is more expedient for a province or a city to be governed by many or by one. This can be considered with respect to the end of government. The intention of those who govern

should be directed to this, in order to procure the health of that which they undertake to govern. It is the pilot's job to conduct a ship unharmed to the well-being of the port by preserving it against the dangers of the sea. But the good and well-being of a multitude joined in society is that its unity should be preserved, and this is called peace.[22] If this is taken away, the utility of social life perishes, and, moreover, the dissenting multitude becomes onerous to itself. Therefore, a rector of a multitude ought especially to attend to this, so as to procure the unity of peace.

[2] Rectors do not rightly take counsel about whether to make peace within the multitudes subject to them, just as doctors do not take counsel about whether to cure the sick committed to them.[23] No one ought to take counsel about an end to which they are obliged to attend, but rather concerning those things which lead to that end. This is why Paul says, after commending the unity of the faithful people: "You should be solicitous to preserve the unity of the spirit in the chain of peace."[24] Therefore, the more effective a government is in preserving the unity of peace, the more useful it will be. For we say that that which leads to the end is more useful. It is evident that what is one in itself can better bring about unity than can many,[25] just as the most effective cause of heat is that which is hot in itself. Therefore, the government of one is more useful than that of many.

[3] It is also evident that the many could in no way preserve the multitude if there were total dissent among them. A certain unity among the many would be required for them to govern at all; many could not pull a ship in one direction unless they were joined together in some way.[26] But many are said to be united to the degree that they approach to one. So it is better for one to govern than many, who only approach to one.

[4] Besides, those things which are in accord with nature are best, for nature operates for the best in individuals. But all natural government is by one. Among the multitude of members there is one which moves all of them, namely the heart, and among the parts of the spirit one strength principally presides, namely reason. There is also one king among the bees,[27] and in the whole universe one God, maker and rector of all. This is in accord with reason, since every multitude derives from one. So, if those things which exist by art imitate those things that are from nature, and if a work of art is better the closer it comes to that which is in nature,[28] it follows necessarily that a human multitude is best governed by one.

[5] This is also apparent from experience. Provinces and cities that are not governed by one labor under dissentions and are tossed about without peace, so that what the Lord bewailed through the prophet seems to be fulfilled: "Many shepherds have demolished my vineyard."[29] On the contrary, provinces and cities that are governed by one king rejoice in peace, flourish in justice, and are gladdened by their affluence. This is why, as a great gift, the Lord promised his people through the prophets that he would put in place one head for them and that there would be one ruler in their midst.[30]

Chapter 4

Many reasons and arguments prove that just as the lordship of one, so long as it is just, is best, so its opposite is worst.

[1] Just as the government of a king is best, so the government of a tyrant is worst. Democracy is opposed to polity, each being a government exercised by many, as is apparent from what I have said;[31] oligarchy is opposed to aristocracy, each being exercised by a few; and kingdom is opposed to tyranny, each being exercised by one. I have already shown that a kingdom is the best government.[32] If, therefore, the worst is opposed to the best, it follows that tyranny is necessarily the worst.[33]

[2] Moreover, a united force is more efficacious in producing its effect than is a dispersed or divided force. Many gathered together can pull what separate individuals working individually could not pull. Therefore, just as it is more useful for a force working for good to be more one, so that it may work for the good more effectively, so it is more harmful if a force working for evil is one, than if it is divided. But the force of one presiding unjustly works to the disadvantage of the multitude, and such a one twists the common good of the multitude to that one's own good alone. Just as, if the government is just, a kingdom is better than aristocracy and aristocracy better than polity, since the more the governing element is one, the more the government will be useful; so, conversely, if the government is unjust, the more the ruling element is one, the more harm it will do. Therefore, tyranny is more harmful than oligarchy, and oligarchy is more harmful than democracy.

[3] Further, a government becomes unjust when it spurns the common good of the multitude and seeks the private good of the governing element. The more it recedes from the common good, the more it is an unjust government. But it recedes more from the common good in oligarchy, in which it seeks the good of a few, than in democracy, in which it seeks the good of the many, and it recedes even more from the common good in tyranny, in which it seeks the good of one alone: for the many is closer to the whole than the few is, and the few are closer than one alone. Therefore the government of tyranny is the most unjust.

[4] Likewise, this is apparent to those who consider the order of divine providence, which disposes all things for the best. Good arises in things from one perfect cause in which everything which can help to effect the good is united, but evil arises from any individual defect.[34] No body possesses beauty unless all its members are properly disposed, but ugliness is present when any member is improperly disposed. Thus, ugliness arises from many causes and in different ways, but beauty arises only in one mode and from one perfect cause. This is the way it is with all good and evil things, as if God provided this so that the good, arising from one cause, should be stronger, but evil, arising from many, should be weaker. Therefore, it is expedient for just government to be of one alone, so that it will be stronger. But if it should decline into unjust government, it is more expedient for it to be of many, so that it will be weaker, and so that the many will mutually impede each other. Therefore, among the unjust governments democracy is more tolerable, and the worst is tyranny.

[5] This is especially apparent if you consider the evils that arise from tyrants. The

consequence of tyrants having contempt for the common good and seeking their private good is that they burden their subjects in various ways, depending on the various passions to which they are subject for obtaining certain goods. Those controlled by the passion of cupidity snatch away the goods of their subjects. As Solomon says: "A just king will build up the earth, but an avaricious man will destroy it."[35] One who is subject to the passion of wrath will shed blood for nothing, so that, as Ezekiel says: "Its rulers in its midst are like wolves snatching their prey to shed blood."[36]

[6] Therefore, we must flee this government, as the Wise One warns, saying: "Keep far away from persons who have the power to kill,"[37] because they kill not for justice but use their power to satisfy the lust of their will. Therefore, there will be no security, for all things are uncertain when there is deviation from what is right, and nothing can be made firm that depends on the will of others, still less on their lust. Such ones not only burden their subjects in temporal things, they also impede their spiritual goods. Since those who have precedence desire that which profits them, they impede all progress of their subjects, suspecting any excellence among their subjects to be prejudicial to their own iniquitous dominance. Tyrants "suspect the good more than the evil, and they always dread another's virtue."[38]

[7] These tyrants attempt to prevent those subjects who become virtuous from acquiring the spirit of magnanimity and not putting up with their iniquitous dominance, and to keep their subjects from joining in a compact of friendship and mutually rejoicing in the advantage of peace. For if their subjects have no trust in one another, they can not take any concerted measures against their lordship. For this reason they sow discord among their subjects, they nourish the discord that has arisen, and they prohibit those things which promote human association, such as marriages and common meals, and other similar things which commonly generate familiarity and trust among human beings.[39] They also try to keep their subjects from becoming mighty or rich. Conscious of their own evil, they suspect others; they fear that just as they use their might and riches for harm, the might and riches of their subjects might become harmful to them. As is said in Job about tyrants: "The sound of dread is always in their ears, and when there is peace," that is, when no one intends evil against them, "they always expect treacheries."[40]

[8] The result is that few virtuous ones are found under tyrants, since those presiding, who ought to lead their subjects to virtue,[41] instead despicably envy the virtue of their subjects and impede it as much as they can. In Aristotle's opinion, brave men are found among those who honor those who are most brave.[42] And as Cicero says, those things of which everyone disapproves are always neglected and flourish too little.[43] It is also natural that persons who are nourished by fear degenerate and develop a servile spirit, and that they become fainthearted in performing all manly and difficult work. Experience shows this clearly in provinces that were under tyrants for a long time. As Paul says in Colossians: "Fathers, don't provoke your children to indignation, lest they become weak in spirit."[44]

[9] Considering these harmful effects of tyranny, king Solomon says, "When the ungodly reign, it is the ruin of persons,"[45] because through the wickedness of tyrants subjects abandon the perfection of virtues. He also says: "When the ungodly take up rule, the people will groan,"[46] having been led, as it were, into servitude. And again he says: "When the ungodly rise up, persons will hide,"[47] so that they might evade the cruelty of

the tyrants. We should not wonder at this, because persons who preside without reason according to the lust of their souls differ in no way from beasts. As Solomon says: "An ungodly ruler over a poor people is like a roaring lion or a hungry bear";[48] for that reason, persons hide themselves from tyrants just as from cruel beasts, and it seems that to be subject to a tyrant is the same thing as to be placed under a raging beast.

Notes

[1] Psalms 94.3 (95.3), Apocalypse (Revelation) 17.14.

[2] Aristotle, *Politics*, 1.2.1253a.2–3, 7–8. See also *Ethics*, 1.7.1097b.11–12, 9.9.1169b.18; *History of Animals*, 1.1.488a.7, 10, and the introduction under "Political Thought of the First Contributor."

[3] Aristotle, *On the Parts of Animals*, 4.10.687a.19.

[4] The emphasis on speech as the characteristic act of human beings probably derives from Cicero.

[5] Aristotle, *History of Animals*, 1.1.488a.10.

[6] Ecclesiastes 4.9.

[7] Proverbs 11.14.

[8] Aristotle, *Politics*, 1.5.1254a.28–31. Aristotle says that all wholes made up of parts have ruling and subject elements.

[9] See Thomas Aquinas, *Summa contra Gentiles*, 3.78, 3.23. In the first reference Thomas explains more clearly that divine providence rules through a universal hierarchy reaching from God to the lowest creatures, and that of all creatures the intellectual ones are highest. Therefore, all are under rational creatures. In 3.23 he explains that the motion of the heavens, that is, the first body, must itself be moved by an intellectual substance above it.

[10] See, for example, Thomas Aquinas, *Summa Theologiae*, 1.81.3, ad 2; 1.2.9.2, ad 3; 1.2.17.2 in 2; and passim. In the first place cited, Thomas repeats Aristotle's statement that the rule of spirit over body is despotic, in the sense that the will need only command the movement of any part subject to the will and it will immediately respond, without any ability to resist. The spirit, however, is different from the body in that it is free and its parts must consequently be able to resist. The irascible and concupiscible tendencies of the spirit, not being slaves, are able to resist their ruler, reason, which rules regally but not despotically. See Blythe, *Ideal Government*, 44–45.

[11] Aristotle, *Metaphysics*, 5.1.1013a.5–6, where, however, Aristotle explains that the heart or head, like the foundation of a house, is an imminent part, from which a person, like a house, takes its beginning, and in fact contrasts this usage of "beginning" with that when we refer to that whose will determines motion, such as the magistrates in cities.

[12] Aristotle, *Politics*, 3.6.1279a.17–21. Aristotle expresses this idea frequently in both the *Politics* and the *Ethics*.

[13] Aristotle, *Metaphysics*, 1.2.982b.25–27.

[14] The classification of government according to the number of rulers and whether or not they serve the common good comes from Aristotle, *Politics*, 3.7.1279a.22–b.10, and the writer takes most of what he says in the next few paragraphs from this. In *Ethics*, 8.10, 1159b.31–1160a.23, Aristotle gives the same classification, but also calls polity "timocracy," and characterizes it by a property qualification.

[15] Ezechiel (Ezekiel) 34.2.

[16] Isidore of Seville, *Etymologies*, 9.19. See also Augustine, *The City of God*, 5.19, where

Augustine explains that the word "tyrant" in its ancient meaning signified a man of power.

[17] "Best" is *optimus* in Latin. "Optimate" was a common term for the powerful in the northern Italian city-states of the author's day.

[18] Ezechiel (Ezekiel) 37.24.

[19] Most of this discussion comes from Aristotle, *Politics*, 1.2.1252b.9–30, but the author of this book adds the part about a province in order to bring Aristotle's scheme of the completion of a political entity in the city-state more into line with medieval kingdoms — to say, in effect, that although the city may be complete, the kingdom is more complete. Aristotle also speaks of the village as less complete than the city, whereas the writer here speaks of the neighborhood. The word used, "*vicus*," could refer to either, but the writer has in mind the medieval arrangement of a city in which each quarter, street, or neighborhood was associated with a trade.

[20] The author says that such a one is called "the king" antonomastically, that is, by the figure of speech whereby an epithet is substituted for a person's or thing's proper name, e.g., "His Holiness" for the pope, or "the City" for Rome, or conversely whereby a proper name is applied to another, e.g., "an Einstein." The former mode is used when the epithet is considered to belong to the one to which it is applied in an essential way, although it may be used for others generically.

[21] Ecclesiastes 5.8.

[22] Augustine, *The City of God*, 19.12. See also Thomas Aquinas, *Summa contra Gentiles*, 4.76.4. In the Latin version of the *Ethics* that Thomas used, the word for the observance of good laws (3.3.1112b.13–14) is translated as "*pax*," peace, which allowed him to claim an Aristotelian ancestry for his position.

[23] Aristotle, *Ethics*, 3.3.1112b.13–14.

[24] Ephesians 4.3.

[25] Thomas Aquinas, *Summa contra Gentiles*, 4.76.4; *Summa Theologiae*, 1.103.3.

[26] Aristotle, *Politics*, 3.4.1276.b.20–27 makes a similar analogy about the different functions of sailors.

[27] A common misconception in ancient times and the Middle Ages. See, e.g., Aristotle, *History of Animals*, 5.21.553b.6.

[28] Aristotle, *Physics*, 2.2.194a.21–22.

[29] Jeremias (Jeremiah) 12.10.

[30] Jeremias (Jeremiah) 30.21; Ezechiel (Ezekiel) 34.23, 37.25.

[31] 1.2.2–3.

[32] 1.3.

[33] Aristotle, *Ethics*, 8.10.1160b.9.

[34] Pseudo-Dionysius the Areopagite (or Dionysius the pseudo-Areopagite), *On the Divine Names*, 4.30. Dionysius was a fifth- or sixth-century Christian Neoplatonist who was incorrectly believed in the Middle Ages to be the same as Dionysius the Areopagite, an Athenian follower of Paul (Acts 17.34). He was immensely influential in the Middle Ages.

[35] Proverbs 29.4.

[36] Ezechiel (Ezekiel) 22.27.

[37] Ecclesiasticus (Sirach) 9.18.

[38] Sallust, *The War with Cataline*, 7.2. The author of this part does not acknowledge that he is quoting anyone. The only difference in this sentence, and it is a interesting one, is that Sallust writes "kings," meaning any king, instead of "tyrants."

[39] Aristotle, *Politics*, 5.11.1313a.39–1313b.21, except for the prohibition of marriage. In medieval society, upper-class and many other marriages were arranged, most often in an attempt to increase the power and prestige of a family. Naturally a tyrant would be suspicious of this and

perhaps the writer here also had in mind large marriage feasts that would bring potentially powerful rivals together. Obviously he does not mean that tyrants would ban marriage altogether, but simply try to prevent disadvantageous unions and encourage ones to their own benefit.

[40] Job 15.21.

[41] Aristotle, *Ethics*, 2.1.1103b.3–6.

[42] Aristotle, *Ethics*, 1.3.1095b.28–30, 3.8.1116a.20–21.

[43] Cicero, *Tusculan Disputations*, 1.2.

[44] Colossians 3.21.

[45] Proverbs 28.12.

[46] Proverbs 29.2.

[47] Proverbs 28.28.

[48] Proverbs 28.15.

9. The Prince[*]

Niccolo Machiavelli

Chapter XV.
What deserves praise or blame in men, and above all in princes.

It now remains to show in what manner a prince should behave to his subjects and friends. This matter having been already discussed by others, it may seem arrogant in me to pursue it farther, especially if I should differ in opinion from them; but as I write only for those who possess sound judgment, I thought it better to treat this subject as it really is, in fact, than to amuse the imagination with visionary models of republics and governments which have never existed. For the manner in which men now live is so different from the manner in which they ought to live, that he who deviates from the common course of practice, and endeavours to act as duty dictates, necessarily ensures his own destruction. Thus, a good man, and one who wishes to prove himself so in all respects, must be undone in a contest with so many who are evily disposed. A prince who wishes to maintain his power ought therefore to learn that he should not be always good, and must use that knowledge as circumstances and the exigencies of his own affairs may seem to require.

Laying aside, then, the false ideas which have been formed as to princes, and adhering only to those which are true, I say, that all men, and especially princes, are marked and distinguished by some quality or other which entails either reputation or dishonour. For instance, men are liberal or parsimonious, honourable or dishonourable, effeminate or pusillanimous, courageous or enterprising, humane or cruel, affable or haughty, wise or debauched, honest or dishonest, good tempered or surly, sedate or inconsiderate, religious or impious, and so forth.

It would, doubtless, be happy for a prince to unite in himself every species of good

[*] Niccolo Machiavelli wrote *The Prince*, arguably his most famous work, circa 1513, but it was not published until 1532, several years after his death. This particular selection comes from Machiavelli, *The History of Florence, and of the Affairs of Italy, from the Earliest Times to the Death of Lorenzo the Magnificent; Together with the Prince. And Various Historical Tracts*, Chapters XV–XIX (London: Henry G. Bohn, 1854), 452–469.

quality; but as our nature does not allow so great a perfection, a prince should have prudence enough to avoid those defects and vices which may occasion his ruin; and as to those who can only compromise his safety and the possession of his dominions, he ought, if possible, to guard against them; but if he cannot succeed in this, he need not embarrass himself in escaping the scandal of those vices, but should devote his whole energies to avoid those which may cause his ruin. He should not shrink from encountering some blame on account of vices which are important to the support of his states; for everything well considered, there are some things having the appearance of virtues, which would prove the ruin of a prince, should he put them in practice, and others, upon which, though seemingly bad and vicious, his actual welfare and security entirely depend.

Chapter XVI.
Of liberality and economy.

To begin with the first qualities of the above-mentioned, I must observe that it is for the interest of a prince to be accounted liberal, but dangerous so to exercise his liberality, that he is thereby neither feared nor respected. I will explain myself. If a prince be only liberal, as far as it suits his purposes, that is to say, within certain bounds, he will please but few, and will be called selfish. A prince who wishes to gain the reputation of being liberal, should be regardless of expense; but then to support this reputation, he will often be reduced to the necessity of levying taxes on his subjects, and adopting every species of fiscal resource which cannot fail to make him odious. Besides exhausting the public treasure by his prodigality, his credit will be destroyed, and he will run the risk of losing his dominions on the first reverse of fortune, his liberality, as it always happens, having ensured him more enemies than friends. And which is worse, he cannot retrace his steps and replenish his finances, without being charged with avarice.

A prince, therefore, who cannot be liberal without prejudicing his state, should not trouble himself much about the imputation of being covetous; for he will be esteemed liberal in time, when people see that by parsimony he has improved his revenue, become able to defend his dominions, and even to undertake useful enterprises without the aid of new taxes; then the many from whom he takes nothing will deem him sufficiently liberal, and the few only, whose expectations he has failed to realize, will accuse him of avarice. In our own times we have seen no great exploits performed, except by those who have been accounted avaricious; all the others have failed. Julius II. attained the pontifical chair by means of his bounty; but he judged rightly in supposing, that in order to enable him to prosecute the war against France, it would do him injury to preserve his reputation for liberality. By his parsimony he was able to support the expense of all his wars without the imposition of new taxes. The present king of Spain could never have accomplished all his great enterprises, if he had felt any ambition to be thought liberal.

A prince, then, who would avoid poverty, and always be in a condition to defend his dominions without imposing new taxes on his subjects, should care little for being charged with avarice, since the imputed vice may be the very means of securing the prosperity and stability of his government.

It may however be alleged that Cæsar would never have attained the empire but by his liberality, and that many others have arrived at the highest honours by the same means. I answer, you are either in possession of dominion already, or you are not. In the first place, liberality would be prejudicial; in the second, the reputation of it is serviceable and necessary. Cæsar endeavoured to appear liberal whilst he aspired to the empire of Rome. But if he had lived longer, he would have lost that reputation for liberality which had paved him the way to empire, or he would have lost himself in the attempt to preserve it.

There have been, however, some princes who have performed splendid actions, and who have distinguished themselves by their liberality; but then their prodigality did not come from the public purse. Such were Cyrus, Alexander, and Cæsar. A prince ought to be very sparing of his own and his subjects' property; but he should be equally lavish of that which he takes from the enemy, if he desires to be popular with his troops; for that will not diminish his reputation, but rather add to it. He who is too liberal cannot long continue so; he will become poor and contemptible unless he grinds his subjects with new taxes — which cannot fail to render him odious to them. Now there is nothing a prince ought to dread so much as his subjects' hatred; unless, indeed, it be their contempt. And both these evils may be occasioned by over liberality. If he must choose between extremes, it is better to submit to the imputation of parsimony than to make a show of liberality; since the first, though it may not be productive of honour, never gives birth to hatred and contempt.

Chapter XVII.
Of cruelty and clemency, and whether it is better to be loved than feared.

To proceed to other qualities which are requisite in those who govern. A prince ought unquestionably to be merciful, but should take care how he executes his clemency. Cæsar Borgia was accounted cruel; but it was to that cruelty that he was indebted for the advantage of uniting Romagna to his other dominions, and of establishing in that province peace and tranquillity, of which it had been so long deprived. And, every thing well considered, it must be allowed that this prince showed greater clemency than the people of Florence, who, to avoid the reproach of cruelty, suffered Pistoia to be destroyed. When it is necessary for a prince to restrain his subjects within the bounds of duty, he should not regard the imputation of cruelty, because by making a few examples, he will find that he really showed more humanity in the end, than he, who by too great indulgence, suffers disorders to arise, which commonly terminate in rapine and murder. For such disorders disturb a whole community, whilst punishments inflicted by the prince affect only a few individuals.

This is particularly true with respect to a new prince, who can scarcely avoid the reproach of cruelty, every new government being replete with dangers. Thus Virgil makes Dido excuse her severity, by the necessity to which she was reduced of maintaining the interests of a throne which she did not inherit from her ancestors: —

Res dura et regni novitas me talia cogunt
Moliri, et latè fines custode tueri. — *Æn*. lib. i.

A prince, however, should not be afraid of phantoms of his own raising; neither should he lend too ready an ear to terrifying tales which may be told him, but should temper his mercy with prudence, in such a manner, that too much confidence may not put him off his guard, nor causeless jealousies make him insupportable. There is a medium between a foolish security and an unreasonable distrust.

It has been sometimes asked, whether it is better to be loved than feared; to which I answer, that one should wish to be both. But as that is a hard matter to accomplish, I think, if it is necessary to make a selection, that it is safer to be feared than be loved. For it may be truly affirmed of mankind in general, that they are ungrateful, fickle, timid, dissembling, and self-interested; so long as you can serve them, they are entirely devoted to you; their wealth, their blood, their lives, and even their offspring are at your disposal, when you have no occasion for them; but in the day of need, they turn their back upon you. The prince who relies on professions, courts his own destruction, because the friends whom he acquires by means of money alone, and whose attachment does not spring from a regard for personal merit, are seldom proof against reverse of fortune, but abandon their benefactor when he most requires their services. Men are generally more inclined to submit to him who makes himself dreaded, than to one who merely strives to be beloved; and the reason is obvious, for friendship of this kind, being a mere moral tie, a species of duty resulting from a benefit, cannot endure against the calculations of interest: whereas fear carries with it the dread of punishment, which never loses its influence. A prince, however, ought to make himself feared, in such a manner, that if he cannot gain the love, he may at least avoid the hatred, of his subjects; and he may attain this object by respecting his subjects' property and the honour of their wives. If he finds it absolutely necessary to inflict the punishment of death, he should avow the reason for it, and above all things, he should abstain from touching the property of the condemned party. For certain it is that men sooner forget the death of their relations than the loss of their patrimony. Besides, when he once begins to live by means of rapine, many occasions offer for seizing the wealth of his subjects; but there will be little or no necessity for shedding blood.

But when a prince is at the head of his army, and has under his command a multitude of soldiers, he should make little account of being esteemed cruel; such a character will be useful to him, by keeping his troops in obedience, and preventing every species of faction.

Hannibal, among many other admirable talents, possessed in a high degree, that of making himself feared by his troops; insomuch, that having led a very large army, composed of all kinds of people, into a foreign country, he never had occasion, either in prosperity or adversity, to punish the least disorder or the slightest want of discipline: and this can only be attributed to his extreme severity, and such other qualities as caused him to be feared and respected by his soldiers, and without which his extraordinary talents and courage would have been unavailing.

There have been writers notwithstanding, but, in my opinion, very injudicious ones, who, whilst they render every degree of justice to his talents and his splendid achievements, still condemn the principle on which he acted. But nothing can in this respect more fully justify him than the example of Scipio, one of the greatest generals mentioned in history. His extreme indulgence towards the troops he commanded in Spain occasioned disorders, and at length a revolt, which drew on him from Fabius Maximus, in full senate, the reproach of having destroyed the Roman soldiery. This general having suffered the barbarous conduct of one of his lieutenants towards the Locrians to go unpunished, a senator, in his justification, observed that there were some men who knew better how to avoid doing ill themselves than to punish it in others. This excess of indulgence would in time have tarnished the glory and reputation of Scipio, if he had been a prince; but as he lived under a republican government, it was not only connived at, but redounded to his glory.

I conclude, then, with regard to the question, whether it is better to be loved than feared, — that it depends on the inclinations of the subjects themselves, whether they will love their prince or not; but the prince has it in his own power to make them fear him, and if he is wise, he will rather rely on his own resources than on the caprice of others, remembering that he should at the same time so conduct himself as to avoid being hated.

Chapter XVIII.
Whether princes ought to be faithful to their engagements.

It is unquestionably very praiseworthy in princes to be faithful to their engagements; but among those of the present day, who have been distinguished for great exploits, few indeed have been remarkable for this virtue, or have scrupled to deceive others who may have relied on their good faith.

It should therefore, be known, that there are two ways of deciding any contest: the one by laws, the other by force. The first is peculiar to men, the second to beasts; but when laws are not sufficiently powerful, it is necessary to recur to force: a prince ought therefore to understand how to use both these descriptions of arms. This doctrine is admirably illustrated to us by the ancient poets in the allegorical history of the education of Achilles, and many other princes of antiquity, by the centaur Chiron, who, under the double form of man and beast, taught those who were destined to govern, that it was their duty to use by turns the arms adapted to both these natures, seeing that one without the other cannot be of any durable advantage. Now, as a prince must learn how to act the part of a beast sometimes, he should make the fox and the lion his patterns. The first can but feebly defend himself against the wolf, and the latter readily falls into such snares as are laid for him. From the fox, therefore, a prince will learn dexterity in avoiding snares; and from the lion, how to employ his strength to keep the wolves in awe. But they who entirely rely upon the lion's strength, will not always meet with success: in other words, a prudent prince cannot and ought not to keep his word, except when he can do it without injury to himself, or when the circumstances under which he contracted the engagement still exist.[1]

I should be cautious in inculcating such a precept if all men were good; but as the generality of mankind are wicked, and ever ready to break their words, a prince should not pique himself in keeping his more scrupulously, especially as it is always easy to justify a breach of faith on his part. I could give numerous proofs of this, and show numberless engagements and treaties which have been violated by the treachery of princes, and that those who enacted the part of the fox, have always succeeded best in their affairs. It is necessary, however, to disguise the appearance of craft, and thoroughly to understand the art of feigning and dissembling; for men are generally so simple and so weak, that he who wishes to deceive easily finds dupes.

One example, taken from the history of our own times, will be sufficient. Pope Alexander VI. played during his whole life a game of deception; and notwithstanding his faithless conduct was extremely well known, his artifices always proved successful. Oaths and protestations cost him nothing; never did a prince so often break his word or pay less regard to his engagements. This was because he so well understood this chapter in the art of government.

It is not necessary, however, for a prince to possess all the good qualities I have enumerated, but it is indispensable that he should appear to have them. I will even venture to affirm, that it is sometimes dangerous to use, though it is always useful to seem to possess them. A prince should earnestly endeavour to gain the reputation of kindness, clemency, piety, justice, and fidelity to his engagements. He ought to possess all these good qualities, but still retain such power over himself as to display their opposites whenever it may be expedient. I maintain, that a prince, and especially a new prince, cannot with impunity exercise all the virtues, because his own self-preservation will often compel him to violate the laws of charity, religion, and humanity. He should habituate himself to bend easily to the various circumstances which may from time to time surround him. In a word, it will be as useful to him to persevere in the path of rectitude, while he feels no inconvenience in doing so, as to know how to deviate from it when circumstances dictate such a course. He should make it a rule above all things, never to utter anything which does not breathe of kindness, justice, good faith, and piety: this last quality it is most important for him to appear to possess, as men in general judge more from appearances than from reality. All men have eyes, but few have the gift of penetration. Every one sees your exterior, but few can discern what you have in your heart; and those few dare not oppose the voice of the multitude, who have the majesty of their prince on their side. Now, in forming a judgment of the minds of men, and more especially of princes, as we cannot recur to any tribunal, we must attend only to results. Let it then be the prince's chief care to maintain his authority; the means he employs, be what they may, will, for this purpose, always appear honourable and meet applause; for the vulgar are ever caught by appearances, and judge only by the event. And as the world is chiefly composed of such as are called the vulgar, the voice of the few is seldom or never heard or regarded.

There is a prince now alive (whose name it may not be proper to mention) who ever preaches the doctrines of peace and good faith; but if he had observed either the one or the other, he would long ago have lost both his reputation and dominions.[2]

Chapter XIX.

That it is necessary to avoid being hated and despised.

Having distinctly considered the principal qualities with which a prince should be endowed, I shall briefly discuss the rest in a general discourse under the following heads, viz. that a prince ought sedulously to avoid every thing which may make him odious or despicable. If he succeed in this, he may fill his part with reasonable success, and need not fear danger from the infamy of other vices.

Nothing, in my opinion, renders a prince so odious as the violation of the right of property and a disregard to the honour of married women. Subjects will live contentedly enough under a prince who neither invades their property nor their honour; and then he will only have to contend against the pretensions of a few ambitious persons, whom he can easily find means to restrain.

A prince whose conduct is light, inconstant, pusillanimous, irresolute, and effeminate, is sure to be despised: these defects he ought to shun as he would so many rocks, and endeavour to display a character for courage, gravity, energy, and magnificence in all his actions. His decisions in matters between individuals should be irrevocable, so that none may dare to think of abusing or deceiving him. By these means he will conciliate the esteem of his subjects, and prevent any attempts to subvert his authority. He will then have less to apprehend from external enemies, who will be cautious in their attacks upon a prince who has secured the affection of his subjects. A prince has two things to guard against, the machinations of his own subjects and the attempts of powerful foreigners. The latter he will be able to repel by means' of good friends and good troops; and these he will be sure to have as long as his arms are respectable. Besides, internal peace can only be interrupted by conspiracies, which are only dangerous when they are encouraged and supported by foreign powers. The latter, however, dare not stir, if the prince but conform to the rules I have laid down, and follow the example of Nabis, the tyrant of Sparta.

With regard to his subjects, if all be at peace without his dominions, a prince has nothing to dread but secret conspiracies, from which he may always secure himself by avoiding whatever can render him odious or contemptible. Conspiracies are seldom formed except against princes whose ruin and death would be acceptable to the people, otherwise men would not expose themselves to the dangers inseparable from such machinations.

History is filled with conspiracies; but how few have been crowned with success? No one can carry on such a design alone, nor trust any accomplices but malcontents. These frequently denounce their confederates and frustrate their designs, in the hope of obtaining a large remuneration from him against whom they are leagued; so that those with whom you are necessarily associated in a conspiracy are placed between the temptation of a considerable reward and the dread of a great danger; so that to keep the secret it must either be entrusted to a very extraordinary friend or an irreconcileable enemy of the prince.

In short, conspirators live in continual fear, jealousy, and suspicion, whilst the prince is supported by all the splendour and majesty of the government, the laws, customs, and the assistance of his friends, not to mention the affection which subjects naturally entertain towards those who govern them. So that conspirators have reason to fear both before and after the execution of their designs, for when the people have been once exasperated, there is no resource left to which they may fly. Of this I might give many examples, but I shall content myself with one only which occurred in the last century.

Hannibal Bentivoglio, the grandfather of the reigning prince of Bologna, had been murdered by the Canneschi, and the only member of the family who survived was John Bentivoglio, then an infant in the cradle. The people rose against the conspirators, and massacred the whole family of the murderers; and in order still more strongly to show their attachment to the house of Bentivoglio, as there was none of the family left who was capable of governing the state, the Bolonese having received information that a natural son of that prince then lived at Florence, sent deputies thither to demand him, though he lived in that city under the name of an artisan who passed for his father, and to him they confided the direction of the state till John Bentivoglio should be of age to govern.

A prince has therefore little to fear from conspiracies when he possesses the affections of the people; but he has no resource left, if this support should fail him. Content the people and manage the nobles, and you have the maxim of wise governors.

France holds the first rank amongst well governed states. One of the wisest institutions they possess is unquestionably that of the parliaments, whose object is to watch over the security of the government and the liberties of the people. The founders of this institution were aware, on the one hand, of the insolence and ambition of the nobles, and, on the other, of the excess to which the people are liable to be transported against them, and they endeavoured to restrain both, without the intervention of the king, who never could have taken part with the people, as he must thereby render the nobles discontented; nor could he favour the latter, without exciting the hatred of the people. Upon this account they have instituted an authority which, without the interference of the king, may favour the people and repress the insolence of the nobles. It must be confessed that nothing is more likely to give consistency to the government, and ensure the tranquillity of the people. And we may learn from hence, that princes should reserve to themselves distribution of favours and employments, and leave to the magistrates the care of pronouncing punishments, and, indeed, the general disposal of all things likely to excite discontent.

I repeat that a prince ought to cherish and support the nobility, but without attracting the hatred of the people. It may perhaps be objected that several Roman emperors were deposed and murdered by conspirators, though their conduct was replete with wisdom, talents, and courage. In answer to this objection, let us examine the character of some of these emperors, such as Marcus the philosopher, Commodus his son, Pertinax, Julian, Severus, Antoninus, Caracalla his son, Macrinus, Heliogabalus, Alexander, and Maximinus. This examination will naturally lead me to unfold the causes of their downfall, and to justify what I have before said in this chapter, respecting the conduct that princes ought to adopt.

I must first observe, that the Roman emperors had not only to restrain the ambition of the nobles and the insolence of the people, but they had also to contend with the cruelty and avarice of the soldiery, which was the ruin of several of those princes, it being almost impossible to please the soldiery without discontenting the people, who wished for peace as much as the former panted for war. The people sighed for a pacific prince, and the soldiers for one who delighted in war, ambitious, cruel, and insolent, not certainly to themselves, but opposed to the people, as from such a one they might hope for double pay, and an opportunity of satiating their avarice and cruelty at the expense of their fellow subjects. From hence it happened that those emperors, whose nature was averse to harsh measures, were unable to retain either soldiery or people in subjection, and their own inevitable ruin was the result. Most of them, indeed, particularly those who were advanced to the throne from a private condition, despairing to reconcile interests totally opposite, determined to take part with the troops, and troubled themselves but little about the discontents of the people; and this conduct was the safest, for in the alternative of exciting the hatred of the greater or lesser number, it is better to take part with the strongest side. Those emperors, therefore, who raised themselves to empire, and stood in need of extraordinary support to maintain their power, chose rather to adhere to the soldiery than the people, which turned to their profit a disadvantage according to the degree of reputation they had with the military.

Marcus, the philosopher, Pertinax, and Alexander, princes as remarkable for their clemency as their love of justice and the simplicity of their manners, all came to unfortunate ends, except the first, and he indeed lived and died in peace and honour, because he succeeded to the empire by hereditary right, and was under no obligation either to the troops or to the people; and this circumstance, joined to his own excellent qualities, rendered him dear to all, and enabled him to restrain the soldiery within the bounds of duty. But Pertinax being desirous to subject the military (against whose inclination, moreover, he had been elected emperor) to a very different and more severe discipline than had been observed by his predecessor Commodus, a few months after his elevation, fell a victim to their hatred, increased, perhaps, by the contempt which his great age inspired. We may here remark, that hatred is as easily incurred by good actions as by evil; and hence, as I have said before, a prince is often compelled to be wicked in order to maintain his power. For when the strongest party is corrupt (whether it be the people, the nobles, or the troops) he must comply with their disposition and content them, and from that moment he must renounce doing good, or it will prove his ruin.

As to Alexander, his clemency has been much praised by historians, but he was nevertheless an object of contempt, on account of his effeminacy, and because he suffered himself to be governed by his mother. The army conspired against this prince, who was so good and so humane that in the course of a reign of fourteen years not one person was put to death without a trial. He was however sacrificed by his soldiers. On the other hand, Commodus, Severus, Caracalla, and Maximinus, having indulged themselves in all kinds of excess to satisfy the avarice and cruelty of the troops, experienced no happier fate; with the exception of Severus, who reigned peaceably, though in order to satisfy the cupidity of the troops he oppressed the people; but he had excellent qualities, which gained him at once the affection of the soldiers and the admiration of his subjects. Now, as he raised himself to empire from a private station, and may for that reason serve as a model for those who may hereafter be in the same situation, I think it necessary to show briefly in what manner he assumed by turns, the qualities of the fox and the lion, the two animals which, as I have said before, ought to serve as a model to princes.

Severus, knowing the cowardice of the emperor Julian, persuaded the army under his command, in Illyria, to march to Rome, in order to avenge the death of Pertinax, who had been massacred by the pretorian guard. Under this pretence, and without any suspicion, that he aimed at empire, this general arrived in Italy, before any one had intelligence of his departure from Illyria. He entered Rome, and the intimidated senate named him emperor, and put Julian to death. But he had still two obstacles to surmount before he became master of the whole empire. Pescennius Niger, and Albinus, one of whom commanded in Asia, and the other in the western part of the empire, were both his competitors. The first of these had even been proclaimed emperor by his own legions. Severus perceiving that he could not without danger attack them both at the same time, determined to march against Niger, and to deceive Albinus by a proposal to share the government with him; and this offer was accepted by Albinus without hesitation. But he had no sooner vanquished and put Pescennius Niger to death, and pacified the eastern district, than returning to Rome, he complained bitterly of Albinus's ingratitude, whom he did not hesitate to accuse of an attempt upon his life; upon which account he said he was obliged to pass the Alps, in order to punish him for his ingratitude. Severus arrived in Gaul, and Albinus lost at once the empire and his life.

If we attentively examine the conduct of this emperor, we shall find him as fierce as a lion and as cunning as a fox; feared and respected by his troops as well as by the people; but it will not seem strange that a private individual should maintain so difficult a post, if we recollect that it was by commanding esteem and admiration that he disarmed the hatred which his rapacity would otherwise have excited.

Antoninus (Caracalla his son) possessed also many excellent qualities, which made him dear to the legions and respected by the people; he was a warrior, an indefatigable enemy of effeminacy and high living, which rendered him the idol of the army; but then he carried his ferocity to such a pitch, that not only the people but the soldiery, and even his own officers, bore him an irreconcileable hatred. He perished by the hand of a centurion; a feeble vengeance for all the blood he had caused to be shed in Rome and Alexandria, where none of the inhabitants escaped carnage.

From hence we may observe that it is difficult for princes to escape such attempts at assassination as proceed from an obstinate and determined resolution. Their lives are at the mercy of every one who despises death; but as these attempts are but rare, princes should not be very uneasy about them. They should however avoid giving any grievous offence to those who are constantly about their persons. This was peculiarly the error of Antoninus, who retained among his body guard a centurion whose brother he had put to an ignominious death, and whom he was continually terrifying with menaces, an imprudence which cost him his life.

As to Commodus, he might easily have maintained his power had he but trod in the steps of his father, to whom alone he was indebted for the empire; but as he was cruel, brutal, and avaricious, the discipline which prevailed in the army soon gave way to the most unbridled licentiousness; he had also rendered himself contemptible to the army by his total disregard of his own dignity, of which he thought so little, that he was not ashamed to descend into the arena, and there combat with the common gladiators: he fell a sacrifice to a conspiracy provoked by the hatred and contempt which he had excited by his meanness, his avarice, and his ferocity. It now only remains to consider the character of Maximinus.

The legions having rid themselves of Alexander, whom they deemed too effeminate, made choice of Maximinus, a great warrior; but he becoming odious and contemptible, soon lost both his life and the empire. The meanness of his birth (he was known to have been a Thracian shepherd), his great delay in appearing at Rome to take possession of the empire, but above all, the cruelties of his lieutenants, both in the capital and in the rest of the empire, rendered him so vile and odious, that Africa, in the first place, and afterwards the whole senate and people of Rome, and all Italy, conspired against him, and were supported by his own army, who, disgusted with his cruelties and fatigued with the length of the siege of Aquileia, put him to death with the less apprehension, as they saw how universally he was detested.

I shall say nothing of Heliogabalus, Macrinus, or Julian, who all died covered with ignominy. But I shall add, in conclusion, that princes of the present day are under no necessity of gratifying the soldiery in their governments, because they do not form, as at Rome, an independent body, nor do they continue for years in the same governments and provinces, and are not therefore to be dreaded, provided they are treated with a suitable degree of respect. At Rome, the chief policy of the emperors was to content the soldiery; but in our modern states the people are the class whose affection it is most important to obtain, as being the strongest and most powerful. I except Turkey and Egypt. We know that the Grand Signior is obliged to keep on foot an army of twelve thousand infantry and fifteen thousand cavalry, which constitute the strength and security of his government, and it is consequently of the highest importance to him to conciliate their affections. It is the same with respect to the soldan of Egypt, whose troops have, as we may say, the power in their own hands, and he is consequently obliged to treat them with great respect, and to humour them moreover at the expense of the people, from whom he has nothing to apprehend. This government resembles no other, unless perhaps the Roman pontificate. It cannot properly be called either hereditary or new, since, at the soldan's death, his children do not succeed, but he who is chosen by particular persons, vested with the power of election; nor is it subject to those inconveniences which are incident to a new state, because the person of the prince is new, yet the government having been long established, he is received as if he enjoyed an hereditary right.

To return however to my subject, upon attentive examination, it will be seen, that the Roman emperors, whose unfortunate fate has been objected to me, have chiefly perished by having made themselves odious and contemptible. This is the reason why several of them, whether their characters were good or bad, experienced a fate so different from those in whose steps they endeavoured to tread. It was thus that Alexander and Pertinax, who had elevated themselves, were destroyed by attempting to tread in the steps of Marcus, who came to the empire by hereditary right, and who therefore owed no obligation either to the people or the legions. Caracalla, Commodus, and Maximinus, were severally sacrificed by an attempt to imitate the conduct of Severus, to whom they were far from equal in talent.

A new prince should therefore conduct himself differently from Marcus and Severus; but he may learn from the first how to elevate himself, and from the second, by what means he may maintain himself in that elevation.

Notes

[1] The reader will remember the circumstances in which Machiavelli was placed, and that all those maxims which appear revolting are only intended for a prince who is a conqueror and a usurper, and therefore he inculcates them; he must not forget that it was against most cruel and most numerous tyrants, a thousand times more false and perfidious than their conqueror, that he deemed it his duty to put such arms into the hands of his prince as should effectually defend him against the perfidies of his enemies. The utility of this advice was therefore peculiarly adapted to the time and circumstances in which it was written; and he himself felt strongly, that he might seem to equivocate, one may say, in giving this counsel and supporting it by such very weak props. In fact, he has recourse to a fable and a miserable allegory; but the political writers who have followed him, in presenting similar maxims in an absolute way, and as applicable to all times, places, and princes, have by not understanding him done all the mischief which they have attributed to him, or rather these culpable princes have committed the evil without reading him; for to that end there is no need of the instruction of a centaur. It would be easy to prove, even by examples, that the success of perfidy cannot be durable, and that moral laws which exclude not prudence may be usefully applied to internal and external policy. It should first be observed, that this point cannot be settled or appreciated by the success of one man during his life, or of several men during their lives, but, to develop it effectually, it is from the life of a people that these calculations should be made: now the life of a people is the period of its duration as a people. — *Note of the French translator, Guiraudet.*

[2] He alludes to Ferdinand V. king of Arragon and Castile, who by such means acquired the kingdoms of Naples and Navarre.

10. The Theory of Moral Sentiments*

Adam Smith

Finally someone defines what a leader is and is not. What are the characteristics of an international or domestic leader + how does such a leader differ from an ideologue

Chapter II.

Of the order in which Societies are by nature recommended to our Beneficence.

The same principles that direct the order in which individuals are recommended to our beneficence, direct that likewise in which societies are recommended to it. Those to which it is, or may be of most importance, are first and principally recommended to it.

The state or sovereignty in which we have been born and educated, and under the protection of which we continue to live, is, in ordinary cases, the greatest society upon whose happiness or misery our good or bad conduct can have much influence. It is accordingly by nature most strongly recommended to us. Not only we ourselves, but all the objects of our kindest affections, our children, our parents, our relations, our friends, our benefactors, all those whom we naturally love and revere the most, are commonly comprehended within it; and their prosperity and safety depend, in some measure, upon its prosperity and safety. It is by nature, therefore, endeared to us, not only by all our selfish, but by all our private benevolent affections. Upon account of our own connection with it, its prosperity and glory seem to reflect some sort of honour upon ourselves. When we compare it with other societies of the same kind, we are proud of its superiority, and mortified, in some degree, if it appears in any respect below them. All the illustrious characters which it has produced in former times (for against those of our own times envy

---

* Adam Smith first published *The Theory of Moral Sentiments* in 1759. Smith was continually revising it and published a total of six editions of this work in his lifetime. This particular selection is taken from Smith, *The Theory of Moral Sentiments; or, an Essay towards an Analysis of the Principles by Which Men Naturally Judge Concerning the Conduct and Character, First of Their Neighbours, and Afterwards of Themselves. To Which Is Added, a Dissertation on the Origin of Languages*, Part VI, Section II, Chapter II (London: Henry G. Bohn, 1853), 334–344.

may sometimes prejudice us a little), its warriors, its statesmen, its poets, its philosophers, and men of letters of all kinds, we are disposed to view with the most partial admiration, and to rank them (sometimes most unjustly) above those of all other nations. The patriot who lays down his life for the safety, or even for the vainglory of this society, appears to act with the most exact propriety. He appears to view himself in the light in which the impartial spectator naturally and necessarily views him, as but one of the multitude, in the eye of that equitable judge, of no more consequence than any other in it, but bound at all times to sacrifice and devote himself to the safety, to the service, and even to the glory, of the greater number. But though this sacrifice appears to be perfectly just and proper, we know how difficult it is to make it, and how few people are capable of making it. His conduct, therefore, excites not only our entire approbation, but our highest wonder and admiration, and seems to merit all the applause which can be due to the most heroic virtue. The traitor, on the contrary, who, in some peculiar situation, fancies he can promote his own little interest by betraying to the public enemy that of his native country; who, regardless of the judgment of the man within the breast, prefers himself, in this respect, so shamefully and so basely, to all those with whom he has any connection, appears to be of all villains the most detestable.

The love of our own nation often disposes us to view, with the most malignant jealousy and envy, the prosperity and aggrandisement of any other neighbouring nation. Independent and neighbouring nations, having no common superior to decide their disputes, all live in continual dread and suspicion of one another. Each sovereign, expecting little justice from his neighbours, is disposed to treat them with as little as he expects from them. The regard for the laws of nations, or for those rules which independent states profess or pretend to think themselves bound to observe in their dealings with one another, is often very little more than mere pretence and profession. From the smallest interest, upon the slightest provocation, we see those rules every day either evaded or directly violated without shame or remorse. Each nation foresees, or imagines it foresees, its own subjugation in the increasing power and aggrandisement of any of its neighbours; and the mean principle of national prejudice is often founded upon the noble one of the love of our own country. The sentence with which the elder Cato is said to have concluded every speech which he made in the senate, whatever might be the subject, *"It is my opinion, likewise, that Carthage ought to be destroyed,"* was the natural expression of the savage patriotism of a strong but coarse mind, enraged almost to madness against a foreign nation from which his own had suffered so much. The more humane sentence with which Scipio Nasica is said to have concluded all his speeches, *"It is my opinion, likewise, that Carthage ought not to be destroyed,"* was the liberal expression of a more enlarged and enlightened mind, who felt no aversion to the prosperity even of an old enemy, when reduced to a state which could no longer be formidable to Rome. France and England may each of them have some reason to dread the increase of the naval and military power of the other; but for either of them to envy the internal happiness and prosperity of the other, the cultivation of its lands, the advancement of its manufactures, the increase of its commerce, the security and number of its ports and harbours, its proficiency in all the liberal arts and sciences, is surely beneath the dignity of two such great nations. These are the real improvements of the world we live in. Mankind are benefited, human nature is ennobled by them. In such improvements each nation ought not only to endeavour itself to excel, but, from the love of mankind, to promote, instead of obstructing, the excellence of its neighbours. These are all proper objects of national emulation, not of national prejudice or envy.

The love of our own country seems not to be derived from the love of mankind. The former sentiment is altogether independent of the latter, and seems sometimes even to dispose us to act inconsistently with it. France may contain, perhaps, near three times the number of inhabitants which Great Britain contains. In the great society of mankind, therefore, the prosperity of France should appear to be an object of much greater importance than that of Great Britain. The British subject, however, who upon that account should prefer upon all occasions the prosperity of the former to that of the latter country, would not be thought a good citizen of Great Britain. We do not love our country merely as a part of the great society of mankind — we love it for its own sake, and independently of any such consideration. That wisdom which contrived the system of human affections, as well as that of every other part of nature, seems to have judged that the interest of the great society of mankind would be best promoted by directing the principal attention of each individual to that particular portion of it which was most within the sphere both of his abilities and of his understanding.

National prejudices and hatreds seldom extend beyond neighbouring nations. We very weakly and foolishly, perhaps, call the French our natural enemies; and they, perhaps, as weakly and foolishly consider us in the same manner. Neither they nor we bear any sort of envy to the prosperity of China or Japan. It very rarely happens, however, that our good-will towards such distant countries can be exerted with much effect.

The most extensive public benevolence which can commonly be exerted with any considerable effect is that of the statesmen, who project and form alliances among neighbouring or not very distant nations, for the preservation either of what is called the balance of power, or of the general peace and tranquillity of the states within the circle of their negotiations. The statesmen, however, who plan and execute such treaties, have seldom any thing in view but the interest of their respective countries. Sometimes, indeed, their views are more extensive. The Count d'Avaux, the plenipotentiary of France, at the treaty of Munster, would have been willing to sacrifice his life (according to the Cardinal de Retz, a man not over-credulous in the virtue of other people), in order to have restored, by that treaty, the general tranquillity of Europe. King William seems to have had a real zeal for the liberty and independency of the greater part of the sovereign states of Europe; which, perhaps, might be a good deal stimulated by his particular aversion to France, the state from which, during his time, that liberty and independency were principally in danger. Some share of the same spirit seems to have descended to the first ministry of Queen Anne.

Every independent state is divided into many different orders and societies, each of which has its own particular powers, privileges, and immunities. Every individual is naturally more attached to his own particular order or society than to any other. His own interest, his own vanity, the interest and vanity of many of his friends and companions, are commonly a good deal connected with it: he is ambitious to extend its privileges and immunities — he is zealous to defend them against the encroachments of every other order or society.

Upon the manner in which any state is divided into the different orders and societies which compose it, and upon the particular distribution which has been made of their respective powers, privileges, and immunities, depends what is called the constitution of that particular state.

Upon the ability of each particular order or society to maintain its own powers, privileges, and immunities, against the encroachments of every other, depends the stability of that particular constitution. That particular constitution is necessarily more or less altered, whenever any of its subordinate parts is either raised above or depressed below whatever had been its former rank and condition.

All those different orders and societies are dependent upon the state to which they owe their security and protection. That they are all subordinate to that state, and established only in subserviency to its prosperity and preservation, is a truth acknowledged by the most partial member of every one of them. It may often, however, be hard to convince him that the prosperity and preservation of the state require any diminution of the powers, privileges, and immunities of his own particular order or society. This partiality, though it may sometimes be unjust, may not upon that account be useless. It checks the spirit of innovation. It tends to preserve whatever is the established balance among the different orders and societies into which the state is divided; and while it sometimes appears to obstruct some alterations of government which may be fashionable and popular at the time, it contributes in reality to the stability and permanency of the whole system.

The love of our country seems, in ordinary cases, to involve in it two different principles; first, a certain respect and reverence for that constitution or form of government which is actually established; and, secondly, an earnest desire to render the condition of our fellow-citizens as safe, respectable, and happy as we can. He is not a citizen who is not disposed to respect the laws and to obey the civil magistrate; and he is certainly not a good citizen who does not wish to promote, by every means in his power, the welfare of the whole society of his fellow-citizens.

In peaceable and quiet times those two principles generally coincide and lead to the same conduct. The support of the established government seems evidently the best expedient for maintaining the safe, respectable, and happy situation of our fellow-citizens — when we see that this government actually maintains them in that situation. But in times of public discontent, faction, and disorder, those two different principles may draw different ways, and even a wise man may be disposed to think some alteration necessary in that constitution or form of government which, in its actual condition, appears plainly unable to maintain the public tranquillity. In such cases, however, it often requires, perhaps, the highest effort of political wisdom to determine when a real patriot ought to support and endeavour to re-establish the authority of the old system, and when he ought to give way to the more daring, but often dangerous, spirit of innovation.

Foreign war and civil faction are the two situations which afford the most splendid opportunities for the display of public spirit. The hero who serves his country successfully in foreign war gratifies the wishes of the whole nation, and is upon that account the object of universal gratitude and admiration. In times of civil discord the leaders of the contending parties, though they may be admired by one-half of their fellow-citizens, are commonly execrated by the other. Their characters, and the merit of their respective services, appear commonly more doubtful. The glory which is acquired by foreign war is, upon this account, almost always more pure and more splendid than that which can be acquired in civil faction.

The leader of the successful party, however, if he has authority enough to prevail upon his own friends to act with proper temper and moderation (which he frequently has not), may sometimes render to his country a service much more essential and important than the greatest victories and the most extensive conquests. He may re-establish and improve the constitution, and from the very doubtful and ambiguous character of the leader of a party, he may assume the greatest and noblest of all characters, that of the reformer and legislator of a great state; and, by the wisdom of his institutions, secure the internal tranquillity and happiness of his fellow-citizens for many succeeding generations.

Amidst the turbulence and disorder of faction, a certain spirit of system is apt to mix itself with that public spirit which is founded upon the love of humanity, upon a real fellow-feeling with the inconveniencies and distresses to which some of our fellow-citizens may be exposed. This spirit of system commonly takes the direction of that more gentle public spirit, always animates it, and often inflames it, even to the madness of fanaticism. The leaders of the discontented party seldom fail to hold out some plausible plan of reformation, which, they pretend, will not only remove the inconveniencies and relieve the distresses immediately complained of, but will prevent in all time coming any return of the like inconveniencies and distresses. They often propose, upon this account, to new-model the constitution, and to alter in some of its most essential parts that system of government under which the subjects of a great empire have enjoyed, perhaps, peace, security, and even glory, during the course of several centuries together. The great body of the party are commonly intoxicated with the imaginary beauty of this ideal system, of which they have no experience, but which has been represented to them in all the most dazzling colours in which the eloquence of their leaders could paint it. Those leaders themselves, though they originally may have meant nothing but their own aggrandizement, become, many of them, in time the dupes of their own sophistry, and are as eager for this great reformation as the weakest and foolishest of their followers. Even though the leaders should have preserved their own heads, as, indeed, they commonly do, free from this fanaticism, yet they dare not always disappoint the expectation of their followers, but are often obliged, though contrary to their principle and their conscience, to act as if they were under the common delusion. The violence of the party refusing all palliatives, all temperaments, all reasonable accommodations, by requiring too much, frequently obtains nothing; and those inconveniencies and distresses which, with a little moderation, might, in a great measure, have been removed and relieved, are left altogether without the hope of a remedy.

The man whose public spirit is prompted altogether by humanity and benevolence, will respect the established powers and privileges even of individuals, and still more those of the great orders and societies into which the state is divided. Though he should consider some of them as in some measure abusive, he will content himself with moderating, what he often cannot annihilate without great violence. When he cannot conquer the rooted prejudices of the people by reason and persuasion, he will not attempt to subdue them by force, but will religiously observe what by Cicero is justly called the divine maxim of Plato, never to use violence to his country, no more than to his parents. He will accommodate, as well as he can, his public arrangements to the confirmed habits and prejudices of the people, and will remedy, as well as he can, the inconveniencies which may flow from the want of those regulations which the people are averse to submit to. When he cannot establish the right, he will not disdain to ameliorate the wrong; but, like

Solon, when he cannot establish the best system of laws, he will endeavour to establish the best that the people can bear.

The man of system, on the contrary, is apt to be very wise in his own conceit, and is often so enamoured with the supposed beauty of his own ideal plan of government, that he cannot suffer the smallest deviation from any part of it. He goes on to establish it completely and in all its parts, without any regard either to the great interests or to the strong prejudices which may oppose it: he seems to imagine that he can arrange the different members of a great society with as much ease as the hand arranges the different pieces upon a chess-board; he does not consider that the pieces upon the chess-board have no other principle of motion besides that which the hand impresses upon them; but that, in the great chess-board of human society, every single piece has a principle of motion of its own, altogether different from that which the legislature might choose to impress upon it. If those two principles coincide and act in the same direction, the game of human society will go on easily and harmoniously, and is very likely to be happy and successful. If they are opposite or different, the game will go on miserably, and the society must be at all times in the highest degree of disorder.

Some general, and even systematical, idea of the perfection of policy and law, may no doubt be necessary for directing the views of the statesman. But to insist upon establishing, and upon establishing all at once, and in spite of all opposition, every thing which that idea may seem to require, must often be the highest degree of arrogance. It is to erect his own judgment into the supreme standard of right and wrong. It is to fancy himself the only wise and worthy man in the commonwealth, and that his fellow-citizens should accommodate themselves to him, and not he to them. It is upon this account that of all political speculators sovereign princes are by far the most dangerous. This arrogance is perfectly familiar to them. They entertain no doubt of the immense superiority of their own judgment. When such imperial and royal reformers, therefore, condescend to contemplate the constitution of the country which is committed to their government, they seldom see any thing so wrong in it as the obstructions which it may sometimes oppose to the execution of their own will. They hold in contempt the divine maxim of Plato, and consider the state as made for themselves, not themselves for the state. The great object of their reformation, therefore, is to remove those obstructions — to reduce the authority of the nobility — to take away the privileges of cities and provinces, and to render both the greatest individuals and the greatest orders of the state as incapable of opposing their commands as the weakest and most insignificant.

11. Considerations on Representative Government[*]

John Stuart Mill *[handwritten: similar to Aristotle]*

[handwritten: Argument against Plato, James, or Hobbes? why does he champion representative gov?]

Chapter III.
That the Ideally Best Form of Government Is Representative Government.

It has long (perhaps throughout the entire duration of British freedom) been a common saying, that if a good despot could be ensured, despotic monarchy would be the best form of government. I look upon this as a radical and most pernicious misconception of what good government is; which, until it can be got rid of, will fatally vitiate all our speculations on government.

The supposition is, that absolute power, in the hands of an eminent individual, would ensure a virtuous and intelligent performance of all the duties of government. Good laws would be established and enforced, bad laws would be reformed; the best men would be placed in all situations of trust; justice would be as well administered, the public burthens would be as light and as judiciously imposed, every branch of administration would be as purely and as intelligently conducted, as the circumstances of the country and its degree of intellectual and moral cultivation would admit. I am willing, for the sake of the argument, to concede all this; but I must point out how great the concession is; how much more is needed to produce even an approximation to these results, than is conveyed in the simple expression, a good despot. Their realization would in fact imply, not merely a good monarch, but an all-seeing one. He must be at all times informed correctly, in

[handwritten margin note: assumptions about a monarchy]

[*] John Stuart Mill published *Considerations on Representative Government* in 1861. This particular excerpt is taken from Mill, *Considerations of Representative Government*, part of Chapter III (London: Longmans, Green, and Co., 1867), 18–22.

(margin handwritten note: one man can't handle everything well)

considerable detail, of the conduct and working of every branch of administration, in every district of the country, and must be able, in the twenty-four hours per day which are all that is granted to a king as to the humblest labourer, to give an effective share of attention and superintendence to all parts of this vast field; or he must at least be capable of discerning and choosing out, from among the mass of his subjects, not only a large abundance of honest and able men, fit to conduct every branch of public administration under supervision and control, but also the small number of men of eminent virtues and talents who can be trusted not only to do without that supervision, but to exercise it themselves over others. So extraordinary are the faculties and energies required for performing this task in any supportable manner, that the good despot whom we are supposing can hardly be imagined as consenting to undertake it, unless as a refuge from intolerable evils, and a transitional preparation for something beyond. But the argument can do without even this immense item in the account. Suppose the difficulty vanquished. What should we then have? One man of superhuman mental activity managing the entire affairs of a mentally passive people. Their passivity is implied in the very idea of absolute power. The nation as a whole, and every individual composing it, are without any potential voice in their own destiny. They exercise no will in respect to their collective interests. All is decided for them by a will not their own, which it is legally a crime for them to disobey. What sort of human beings can be formed under such a regimen? What development can either their thinking or their active faculties attain under it? On matters of pure theory they might perhaps be allowed to speculate, so long as their speculations either did not approach politics, or had not the remotest connexion with its practice. On practical affairs they could at most be only suffered to suggest; and even under the most moderate of despots, none but persons of already admitted or reputed superiority could hope that their suggestions would be known to, much less regarded by, those who had the management of affairs. A person must have a very unusual taste for intellectual exercise in and for itself, who will put himself to the trouble of thought when it is to have no outward effect, or qualify himself for functions which he has no chance of being allowed to exercise. The only sufficient incitement to mental exertion, in any but a few minds in a generation, is the prospect of some practical use to be made of its results. It does not follow that the nation will be wholly destitute of intellectual power. The common business of life, which must necessarily be performed by each individual or family for themselves, will call forth some amount of intelligence and practical ability, within a certain narrow range of ideas. There may be a select class of *savants*, who cultivate science with a view to its physical uses, or for the pleasure of the pursuit. There will be a bureaucracy, and persons in training for the bureaucracy, who will be taught at least some empirical maxims of government and public administration. There may be, and often has been, a systematic organization of the best mental power in the country in some special direction (commonly military) to promote the grandeur of the despot. But the public at large remain without information and without interest on all the greater matters of practice; or, if they have any knowledge of them, it is but a *dilettante* knowledge, like that which people have of the mechanical arts who have never handled a tool. Nor is it only in their intelligence that they suffer. Their moral capacities are equally stunted. Wherever the sphere of action of human beings is artificially circumscribed, their sentiments are narrowed and dwarfed in the same proportion. The food of feeling is action; even domestic affection lives upon voluntary good offices. Let a person have nothing to do for his country, and he will not care for it, It has been said of old that in a despotism there is at most but one patriot, the despot himself; and the saying rests on a just appreciation of the effects of absolute subjection, even to a good and wise master. Religion remains: and here at least, it may be thought, is an agency that may be relied on for lifting men's eyes and minds above the dust at their feet. But religion, even supposing it to escape perversion for the purposes of despotism, ceases in these circumstances to be a social concern, and narrows into a personal affair between an individual and his Maker, in which the issue at stake is but his private salvation. Religion in this shape is quite consistent with the most selfish and contracted egoism, and identifies the votary as little in feeling with the rest of his kind as sensuality itself.

A good despotism means a government in which, so far as depends on the despot, there is no positive oppression by officers of state, but in which all the collective interests of the people are managed for them, all the thinking that has relation to collective interests done for them, and in which their minds are formed by, and consenting to, this abdication of their own energies. Leaving things to the Government, like leaving them to Providence, is synonymous with caring nothing about them, and accepting their results, when disagreeable, as visitations of Nature. With the exception, therefore, of a few studious men who take an intellectual interest in speculation for its own sake, the intelligence and sentiments of the whole people are given up to the material interests, and when these are provided for, to the amusement and ornamentation, of private life. But to say this is to say, if the whole testimony of history is worth anything, that the era of national decline has arrived: that is, if the nation had ever attained anything to decline from. If it has never risen above the condition of an Oriental people, in that condition it continues to stagnate. But if, like Greece or Rome, it had realized anything higher, through the energy, patriotism, and enlargement of mind, which as national qualities are the fruits solely of freedom, it relapses in a few generations into the Oriental state. And that state does not mean stupid tranquillity, with security against change for the worse; it often means being overrun, conquered, and reduced to domestic slavery, either by a stronger despot, or by the nearest barbarous people who retain along with their savage rudeness the energies of freedom.

Such are not merely the natural tendencies, but the inherent necessities of despotic government; from which there is no outlet, unless in so far as the despotism consents not to be despotism; in so far as the supposed good despot abstains from exercising his power, and, though holding it in reserve, allows the general business of government to go on as if the people really governed themselves. However little probable it may be, we may imagine a despot observing many of the rules and restraints of constitutional government. He might allow such freedom of the press and of discussion as would enable a public opinion to form and express itself on national affairs. He might suffer local interests to be managed, without the interference of authority, by the people themselves. He might even surround himself with a council or councils of government, freely chosen by the whole or some portion of the nation; retaining in his own hands the power of taxation, and the supreme legislative as well as executive authority. Were he to act thus, and so far abdicate as a despot, he would do away with a considerable part of the evils characteristic of despotism. Political activity and capacity for public affairs would no longer be prevented from growing up in the body of the nation; and a public opinion would form itself, not the mere echo of the government. But such improvement would be the beginning of new difficulties. This public opinion, independent of the monarch's dictation, must be either with him or against him; if not the one, it will be the other. All governments must displease many persons, and these having now regular organs, and being able to express their sentiments, opinions adverse to the measures of government would often be expressed. What is the monarch to do when these unfavourable opinions happen to be in the majority? Is he to alter his course? Is he to defer to the nation? If so, he is no longer a despot, but a constitutional king; an organ or first minister of the people, distinguished only by being irremovable. If not, he must either put down opposition by his despotic power, or there will arise a permanent antagonism between the people and one man, which can have but one possible ending. Not even a religious principle of passive obedience and 'right divine' would long ward off the natural consequences of such a position. The monarch would have to succumb, and conform to the conditions of constitutional royalty, or give place to some one who would. The despotism, being thus chiefly nominal, would possess few of the advantages supposed to belong to absolute monarchy; while it would realize in a very imperfect degree those of a free government; since however great an amount of liberty the citizens might practically enjoy, they could never forget that they held it on sufferance, and by a concession which under the existing constitution of the state might at any moment be resumed; that they were legally slaves, though of a prudent, or indulgent, master.

It is not much to be wondered at, if impatient or disappointed reformers, groaning under the impediments opposed to the most salutary public improvements by the ignorance, the indifference, the intractableness, the perverse obstinacy of a people, and the corrupt combinations of selfish private interests armed with the powerful weapons afforded by free institutions, should at times sigh for a strong hand to bear down all these obstacles, and compel a recalcitrant people to be better governed. But (setting aside the fact, that for one despot who now and then reforms an abuse, there are ninety-nine who do nothing but create them) those who look in any such direction for the realization of their hopes leave out of the idea of good government its principal element, the improvement of the people themselves. One of the benefits of freedom is that under it the ruler cannot pass by the people's minds, and amend their affairs for them without amending them. If it were possible for the people to be well governed in spite of themselves, their good government would last no longer than the freedom of a people usually lasts who have been liberated by foreign arms without their own cooperation. It is true, a despot may educate the people; and to do so really, would be the best apology for his despotism. But any education which aims at making human beings other than machines, in the long run makes them claim to have the control of their own actions. The leaders of French philosophy in the eighteenth century had been educated by the Jesuits. Even Jesuit education, it seems, was sufficiently real to call forth the appetite for freedom. Whatever invigorates the faculties, in however small a measure, creates an increased desire for their more unimpeded exercise: and a popular education is a failure, if it educates the people for any state but that which it will certainly induce them to desire, and most probably to demand.

I am far from condemning, in cases of extreme exigency, the assumption of absolute power in the form of a temporary dictatorship. Free nations have, in times of old, conferred such power by their own choice, as a necessary medicine for diseases of the body politic which could not be got rid of by less violent means. But its acceptance, even for a time strictly limited, can only be excused, if, like Solon or Pittacus, the dictator employs the whole power he assumes in removing the obstacles which debar the nation from the enjoyment of freedom. A good despotism is an altogether false ideal, which practically (except as a means to some temporary purpose) becomes the most senseless and dangerous of chimeras. Evil for evil, a good despotism, in a country at all advanced in civilization, is more noxious than a bad one; for it is far more relaxing and enervating to the thoughts, feelings, and energies of the people. The despotism of Augustus prepared the Romans for Tiberius. If the whole tone of their character had not first been prostrated by nearly two generations of that mild slavery, they would probably have had spirit enough left to rebel against the more odious one.

There is no difficulty in showing that the ideally best form of government is that in which the sovereignty, or supreme controlling power in the last resort, is vested in the entire aggregate of the community; every citizen not only having a voice in the exercise of that ultimate sovereignty, but being, at least occasionally, called on to take an actual part in the government, by the personal discharge of some public function, local or general.

To test this proposition, it has to be examined in reference to the two branches into which, as pointed out in the last chapter, the inquiry into the goodness of a government conveniently divides itself, namely, how far it promotes the good management of the affairs of society by means of the existing faculties, moral, intellectual, and active, of its various members, and what is its effect in improving or deteriorating those faculties.

The ideally best form of government, it is scarcely necessary to say, does not mean one which is practicable or eligible in all states of civilization, but the one which, in the circumstances in which it is practicable and eligible, is attended with the greatest amount of beneficial consequences, immediate and prospective. A completely popular government is the only polity which can make out any claim to this character. It is pre-eminent in both the departments between which the excellence of a political constitution is divided. It is both more favourable to present good government, and promotes a better and higher form of national character, than any other polity whatsoever. . . .

12. The Book of the Three Virtues[*]

Christine de Pizan

---

8. Which shows how the good princess wishes to attract virtue to her.

Guided by divine inspiration, the good princess will think of all these things. Here is how she will act. She will choose well-informed, ethical, and wise advisers to help her elect what is good and avoid what is evil. Although every mortal creature, by nature, is inclined to sin, she will strive to avoid specific mortal sins. As in medicine, she will be the good doctor who cures ills by their opposites. She will follow Chrysostom's *Commentary on the Gospel of Saint Matthew* which says: "Whoever wishes importance in Heaven must observe humility on earth." The most significant in the eyes of God is not the most honored on earth, but whoever is most just on earth will be exalted in Heaven. Since the good princess knows that honors generally inflate pride yet befit her husband's status and her own authority, she will direct her heart toward humility, protecting it from damage by arrogance and puffery by pride. She will thank God and attribute all honor to Him, never ceasing to recognize that she is poor, mortal, frail, and sinful, and that her worldly status is only an office for which she will be accountable to God shortly. In the eyes of eternity, her life's span is very short.

Though the dignity of her position requires this noble princess to receive homage from others, she will not take undue pleasure when it is rendered to her. She will avoid it whenever possible. Her manner, her bearing, and her speech will be gentle and kindly,

---

[*] Christine de Pizan penned *Le Livre des Trois Vertus* (*The Book of the Three Virtues*) in 1405 as a sequel to her book *Le Livre de la Cité des Dames* (*The Book of the City of Ladies*), which she wrote in 1404–1405. The first printed version of the sequel appeared in the year 1497 under the title *Le Trésor de la Cité des Dames* (*The Treasury of the City of Ladies*). This particular selection is taken from de Pizan, *A Medieval Woman's Mirror of Honor: The Treasury of the City of Ladies*, Chapters 8–10, edited by Madeleine Pelner Cosman and translated by Charity Cannon Willard (New York: Bard Hall Press and Persea Books, 1989), 83–90.

1) well-informed, ethical, + wise advisors
2) not sin
3) be humble
4) forgive others easily, be merciful
5) charitable, protect the ppl from husband's wrath

her face friendly, her eyes lowered. Returning greetings to all who greet her, she will be so humane and courteous that her words will be pleasing to God and to all the world. This virtue of humility will make the noble lady patient. Although the world brings ample adversity to great lords and ladies as well as to the lowly, she never will be resentful no matter what happens. She will accept all adversity for the love of Our Lord, thanking Him humbly. If people wrong or injure her, as they might by accident or intention, she will not punish or pursue them. If they are rightfully and justly punished, she will pity them, remembering that God commands one to love one's enemies. Saint Paul says that charity is not self-seeking. Therefore she will pray to God to give them patience in suffering and to be merciful to them.

This noble lady's great constancy, courage, and force of character will not heed the darts of the envious. If she learns of frivolous slander against her, as happens every day to the best of people no matter how great they are, she will not be troubled nor take offence but will pardon readily. Nor because of her greatness will she suspect ill will if anyone slights her, recalling what Our Lord suffered for us and nevertheless prayed for His tormenters. Instead, this humble lady will question whether she could have offended in any manner, remembering virtuous Seneca's teaching to princes, princesses, and people in power: "It is great merit in the sight of God, praiseworthy in the world, and a sign of nobility to let pass lightly the slight which might easily be avenged." That is also a good example to lesser people.

Saint Gregory speaks similarly in the twenty-second book of the *Moralia:* "Nobody is perfect who does not have patience with the damage his neighbors may inflict upon him." He who cannot bear the trespasses of others shows by impatience that he is far from virtuous himself. The same saint's praise of patience says that just as the rose smells sweet and looks beautiful among sharp thorns, a patient creature shines victoriously among those who attempt to wrong her. The princess trying to amass virtue upon virtue should remember that Saint Paul says: "Whoever has all the other virtues, prays unceasingly, goes on pilgrimages, fasts at length, and does all good, but has no charity, profits in nothing."

Therefore, the princess contemplating all this will be so merciful toward everyone that she will suffer for them as for herself. Not content merely to note people in trouble, she will put her hand to the task of helping. As a sage said: "Charity is extended not only through aiding others with money from one's purse but also through comforting words, fitting advice, and all other good one can do." Through charity, this great lady will be the advocate of peace between the prince, her husband (or her son, if she is a widow), and her people, those to whom she has a duty to offer her assistance. If the prince, because of poor advice or for any other reason, should be tempted to harm his subjects, they will know their lady to be full of kindness, pity, and charity. They will come to her, humbly petitioning her to intercede for them before the prince. Poor and unable to request it themselves, they merit the lady's clemency.

9. Wherein it is explained how the good and wise princess will attempt to make peace between the prince and his barons if there is any difficulty between them.

If any neighboring or foreign prince wars for any grievance against her lord, or if her lord wages war against another, the good lady will weigh the odds carefully. She will balance the great ills, infinite cruelties, losses, deaths, and destruction to property and people against the war's outcome, which is usually unpredictable. She will seriously consider whether she can preserve the honor of her lord and yet prevent the war. Working wisely and calling on God's aid, she will strive to maintain peace. So also, if any prince of the realm or the country, or any baron, knight, or powerful subject should hold a grudge against her lord, or if he is involved in any such quarrel and she foresees that for her lord to take a prisoner or make a battle would lead to trouble in the land, she will strive toward peace. In France the discontent of an insignificant baron (named Bouchart) against the King of France, the great prince, has recently resulted in great trouble and damage to the kingdom. The *Chronicles of France* recount the tale of many such misadventures. Again, not long ago, in the case of Lord Robert of Artois, a disagreement with the king harmed the French realm and gave comfort to the English.

Mindful of such terrible possibilities, the good lady will strive to avoid destruction of her people, making peace and urging her lord (the prince) and his council to consider the potential harm inherent in any martial adventure. Furthermore, she must remind him that every good prince should avoid shedding blood, especially that of his subjects. Since making a new war is a grave matter, only long thought and mature deliberation will devise the better way toward the desired result. Thus, always saving both her own honor and her lord's, the good lady will not rest until she has spoken, or has had someone else speak to those who have committed the misdeed in question, alternately soothing and reproving them. While their error is great and the prince's displeasure reasonable, and though he ought to punish them, she would always prefer peace. Therefore, if they would be willing to correct their ways or make suitable amends, she gladly would try to restore them to her lord's good graces.

With such words as these, the good princess will be peacemaker. In such manner, Good Queen Blanche, mother of Saint Louis, always strove to reconcile the king with his barons, and, among others, the Count of Champagne. The proper role of a good, wise queen or princess is to maintain peace and concord and to avoid wars and their resulting disasters. Women particularly should concern themselves with peace because men by nature are more foolhardy and headstrong, and their overwhelming desire to avenge themselves prevents them from foreseeing the resulting dangers and terrors of war. But woman by nature is more gentle and circumspect. Therefore, if she has sufficient will and wisdom she can provide the best possible means to pacify man. Solomon speaks of peace in the twenty-fifth chapter of the *Book of Proverbs*. Gentleness and humility assuage the prince. The gentle tongue (which means the soft word) bends and breaks harshness. So water extinguishes fire's heat by its moisture and chill.

Queens and princesses have greatly benefitted this world by bringing about peace between enemies, between princes and their barons, or between rebellious subjects and their lords. The Scriptures are full of examples. The world has no greater benevolence than a good and wise princess. Fortunate is that land which has one. I have listed as examples many of these wondrous women in *The Book of the City of Ladies*.

What results from the presence of such a princess? All her subjects who recognize her wisdom and kindness come to her for refuge, not only as their mistress but almost as the goddess on earth in whom they have infinite hope and confidence. Keeping the land in peace and tranquility, she and her works radiate charity.

10. Which speaks of the paths of devout charity which are to be followed by a good princess.

The good princess will do even more than tread the pathway of charity. She will personify Saint Basil's words to the rich: "Your temporal possessions come from God." You have more of them than others more deserving. Was God not just in dividing them unequally? Not at all. By sharing with the poor you can merit God's gifts to you; and because of their suffering, the poor will be crowned with a diadem of Patience. Do not let the bread of the hungry mildew in your larder! Do not let moths eat the poor man's cloak. Do not store the shoes of the barefoot. Do not hoard the money of the needy. Things you possess in too great abundance belong to the poor and not to you. You are the thief who steals from God if you are able to help your neighbor and refuse to do it.

Therefore, the well-guided princess must hire fine administrators to help her in her good works. No matter how deserving of compassion are princes who act on bad advice or who are betrayed by dishonest ministers, I believe that the truly good-intentioned select competent counsellors who would not dare to give them bad advice. Ordinarily, a master chooses servants according to his own disposition, and they counsel their master to good or evil according to what they think he wills. Likewise, a good lady will retain servants in her own likeness. She will commission them to inquire throughout the town or elsewhere to find the destitute people, gentlefolk who have fallen on hard times, neglected widows, unfortunate wives, poor girls of an age to be married, women in childbed, students, priests, and monks living in poverty. She will send them help by her almoner, whom she will know to be devout, charitable, and generous even before she appoints him. She will not imitate the custom of certain lords, noblemen, and prelates, who make the most dishonest servant master.

The noble lady will send her almoner secretly to these poor, good people so that even they themselves will not know whence the help is coming; that was what Saint Nicholas counseled. Nor will the good lady, accompanied by her ladies, be ashamed occasionally to visit hospitals and the poor in their homes. Speaking to the poverty-stricken and the ill, touching them and gently comforting them, she will be distributing the greatest charity of all. For the poor feel especially comforted and prefer the kind word, the visit, and the attention of the great and powerful personage over anything else. They think the world despises them. If someone of importance deigns to visit and speak with them, they thereby recover a certain self-respect, which everyone naturally desires.

So doing, the princess or great lady acquires greater merit than a lesser person who performs the same good deed. Three reasons justify that disparity. First, the more exalted the donor, the deeper comfort the poor person receives. Second, the greater the person,

[handwritten margin note: being humble when being charitable]

the more she must humble herself, and thus the more profound the virtue. Third, and most important, she sets a good example for those who see a good work performed with such spirit of humility. Nothing so well instructs subjects as observation of their lord or lady. Therefore, it is as great a benefit when the highborn or others in authority are graciously well-bred as it is a great misfortune when the opposite is true. No lady is so important that it is shameful or unsuitable for her to go devoutly and humbly to pardons or to visit churches or holy places. A lady ashamed to do good is ashamed to work for her own salvation.

Perhaps you will ask me how a great lady can give alms if she has no money, for I have already said that it is dangerous to amass worldly treasure. But, of course, there is no inevitable harm in the princess gathering treasure through revenues or income rightfully her own and gotten without extortion. The question is what she does with these treasures. Certainly God does not oblige her to give all to the poor if she does not want to. She can rightfully use it for her own necessities, to preserve her worldly station, to pay her servants, to give suitable gifts, and to pay her debts. Debts must be paid even before alms are distributed, for there is no merit in giving as alms what truly is due another. The good lady, however, should avoid the temptation of extravagances. Denying herself numerous robes and superfluous jewels and using her money instead for alms is true generosity. Admirable is she who so acts!

She might be compared to the wise man elected governor of a city who, being prudent and clever, realized that former holders of that office later had been deposed, banished, and exiled. Deprived of everything, they were left to die of hunger in a poor country. He thus provided for such a contingency, so that if ever he were exiled he would not starve. He arranged that his pay and the wealth earned in office that was left over after providing for necessities was stored safely. In the end it happened to him as to the others, but his wise provision preserved him from want. Likewise, what one saves out of abundance to give to the poor and to other works of merit is the treasure laid aside in holy provision to serve after death as protection against the exile of hell. This is the incessant message of the Scriptures: "Lay up treasures in Heaven! Lay up treasures in Heaven!" One can take along nothing but such treasures. As the Bible truly demonstrates, not only princesses but all women who are good housekeepers understand this manner of thrift.

In short, then, charity (joined to other noble virtues in her heart) will provide the benevolent princess with such good will that she will celebrate other people's worthiness as greater than her own and rejoice in their welfare as if it were her own. Their good reputation also will delight her. Accordingly, she will encourage the good to persevere in their virtue and the wicked to desist.

13. A Room of One's Own[*]

Virginia Woolf

Chapter Six

Next day the light of the October morning was falling in dusty shafts through the uncurtained windows, and the hum of traffic rose from the street. London then was winding itself up again; the factory was astir; the machines were beginning. It was tempting, after all this reading, to look out of the window and see what London was doing on the morning of the twenty-sixth of October 1928. And what was London doing? Nobody, it seemed, was reading *Antony and Cleopatra*. London was wholly indifferent, it appeared, to Shakespeare's plays. Nobody cared a straw — and I do not blame them — for the future of fiction, the death of poetry or the development by the average woman of a prose style completely expressive of her mind. If opinions upon any of these matters had been chalked on the pavement, nobody would have stooped to read them. The nonchalance of the hurrying feet would have rubbed them out in half an hour. Here came an errand-boy; here a woman with a dog on a lead. The fascination of the London street is that no two people are ever alike; each seems bound on some private affair of his own. There were the business-like, with their little bags; there were the drifters rattling sticks upon area railings; there were affable characters to whom the streets serve for clubroom, hailing men in carts and giving information without being asked for it. Also there were funerals to which men, thus suddenly reminded of the passing of their own bodies, lifted their hats. And then a very distinguished gentleman came slowly down a doorstep and paused to avoid collision with a bustling lady who had, by some means or other, acquired a splendid fur coat and a bunch of Parma violets. They all seemed separate, self-absorbed, on business of their own.

At this moment, as so often happens in London, there was a complete lull and suspension of traffic. Nothing came down the street; nobody passed. A single leaf

---

[*] Virginia Woolf published *A Room of One's Own* in 1929. This particular selection was taken from Woolf, *A Room of One's Own*, Chapter Six (San Diego, CA: A Harvest Book for Harcourt, Brace and Company, 1981), 95–114.

detached itself from the plane tree at the end of the street, and in that pause and suspension fell. Somehow it was like a signal falling, a signal pointing to a force in things which one had overlooked. It seemed to point to a river, which flowed past, invisibly, round the corner, down the street, and took people and eddied them along, as the stream at Oxbridge had taken the undergraduate in his boat and the dead leaves. Now it was bringing from one side of the street to the other diagonally a girl in patent leather boots, and then a young man in a maroon overcoat; it was also bringing a taxi-cab; and it brought all three together at a point directly beneath my window; where the taxi stopped; and the girl and the young man stopped; and they got into the taxi; and then the cab glided off as if it were swept on by the current elsewhere.

The sight was ordinary enough; what was strange was the rhythmical order with which my imagination had invested it; and the fact that the ordinary sight of two people getting into a cab had the power to communicate something of their own seeming satisfaction. The sight of two people coming down the street and meeting at the corner seems to ease the mind of some strain, I thought, watching the taxi turn and make off. Perhaps to think, as I had been thinking these two days, of one sex as distinct from the other is an effort. It interferes with the unity of the mind. Now that effort had ceased and that unity had been restored by seeing two people come together and get into a taxi-cab. The mind is certainly a very mysterious organ, I reflected, drawing my head in from the window, about which nothing whatever is known, though we depend upon it so completely. Why do I feel that there are severances and oppositions in the mind, as there are strains from obvious causes on the body? What does one mean by "the unity of the mind," I pondered, for clearly the mind has so great a power of concentrating at any point at any moment that it seems to have no single state of being. It can separate itself from the people in the street, for example, and think of itself as apart from them, at an upper window looking down on them. Or it can think with other people spontaneously, as, for instance, in a crowd waiting to hear some piece of news read out. It can think back through its fathers or through its mothers, as I have said that a woman writing thinks back through her mothers. Again if one is a woman one is often surprised by a sudden splitting off of consciousness, say in walking down Whitehall, when from being the natural inheritor of that civilisation, she becomes, on the contrary, outside of it, alien and critical. Clearly the mind is always altering its focus, and bringing the world into different perspectives. But some of these states of mind seem, even if adopted spontaneously, to be less comfortable than others. In order to keep oneself continuing in them one is unconsciously holding something back, and gradually the repression becomes an effort. But there may be some state of mind in which one could continue without effort because nothing is required to be held back. And this perhaps, I thought, coming in from the window, is one of them. For certainly when I saw the couple get into the taxi-cab the mind felt as if, after being divided, it had come together again in a natural fusion. The obvious reason would be that it is natural for the sexes to co-operate. One has a profound, if irrational, instinct in favour of the theory that the union of man and woman makes for the greatest satisfaction, the most complete happiness. But the sight of the two people getting into the taxi and the satisfaction it gave me made me also ask whether there are two sexes in the mind corresponding to the two sexes in the body, and whether they also require to be united in order to get complete satisfaction and happiness. And I went on amateurishly to sketch a plan of the soul so that in each of us two powers preside, one male, one female; and in the man's brain, the man predominates over the woman, and in the woman's brain, the woman predominates over the man. The normal and comfortable state of being is that when the two live in harmony together, spiritually co-operating. If one is a man, still the woman part of the brain must have effect; and a woman also must have intercourse with the man in her. Coleridge perhaps meant this when he said that a great mind is androgynous. It is when this fusion takes place that the mind is fully fertilised and uses all its faculties. Perhaps a mind that is purely masculine cannot create, any more than a mind that is purely feminine, I thought. But it would be well to test what one meant by man-womanly, and conversely by woman-manly, by pausing and looking at a book or two.

Coleridge certainly did not mean, when he said that a great mind is androgynous, that it is a mind that has any special sympathy with women; a mind that takes up their cause or devotes itself to their interpretation. Perhaps the androgynous mind is less apt to make these distinctions than the single-sexed mind. He meant, perhaps, that the androgynous mind is resonant and porous; that it transmits emotion without impediment; that it is naturally creative, incandescent and undivided. In fact one goes back to Shakespeare's mind as the type of the androgynous, of the man-womanly mind, though it would be impossible to say what Shakespeare thought of women. And if it be true that it is one of the tokens of the fully developed mind that it does not think specially or separately of sex, how much harder it is to attain that condition now than ever before. Here I came to the books by living writers, and there paused and wondered if this fact were not at the root of something that had long puzzled me. No age can ever have been as stridently sex-conscious as our own; those innumerable books by men about women in the British Museum are a proof of it. The Suffrage campaign was no doubt to blame. It must have roused in men an extraordinary desire for self-assertion; it must have made them lay an emphasis upon their own sex and its characteristics which they would not have troubled to think about had they not been challenged. And when one is challenged, even by a few women in black bonnets, one retaliates, if one has never been challenged before, rather excessively. That perhaps accounts for some of the characteristics that I remember to have found here, I thought, taking down a new novel by Mr. A, who is in the prime of life and very well thought of, apparently, by the reviewers. I opened it. Indeed, it was delightful to read a man's writing again. It was so direct, so straightforward after the writing of women. It indicated such freedom of mind, such liberty of person, such confidence in himself. One had a sense of physical well-being in the presence of this well-nourished, well-educated, free mind, which had never been thwarted or opposed, but had had full liberty from birth to stretch itself in whatever way it liked. All this was admirable. But after reading a chapter or two a shadow seemed to lie across the page. It was a straight dark bar, a shadow shaped something like the letter "I." One began dodging this way and that to catch a glimpse of the landscape behind it. Whether that was indeed a tree or a woman walking I was not quite sure. Back one was always hailed to the letter "I." One began to be tired of "I." Not but what this "I" was a most respectable "I"; honest and logical; as hard as a nut, and polished for centuries by good teaching and good feeding. I respect and admire that "I" from the bottom of my heart. But — here I turned a page or two, looking for something or other — the worst of it is that in the shadow of the letter "I" all is shapeless as mist. Is that a tree? No, it is a woman. But . . . she has not a bone in her body, I thought, watching Phoebe, for that was her name, coming across the beach. Then Alan got up and the shadow of Alan at once obliterated Phoebe. For Alan had views and Phoebe was quenched in the flood of his views. And then Alan, I thought, has passions; and here I turned page after page very fast, feeling that the crisis was approaching, and so it was. It took place on the beach under the sun. It was done very openly. It was done very vigorously. Nothing could have been more indecent. But . . . I had said "but" too often. One cannot go on saying "but." One must finish the sentence somehow, I rebuked myself. Shall I finish it, "But — I am bored!" But why was I bored? Partly because of the dominance of the letter "I" and the aridity, which, like the giant beech tree, it casts within its shade. Nothing will grow there. And partly for some more obscure reason. There seemed to be some obstacle, some impediment in Mr. A's mind which blocked the fountain of creative energy and shored it within narrow limits. And remembering the lunch party at Oxbridge, and the cigarette ash and the Manx cat and Tennyson and Christina Rossetti all in a bunch, it seemed possible that the impediment lay there. As he no longer hums under his breath, "There has fallen a splendid tear from the passion-flower at the gate," when Phoebe crosses the beach, and she no longer replies, "My heart is like a singing bird whose nest is in a water'd shoot," when Alan approaches what can he do? Being honest as the day and logical as the sun, there is only one thing he can do. And that he does, to do him justice, over and over (I said, turning the pages) and over again. And that, I added, aware of the awful nature of the confession, seems somehow dull. Shakespeare's indecency uproots a thousand other things in one's mind, and is far from being dull. But Shakespeare does it for pleasure; Mr. A, as the nurses say, does it on purpose. He does it in protest. He is protesting against the equality of the other sex by asserting his own superiority. He is therefore impeded and inhibited and self-conscious as Shakespeare might have been if he too had known Miss Clough and Miss Davies. Doubtless Elizabethan literature would have been very different from what it is if the woman's movement had begun in the sixteenth century and not in the nineteenth.

What, then, it amounts to, if this theory of the two sides of the mind holds good, is that virility has now become self-conscious — men, that is to say, are now writing only with the male side of their brains. It is a mistake for a woman to read them, for she will inevitably look for something that she will not find. It is the power of suggestion that one most misses, I thought, taking Mr. B the critic in my hand and reading, very carefully and very dutifully, his remarks upon the art of poetry. Very able they were, acute and full of learning; but the trouble was, that his feelings no longer communicated; his mind seemed separated into different chambers; not a sound carried from one to the other. Thus, when one takes a sentence of Mr. B into the mind it falls plump to the ground — dead; but when one takes a sentence of Coleridge into the mind, it explodes and gives birth to all kinds of other ideas, and that is the only sort of writing of which one can say that it has the secret of perpetual life.

But whatever the reason may be, it is a fact that one must deplore. For it means — here I had come to rows of books by Mr. Galsworthy and Mr. Kipling — that some of the finest works of our greatest living writers fall upon deaf ears. Do what she will a woman cannot find in them that fountain of perpetual life which the critics assure her is there. It is not only that they celebrate male virtues, enforce male values and describe the world of men; it is that the emotion with which these books are permeated is to a woman incomprehensible. It is coming, it is gathering, it is about to burst on one's head, one begins saying long before the end. That picture will fall on old Jolyon's head; he will die of the shock; the old clerk will speak over him two or three obituary words; and all the swans on the Thames will simultaneously burst out singing. But one will rush away before that happens and hide in the gooseberry bushes, for the emotion which is so deep, so subtle, so symbolical to a man moves a woman to wonder. So with Mr. Kipling's officers who turn their backs; and his Sowers who sow the Seed; and his Men who are alone with their Work; and the Flag — one blushes at all these capital letters as if one had been caught eavesdropping at some purely masculine orgy. The fact is that neither Mr. Galsworthy nor Mr. Kipling has a spark of the woman in him. Thus all their qualities seem to a woman, if one may generalise, crude and immature. They lack suggestive power. And when a book lacks suggestive power, however hard it hits the surface of the mind it cannot penetrate within.

And in that restless mood in which one takes books out and puts them back again without looking at them I began to envisage an age to come of pure, of self-assertive virility, such as the letters of professors (take Sir Walter Raleigh's letters, for instance) seem to forebode, and the rulers of Italy have already brought into being. For one can hardly fail to be impressed in Rome by the sense of unmitigated masculinity; and whatever the value of unmitigated masculinity upon the state, one may question the effect of it upon the art of poetry. At any rate, according to the newspapers, there is a certain anxiety about fiction in Italy. There has been a meeting of academicians whose object it is "to develop the Italian novel." "Men famous by birth, or in finance, industry or the Fascist corporations" came together the other day and discussed the matter, and a telegram was sent to the Duce expressing the hope "that the Fascist era would soon give birth to a poet worthy of it." We may all join in that pious hope, but it is doubtful whether poetry can come out of an incubator. Poetry ought to have a mother as well as a father. The Fascist poem, one may fear, will be a horrid little abortion such as one sees in a glass jar in the museum of some county town. Such monsters never live long, it is said; one has never seen a prodigy of that sort cropping grass in a field. Two heads on one body do not make for length of life.

However, the blame for all this, if one is anxious to lay blame, rests no more upon one sex than upon the other. All seducers and reformers are responsible, Lady Bessborough when she lied to Lord Granville; Miss Davies when she told the truth to Mr. Greg. All who have brought about a state of sex-consciousness are to blame, and it is they who drive me, when I want to stretch my faculties on a book, to seek it in that happy age, before Miss Davies and Miss Clough were born, when the writer used both sides of his mind equally. One must turn back to Shakespeare then, for Shakespeare was androgynous; and so was Keats and Sterne and Cowper and Lamb and Coleridge. Shelley perhaps was sexless. Milton and Ben Jonson had a dash too much of the male in them. So had Wordsworth and Tolstoi. In our time Proust was wholly androgynous, if not perhaps a little too much of a woman. But that failing is too rare for one to complain of it, since without some mixture of the kind the intellect seems to predominate and the other faculties of the mind harden and become barren. However, I consoled myself with the reflection that this is perhaps a passing phase; much of what I have said in obedience to my promise to give you the course of my thoughts will seem out of date; much of what flames in my eyes will seem dubious to you who have not yet come of age.

Even so, the very first sentence that I would write here, I said, crossing over to the writing-table and taking up the page headed Women and Fiction, is that it is fatal for any one who writes to think of their sex. It is fatal to be a man or woman pure and simple; one must be woman-manly or man-womanly. It is fatal for a woman to lay the least stress on any grievance; to plead even with justice any cause; in any way to speak consciously as a woman. And fatal is no figure of speech; for anything written with that conscious bias is doomed to death. It ceases to be fertilised. Brilliant and effective, powerful and masterly, as it may appear for a day or two, it must wither at nightfall; it cannot grow in the minds of others. Some collaboration has to take place in the mind between the woman and the man before the act of creation can be accomplished. Some marriage of opposites has to be consummated. The whole of the mind must lie wide open if we are to get the sense that the writer is communicating his experience with perfect fullness. There must be freedom and there must be peace. Not a wheel must grate, not a light glimmer. The curtains must be close drawn. The writer, I thought, once his experience is over, must lie back and let his mind celebrate its nuptials in darkness. He must not look or question what is being done. Rather, he must pluck the petals from a rose or watch the swans float calmly down the river. And I saw again the current which took the boat and the undergraduate and the dead leaves; and the taxi took the man and the woman, I thought, seeing them come together across the street, and the current swept them away, I thought, hearing far off the roar of London's traffic, into that tremendous stream.

Here, then, Mary Beton ceases to speak. She has told you how she reached the conclusion — the prosaic conclusion — that it is necessary to have five hundred a year and a room with a lock on the door if you are to write fiction or poetry. She has tried to lay bare the thoughts and impressions that led her to think this. She has asked you to follow her flying into the arms of a Beadle, lunching here, dining there, drawing pictures in the British Museum, taking books from the shelf, looking out of the window. While she has been doing all these things, you no doubt have been observing her failings and foibles and deciding what effect they have had on her opinions. You have been contradicting her and making whatever additions and deductions seem good to you. That is all as it should be, for in a question like this truth is only to be had by laying together many varieties of error. And I will end now in my own person by anticipating two criticisms, so obvious that you can hardly fail to make them.

No opinion has been expressed, you may say, upon the comparative merits of the sexes even as writers. That was done purposely, because, even if the time had come for such a valuation — and it is far more important at the moment to know how much money women had and how many rooms than to theorise about their capacities — even if the time had come I do not believe that gifts, whether of mind or character, can be weighed like sugar and butter, not even in Cambridge, where they are so adept at putting people into classes and fixing caps on their heads and letters after their names. I do not believe that even the Table of Precedency which you will find in Whitaker's *Almanac* represents a final order of values, or that there is any sound reason to suppose that a Commander of the Bath will ultimately walk in to dinner behind a Master in Lunacy. All this pitting of sex against sex, of quality against quality; all this claiming of superiority and imputing of inferiority, belong to the private-school stage of human existence where there are "sides," and it is necessary for one side to beat another side, and of the utmost importance to walk up to a platform and receive from the hands of the Headmaster himself a highly ornamental pot. As people mature they cease to believe in sides or in Headmasters or in highly ornamental pots. At any rate, where books are concerned, it is notoriously difficult to fix labels of merit in such a way that they do not come off. Are not reviews of current literature a perpetual illustration of the difficulty of judgment? "This great book," "this worthless book," the same book is called by both names. Praise and blame alike mean nothing. No, delightful as the pastime of measuring may be, it is the most futile of all occupations, and to submit to the decrees of the measurers the most servile of attitudes. So long as you write what you wish to write, that is all that matters; and whether it matters for ages or only for hours, nobody can say. But to sacrifice a hair of the head of your vision, a shade of its colour, in deference to some Headmaster with a silver pot in his hand or to some professor with a measuring-rod up his sleeve, is the most abject treachery, and the sacrifice of wealth and chastity which used to be said to be the greatest of human disasters, a mere flea-bite in comparison.

Next I think that you may object that in all this I have made too much of the importance of material things. Even allowing a generous margin for symbolism, that five hundred a year stands for the power to contemplate, that a lock on the door means the power to think for oneself, still you may say that the mind should rise above such things; and that great poets have often been poor men. Let me then quote to you the words of your own Professor of Literature, who knows better than I do what goes to the making of a poet. Sir Arthur Quiller-Couch writes:[1]

"What are the great poetical names of the last hundred years or so? Coleridge, Wordsworth, Byron, Shelley, Landor, Keats, Tennyson, Browning, Arnold, Morris, Rossetti, Swinburne — we may stop there. Of these, all but Keats, Browning, Rossetti were University men; and of these three, Keats, who died young, cut off in his prime, was the only one not fairly well to do. It may seem a brutal thing to say, and it is a sad thing to say: but, as a matter of hard fact, the theory that poetical genius bloweth where it listeth, and equally in poor and rich, holds little truth. As a matter of hard fact, nine out of those twelve were University men: which means that somehow or other they procured the means to get the best education England can give. As a matter of hard fact, of the remaining three you know that Browning was well to do, and I challenge you that, if he had not been well to do, he would no more have attained to write *Saul* or *The Ring and the Book* than Ruskin would have attained to writing *Modern Painters* if his father had not dealt prosperously in business. Rossetti had a small private income; and, moreover, he painted. There remains but Keats; whom Atropos slew young, as she slew John Clare in a mad-house, and James Thomson by the laudanum he took to drug disappointment. These are dreadful facts, but let us face them. It is — however dishonouring to us as a nation — certain that, by some fault in our commonwealth, the poor poet has not in these days, nor has had for two hundred years, a dog's chance. Believe me — and I have spent a great part of ten years in watching some three hundred and twenty elementary schools — we may prate of democracy, but actually, a poor child in England has little more hope than had the son of an Athenian slave to be emancipated into that intellectual freedom of which great writings are born."

Nobody could put the point more plainly. "The poor poet has not in these days, nor has had for two hundred years, a dog's chance . . . a poor child in England has little more hope than had the son of an Athenian slave to be emancipated into that intellectual freedom of which great writings are born." That is it. Intellectual freedom depends upon material things. Poetry depends upon intellectual freedom. And women have always been poor, not for two hundred years merely, but from the beginning of time. Women have had less intellectual freedom than the sons of Athenian slaves. Women, then, have not had a dog's chance of writing poetry. That is why I have laid so much stress on money and a room of one's own. However, thanks to the toils of those obscure women in the past, of whom I wish we knew more, thanks, curiously enough, to two wars, the Crimean which let Florence Nightingale out of her drawing-room, and the European War which opened the doors to the average woman some sixty years later, these evils are in the way to be bettered. Otherwise you would not be here tonight, and your chance of earning five hundred pounds a year, precarious as I am afraid that it still is, would be minute in the extreme.

Still, you may object, why do you attach so much importance to this writing of books by women when, according to you, it requires so much effort, leads perhaps to the murder of one's aunts, will make one almost certainly late for luncheon, and may bring one into very grave disputes with certain very good fellows? My motives, let me admit, are partly selfish. Like most uneducated Englishwomen, I like reading — I like reading books in the bulk. Lately my diet has become a trifle monotonous; history is too much about wars; biography too much about great men; poetry has shown, I think, a tendency to sterility, and fiction — but I have sufficiently exposed my disabilities as a critic of modern fiction and will say no more about it. Therefore I would ask you to write all kinds of books, hesitating at no subject however trivial or however vast. By hook or by crook, I hope that you will possess yourselves of money enough to travel and to idle, to contemplate the future or the past of the world, to dream over books and loiter at street corners and let the line of thought dip deep into the stream. For I am by no means confining you to fiction. If you would please me — and there are thousands like me — you would write books of travel and adventure, and research and scholarship, and history and biography, and criticism and philosophy and science. By so doing you will certainly profit the art of fiction. For books have a way of influencing each other. Fiction will be much the better for standing cheek by jowl with poetry and philosophy. Moreover, if you consider any great figure of the past, like Sappho, like the Lady Murasaki, like Emily Brontë, you will find that she is an inheritor as well as an originator, and has come into existence because women have come to have the habit of writing naturally; so that even as a prelude to poetry such activity on your part would be invaluable.

But when I look back through these notes and criticise my own train of thought as I made them, I find that my motives were not altogether selfish. There runs through these comments and discursions the conviction — or is it the instinct? — that good books are desirable and that good writers, even if they show every variety of human depravity, are still good human beings. Thus when I ask you to write more books I am urging you to do what will be for your good and for the good of the world at large. How to justify this instinct or belief I do not know, for philosophic words, if one has not been educated at a university, are apt to play one false. What is meant by "reality"? It would seem to be something very erratic, very undependable — now to be found in a dusty road, now in a scrap of newspaper in the street, now in a daffodil in the sun. It lights up a group in a room and stamps some casual saying. It overwhelms one walking home beneath the stars and makes the silent world more real than the world of speech — and then there it is again in an omnibus in the uproar of Piccadilly. Sometimes, too, it seems to dwell in shapes too far away for us to discern what their nature is. But whatever it touches, it fixes and makes permanent. That is what remains over when the skin of the day has been cast into the hedge; that is what is left of past time and of our loves and hates. Now the writer, as I think, has the chance to live more than other people in the presence of this reality. It is his business to find it and collect it and communicate it to the rest of us. So at least I infer from reading *Lear* or *Emma* or *La Recherche du Temps Perdu*. For the reading of these books seems to perform a curious couching operation on the senses; one sees more intensely afterwards; the world seems bared of its covering and given an intenser life. Those are the enviable people who live at enmity with unreality; and those are the pitiable who are knocked on the head by the thing done without knowing or caring. So that when I ask you to earn money and have a room of your own, I am asking you to live in the presence of reality, an invigorating life, it would appear, whether one can impart it or not.

Here I would stop, but the pressure of convention decrees that every speech must end with a peroration. And a peroration addressed to women should have something, you will agree, particularly exalting and ennobling about it. I should implore you to remember your responsibilities, to be higher, more spiritual; I should remind you how much depends upon you, and what an influence you can exert upon the future. But those exhortations can safely, I think, be left to the other sex, who will put them, and indeed have put them, with far greater eloquence than I can compass. When I rummage in my own mind I find no noble sentiments about being companions and equals and influencing the world to higher ends. I find myself saying briefly and prosaically that it is much more important to be oneself than anything else. Do not dream of influencing other people, I would say, if I knew how to make it sound exalted. Think of things in themselves.

And again I am reminded by dipping into newspapers and novels and biographies that when a woman speaks to women she should have something very unpleasant up her sleeve. Women are hard on women. Women dislike women. Women — but are you not sick to death of the word? I can assure you that I am. Let us agree, then, that a paper read by a woman to women should end with something particularly disagreeable.

But how does it go? What can I think of? The truth is, I often like women. I like their unconventionality. I like their subtlety. I like their anonymity. I like — but I must not run on in this way. That cupboard there, — you say it holds clean table-napkins only; but what if Sir Archibald Bodkin were concealed among them? Let me then adopt a sterner tone. Have I, in the preceding words, conveyed to you sufficiently the warnings and reprobation of mankind? I have told you the very low opinion in which you were held by Mr. Oscar Browning. I have indicated what Napoleon once thought of you and what Mussolini thinks now. Then, in case any of you aspire to fiction, I have copied out for your benefit the advice of the critic about courageously acknowledging the limitations of your sex. I have referred to Professor X and given prominence to his statement that women are intellectually, morally and physically inferior to men. I have handed on all that has come my way without going in search of it, and here is a final warning — from Mr. John Langdon Davies.[2] Mr. John Langdon Davies warns women "that when children cease to be altogether desirable, women cease to be altogether necessary." I hope you will make a note of it.

How can I further encourage you to go about the business of life? Young women, I would say, and please attend, for the peroration is beginning, you are, in my opinion, disgracefully ignorant. You have never made a discovery of any sort of importance. You have never shaken an empire or led an army into battle. The plays of Shakespeare are not by you, and you have never introduced a barbarous race to the blessings of civilisation.

What is your excuse? It is all very well for you to say, pointing to the streets and squares and forests of the globe swarming with black and white and coffee-coloured inhabitants, all busily engaged in traffic and enterprise and love-making, we have had other work on our hands. Without our doing, those seas would be unsailed and those fertile lands a desert. We have borne and bred and washed and taught, perhaps to the age of six or seven years, the one thousand six hundred and twenty-three million human beings who are, according to statistics, at present in existence, and that, allowing that some had help, takes time.

There is truth in what you say — I will not deny it. But at the same time may I remind you that there have been at least two colleges for women in existence in England since the year 1866; that after the year 1880 a married woman was allowed by law to possess her own property; and that in 1919 — which is a whole nine years ago — she was given a vote? May I also remind you that the most of the professions have been open to you for close on ten years now? When you reflect upon these immense privileges and the length of time during which they have been enjoyed, and the fact that there must be at this moment some two thousand women capable of earning over five hundred a year in one way or another, you will agree that the excuse of lack of opportunity, training, encouragement, leisure and money no longer holds good. Moreover, the economists are telling us that Mrs. Seton has had too many children. You must, of course, go on bearing children, but, so they say, in twos and threes, not in tens and twelves.

Thus, with some time on your hands and with some book learning in your brains — you have had enough of the other kind, and are sent to college partly, I suspect, to be un-educated — surely you should embark upon another stage of your very long, very laborious and highly obscure career. A thousand pens are ready to suggest what you should do and what effect you will have. My own suggestion is a little fantastic, I admit; I prefer, therefore, to put it in the form of fiction.

I told you in the course of this paper that Shakespeare had a sister; but do not look for her in Sir Sidney Lee's life of the poet. She died young — alas, she never wrote a word. She lies buried where the omnibuses now stop, opposite the Elephant and Castle. Now my belief is that this poet who never wrote a word and was buried at the crossroads still lives. She lives in you and in me, and in many other women who are not here tonight, for they are washing up the dishes and putting the children to bed. But she lives; for great poets do not die; they are continuing presences; they need only the opportunity to walk among us in the flesh. This opportunity, as I think, it is now coming within your power to give her. For my belief is that if we live another century or so — I am talking of the common life which is the real life and not of the little separate lives which we live as individuals — and have five hundred a year each of us and rooms of our own; if we have the habit of freedom and the courage to write exactly what we think; if we escape a little from the common sitting-room and see human beings not always in their relation to each other but in relation to reality; and the sky, too, and the trees or whatever it may be in themselves; if we look past Milton's bogey, for no human being should shut out the view; if we face the fact, for it is a fact, that there is no arm to cling to, but that we go alone and that our relation is to the world of reality and not only to the world of men and women, then the opportunity will come and the dead poet who was Shakespeare's sister will put on the body which she has so often laid down. Drawing her life from the lives of the unknown who were her forerunners, as her brother did before her, she will be born. As for her coming without that preparation, without that effort on our part, without that determination that when she is born again she shall find it possible to live and write her poetry, that we cannot expect, for that would be impossible. But I maintain that she would come if we worked for her, and that so to work, even in poverty and obscurity, is worth while.

Notes

[1] *The Art of Writing*, by Sir Arthur Quiller-Couch.
[2] *A Short History of Women*, by John Langdon Davies.

14. Moses and Monotheism[*]

Sigmund Freud

what are the 2 traits moses' leadership was born from?

How did they create a leader/liberator

Section II

I. Summary

The following part of this essay cannot be sent forth into the world without lengthy explanations and apologies. For it is no other than a faithful, often literal repetition of the first part, save that some of the critical investigations have been condensed and that there are additions referring to the problem of how and why the character of the Jewish people developed in the form it did. I know that this way of presenting my subject is as ineffectual as it is inartistic. I myself disapprove of it wholeheartedly. Why have I not avoided it? The answer to this question is easy for me to find, but rather hard to admit. I have not been able to efface the traces of the unusual way in which this book came to be written.

In truth it has been written twice over. The first time was a few years ago in Vienna, where I did not believe in the possibility of publishing it. I decided to put it away, but it haunted me like an unlaid ghost, and I compromised by publishing two parts of the book independently in the periodical *Imago*. They were the psychoanalytical starting-points of the whole book: "Moses an Egyptian" and the historical essay built on it, "If Moses Was an Egyptian." The rest, which might give offence and was dangerous — namely, the application of my theory to the genesis of monotheism and my interpretation of religion — I kept back, as I thought, for ever. Then in March 1938 came the unexpected German invasion. It forced me to leave my home, but it also freed me of the fear lest my publishing the book might cause psychoanalysis to be forbidden in a country where its practice was still allowed. No sooner had I arrived in England than I found the temptation of making my withheld knowledge accessible to the world irresistible, and so I started to rewrite the third part of my essay, to follow the two already published. This naturally

[*] Sigmund Freud published *Moses and Monotheism* in 1939. This particular selection was taken from Freud, 'Moses, His People, and Monotheistic Religion,' in *Moses and Monotheism*, Part III, Section II, I–IV, translated by Katherine Jones (New York: Alfred A. Knopf, 1939), 162–182.

necessitated a regrouping of the material, if only in part. I did not succeed, however, in fitting in the whole material in this secondary re-editing. On the other hand, I could not make up my mind to relinquish the two former contributions altogether, and that is how the compromise came about of adding unaltered a whole piece of the first version to the second, a device which has the disadvantage of extensive repetition.

I might, it is true, find comfort in the reflection that the matter I treated of was so new and significant — quite apart from whether my presentation of it was correct or not — that it must count as only a minor misfortune if people are made to read about it twice over. There are things that should be said more than once and cannot be repeated often enough. It should, however, be left to the reader's free will whether he wishes to linger with a subject or return to it. A conclusion should not be emphasized by the sly device of dishing up the same subject twice in the same book. By doing so one proves oneself a clumsy writer and has to bear the blame for it. However, the creative power of an author does not, alas, always follow his goodwill. A work grows as it will and sometimes confronts its author as an independent, even an alien creation.

II. The People of Israel

If we are quite clear in our minds that a procedure like the present one — to take from the traditional material what seems useful and to reject what is unsuitable, and then to put the individual pieces together according to their psychological probability — does not afford any security for finding the truth, then one is quite right to ask why such an attempt was undertaken. In answer to this I must cite the result. If we substantially reduce the severe demands usually made on a historical and psychological investigation, then it might be possible to clear up problems that have always seemed worthy of attention and that, in consequence of recent events, force themselves again on our observation. We know that of all the peoples who lived in antiquity in the basin of the Mediterranean the Jewish people is perhaps the only one that still exists in name and probably also in nature. With an unexampled power of resistance it has defied misfortune and ill-treatment, developed special character traits, and, incidentally, earned the hearty dislike of all other peoples. Whence comes this resistance of the Jew and how his character is connected with his fate are things one would like to understand better.

We may start from one character trait of the Jews which governs their relationship to other people. There is no doubt that they have a very good opinion of themselves, think themselves nobler, on a higher level, superior to the others, from whom they are also separated by many of their customs.[1] With this they are animated by a special trust in life, such as is bestowed by the secret possession of a precious gift; it is a kind of optimism. Religious people would call it trust in God.

We know the reason for this attitude of theirs and what their precious treasure is. They really believe themselves to be God's chosen people; they hold themselves to be specially near to him, and this is what makes them proud and confident. According to trustworthy accounts, they behaved in Hellenistic times as they do today. The Jewish character, therefore, even then was what it is now, and the Greeks, among whom and alongside whom they lived, reacted to the Jewish qualities in the same way as their "hosts" do today. They reacted, one might think, as if they too believed in the preference which the Israelites claimed for themselves. When one is the declared favourite of the dreaded father one need not be surprised that the other brothers and sisters are jealous. What this jealousy can lead to is exquisitely shown in the Jewish legend of Joseph and his brethren. The subsequent course of world history seemed to justify this Jewish arrogance, for when, later on, God consented to send mankind a Messiah and Redeemer, he again chose him from among the Jewish people. The other peoples would then have had reason to say: "Indeed, they were right; they are God's chosen people." Instead of which it happened that the salvation through Jesus Christ brought on the Jews nothing but a stronger hatred, while the Jews themselves derived no advantage from this second proof of being favoured, because they did not recognize the Redeemer.

On the strength of my previous remarks we may say that it was the man Moses who stamped the Jewish people with this trait, one which became so significant to them for all time. He enhanced their self-confidence by assuring them that they were the chosen people of God; he declared them to be holy and laid on them the duty to keep apart from others. Not that the other peoples on their part lacked self-confidence. Then, just as now, each nation thought itself superior to all the others. The self-confidence of the Jews, however, became through Moses anchored in religion; it became a part of their religious belief. By the particularly close relationship to their God they acquired a part of his grandeur. And since we know that behind the God who chose the Jews and delivered them from Egypt stood the man Moses, who achieved that deed, ostensibly at God's command, I venture to say this: it was one man, the man Moses, who created the Jews. To him this people owes its tenacity in supporting life; to him, however, also much of the hostility which it has met with and is meeting still.

Very good self opinion → creates self-confidence in Jews

III. The Great Man

How is it possible that one single man can develop such extraordinary effectiveness, that he can create out of indifferent individuals and families one people, can stamp this people with its definite character and determine its fate for millennia to come? Is not such an assumption a retrogression to the manner of thinking that produced creation myths and hero-worship, to times in which historical writing exhausted itself in narrating the dates and life-histories of certain individuals — sovereigns or conquerors? The inclination of modern times tends rather to trace back the events of human history to more hidden, general, and impersonal factors — the forcible influence of economic circumstances, changes in food supply, progress in the use of materials and tools, migrations caused by increase in population and change of climate. In these factors individuals play no other part than that of exponents or representatives of mass tendencies which must come to expression and which found that expression as it were by chance in such persons.

These are quite legitimate points of view, but they remind us of a significant discrepancy between the nature of our thinking-apparatus and the organization of the world which we are trying to apprehend. Our imperative need for cause and effect is satisfied when each process has one demonstrable cause. In reality, outside us this is hardly so; each event seems to be over-determined and turns out to be the effect of several converging causes. Intimidated by the countless complications of events, research takes the part of one chain of events against another, stipulates contrasts that do not exist and that are created merely through tearing apart more comprehensive relations.[2]

If, therefore, the investigation of one particular case demonstrates the outstanding influence of a single human personality, our conscience need not reproach us that through accepting this conclusion we have dealt a blow at the doctrine of the significance of those general impersonal factors. In point of fact there is without doubt room for both. In the genesis of monotheism we cannot, it is true, point to any other external factor than those I have already mentioned: namely, that this development has to do with the establishing of closer connections among different nations and the existence of a great empire.

We will keep, therefore, a place for "the great man" in the chain, or rather in the network, of determining causes. It may not be quite useless, however, to ask under what condition we bestow this title of honour. We may be surprised to find that it is not so easy to answer this question. A first formulation which would define as great a human being specially endowed with qualities we value highly is obviously in all respects unsuitable. Beauty, for instance, and muscular strength, much as they may be envied, do not establish a claim to "greatness." There should perhaps be mental qualities present, psychical and intellectual distinction. In the latter respect we have misgivings: a man who has an outstanding knowledge in one particular field would not be called a great man without any further reason. We should certainly not apply the term to a master of chess or to a virtuoso on a musical instrument, and not necessarily to a distinguished artist or a man of science. In such a case we should be content to say he is a great writer, painter, mathematician, or physicist, a pioneer in this field or that, but we should pause before pronouncing him a great man. When we declare, for instance, Goethe, Leonardo da Vinci, and Beethoven to be great men, then something else must move us to do so beyond the admiration of their grandiose creations. If it were not for just such examples one might very well conceive the idea that the title "a great man" is reserved by preference for men of action — that is to say, conquerors, generals, and rulers — and was intended as a recognition of the greatness of their achievements and the strength of the influence that emanated from them. However, this, too, is unsatisfying, and is fully contradicted by our condemnation of so many worthless people of whom one cannot deny that they exercised a great influence on their own and later times. Nor can success be chosen as a distinguishing feature of greatness, if one thinks of the vast number of great men who, instead of being successful, perished after being dogged by misfortune.

We should therefore, tentatively, incline to the conclusion that is hardly worth while to search for an unequivocal definition of the concept: "a great man." It seems to be a rather loosely used term, one bestowed without due consideration and given to the supernormal development of certain human qualities; in doing so we keep close to the original literal sense of the word "greatness." We may also remember that it is not so much the nature of the great man that arouses our interest as the question of what are the qualities by virtue of which he influences his contemporaries. I propose to shorten this investigation, however, since it threatens to lead us far from our goal.

Let us agree, therefore, that the great man influences his contemporaries in two ways: through his personality and through the idea for which he stands. This idea may lay stress on an old group of wishes in the masses, or point to a new aim for their wishes, or, again,

Great man influences others with his personality + ideas

lure the masses by other means. Sometimes — and this is surely the more primitive effect — the personality alone exerts its influence, and the idea plays a decidedly subordinate part. Why the great man should rise to significance at all we have no doubt whatever. We know that the great majority of people have a strong need for authority which they can admire, to which they can submit, and which dominates and sometimes even ill-treats them. We have learned from the psychology of the individual whence comes this need of the masses. It is the longing for the father that lives in each of us from his childhood days, for the same father whom the hero of legend boasts of having overcome. And now it begins to dawn on us that all the features with which we furnish the great man are traits of the father, that in this similarity lies the essence, which so far has eluded us, of the great man. The decisiveness of thought, the strength of will, the forcefulness of his deeds, belong to the picture of the father; above all other things, however, the self-reliance and independence of the great man, his divine conviction of doing the right thing, which may pass into ruthlessness. He must be admired, he may be trusted, but one cannot help also being afraid of him. We should have taken a cue from the word itself; who else but the father should in childhood have been the great man?

Without doubt it must have been a tremendous father imago that stooped in the person of Moses to tell the poor Jewish labourers that they were his dear children. And the conception of a unique, eternal, omnipotent God could not have been less overwhelming for them; he who thought them worthy to make a bond with him promised to take care of them if only they remained faithful to his worship. Probably they did not find it easy to separate the image of the man Moses from that of his God, and their instinct was right in this, since Moses might very well have incorporated into the character of his God some of his own traits, such as his irascibility and implacability. And when they killed this great man they only repeated an evil deed which in primeval times had been a law directed against the divine king, and which, as we know, derives from a still older prototype.

When, on the one hand, the figure of the great man has grown into a divine one, it is time to remember, on the other hand, that the father also was once a child. The great religious idea for which the man Moses stood was, as I have stated, not his own; he had taken it over from his king Ikhnaton. And the latter — whose greatness as a founder of religion is proved without a doubt — perhaps followed intimations which through his mother or by other ways had reached him from the Near or the Far East.

We cannot trace the network any further. If the present argument, however, is correct so far, the idea of monotheism must have returned in the fashion of a boomerang into the country of its origin. It appears fruitless to attempt to ascertain what merit attaches to an individual in a new idea. Obviously many have taken part in its development and made contributions to it. On the other hand it would be wrong to break off the chain of causation with Moses and to neglect what his successors, the Jewish Prophets, achieved. Monotheism had not taken root in Egypt. The same failure might have happened in Israel after the people had thrown off the inconvenient and pretentious religion imposed on them. From the mass of the Jewish people, however, there arose again and again men who lent new colour to the fading tradition, renewed the admonishments and demands of Moses, and did not rest until the lost cause was once more regained. In the constant endeavour of centuries, and last but not least through two great reforms — the one before, the other after the Babylonian exile — there took place the change of the popular God Jahve into the God whose worship Moses had forced upon the Jews. And it is the proof of a special psychical fitness in the mass which had become the Jewish people that it could bring forth so many persons who were ready to take upon themselves the burden of the Mosaic religion for the reward of believing that their people was a chosen one and perhaps for other benefits of a similar order.

IV. The Progress in Spirituality

To achieve lasting psychical effects in a people it is obviously not sufficient to assure them that they were specially chosen by God. This assurance must be proved if they are to attach belief to it and draw their conclusions from that belief. In the religion of Moses the Exodus served as such a proof; God, or Moses in his name, did not tire of citing this proof of favour. The feast of the Passover was established to keep this event in mind, or, rather, an old feast was endowed with this memory. Yet it was only a memory. The Exodus itself belonged to a dim past. At the time the signs of God's favour were meagre enough; the fate of the people of Israel would rather indicate his disfavour. Primitive peoples used to depose or even punish their gods if they did not fulfil their duty of granting them victory, fortune, and comfort. Kings have often been treated similarly to gods in every age; the ancient identity of king and god — that is, their common origin — thus becomes manifest. Modern peoples also are in the habit of thus getting rid of their kings if the splendour of their reign is dulled by defeats accompanied by the loss of land and money. Why the people of Israel, however, adhered to their God all the more devotedly the worse they were treated by him — that is a question which we must leave open for the moment.

It may stimulate us to inquire whether the religion of Moses had given the people nothing but an increase in self-confidence through the consciousness of being "chosen." The next element is indeed easily found. Their religion also gave to the Jews a much more grandiose idea of their God or, to express it more soberly, the idea of a more august God. Whoever believed in this God took part in his greatness, so to speak, might feel uplifted himself. This may not be quite obvious to unbelievers, but it may be illustrated by the simile of the high confidence a Briton would feel in a foreign land made unsafe by revolt, a confidence in which a subject of some small Continental state would be entirely lacking. The Briton counts on his government to send a warship if a hair of his head is touched, and also on the rebels' knowing very well that this is so, while the small state does not even own a warship. The pride in the greatness of the British Empire has therefore one of its roots in the consciousness of the greater security and protection that a British subject enjoys. The same may be true of the idea of the great God, and — since one would hardly presume to assist God in his conduct of the world — pride in the greatness of God goes together with that of being "chosen."

Among the precepts of Mosaic religion is one that has more significance than is at first obvious. It is the prohibition against making an image of God, which means the compulsion to worship an invisible God. I surmise that in this point Moses surpassed the Aton religion in strictness. Perhaps he meant to be consistent; his God was to have neither a name nor a countenance. The prohibition was perhaps a fresh precaution against magic malpractices. If this prohibition was accepted, however, it was bound to exercise a profound influence. For it signified subordinating sense perception to an abstract idea; it was a triumph of spirituality over the senses; more precisely, an instinctual renunciation[3] accompanied by its psychologically necessary consequences.

To make more credible what at first glance does not appear convincing we must call to mind other processes of similar character in the development of human culture. The earliest among them, and perhaps the most important, we can discern only in dim outline in the obscurity of primeval times. Its surprising effects make it necessary to conclude that it happened. In our children, in adult neurotics, as well as in primitive people, we find the mental phenomenon which I have called the belief in the "omnipotence of thoughts." We judge it to be an over-estimation of the influence which our mental faculties — the intellectual ones in this case — can exert on the outer world by changing it. All magic, the predecessor of science, is basically founded on these premises. All magic of words belongs here, as does the conviction of the power connected with the knowledge and the pronouncing of a name. We surmise that "omnipotence of thoughts" was the expression of the pride mankind took in the development of language, which had brought in its train such an extraordinary increase in the intellectual faculties. There opened then the new realm of spirituality where conceptions, memories, and deductions became of decisive importance, in contrast to the lower psychical activity which concerned itself with the immediate perceptions of the sense organs. It was certainly one of the most important stages on the way to becoming human.

Another process of later time confronts us in a much more tangible form. Under the influence of external conditions — which we need not follow up here and which in part are also not sufficiently known — it happened that the matriarchal structure of society was replaced by a patriarchal one. This naturally brought with it a revolution in the existing state of the law. An echo of this revolution can still be heard, I think, in the *Oresteia of Æschylus*. This turning from the mother to the father, however, signifies above all a victory of spirituality over the senses — that is to say, a step forward in culture, since maternity is proved by the senses whereas paternity is a surmise based on a deduction and a premiss. This declaration in favour of the thought-process, thereby raising it above sense perception, was proved to be a step charged with serious consequences.

Some time between the two cases I have mentioned, another event took place which shows a closer relationship to the ones we have investigated in the history of religion. Man found that he was faced with the acceptance of "spiritual" forces — that is to say, such forces as cannot be apprehended by the senses, particularly not by sight, and yet having undoubted, even extremely strong effects. If we may trust to language, it was the movement of the air that provided the image of spirituality, since the spirit borrows its name from the breath of wind (*animus, spiritus*, Hebrew *ruach* = smoke). The idea of the soul was thus born as the spiritual principle in the individual. Observation found the breath of air again in the human breath, which ceases with death; even today we talk of a dying man breathing his last. Now the realm of spirits had opened for man, and he was ready to endow everything in nature with the soul he had discovered in himself. The whole world became animated, and science, coming so much later, had enough to do in disestablishing the former state of affairs and has not yet finished this task.

Through the Mosaic prohibition, God was raised to a higher level of spirituality; the door was opened to further changes in the idea of God, of which I shall speak later. At present another of its effects will occupy us. All such progress in spirituality results in increasing self-confidence, in making people proud so that they feel superior to those who have remained in the bondage of the senses. We know that Moses had given the Jews the proud feeling of being God's chosen people; by dematerializing God a new, valuable contribution was made to the secret treasure of the people. The Jews preserved their inclination towards spiritual interests. The political misfortune of the nation taught them to appreciate the only possession they had retained, their written records, at its true value. Immediately after the destruction of the Temple in Jerusalem by Titus, Rabbi Jochanan ben Sakkai asked for permission to open at Jabneh the first school for the study of the Torah. From now on, it was the Holy Book, and the study of it, that kept the scattered people together.

So much is generally known and accepted. I only wished to add that this whole development, so characteristic of the Jews, had been initiated by Moses' prohibition against worshipping God in a visible form.

The preference which through two thousand years the Jews have given to spiritual endeavour has, of course, had its effect; it has helped to build a dike against brutality and the inclination to violence which are usually found where athletic development becomes the ideal of the people. The harmonious development of spiritual and bodily activity, as achieved by the Greeks, was denied to the Jews. In this conflict their decision was at least made in favour of what is culturally the more important....

Notes

[1] The insult frequently hurled at them in ancient times that they were lepers (cf. Manetho) must be read as a projection: "They keep apart from us as if we were lepers."

[2] I would guard myself, however, against a possible misunderstanding. I do not mean to say that the world is so complicated that every assertion must hit the truth somewhere. No, our thinking has preserved the liberty of inventing dependencies and connections that have no equivalent in reality. It obviously prizes this gift very highly, since it makes such ample use of it — inside as well as outside of science.

[3] I use this phrase (*Triebverzicht*) as an abbreviation for "renouncing the satisfaction of an urge derived from an instinct." — Translator

Part III
The Nature of Legitimate Authority

15. Institutes of the Christian Religion*

John Calvin

Chapter XX.
On Civil Government.

Having already stated that man is the subject of two kinds of government, and having sufficiently discussed that which is situated in the soul, or the inner man, and relates to eternal life; we are, in this chapter, to say something of the other kind, which relates to civil justice, and the regulation of the external conduct. For, though the nature of this argument seems to have no connection with the spiritual doctrine of faith which I have undertaken to discuss, the sequel will shew that I have sufficient reason for connecting them together, and, indeed, that necessity obliges me to it: especially since, on the one hand, infatuated and barbarous men madly endeavour to subvert this ordinance established by God; and, on the other hand, the flatterers of princes, extolling their power beyond all just bounds, hesitate not to oppose it to the authority of God himself. Unless both those errors be resisted, the purity of the faith will be destroyed. Besides, it is of no small importance for us to know what benevolent provision God hath made for mankind in this instance, that we may be stimulated by a greater degree of pious zeal to testify our gratitude. In the first place, before we enter on the subject itself, it is necessary for us to recur to the distinction which we have already established, lest we fall into an error very common in the world, and injudiciously confound together these two things, the nature of which is altogether different. For some men, when they hear that the gospel promises a

* John Calvin published his first edition of *Institutes of the Christian Religion* in 1536. He continued revising it in the ensuing years and published many other editions. This particular selection was taken from Calvin, 'On Civil Government,' in *Institutes of the Christian Religion*, Volume I, Book IV, Chapter XX, Sections I–XIII and XXII–XXXII, translated by John Allen (New Haven, CT: Hezekiah Howe and Philadelphia, PA: Philip H. Nicklin, 1816), 515–533 and 541–552.

liberty which acknowledges no king or master among men, but submits to Christ alone, think they can enjoy no advantage of their liberty, while they see any power exalted above them. They imagine, therefore, that nothing will prosper, unless the whole world be modelled in a new form, without any tribunals, or laws, or magistrates, or any thing of a similar kind, which they consider injurious to their liberty. But he, who knows how to distinguish between the body and the soul, between this present transitory life and the future eternal one, will find no difficulty in understanding, that the spiritual kingdom of Christ and civil government are things very different and remote from each other. Since it is a jewish folly, therefore, to seek and include the kingdom of Christ under the elements of this world; let us, on the contrary, considering what the scripture clearly inculcates, that the benefit which is received from the grace of Christ is spiritual; let us, I say, remember to confine within its proper limits all this liberty which is promised and offered to us in him. For why is it that the same apostle who, in one place exhorts to "stand fast in the liberty wherewith Christ hath made us free, and be not entangled again with the yoke of bondage,"[1] in another, enjoins servants to "care not for" their servile condition;[2] except, that spiritual liberty may very well consist with civil servitude? In this sense we are likewise to understand him in these passages. "There is neither Jew nor Greek, there is neither bond nor free, there is neither male nor female:"[3] Again: "There is neither Greek nor Jew, circumcision nor uncircumcision, Barbarian, Scythian, bond nor free: but Christ is all, and in all:"[4] in which he signifies that it is of no importance, what is our condition among men, or under the laws of what nation we live, as the kingdom of Christ consists not in these things.

II. Yet this distinction does not lead us to consider the whole system of civil government as a polluted thing, which has nothing to do with Christian men. Some fanatics, who are pleased with nothing but liberty, or rather licentiousness without any restraint, do indeed boast and vociferate, That since we are dead with Christ to the elements of this world, and being translated into the kingdom of God, sit among the celestials, they think it a degradation to us, and far beneath our dignity, to be occupied with those secular and impure cares which relate to things altogether uninteresting to a Christian man. Of what use, they ask, are laws without judgments and tribunals? But what have judgments to do with a Christian man? And if it be unlawful to kill, of what use are laws and judgments to us? But as we have just suggested that this kind of government is distinct from that spiritual and internal reign of Christ, so it ought to be known that they are in no respect at variance with each other. For that spiritual reign even, now upon earth, commences within us some preludes of the heavenly kingdom, and in this mortal and transitory life affords us some prelibations of immortal and incorruptible blessedness: but this civil government is designed, as long as we live in this world, to cherish and support the external worship of God, to preserve the pure doctrine of religion, to defend the constitution of the Church, to regulate our lives in a manner requisite for the society of men, to form our manners to civil justice, to promote our concord with each other, and to establish general peace and tranquillity: all which I confess to be superfluous, if the kingdom of God, as it now exists in us, extinguish the present life. But if it be the will of God, that while we are aspiring towards our true country, we be pilgrims on the earth, and if such aids be necessary to our pilgrimage; they who take them from man deprive him of his human nature. They plead that there is so much perfection in the Church of God, that its order is sufficient to supply the place of all laws; but they foolishly imagine a perfection, which can never be found in any community of men. For since the insolence of the wicked is so great, and their iniquity so obstinate that it can scarcely be restrained by all the severity of the laws, what may we expect they would do, if they found themselves at liberty to perpetrate crimes with impunity, whose outrages even the arm of power cannot altogether prevent?

III. But for speaking of the exercise of civil polity, there will be another place more suitable. At present we only wish it to be understood, that to entertain a thought of its extermination, is inhuman barbarism; it is equally as necessary to mankind as bread and water, light and air, and far more excellent. For it not only tends to secure the accommodations arising from all these things, that men may breathe, eat, drink, and be sustained in life, though it comprehends all these things while it causes them to live together, yet I say this is not its only tendency; its objects also are, that idolatry, sacrileges against the name of God, blasphemies against his truth, and other offences against religion, may not openly appear and be disseminated among the people; that the public tranquillity may not be disturbed; that every person may enjoy his property without molestation; that men may transact their business together without fraud or injustice; that integrity and modesty may be cultivated between them: in short, that there may be a public form of religion among Christians, and that humanity may be maintained among men. Nor let any one think it strange that I now refer to human polity the charge of the due maintenance of religion, which I may appear to have placed beyond the jurisdiction of men. For I do not allow men to make laws respecting religion and the worship of God now, any more than I did before; though I approve of civil government, which provides that the true religion which is contained in the law of God, be not violated, and polluted by public blasphemies, with impunity. But the perspicuity of order will assist the readers to attain a clearer understanding of what sentiments ought to be entertained respecting the whole system of civil administration, if we enter on a discussion of each branch of it. These are three: The Magistrate, who is the guardian and conservator of the laws: The Laws, according to which he governs: The People, who are governed by the laws, and obey the magistrate. Let us, therefore, examine, first, the function of a magistrate, whether it be a legitimate calling and approved by God, the nature of the duty, and the extent of the power: secondly, by what laws Christian government ought to be regulated: and lastly, what advantage the people derive from the laws, and what obedience they owe to the magistrate.

IV. The Lord hath not only testified that the function of magistrates has his approbation and acceptance, but hath eminently commended it to us, by dignifying it with the most honourable titles. We will mention a few of them. When all who sustain the magistracy are called "gods,"[5] it ought not to be considered as an appellation of trivial importance: for it implies, that they have their command from God, that they are invested with his authority, and are altogether his representatives, and act as his vicegerents. This is not an invention of mine, but the interpretation of Christ, who says; "If he called them gods, unto whom the word of God came, and the Scripture cannot be broken."[6] What is the meaning of this, but that their commission has been given to them by God, to serve him in their office, and, as Moses and Jehoshaphat said to the judges whom they appointed, to "judge not for man, but for the Lord?"[7] To the same purpose is the declaration of the wisdom of God by the mouth of Solomon: "By me kings reign, and princes decree justice. By me princes rule, and nobles, even all the judges of the earth."[8] This is just as if it had been affirmed, that the authority possessed by kings and other governors over all things upon earth is not a consequence of the perverseness of men, but of the providence and holy ordinance of God; who hath been pleased to regulate human affairs in this manner; forasmuch as he is present, and also presides among them, in making laws and in executing equitable judgments. This is clearly taught by Paul, when he enumerates governments (ο προιστομενος)[9] among the gifts of God, which being variously distributed according to the diversity of grace, ought to be employed by the servants of Christ to the edification of the Church. For though in that place he is properly speaking of the council of elders, who were appointed in the primitive Church to preside over the regulation of the public discipline, the same office which in writing to the Corinthians he calls κυβερνησεις "governments;"[10] yet as we see that civil government tends to promote the same object, there is no doubt that he recommends to us every kind of just authority. But he does this in a manner much more explicit, where he enters on a full discussion of that subject. For he says, "There is no power but of God; the powers that be are ordained of God. Rulers are ministers of God, revengers to execute wrath upon him that doeth evil. Do that which is good, and thou shalt have praise of the same."[11] This is corroborated by the examples of holy men; of whom some have been kings, as David, Josiah, Hezekiah; some have been viceroys, as Joseph and Daniel; some have held civil offices in a commonwealth, as Moses, Joshua, and the Judges; whose functions God declared to be approved by him. Wherefore no doubt ought now to be entertained by any person that civil magistracy is a calling, not only holy and legitimate, but far the most sacred and honourable in human life.

V. Those who would wish to introduce anarchy, reply, that though in ancient times kings and judges presided over a rude people, that servile kind of government is now quite incompatible with the perfection which accompanies the gospel of Christ. Here they betray not only their ignorance, but their diabolical pride, in boasting of perfection, of which not the smallest particle can be discovered in them. But whatever their characters may be, they are easily refuted. For when David exhorts kings and judges to kiss the Son of God,[12] he does not command them to abdicate their authority and retire to private life, but to submit to Christ the power with which they are invested, that he alone may have the pre-eminence over all. In like manner Isaiah, when he predicts that "kings shall be nursing-fathers and queens nursing-mothers" to the Church,[13] does not depose them from their thrones; but rather establishes them by an honourable title, as patrons and protectors of the pious worshippers of God: for that prophecy relates to the advent of Christ. I purposely omit numerous testimonies, which often occur, and especially in the Psalms, in which the rights of all governors are asserted. But the most remarkable of all is that passage where Paul, admonishing Timothy that in the public congregation, "supplications, prayers, intercessions, and giving of thanks be made for kings and for all that are in authority," assigns as a reason, "that we may lead a quiet and peaceable life in all godliness and honesty:"[14] language in which he recommends the state of the Church to their patronage and defence.

VI. This consideration ought continually to occupy the magistrates themselves, since it is calculated to furnish them with a powerful stimulus, by which they may be excited to their duty, and to afford them peculiar consolation, by which the difficulties of their office, which certainly are many and arduous, may be alleviated. For what an ardent pursuit of integrity, prudence, clemency, moderation, and innocence ought they to prescribe to themselves, who are conscious of having been constituted ministers of the divine justice! With what confidence will they admit iniquity to their tribunal, which they understand to be the throne of the living God!

With what audacity will they pronounce an unjust sentence with that mouth which they know to be the destined organ of divine truth? With what conscience will they subscribe to impious decrees with that hand which they know to be appointed to register the edicts of God? In short, if they remember that they are the vicegerents of God, it behoves them to watch with all care, earnestness, and diligence, that in their administration they may exhibit to men an image, as it were, of the providence, care, goodness, benevolence, and justice of God. And they must constantly bear this in mind, that if in all cases "he be cursed that doeth the work of the Lord deceitfully,"[15] a far heavier curse awaits those who act fraudulently in a righteous calling. Therefore when Moses and Jehoshaphat wished to exhort their judges to the discharge of their duty, they had nothing to suggest more efficacious than the principle which we have already mentioned. Moses says, "Judge righteously between every man and his brother, and the stranger that is with him. For the judgment is God's."[16] Jehoshaphat says, "Take heed what ye do: for ye judge not for man, but for the Lord, who is with you in the judgment. Wherefore now let the fear of the Lord be upon you: take heed and do it: for there is no iniquity with the Lord our God."[17] And in another place it is said, "God standeth in the congregation of the mighty: he judgeth among the gods;"[18] that they may be animated to their duty, when they understand that they are delegated by God, to whom they must one day render an account of their administration. And this admonition is entitled to have considerable weight with them: for if they fail in their duty, they not only injure men by criminally distressing them, but even offend God by polluting his sacred judgments. On the other hand, it opens a source of peculiar consolation to them to reflect, that they are not employed in profane things, or occupations unsuitable to a servant of God, but in a most sacred function, inasmuch as they execute a divine commission.

VII. Those who are not restrained by so many testimonies of Scripture, but still dare to stigmatise this sacred ministry as a thing incompatible with religion and Christian piety, do they not offer an insult to God himself, who cannot but be involved in the reproach cast upon his ministry? And in fact they do not reject magistrates, but they reject God, "that he should not reign over them."[19] For if this was truly asserted by the Lord respecting the people of Israel, because they refused the government of Samuel, why shall it not now be affirmed with equal truth of those who take the liberty to outrage all the authorities which God hath instituted? But they object that our Lord said to his disciples, "The kings of the Gentiles exercise lordship over them: but ye shall not be so; but he that is greatest among you, let him be as the younger; and he that is chief, as he that doth serve:"[20] and they contend that these words prohibit the exercise of royalty, or any other authority, by any Christians. Admirable expositors! A contention had arisen among the disciples "which of them should be accounted the greatest:" To repress this vain ambition, our Lord taught them that their ministry was not like temporal kingdoms, in which one person has the pre-eminence over all others. Now what dishonour does this comparison cast upon regal dignity? What does it prove at all, except that the regal office is not the apostolic ministry? Moreover, though there are various forms of magistracy, yet there is no difference in this respect, but we ought to receive them all as ordinances of God. For Paul comprehends them all together, when he says, that "there is no power but of God:"

and that which was furthest from giving general satisfaction, is recommended to us in a remarkable manner beyond all others; namely, the government of one man: which, as it is attended with the common servitude of all, except the single individual to whose will all others are subjected, has never been so highly approved by heroic and noble minds. But the Scripture, on the contrary, to correct these unjust sentiments, expressly affirms, that it is by the providence of Divine wisdom that kings reign, and particularly commands us to "honour the king."[21]

VIII. And for private men, who have no authority to deliberate on the regulation of any public affairs, it would surely be a vain occupation to dispute which would be the best form of government in the place where they live. Besides, this could not be simply determined, as an abstract question, without great impropriety, since the principle to guide the decision must depend on circumstances. And even if we compare the different forms together, without their circumstances, their advantages are so nearly equal, that it will not be easy to discover of which the utility preponderates. The forms of civil government are considered to be of three kinds: Monarchy, which is the dominion of one person, whether called a king, or a duke, or any other title: Aristocracy, or the dominion of the principal persons of a nation: and Democracy, or popular government, in which the power resides in the people at large. It is true that the transition is easy from monarchy to despotism; it is not much more difficult from aristocracy to oligarchy, or the faction of a few; but it is most easy of all from democracy to sedition. Indeed, if these three forms of government, which are stated by philosophers, be considered in themselves, I shall by no means deny, that either aristocracy or a mixture of aristocracy and democracy far excels all others; and that indeed not of itself, but because it very rarely happens that kings regulate themselves so that their will is never at variance with justice and rectitude; or in the next place, that they are endued with such penetration and prudence, as in all cases to discover what is best. The vice or imperfection of men therefore renders it safer and more tolerable for the government to be in the hands of many, that they may afford each other mutual assistance and admonition, and that if any one arrogate to himself more than is right, the many may act as censors and masters to restrain his ambition. This has always been proved by experience, and the Lord confirmed it by his authority, when he established a government of this kind among the people of Israel, with a view to preserve them in the most desirable condition, till he exhibited in David a type of Christ. And as I readily acknowledge that no kind of government is more happy than this, where liberty is regulated with becoming moderation, and properly established on a durable basis, so also I consider those as the most happy people, who are permitted to enjoy such a condition; and if they exert their strenuous and constant efforts for its preservation and retention, I admit that they act in perfect consistence with their duty. And to this object the magistrates likewise ought to apply their greatest diligence, that they suffer not the liberty, of which they are constituted guardians, to be in any respect diminished, much less to be violated: if they are inactive and unconcerned about this, they are perfidious to their office, and traitors to their country. But if those, to whom the will of God has assigned another form of government, transfer this to themselves so as to be tempted to desire a revolution, the very thought will be not only foolish and useless, but altogether criminal. If we limit not our views to one city, but look round and take a comprehensive survey of the whole world, or at least extend our observations to distant lands, we shall certainly find it to be a wise arrangement of Divine providence that various countries are governed by different forms of civil polity: for they are admirably held together with a certain inequality, as the elements are combined in very unequal proportions. All these remarks, however, will be unnecessary to those who are satisfied with the will of the Lord. For if it be his pleasure to appoint kings over kingdoms, and senators or other magistrates over free cities, it is our duty to be obedient to any governors whom God hath established over the places in which we reside.

IX. Here it is necessary to state in a brief manner the nature of the office of magistracy, as described in the word of God, and wherein it consists. If the Scripture did not teach that this office extends to both tables of the law, we might learn it from heathen writers: for not one of them has treated of the office of magistrates, of legislation, and civil government, without beginning with religion and divine worship. And thus they have all confessed that no government can be happily constituted, unless its first object be the promotion of piety, and that all laws are preposterous which neglect the claims of God, and merely provide for the interests of men. Therefore as religion holds the first place among all the philosophers, and as this has always been regarded by the universal consent of all nations, Christian princes and magistrates ought to be ashamed of their indolence, if they do not make it the object of their most serious care. We have already shewn that this duty is particularly enjoined upon them by God; for it is reasonable that they should employ their utmost efforts in asserting and defending the honour of him, whose vicegerents they are, and by whose favour they govern. And the principal commendations given in the Scripture to the good kings are for having restored the worship of God when it had been corrupted or abolished, or for having devoted their attention to religion, that it might flourish in purity and safety under their reigns. On the contrary, the sacred history represents it as one of the evils arising from anarchy, or a want of good government, that when "there was no king in Israel, every man did that which was right in his own eyes."[22] These things evince the folly of those who would wish magistrates to neglect all thoughts of God, and to confine themselves entirely to the administration of justice among men: as though God appointed governors in his name to decide secular controversies, and disregarded that which is of far greater importance, the pure worship of himself according to the rule of his law. But a rage for universal innovation, and a desire to escape with impunity, instigate men of turbulent spirits to wish that all the avengers of violated piety were removed out of the world. With respect to the second table, Jeremiah admonishes kings in the following manner: "Execute ye judgment and righteousness, and deliver the spoiled out of the hand of the oppressor: and do no wrong, do no violence to the stranger, the fatherless, nor the widow, neither shed innocent blood."[23] To the same purpose is the exhortation in the eighty-second Psalm: "Defend the poor and fatherless: do justice to the afflicted and needy: deliver the poor and needy: rid them out of the hand of the wicked."[24] And Moses "charged the judges" whom he appointed to supply his place, "saying, Hear the causes between your brethren, and judge righteously between every man and his brother, and the stranger that is with him: ye shall not respect persons in judgment; but ye shall hear the small as well as the great; ye shall not be afraid of the face of man; for the judgment is God's."[25] I forbear to remark the directions given by him in another place respecting their future kings: "He shall not multiply horses to himself: neither shall he greatly multiply to himself silver and gold: his heart shall not be lifted up above his brethren: he shall read in the law all the days of his life:"[26] also that judges show no partiality, nor take bribes, with similar injunctions which abound in the Scriptures:

because in describing the office of magistrates in this treatise, my design is not so much to instruct magistrates themselves, as to shew to others what magistrates are, and for what end God hath appointed them. We see therefore that they are constituted the protectors and vindicators of the public innocence, modesty, probity, and tranquillity, whose sole object it ought to be to promote the common peace and security of all. Of these virtues, David declares that he will be an example, when he shall be exalted to the royal throne. "I will set no wicked thing before mine eyes. I will not know a wicked person. Whoso privily slandereth his neighbour, him will I cut off: him that hath an high look and a proud heart will I not suffer. Mine eyes shall be upon the faithful of the land, that they may dwell with me: he that walketh in a perfect way, he shall serve me."[27] But as they cannot do this, unless they defend good men from the injuries of the wicked, and aid the oppressed by their relief and protection; they are likewise armed with power for the suppression of crimes, and the severe punishment of male-factors, whose wickedness disturbs the public peace. For experience fully verifies the observation of Solon: "That all states are supported by reward and punishment; and that when these two things are removed, all the discipline of human societies is broken and destroyed." For the minds of many lose their regard for equity and justice, unless virtue be rewarded with due honour; nor can the violence of the wicked be restrained, unless crimes are followed by severe punishments. And these two parts are included in the injunction of the prophet to kings and other governors, to "execute judgment and righteousness."[28] *Righteousness* means the care, patronage, defence, vindication, and liberation of the innocent: *judgment* imports the repression of the audacity, the coercion of the violence, and the punishment of the crimes of the impious.

X. But here, it seems, arises an important and difficult question. If by the law all Christians are forbidden to kill,[29] and the prophet predicts respecting the Church, that "they shall not hurt nor destroy in all my holy mountain, saith the Lord;"[30] how can it be compatible with piety for magistrates to shed blood? But if we understand, that in the infliction of punishments, the magistrate does not act at all from himself, but merely executes the judgments of God, we shall not be embarrassed with this scruple. The law of the Lord commands, "Thou shalt not kill:" but that homicide may not go unpunished, the legislator himself puts the sword into the hands of his ministers, to be used against all homicides.[31] *To hurt* and *to destroy* are incompatible with the character of the faithful: but to avenge the afflictions of the righteous at the command of God, is neither *to hurt* nor *to destroy*. Therefore it is easy to conclude that in this respect magistrates are not subject to the common law; by which, though the Lord binds the hands of men, he does not bind his own justice which he exercises by the hands of magistrates. So when a prince forbids all his subjects to strike or wound any one, he does not prohibit his officers from executing that justice which is particularly committed to them. I sincerely wish that this consideration were constantly in our recollection, that nothing is done here by the temerity of men, but every thing by the authority of God who commands it, and under whose guidance we never err from the right way. For we can find no valid objection to the infliction of public vengeance, unless the justice of God be restrained from the punishment of crimes. But if it be unlawful for us to impose restraints upon him, why do we calumniate his ministers? Paul says of the magistrate, that "He beareth not the sword in vain; for he is the minister of God, a revenger to execute wrath upon him that doeth evil."[32] Therefore, if princes and other governors know that nothing will be more acceptable to God than their obedience, and if they desire to approve their piety, justice, and integrity before God, let them devote themselves to this duty. This motive influenced Moses, when knowing himself to be destined to become the liberator of his people by the power of the Lord, "he slew the Egyptian;"[33] and when he punished the idolatry of the people by the slaughter of three thousand men in one day.[34] The same motive actuated David when at the close of his life he commanded his son Solomon to put to death Joab and Shimei.[35] Hence also it is enumerated among the virtues of a king, to "destroy all the wicked of the land, that he may cut off all wicked doers from the city of the Lord."[36] The same topic furnishes the eulogium given to Solomon: "Thou lovest righteousness, and hatest wickedness."[37] How did the meek and placid disposition of Moses burn with such cruelty, that after having his hands imbrued in the blood of his brethren, he continued to go through the camp till three thousand were slain? How did David, who discovered such humanity all his life-time, in his last moments bequeath such a cruel injunction to his son respecting Joab; "Let not his hoar head go down to the grave in peace:" and respecting Shimei; "His hoar head bring down to the grave with blood." Both Moses and David, in executing the vengeance committed to them by God, by this severity sanctified their hands, which had been defiled by their former lenity. Solomon says, "It is an abomination to kings to commit wickedness; for the throne is established by righteousness."[38] Again: "A king that sitteth in the throne of judgment, scattereth away all evil with his eyes."[39] Again: "A wise king scattereth the wicked, and bringeth the wheel over them."[40] Again: "Take away the dross from the silver, and there shall come forth a vessel for the finer. Take away the wicked from before the king, and his throne shall be established in righteousness."[41] Again: "He that justifieth the wicked, and he that condemneth the just, even they both are an abomination to the Lord."[42] Again: "An evil man seeketh only rebellion; therefore a cruel messenger shall be sent against him."[43] Again: "He that saith unto the wicked, Thou art righteous; him shall the people curse, nations shall abhor him."[44] Now if it be true justice for them to pursue the wicked with a drawn sword, let them sheath the sword, and keep their hands from shedding blood, while the swords of desperadoes are drenched in murders; and they will be so far from acquiring the praise of goodness and justice by this forbearance, that they will involve themselves in the deepest impiety. There ought not however to be any excessive or unreasonable severity, nor ought any cause to be given for considering the tribunal as a gibbet prepared for all who are accused. For I am not an advocate for unnecessary cruelty, nor can I conceive the possibility of an equitable sentence being pronounced without mercy; of which Solomon affirms, that "mercy and truth preserve the king: and his throne is upholden by mercy."[45] Yet it behoves the magistrate to be on his guard against both these errors; that he do not, by excessive severity, wound rather than heal; or through a superstitious affectation of clemency, fall into a mistaken humanity, which is the worst kind of cruelty, by indulging a weak and ill-judged lenity, to the detriment of multitudes. For it is a remark not without foundation, that was anciently applied to the government of Nerva, that it is bad to live under a prince who permits nothing, but much worse to live under one who permits every thing.

XI. Now as it is sometimes necessary for kings and nations to take up arms for the infliction of such public vengeance, the same reason will lead us to infer the lawfulness of wars which are undertaken for this end. For if they have been entrusted with power to preserve the tranquillity of their own territories, to suppress the seditious tumults of disturbers, to succour the victims of oppression, and to punish crimes; can they exert this power for a better purpose, than to repel the violence of him, who disturbs both the private repose of individuals and the general tranquillity of the nation; who excites insurrections, and perpetrates acts of oppression, cruelty, and every species of crime? If they ought to be the guardians and defenders of the laws, it is incumbent upon them to defeat the efforts of all by whose injustice the discipline of the laws is corrupted. And if they justly punish those robbers, whose injuries have only extended to a few persons; shall they suffer a whole district to be plundered and devastated with impunity? For there is no difference, whether he, who in a hostile manner invades, disturbs, and plunders the territory of another to which he has no right, be a king, or one of the meanest of mankind: all persons of this description are equally to be considered as robbers, and ought to be punished as such. It is the dictate both of natural equity, and of the nature of the office, therefore, that princes are armed, not only to restrain the crimes of private individuals by judicial punishments, but also to defend the territories committed to their charge by going to war against any hostile aggression: and the Holy Spirit in many passages of Scripture declares such wars to be lawful.

XII. If it be objected, that the New Testament contains no precept or example, which proves war to be lawful to Christians: I answer, first, that the reason for waging war which existed in ancient times, is equally valid in the present age; and that, on the contrary, there is no cause to prevent princes from defending their subjects. Secondly, that no express declaration on this subject is to be expected in the writings of the apostles, whose design was, not to organise civil governments, but to describe the spiritual kingdom of Christ. Lastly, that in those very writings it is implied by the way, that no change has been made in this respect by the coming of Christ. "For," to use the words of Augustine, "if Christian discipline condemned all wars, the soldiers who inquired respecting their salvation ought rather to have been directed to cast away their arms, and entirely to renounce the military profession; whereas the advice given them was; 'Do violence to no man, neither accuse any falsely; and be content with your wages.'[46] An injunction to be content with their wages was certainly not a prohibition of the military life." But here all magistrates ought to be very cautious, that they follow not in any respect the impulse of their passions. On the contrary, if punishments are to be inflicted, they ought not to be precipitated with anger, exasperated with hatred, or inflamed with implacable severity: they ought, as Augustine says, "to commiserate our common nature, even in him whom they punish for his crime." Or if arms are to be resorted to against an enemy, that is, an armed robber, they ought not to seize a trivial occasion, nor even to take it when presented, unless they are driven to it by extreme necessity. For if it be our duty to exceed what was required by that heathen writer, who maintained that the evident object of war ought to be the restoration of peace; certainly we ought to make every other attempt before we have recourse to the decision of arms. In short, in both cases they must not suffer themselves to be carried away by any private motive, but be wholly guided by public spirit: otherwise they grossly abuse their power, which is given them, not for their own particular advantage, but for the benefit and service of others. Moreover on this right of war, depends the lawfulness of garrisons, alliances, and other civil munitions. By *garrisons*, I mean soldiers who are stationed in towns to defend the boundaries of a country. By *alliances*, I mean confederations which are made between neighbouring princes, that, if any disturbance arise in their territories, they will render each other mutual assistance, and will unite their forces together for the common resistance of the common enemies of mankind. By *civil munitions*, I mean all the provisions which are employed in the art of war.

XIII. In the last place, I think it necessary to add, that tributes and taxes are the legitimate revenues of princes; which indeed they ought principally to employ in sustaining the public expenses of their office, but which they may likewise use for the support of their domestic splendour, which is closely connected with the dignity of the government that they hold. Thus we see that David, Jehoshaphat, Hezekiah, Josiah, and other pious kings, and likewise Joseph and Daniel, without any violation of piety, on account of the office which they filled, lived at the public expense; and we read in Ezekiel of a very ample portion of land being assigned to the kings:[47] in which passage, though the prophet is describing the spiritual kingdom of Christ, yet he borrows the model of it from the legitimate kingdoms of men. On the other hand, princes themselves ought to remember, that their finances are not so much private incomes, as the revenues of the whole people, according to the testimony of Paul,[48] and therefore cannot be lavished, or dilapidated, without manifest injustice: or rather that they are to be considered as the blood of the people, which not to spare is the most inhuman cruelty: and their various imposts and tributes ought to be regarded merely as aids of the public necessity, to burden the people with which without cause, would be tyrannical rapacity. These things give no encouragement to princes to indulge profusion and luxury, and certainly there is no need to add fuel to their passions, which of themselves are more than sufficiently inflamed: but as it is of very great importance that whatever they undertake, they attempt it with a pure conscience before God, it is necessary, in order to their avoiding vain confidence and contempt of God, that they be taught how far their rights extend. Nor is this doctrine useless to private persons, who learn from it not to pronounce rash and insolent censures on the expenses of princes, notwithstanding they exceed the limits of common life....

XXII. The first duty of subjects towards their magistrates is to entertain the most honourable sentiments of their function, which they know to be a jurisdiction delegated to them from God, and on that account to esteem and reverence them as God's ministers and vicegerents. For there are some persons to be found, who shew themselves very obedient to their magistrates, and have not the least wish that there were no magistrates for them to obey, because they know them to be so necessary to the public good; but who, nevertheless, consider the magistrates themselves as no other than necessary evils. But something more than this is required of us by Peter, when he commands us to "honour the king;"[49] and by Solomon when he says, "Fear thou the Lord and the king:"[50] for Peter, under the term *honour*, comprehends a sincere and candid esteem; and Solomon, by connecting the king with the Lord, attributes to him a kind of sacred veneration and dignity. It is also a remarkable commendation of magistrates which is given by Paul, when he says, that we "must needs be subject, not only for wrath, but also for conscience sake:"[51] by which he means, that subjects ought to be induced to submit to princes and governors, not merely from a dread of their power, as persons are accustomed to yield to an armed enemy, who they know will immediately take vengeance upon them if they resist; but because the obedience which is rendered to princes and magistrates is rendered to God, from whom they have received their authority. I am not speaking of the persons, as if the mask of dignity ought to palliate or excuse folly, ignorance, or cruelty, and conduct the most nefarious and flagitious, and so to acquire for vices the praise due to virtues: but I affirm that the station itself is worthy of honour and reverence: so that, whoever our governors are, they ought to possess our esteem and veneration on account of the office which they fill.

XXIII. Hence follows another duty, that, with minds disposed to honour and reverence magistrates, subjects approve their obedience to them, in submitting to their edicts, in paying taxes, in discharging public duties and bearing burdens which relate to the common defence, and in fulfilling all their other commands. Paul says to the Romans, "Let every soul be subject unto the higher powers. Whosoever resisteth the power, resisteth the ordinance of God."[52] He writes to Titus; "Put them in mind to be subject to principalities and powers, to obey magistrates, to be ready to every good work."[53] Peter exhorts; "Submit yourselves to every ordinance of man for the Lord's sake: whether it be to the king as supreme; or unto governors, as unto them that are sent by him for the punishment of evil doers, and for the praise of them that do well."[54] Moreover, that subjects may testify that theirs is not a hypocritical but a sincere and cordial submission, Paul teaches, that they ought to pray to God for the safety and prosperity of those under whose government they live. "I exhort," he says, "that supplications, prayers, intercessions, and giving of thanks be made for all men; for kings, and for all that are in authority; that we may lead a quiet and peaceable life in all godliness and honesty."[55] Here let no man deceive himself. For as it is impossible to resist the magistrate without, at the same time, resisting God himself; though an unarmed magistrate may seem to be despised with impunity, yet God is armed to inflict exemplary vengeance on the contempt offered to himself. Under this obedience I also include the moderation which private persons ought to prescribe to themselves in relation to public affairs, that they do not, without being called upon, intermeddle with affairs of state, or rashly intrude themselves into the office of magistrates, or undertake any thing of a public nature. If there be any thing in the public administration which requires to be corrected, let them not raise any tumults, or take the business into their own hands, which ought to be all bound in this respect, but let them refer it to the cognizance of the magistrate, who is alone authorised to regulate the concerns of the public. I mean, that they ought to attempt nothing without being commanded: for when they have the command of a governor, then they also are invested with public authority. For, as we are accustomed to call the counsellors of a prince *his eyes and ears*: so they may not unaptly be called *his hands* whom he has commissioned to execute any of his commands.

XXIV. Now as we have hitherto described a magistrate who truly answers to his title; who is the father of his country, and, as the poet calls him, the pastor of his people, the guardian of peace, the protector of justice, the avenger of innocence; he would justly be deemed insane who disapproved of such a government. But, as it has happened in almost all ages, that some princes, regardless of every thing to which they ought to have directed their attention and provision, give themselves up to their pleasures in indolent exemption from every care; others, absorbed in their own interest, expose to sale all laws, privileges, rights, and judgments; others plunder the public of wealth, which they afterwards lavish in mad prodigality; others commit flagrant outrages, pillaging houses, violating virgins and matrons, and murdering infants: many persons cannot be persuaded that such ought to be acknowledged as princes, whom, as far possible, they ought to obey. For in such enormities, and actions so completely incompatible, not only with the office of a magistrate, but with the duty of every man, they discover no appearance of the image of

God, which ought to be conspicuous in a magistrate; while they perceive no vestige of that minister of God who is "not a terror to good works but to the evil," who is sent "for the punishment of evil-doers, and for the praise of them that do well;" nor recognize that governor, whose dignity and authority the Scripture recommends to us. And certainly the minds of men have always been naturally disposed to hate and execrate tyrants as much as to love and reverence legitimate kings.

XXV. But, if we direct our attention to the word of God, it will carry us much further; even to submit to the government, not only of those princes who discharge their duty to us with becoming integrity and fidelity, but of all who possess the sovereignty, even though they perform none of the duties of their function. For though the Lord testifies that the magistrate is an eminent gift of his liberality to preserve the safety of men, and prescribes to magistrates themselves the extent of their duty; yet he, at the same time, declares, that whatever be their characters, they have their government only from him; ~God~ that those who govern for the public good are true specimens and mirrors of his beneficence; and that those who rule in an unjust and tyrannical manner are raised up by him to punish the iniquity of the people; that all equally possess that sacred majesty which he hath invested with legitimate authority. I will not proceed any further till I have subjoined a few testimonies in proof of this point. It is unnecessary, however, to labour much to evince an impious king to be a judgment of God's wrath upon the world, as I have no expectation that any one will deny it: and in this we say no more of a king than of any other robber who plunders our property; or adulterer who violates our bed; or assassin who attempts to murder us; since the Scripture enumerates all these calamities among the curses inflicted by God. But let us rather insist on the proof of that which the minds of men do not so easily admit; that a man of the worst character, and most undeserving of all honour, who holds the sovereign power, really possesses that eminent and divine authority, which the Lord hath given by his word to the ministers of his justice and judgment; and, therefore, that he ought to be regarded by his subjects with the same reverence and esteem which they would shew to the best of kings, if such an one were granted to them.

XXVI. In the first place, I request my readers to observe and consider with attention, what is so frequently and justly mentioned in the Scriptures, the providence of God, and peculiar dispensation of God in distributing kingdoms and appointing whom he pleases to be kings. Daniel says; "God changeth the times and the seasons: he removeth kings and setteth up kings."[56] Again; "That the living may know that the Most High ruleth in the kingdom of men, and giveth it to whomsoever he will."[57] Passages of this kind abound throughout the Scriptures, but particularly in this prophecy. Now the character of Nebuchadnezzar, who conquered Jerusalem, is sufficiently known, that he was an invader and depopulator of the territories of others. Yet by the mouth of Ezekiel the Lord declares that he had given him the land of Egypt, as a reward for the service which he had performed in devastating Tyre.[58] And Daniel said to him; "Thou, O king, art a king of kings: for the God of heaven hath given thee a kingdom, power, and strength, and glory: and wheresoever the children of men dwell, the beasts of the field, and the fowls of the heaven, hath he given into thine hand, and hath made thee ruler over all."[59] Again; to his grandson Belshazzar Daniel said, "The most high God gave Nebuchadnezzar thy father a kingdom, and majesty, and glory, and honour: and for the majesty that he gave him, all people, nations, and languages, trembled and feared before him."[60] When we hear that

Nebuchadnezzer was placed on the throne by God, let us, at the same time, call to mind the celestial edicts which command us to fear and honour the king; and we shall not hesitate to regard the most iniquitous tyrant with the honour due to the station in which the Lord hath deigned to place him. When Samuel denounced to the children of Israel what treatment they would receive from their kings, he said; "This will be the manner of the king that shall reign over you: he will take your sons and appoint them for himself, for his chariots, and to be his horsemen; and to ear his ground, and to reap his harvest, and to make his instruments of war. And he will take your daughters to be confectionaries, and to be cooks, and to be bakers. And he will take your fields, and your vineyards, and your oliveyards, even the best of them, and give them to his servants. And he will take the tenth of your fields, and of your vineyards, and give to his officers, and to his servants. And he will take your men-servants, and your maid-servants, and your goodliest young men, and your asses, and put them to his work. He will take the tenth of your sheep: and ye shall be his servants."[61] Certainly the kings would not do all this as a matter of right, for they were excellently instructed by the law to observe all moderation: but it was called a right with respect to the people who were bound to obey and were not at liberty to resist it. It was just as if Samuel had said; The cupidity of your kings will proceed to all these outrages, which it will not be your province to restrain; nothing will remain for you, but to receive their commands and to obey them.

XXVII. But the most remarkable and memorable passage of all is in the Prophecy of Jeremiah, which, though it is rather long, I shall readily quote, because it most clearly decides the whole question; "I have made the earth, the man and the beast that are upon the ground, by my great power and by my outstretched arm, and have given it unto whom it seemed meet unto me. And now I have given all these lands into the hand of Nebuchadnezzar, the king of Babylon, my servant. And all nations shall serve him, and his son, and his son's son, until the very time of his land come. And it shall come to pass, that the nation and kingdom which will not serve the same king of Babylon, that nation will I punish with the sword, and with the famine, and with the pestilence. Therefore serve the king of Babylon, and live."[62] We see what great obedience and honour the Lord required to be rendered to that pestilent and cruel tyrant, for no other reason than because he possessed the kingdom: and it was by the heavenly decree that he was seated on the throne of the kingdom, and exalted to that regal majesty, which it was not lawful to violate. If we have this constantly present to our eyes and impressed upon our hearts, that the most iniquitous kings are placed on their thrones by the same decree by which the authority of all kings is established, those seditious thoughts will never enter our minds, that a king is to be treated according to his merits, and that it is not reasonable for us to be subject to a king who does not on his part perform towards us those duties which his office requires.

XXVIII. In vain will any one object that this was a special command given to the Israelites. For we must observe the reason upon which the Lord founds it. He says, "I have given these lands to Nebuchadnezzar; therefore serve him, and live." To whomsoever, therefore, a kingdom shall evidently be given, we have no room to doubt that subjection is due to him. And as soon as he exalts any person to royal dignity, he gives us a declaration of his pleasure that he shall reign. The Scripture contains general testimonies on this subject. Solomon says; "For the transgression of a land, many are the princes thereof."[63] Job says; "He looseth the bonds of kings," or divesteth them of their power; "and girdeth their loins with a girdle,"[64] or restoreth them to their former dignity. This being admitted, nothing remains for us but to serve and live. The Prophet Jeremiah likewise records another command of the Lord to his people: "Seek the peace of the city whither I have caused you to be carried away captives, and pray unto the Lord for it: for in the peace of it ye shall have peace."[65] Here, we see, the Israelites, after having been stripped of all their property, torn from their habitations, driven into exile, and forced into a miserable servitude, were commanded to pray for the prosperity of their conqueror; not in the same manner in which we are all commanded to pray for our persecutors; but that his kingdom might be preserved in safety and tranquillity, and that they might live in prosperity under him. Thus David, after having been already designated as king by the ordination of God, and anointed with his holy oil, though he was unjustly persecuted by Saul, without having given him any cause of offence, nevertheless accounted the person of his pursuer sacred, because the Lord had consecrated it by the royal dignity. And he said, "The Lord forbid that I should do this thing unto my master, the Lord's anointed, to stretch forth mine hand against him, seeing he is the anointed of the Lord." Again; "Mine eye spared thee; and I said, I will not put forth mine hand against my Lord; for he is the Lord's anointed."[66] Again; "Who can stretch forth his hand against the Lord's anointed, and be guiltless? As the Lord liveth, the Lord shall smite him; or his day shall come to die, or he shall descend into battle, and perish. The Lord forbid that I should stretch forth mine hand against the Lord's anointed."[67]

XXIX. Finally, we owe these sentiments of affection and reverence to all our rulers, whatever their characters may be: which we the more frequently repeat, that we may learn not to scrutinize the persons themselves, but may be satisfied with knowing that they are invested by the will of the Lord with that function, upon which he hath impressed an inviolable majesty. But it will be said, that rulers owe mutual duties to their subjects. That I have already confessed. But he who infers from this that obedience ought to be rendered to none but just rulers, is a very bad reasoner. For husbands owe mutual duties to their wives, and parents to their children. Now, if husbands and parents violate their obligations, if parents conduct themselves with discouraging severity and fastidious morosenses towards their children, whom they are forbidden to provoke to wrath:[68] if husbands despise and vex their wives, whom they are commanded to love and to spare as the weaker vessels;[69] does it follow that children should be less obedient to their parents; or wives to their husbands? They are still subject, even to those who are wicked and unkind. As it is incumbent on all, not to inquire into the duties of one another, but to confine their attention respectively to their own; this consideration ought particularly to be regarded by those who are subject to the authority of others. Wherefore, if we are inhumanly harassed by a cruel prince, if we are rapaciously plundered by an avaricious or luxurious one, if we are neglected by an indolent one, or if we are persecuted, on account of piety, by an impious and sacrilegious one, let us first call to mind our transgressions against God, which he undoubtedly chastises by these scourges. Thus our impatience will be restrained by humility. Let us, in the next place, consider that it is not our province to remedy these evils; and that nothing remains for us, but to implore the aid of the Lord, in whose hand are the hearts of kings and the revolutions of kingdoms. It is "God" who "standeth in the congregation of the mighty," and "judgeth among the gods;"[70] whose presence shall confound and crush all kings and judges of the earth who shall not have kissed his Son;[71] "that decree unrighteous decrees, to turn aside the needy from judgment, and to take away the right from the poor, that widows may be their prey, and that they may rob the fatherless."[72]

XXX. And here is displayed his wonderful goodness, and power, and providence: for sometimes he raises up some of his servants as public avengers, and arms them with his commission to punish unrighteous domination, and to deliver from their distressing calamities a people who have been unjustly oppressed: sometimes he accomplishes this end by the fury of men who meditate and attempt something altogether different. Thus he liberated the people of Israel from the tyranny of Pharaoh by Moses: from the oppression of Chusan by Othniel; and from other yokes by other kings and judges. Thus he subdued the pride of Tyre by the Egyptians; the insolence of the Egyptians, by the Assyrians; the haughtiness of the Assyrians, by the Chaldeans; the confidence of Babylon, by the Medes and Persians, after Cyrus had subjugated the Medes. The ingratitude of the kings of Israel and Judah, and their impious rebellion, notwithstanding his numerous favours, he repressed and punished sometimes by the Assyrians, sometimes by the Babylonians. These were all the executioners of his vengeance, but not all in the same manner. The former, when they were called forth to the performance of such acts by a legitimate commission from God, in taking arms against kings, were not chargeable with the least violation of that majesty with which kings are invested by the ordination of God; but being armed with authority from heaven, they punished an inferior power by a superior one, as it is lawful for kings to punish their inferior officers. The latter, though they were guided by the hand of God in such directions as he pleased, and performed his work without being conscious of it, nevertheless contemplated in their hearts nothing but evil.

XXXI. But whatever opinion be formed of the acts of men, yet the Lord equally executed his work by them, when he broke the sanguinary sceptres of insolent kings, and overturned tyrannical governments. Let princes hear and fear. But, in the mean while, it behoves us to use the greatest caution, that we do not despise or violate that authority of magistrates, which is entitled to the greatest veneration, which God hath established by the most solemn commands, even though it reside in those who are most unworthy of it, and who, as far as in them lies, pollute it by their iniquity. For though the correction of tyrannical domination is the vengeance of God, we are not, therefore, to conclude that it is committed to us, who have received no other command than to obey and suffer. This observation I always apply to private persons. For if there be, in the present day, any magistrates appointed for the protection of the people and the moderation of the power of kings, such as were, in ancient times, the Ephori who were a check upon the kings among the Lacedæmonians, or the popular tribunes upon the consuls among the Romans, or the Demarchi upon the senate among the Athenians; or with power such as perhaps is now possessed by the three estates in every kingdom when they are assembled; I am so far from prohibiting them in the discharge of their duty to oppose the violence or cruelty of kings, that I affirm, that if they connive at kings in their oppression of their people, such forbearance involves the most nefarious perfidy, because they fraudulently betray the liberty of the people, of which they know that they have been appointed protectors by the ordination of God.

XXXII. But in the obedience which we have shewn to be due to the authority of governors, it is always necessary to make one exception, and that is entitled to our first attention, that it do not seduce us from obedience to him, to whose will the desires of all kings ought to be subject, to whose decrees all their commands ought to yield, to whose majesty all their sceptres ought to submit. And, indeed, how preposterous it would be for us, with a view to satisfy men, to incur the displeasure of him on whose account we yield obedience to men! The Lord, therefore, is the King of kings; who, when he hath opened his sacred mouth, is to be heard alone, above all, for all, and before all: in the next place, we are subject to those men who preside over us; but no otherwise than in him. If they command any thing against him, it ought not to have the least attention; nor, in this case, ought we to pay any regard to all that dignity attached to magistrates; to which no injury is done when it is subjected to the unrivalled and supreme power of God. On this principle Daniel denied that he had committed any crime against the king in disobeying his impious decree;[73] because the king had exceeded the limits of his office, and had not only done an injury to men, but, by raising his arm against God, had degraded his own authority. On the other hand, the Israelites are condemned for having been too submissive to the impious edict of their king. For when Jeroboam had made his golden calves, in compliance with his will, they deserted the temple of God and revolted to new superstitions. Their posterity conformed to the decrees of their idolatrous kings with the same facility. The prophet severely condemns them for having "willingly walked after the commandment:"[74] so far is any praise from being due to the pretext of humility, with which courtly flatterers excuse themselves and deceive the unwary, when they deny that it is lawful for them to refuse compliance with any command of their kings: as if God had resigned his right to mortal men when he made them rulers of mankind; or as if earthly power were diminished by being subordinated to its author, before whom even the principalities of heaven tremble with awe. I know what great and present danger awaits this constancy, for kings cannot bear to be disregarded without the greatest indignation; and "the wrath of a king," says Solomon, "is as messengers of death."[75] But since this edict has been proclaimed by that celestial herald, Peter, "We ought to obey God rather than men:"[76] let us console ourselves with this thought, that we truly perform the obedience which God requires of us, when we suffer any thing rather than deviate from piety. And that our hearts may not fail us, Paul stimulates us with another consideration; that Christ has redeemed us at the immense price which our redemption cost him, that we may not be submissive to the corrupt desires of men, much less be slaves to their impiety.[77]

END OF THE INSTITUTES.

[handwritten:] Old testament in Greek = Septuagint
Apocrypha = not translated, still in Hebrew (Judith, Ester, song of psalms?)

Notes

[handwritten:] Hebrew Bible Old testament
1) law (Torah)
2) prophets (issaiha, jeremiah, ect)
3) wisdom (Book of Job, psalms)

[1] Gal. v.1.
[2] 1 Cor. vii. 21.
[3] Gal. iii. 28.
[4] Col. iii. 11.
[5] Psalm lxxxii, 1, 6.
[6] John x. 35.
[7] Deut. i. 16, 17. 2 Chron. xix. 6.
[8] Prov. viii. 15, 16.
[9] Rom. xii. 8.

[handwritten:] +
New testament = christian Bible
- Gospels
- Acts
- Epistles (paul)
- Revelation / Apocalypse
= bible (RC)

[handwritten:] Only quotes O.T and John. Never Paul quotes jesus

[10] 1 Cor. xii. 28.
[11] Rom. xiii. 1, 3, 4.
[12] Psalm ii. 10–12.
[13] Isaiah xlix. 23.
[14] 1 Tim. ii. 1, 2.
[15] Jer. xlviii. 10.
[16] Deut. i. 16, 17.
[17] 2 Chron. xix. 6, 7.
[18] Psalm lxxxii. 1.
[19] 1 Sam. viii. 7.
[20] Luke xxii. 25, 26.
[21] Rom. xiii. 1, &c. Prov. viii. 15. 1 Pet. ii. 13, 14, 17.
[22] Judges xxi. 25.
[23] Jer. xxii. 3.
[24] Psalm lxxxii. 3, 4.
[25] Deut. i. 16, 17.
[26] Deut. xvii. 16, 17, 19, 20.
[27] Psalm ci. 3–6.
[28] Jer. xxii. 3.
[29] Exod. xx. 13.
[30] Isaiah xi. 9. lxv. 25.
[31] Gen. ix. 6. Exod. xxi. 12.
[32] Rom. xiii. 4.
[33] Exod. ii. 12.
[34] Exod. xxxii. 26–28.
[35] 1 Kings ii. 5–9.
[36] Psalm ci. 8.
[37] Psalm xlv. 7.
[38] Prov. xvi. 12.
[39] Prov. xx. 8.
[40] Prov. xx. 26.
[41] Prov. xxv. 4, 5.
[42] Prov. xvii. 15.
[43] Prov. xvii. 11.
[44] Prov. xxiv. 24.
[45] Prov. xx. 28.
[46] Luke iii. 14.
[47] Ezek. xlviii. 21, 22.
[48] Rom. xiii. 6.
[49] 1 Peter ii. 17.
[50] Prov. xxiv. 21.
[51] Rom. xiii. 5.
[52] Rom. xiii. 1, 2.
[53] Titus iii. 1.
[54] 1 Peter ii. 13, 14.
[55] 1 Tim. ii. 1, 2.
[56] Dan. ii. 21.
[57] Dan. iv. 17.
[58] Ezek. xxix. 18–21.
[59] Dan. ii. 37, 38.
[60] Dan. v. 18, 19.

Old testament

61 1 Sam. viii. 11–17.
62 Jer. xxvii. 5–9. 12.
63 Prov. xxviii. 2.
64 Job xii. 18.
65 Jer. xxix. 7.
66 1 Sam. xxiv. 6, 11.
67 1 Sam. xxvi. 9–11.
68 Ephes. vi. 4. Col. iii. 21.
69 Ephes. v. 25. 1 Pet. iii. 7.
70 Psalm lxxxii. 1.
71 Psalm ii. 10–12.
72 Isaiah x. 1, 2.
73 Dan. vi. 22.
74 Hosea. v. 11.
75 Prov. xvi. 14.
76 Acts v. 29.
77 1 Cor. vii. 23.

* NO Gospels except John

16. The Trew Law of Free Monarchies[*]

James I, King of England

An Advertisement to the Reader.

Accept, I pray you (my deare countreymen) as thankefully this Pamphlet that I offer unto you, as louingly it is written for your weale. I would be loath both to be faschious, and fectlesse: And therefore, if it be not sententious, at least it is short. It may be yee misse many things that yee looke for in it: But for excuse thereof, consider rightly that I onely lay downe herein the trew grounds, to teach you the right-way, without wasting time upon refuting the aduersaries. And yet I trust, if ye will take narrow tent, ye shall finde most of their great gunnes payed home againe, either with contrary conclusions, or tacite obiections, suppose in a dairned forme, and indirectly: For my intention is to instruct, and not irritat, if I may eschew it. The profite I would wish you to make of it, is, as well so to frame all your actions according to these grounds, as may confirme you in the course of honest and obedient Subiects to your King in all times comming, as also, when ye shall fall in purpose with any that shall praise or excuse the by-past rebellions that brake foorth either in this countrey, or in any other, ye shall herewith bee armed against their Sirene songs, laying their particular examples to the square of these grounds. Whereby yee shall soundly keepe the course of righteous Iudgement, decerning wisely of euery action onely according to the qualitie thereof, and not according to your pre-iudged conceits of the committers: So shall ye, by reaping profit to your selues, turne my paine

---

[*] James published this treatise in 1598 when he was ruling over Scotland as King James VI, again in 1603 after becoming King James I of England, and yet again in 1616 in a volume containing many of his other political writings. This particular selection was taken from King James I of England, 'The Trew Law of Free Monarchies: Or the Reciprock and Mvtvall Dvetie betwixt a Free King, and His Naturall Subjects,' in *The Political Works of James I*, reprinted from the edition of 1616, with an introduction by Charles Howard McIlwain (Cambridge: Harvard University Press, 1918), 53–70.

into pleasure. But least the whole Pamphlet runne out at the gaping mouth of this Preface, if it were any more enlarged; I end, with committing you to God, and me to your charitable censures.

The Trew Law of Free Monarchies: Or the Reciprock and Mvtvall Dvetie betwixt a Free King and His Naturall Subjects.

As there is not a thing so necessarie to be knowne by the people of any land, next the knowledge of their God, as the right knowledge of their alleageance, according to the forme of gouernement established among them, especially in a *Monarchie* (which forme of gouernment, as resembling the Diuinitie, approacheth nearest to perfection, as all the learned and wise men from the beginning haue agreed vpon; Vnitie being the perfection of all things,) So hath the ignorance, and (which is worse) the seduced opinion of the multitude blinded by them, who thinke themselues able to teach and instruct the ignorants, procured the wracke and ouerthrow of sundry flourishing Common-wealths; and heaped heauy calamities, threatning vtter destruction vpon others. And the smiling successe, that vnlawfull rebellions haue oftentimes had against Princes in aages past (such hath bene the misery, and iniquitie of the time) hath by way of practise strengthned many in their errour: albeit there cannot be a more deceiueable argument; then to iudge ay the iustnesse of the cause by the euent thereof; as hereafter shall be proued more at length. And among others, no Commonwealth, that euer hath bene since the beginning, hath had greater need of the trew knowledge of this ground, then this our so long disordered, and distracted Common-wealth hath: the misknowledge hereof being the onely spring, from whence haue flowed so many endlesse calamities, miseries, and confusions, as is better felt by many, then the cause thereof well knowne, and deepely considered. The naturall zeale therefore, that I beare to this my natiue countrie, with the great pittie I haue to see the so-long disturbance thereof for lacke of the trew knowledge of this ground (as I haue said before) hath compelled me at last to breake silence, to discharge my conscience to you my deare country men herein, that knowing the ground from whence these your many endlesse troubles haue proceeded, as well as ye haue already too-long tasted the bitter fruites thereof, ye may by knowledge, and eschewing of the cause escape, and diuert the lamentable effects that euer necessarily follow thereupon. I haue chosen then onely to set downe in this short Treatise, the trew grounds of the mutuall duetie, and alleageance betwixt a free and absolute *Monarche*, and his people; not to trouble your patience with answering the contrary propositions, which some haue not bene ashamed to set downe in writ, to the poysoning of infinite number of simple soules, and their owne perpetuall, and well deserued infamie: For by answering them, I could not haue eschewed whiles to pick, and byte wel saltly their persons; which would rather haue bred contentiousnesse among the readers (as they had liked or misliked) then sound instruction of the trewth: Which I protest to him that is the searcher of all hearts, is the onely marke that I shoot at herein.

First then, I will set downe the trew grounds, whereupon I am to build, out of the Scriptures, since *Monarchie* is the trew paterne of Diuinitie, as I haue already said: next, from the fundamental Lawes of our owne Kingdome, which nearest must concerne vs:

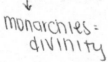

monarchies= divinity

thirdly, from the law of Nature, by diuers similitudes drawne out of the same: and will conclude syne by answering the most waighty and appearing incommodities that can be obiected.

The Princes duetie to his Subiects is so clearely set downe in many places of the Scriptures, and so openly confessed by all the good Princes, according to their oath in their Coronation, as not needing to be long therein, I shall as shortly as I can runne through it.

Kings are called Gods[1] by the propheticall King *Dauid*, because they sit vpon GOD his Throne in the earth, and haue the count of their administration to giue vnto him. Their office is, *To minister Iustice and Iudgement to the people*,[2] as the same *Dauid* saith: *To aduance the good, and punish the euill*,[3] as he likewise saith: *To establish good Lawes to his people, and procure obedience to the same*,[4] as diuers good Kings of *Iudah*[5] did: *To procure the peace of the people*, as the same *Dauid* saith:[6] *To decide all controuersies that can arise among them*[7] as *Salomon* did: *To be the Minister of God for the weale of them that doe well, and as the minister of God, to take vengeance vpon them that doe euill*,[8] as S. *Paul* saith. And finally, *As a good Pastour, to goe out and in before his people*[9] as is said in the first of *Samuel: That through the Princes prosperitie, the peoples peace may be procured*,[10] as *Ieremie* saith.

And therefore in the Coronation of our owne Kings, as well as of euery Christian *Monarche* they giue their Oath, first to maintaine the Religion presently professed within their countrie, according to their lawes, whereby it is established, and to punish all those that should presse to alter, or disturbe the profession thereof; And next to maintaine all the lowable and good Lawes made by their predecessours: to see them put in execution, and the breakers and violaters thereof, to be punished, according to the tenour of the same: And lastly, to maintaine the whole countrey, and euery state therein, in all their ancient Priuiledges and Liberties, as well against all forreine enemies, as among themselues: And shortly to procure the weale and flourishing of his people, not onely in maintaining and putting to execution the olde lowable lawes of the countrey, and by establishing of new (as necessitie and euill maners will require) but by all other meanes possible to fore-see and preuent all dangers, that are likely to fall vpon them, and to maintaine concord, wealth, and ciuilitie among them, as a louing Father, and carefull watchman, caring for them more then for himselfe, knowing himselfe to be ordained for them, and they not for him; and therefore countable to that great God, who placed him as his lieutenant ouer them, vpon the perill of his soule to procure the weale of both soules and bodies, as farre as in him lieth, of all them that are committed to his charge. And this oath in the Coronation is the clearest, ciuill, and fundamentall Law, whereby the Kings office is properly defined.

By the Law of Nature the King becomes a naturall Father to all his Lieges at his Coronation: And as the Father of his fatherly duty is bound to care for the nourishing, education, and vertuous gouernment of his children; euen so is the king bound to care for all his subiects. As all the toile and paine that the father can take for his children, will be thought light and well bestowed by him, so that the effect thereof redound to their profite and weale; so ought the Prince to doe towards his people. As the kindly father ought to foresee all inconuenients and dangers that may arise towards his children, and though with the hazard of his owne person presse to preuent the same; so ought the King towards his people. As the fathers wrath and correction vpon any of his children that offendeth, ought to be by a fatherly chastisement seasoned with pitie, as long as there is any hope of amendment in them; so ought the King towards any of his Lieges that offend in that measure. And shortly, as the Fathers chiefe ioy ought to be in procuring his childrens welfare, reioycing at their weale, sorrowing and pitying at their euill, to hazard for their safetie, trauell for their rest, wake for their sleepe; and in a word, to thinke that his earthly felicitie and life standeth and liueth more in them, nor in himselfe; so ought a good Prince thinke of his people.

As to the other branch of this mutuall and reciprock band, is the duety and alleageance that the Lieges owe to their King: the ground whereof, I take out of the words of *Samuel*, dited by Gods Spirit, when God had giuen him commandement to heare the peoples voice in choosing and annointing them a King. And because that place of Scripture being well vnderstood, is so pertinent for our purpose, I haue insert herein the very words of the Text.

9 *Now therefore hearken to their voice: howbeit yet testifie vnto them, and shew them the maner of the King, that shall raigne ouer them.*

10 *So* Samuel *tolde all the wordes of the Lord vnto the people that asked a King of him.*

11 *And he said, This shall be the maner of the King that shall raigne ouer you: he will take your sonnes, and appoint them to his Charets, and to be his horsemen, and some shall runne before his Charet.*

12 *Also, hee will make them his captaines ouer thousands, and captaines ouer fifties, and to eare his ground, and to reape his haruest, and to make instruments of warre and the things that serue for his charets:*

13 *Hee will also take your daughters, and make them Apothicaries, and Cookes, and Bakers.*

14 *And hee will take your fields, and your vineyards, and your best Oliue trees, and giue them to his seruants.*

15 *And he will take the tenth of your seed, and of your Vineyards, and giue it to his Eunuches, and to his seruants.*

16 *And he will take your men seruants, and your maid-seruants, and the chiefe of your young men, and your asses, and put them to his worke.*

17 *He will take the tenth of your sheepe: and ye shall be his seruants.*

18 *And ye shall cry out at that day, because of your King, whom ye haue chosen you: and the Lord God will not heare you at that day.*

19 *But the people would not heare the voice of* Samuel, *but did say: Nay, but there shalbe a King ouer vs.*

20 *And we also will be all like other Nations, and our King shall iudge vs, and goe out before vs, and fight our battels.*

That these words, and discourses of *Samuel* were dited by Gods Spirit, it needs no further probation, but that it is a place of Scripture; since the whole Scripture is dited by that inspiration, as *Paul* saith: which ground no good Christian will, or dare denie. Whereupon it must necessarily follow, that these speeches proceeded not from any ambition in *Samuel*, as one loath to quite the reines that he so long had ruled, and therefore desirous, by making odious the gouernment of a King, to disswade the people from their farther importunate crauing of one: For, as the text proueth it plainly, he then conueened them to giue them a resolute grant of their demand, as God by his owne mouth commanded him, saying,

> *Hearken to the voice of the people.*

And to presse to disswade them from that, which he then came to grant vnto them, were a thing very impertinent in a wise man; much more in the Prophet of the most high God. And likewise, it well appeared in all the course of his life after, that so long refusing of their sute before came not of any ambition in him: which he well proued in praying, & as it were importuning God for the weale of *Saul*. Yea, after God had declared his reprobation vnto him, yet he desisted not, while God himselfe was wrath at his praying, and discharged his fathers suit in that errand. And that these words of *Samuel* were not vttered as a prophecie of *Saul* their first Kings defection, it well appeareth, as well because we heare no mention made in the Scripture of any his tyrannie and oppression, (which, if it had beene, would not haue been left vnpainted out therein, as well as his other faults were, as in a trew mirrour of all the Kings behauiours, whom it describeth) as likewise in respect that *Saul* was chosen by God for his vertue, and meet qualities to gouerne his people: whereas his defection sprung after-hand from the corruption of his owne nature, & not through any default in God, whom they that thinke so, would make as a step-father to his people, in making wilfully a choise of the vnmeetest for gouerning them, since the election of that King lay absolutely and immediatly in Gods hand. But by the contrary it is plaine, and euident, that this speech of *Samuel* to the people, was to prepare their hearts before the hand to the due obedience of that King, which God was to giue vnto them; and therefore opened vp vnto them, what might be the intollerable qualities that might fall in some of their kings, thereby preparing them to patience, not to resist to Gods ordinance: but as he would haue said; Since God hath granted your importunate suit in giuing you a king, as yee haue else committed an errour in shaking off Gods yoke, and ouer-hastie seeking of a King; so beware yee fall not into the next, in casting off also rashly that yoke, which God at your earnest suite hath laid vpon you, how hard that euer it seeme to be: For as ye could not haue obtained one without the permission and ordinance of God, so may yee no more, for hee be once set ouer you, shake him off without the same warrant. And therefore in time arme your selues with patience and humilitie, since he that hath the only power to make him, hath the onely power to vnmake him; and ye onely to obey, bearing with these straits that I now foreshew you, as with the finger of God, which lieth not in you to take off.

And will ye consider the very wordes of the text in order, as they are set downe, it shall plainely declare the obedience that the people owe to their King in all respects.

First, God commandeth *Samuel* to doe two things: the one, to grant the people their suit in giuing them a king; the other, to forewarne them, what some kings will doe vnto them, that they may not thereafter in their grudging and murmuring say, when they shal feele the snares here fore-spoken; We would neuer haue had a king of God, in case when we craued him, hee had let vs know how wee would haue beene vsed by him, as now we finde but ouer-late. And this is meant by these words:

Now therefore hearken vnto their voice: howbeit yet testifie vnto them, and shew them the maner of the King that shall rule ouer them.

And next, *Samuel* in execution of this commandement of God, hee likewise doeth two things.

First, hee declares vnto them, what points of iustice and equitie their king will breake in his behauiour vnto them: And next he putteth them out of hope, that wearie as they will, they shall not haue leaue to shake off that yoke, which God through their importunitie hath laide vpon them. The points of equitie that the King shall breake vnto them, are expressed in these words:

11 *He will take your sonnes, and appoint them to his Charets, and to be his horsemen, and some shall run before his Charet.*

12 *Also he will make them his captaines ouer thousands, and captaines ouer fifties, and to eare his ground, and to reape his haruest, and to make instruments of warre, and the things that serue for his charets.*

13 *He will also take your daughters, and make them Apothecaries, and Cookes, and Bakers.*

The points of Iustice, that hee shall breake vnto them, are expressed in these wordes:

14 *Hee will take your fields, and your vineyards, and your best Oliue trees, and giue them to his seruants.*

15 *And he will take the tenth of your seede, and of your vineyards, and giue it to his Eunuches and to his seruants: and also the tenth of your sheepe.*

As if he would say; The best and noblest of your blood shall be compelled in slauish and seruile offices to serue him: and not content of his owne patrimonie, will make vp a rent to his owne vse out of your best lands, vineyards, orchards, and store of cattell: So as inuerting the Law of nature, and office of a King, your persons and the persons of your posteritie, together with your lands, and all that ye possesse shall serue his priuate vse, and inordinate appetite.

And as vnto the next point (which is his fore-warning them, that, weary as they will, they shall not haue leaue to shake off the yoke, which God thorow their importunity hath laid vpon them) it is expressed in these words:

18 *And yee shall crie out at that day, because of your King whom yee haue chosen you: and the Lord will not heare you at that day.*

As he would say; When ye shall finde these things in proofe that now I forewarne you of, although you shall grudge and murmure, yet it shal not be lawful to you to cast it off, in respect it is not only the ordinance of God, but also your selues haue chosen him vnto you, thereby renouncing for euer all priuiledges, by your willing consent out of your hands, whereby in any time hereafter ye would claime, and call backe vnto your selues againe that power, which God shall not permit you to doe. And for further taking away of all excuse, and retraction of this their contract, after their consent to vnder-lie this yoke with all the burthens that hee hath declared vnto them, he craues their answere, and consent to his proposition: which appeareth by their answere, as it is expressed in these words:

19 *Nay, but there shall be a King ouer vs.*

20 *And we also will be like all other nations: and our king shall iudge vs, and goe out before vs and fight our battels.*

As if they would haue said; All your speeches and hard conditions shall not skarre vs, but we will take the good and euill of it vpon vs, and we will be content to beare whatsoeuer burthen it shal please our King to lay vpon vs, aswell as other nations doe. And for the good we will get of him in fighting our battels, we will more patiently beare any burden that shall please him to lay on vs.

Now then, since the erection of this Kingdome and Monarchie among the Iewes, and the law thereof may, and ought to bee a paterne to all Christian and well founded Monarchies, as beeing founded by God himselfe, who by his Oracle, and out of his owne mouth gaue the law thereof: what liberty can broiling spirits, and rebellious minds claime iustly to against any Christian Monarchie; since they can claime to no greater libertie on their part, nor the people of God might haue done, and no greater tyranny was euer executed by any Prince or tyrant, whom they can obiect, nor was here fore-warned to the people of God, (and yet all rebellion countermanded vnto them) if tyrannizing ouer mens persons, sonnes, daughters and seruants; redacting noble houses, and men, and women of noble blood, to slauish and seruile offices; and extortion, and spoile of their lands and goods to the princes owne priuate vse and commoditie, and of his courteours, and seruants, may be called a tyrannie?

And that this proposition grounded vpon the Scripture, may the more clearly appeare to be trew by the practise oft prooued in the same booke, we neuer reade, that euer the Prophets perswaded the people to rebell against the Prince, how wicked soeuer he was.

When *Samuel* by Gods command pronounced to the same king *Saul*, that his kingdome was rent from him, and giuen to another (which in effect was a degrading of him) yet his next action following that, was peaceably to turne home, and with floods of teares to pray to God to haue some compassion vpon him.[11]

And *David*, notwithstanding hee was inaugurate in that same degraded Kings roome, not onely (when he was cruelly persecuted, for no offence; but good seruice done vnto him) would not presume, hauing him in his power, skantly, but with great reuerence, to touch the garment of the annoynted of the Lord, and in his words blessed him:[12] but likewise, when one came to him vanting himselfe vntrewly to haue slaine *Saul*, hee, without forme of proces, or triall of his guilt, caused onely for guiltinesse of his tongue, put him to sodaine death.[13]

And although there was neuer a more monstrous persecutor, and tyrant nor *Achab* was: yet all the rebellion, that *Elias* euer raised against him, was to flie to the wildernes: where for fault of sustentation, he was fed with the Corbies. And I thinke no man will doubt but *Samuel, Dauid,* and *Elias,* had as great power to perswade the people, if they had like to haue employed their credite to vproares & rebellions against these wicked kings, as any of our seditious preachers in these daies of whatsoeuer religion, either in this countrey or in France, had, that busied themselues most to stir vp rebellion vnder cloake of religion. This farre the only loue of veritie, I protest, without hatred at their persons, haue mooued me to be somewhat satyricke.

And if any will leane to the extraordinarie examples of degrading or killing of kings in the Scriptures, thereby to cloake the peoples rebellion, as by the deed of *Iehu*, and such like extraordinaries: I answere, besides that they want the like warrant that they had, if extraordinarie examples of the Scripture shall bee drawne in daily practise; murther vnder traist as in the persons of *Ahud*, and *Iael*; theft, as in the persons of the *Israelites* comming out of *Egypt*; lying to their parents to the hurt of their brother, as in the person of *Iacob*, shall all be counted as lawfull and allowable vertues, as rebellion against Princes. And to conclude, the practise through the whole Scripture prooueth the peoples obedience giuen to that sentence in the law of God:

Thou shalt not rayle vpon the Iudges, neither speake euill of the ruler of thy people.

To end then the ground of my proposition taken out of the Scripture, let two speciall, and notable examples, one vnder the law, another vnder the Euangel, conclude this part of my alleageance. Vnder the lawe, *Ieremie* threatneth the people of God with vtter destruction for rebellion to *Nabuchadnezar* the king of Babel:[14] who although he was an idolatrous persecuter, a forraine King, a Tyrant, and vsurper of their liberties; yet in respect they had once receiued and acknowledged him for their king, he not only commandeth them to obey him, but euen to pray for his prosperitie, adioyning the reason to it; because in his prosperitie stood their peace.[15]

And vnder the Euangel, that king, whom *Paul* bids the *Romanes obey* and serue *for conscience sake*, was *Nero* that bloody tyrant, an infamie to his aage, and a monster to the world, being also an idolatrous persecuter, as the King of *Babel* was. If then Idolatrie and defection from God, tyranny ouer their people, and persecution of the Saints, for their profession sake, hindred not the Spirit of God to command his people vnder all highest paine to giue them all due and heartie obedience for conscience sake, giuing to *Cæsar* that which was *Cæsars*, and to God that which was Gods, as Christ saith; and that this practise throughout the booke of God agreeth with this lawe, which he made in the erection of that Monarchie (as is at length before deduced) what shamelesse presumption is it to any Christian people now adayes to claime to that vnlawfull libertie, which God refused to his owne peculiar and chosen people?[16] Shortly then to take vp in two or three sentences, grounded vpon all these arguments, out of the lawe of God, the duetie, and alleageance of the people to their lawfull king, their obedience, I say, ought to be to him, as to Gods Lieutenant in earth, obeying his commands in all thing, except directly against God, as the commands of Gods Minister, acknowledging him a Iudge set by GOD ouer them, hauing power to iudge them, but to be iudged onely by GOD, whom to onely hee must giue count of his iudgement; fearing him as their Iudge, louing him as their father; praying for him as their protectour; for his continuance, if he be good; for his amendement, if he be wicked; following and obeying his lawfull commands, eschewing and flying his fury in his vnlawfull, without resistance, but by sobbes and teares to God, according to that sentence vsed in the primitiue Church in the time of the persecution.

Preces, & Lachrymæ sunt arma Ecclesiæ.

Now, as for the describing the allegeance, that the lieges owe to their natiue King, out of the fundamentall and ciuill Lawe, especially of this contrey, as I promised, the ground must first be set downe of the first maner of establishing the Lawes and forme of gouernement among vs; that the ground being first right laide, we may thereafter build rightly thereupon. Although it be trew (according to the affirmation of those that pryde themselues to be the scourges of Tyrants) that in the first beginning of Kings rising among the Gentiles, in the time of the first aage, diuers commonwealths and societies of men choosed out one among themselues, who for his vertues and valour, being more eminent then the rest, was chosen out by them, and set vp in that roome, to maintaine the weakest in their right, to throw downe oppressours, and to foster and continue the societie among men; which could not otherwise, but by vertue of that vnitie be wel done: yet these examples are nothing pertinent to vs; because our Kingdome and diuers other Monarchies are not in that case, but had their beginning in a farre contrary fashion.

For as our Chronicles beare witnesse, this Ile, and especially our part of it, being scantly inhabited, but by very few, and they as barbarous and scant of ciuilitie, as number, there comes our first King *Fergus*, with a great number with him, out of *Ireland*, which was long inhabited before vs, and making himself master of the countrey, by his owne friendship, and force, as well of the *Irelandmen* that came with him, as of the countrey-men that willingly fell to him, hee made himselfe King and Lord, as well of the whole landes, as of the whole inhabitants within the same. Thereafter he and his successours, a long while after their being Kinges, made and established their lawes from time to time, and as the occasion required. So the trewth is directly contrarie in our state to the false affirmation of such seditious writers, as would perswade vs, that the Lawes and state of our countrey were established before the admitting of a king: where by the countrarie ye see it plainely prooued, that a wise king comming in among barbares, first established the estate and forme of gouernement, and thereafter made lawes by himselfe, and his successours according thereto.

The kings therefore in *Scotland* were before any estates or rankes of men within the same, before any Parliaments were holden, or lawes made: and by them was the land distributed (which at the first was whole theirs) states erected and decerned, and formes of gouernement deuised and established: And so it followes of necessitie, that the kings were the authors and makers of the Lawes, and not the Lawes of the kings. And to prooue this my assertion more clearly, it is euident by the rolles of our Chancellery (which containe our eldest and fundamentall Lawes) that the King is *Dominus omnium bonorum*, and *Dominus directus totius Dominij*, the whole subiects being but his vassals, and from him holding all their lands as their ouer-lord, who according to good seruices done vnto him, chaungeth their holdings from tacke to few, from ward to blanch, erecteth new Baronies, and vniteth olde, without aduice or authoritie of either Parliament or any other subalterin iudiciall seate: So as if wrong might bee admitted in play (albeit I grant wrong should be wrong in all persons) the King might haue a better colour for his pleasure, without further reason, to take the land from his lieges, as ouer-lord of the whole, and doe with it as pleaseth him, since all that they hold is of him, then, as foolish writers say, the people might vnmake the king, and put an other in his roome: But either of them as vnlawful, and against the ordinance of God, ought to be alike odious to be thought, much lesse put in practise.

And according to these fundamentall Lawes already alledged, we daily see that in the Parliament (which is nothing else but the head Court of the king and his vassals) the lawes are but craued by his subiects, and onely made by him at their rogation, and with their aduice: For albeit the king make daily statutes and ordinances, enioyning such paines thereto as hee thinkes meet, without any aduice of Parliament or estates; yet it lies in the power of no Parliament, to make any kinde of Lawe or Statute, without his Scepter be to it, for giuing it the force of a Law: And although diuers changes haue beene in other countries of the blood Royall, and kingly house, the kingdome being reft by conquest from one to another, as in our neighbour countrey in *England*, (which was neuer in ours) yet the same ground of the kings right ouer all the land, and subiects thereof remaineth alike in all other free Monarchies, as well as in this: For when the Bastard of *Normandie* came into *England*, and made himselfe king, was it not by force, and with a mighty army? Where he gaue the Law, and tooke none, changed the Lawes, inuerted the order of gouernement, set downe the strangers his followers in many of the old possessours roomes, as at this day well appeareth a great part of the Gentlemen in *England*, beeing come of the *Norman* blood, and their old Lawes, which to this day they are ruled by, are written in his language, and not in theirs: And yet his successours haue with great happinesse enioyed the Crowne to this day; Whereof the like was also done by all them that conquested them before.

And for conclusion of this point, that the king is ouer-lord ouer the whole lands, it is likewise daily proued by the Law of our hoordes, of want of Heires, and of Bastardies: For if a hoord be found vnder the earth, because it is no more in the keeping or vse of any person, it of the law pertains to the king. If a person, inheritour of any lands or goods, dye without any sort of heires, all his landes and goods returne to the king. And if a bastard die vnrehabled without heires of his bodie (which rehabling onely lyes in the kings hands) all that hee hath likewise returnes to the king. And as ye see it manifest, that the King is ouer-Lord of the whole land: so is he Master ouer euery person that inhabiteth the same, hauing power ouer the life and death of euery one of them: For although a iust Prince will not take the life of any of his subiects without a cleare law; yet the same lawes whereby he taketh them, are made by himselfe, or his predecessours; and so the power flowes alwaies from him selfe; as by daily experience we see, good and iust Princes will from time to time make new lawes and statutes, adioyning the penalties to the breakers thereof, which before the law was made, had beene no crime to the subiect to haue committed. Not that I deny the old definition of a King, and of a law; which makes the king to bee a speaking law, and the Law a dumbe king: for certainely a king that gouernes not by his lawe, can neither be countable to God for his administration, nor haue a happy and established raigne: For albeit it be trew that I haue at length prooued, that the King is aboue the law, as both the author and giuer of strength thereto, yet a good king will not onely delight to rule his subiects by the lawe, but euen will conforme himselfe in his owne actions thereunto, alwaies keeping that ground, that the health of the common-wealth be his chiefe lawe: And where he sees the lawe doubtsome or rigorous, hee may interpret or mitigate the same, lest otherwise *Summum ius* bee *summa iniuria*: And therefore generall lawes, made publikely in Parliament, may vpon knowen respects to the King by his authoritie bee mitigated, and suspended vpon causes onely knowen to him.

As likewise, although I haue said, a good king will frame all his actions to be according to the Law; yet is hee not bound thereto but of his good will, and for good example-giuing to his subiects: For as in the law of abstaining from eating of flesh in *Lenton*, the king will, for examples sake, make his owne house to obserue the Law; yet no man will thinke he needs to take a licence to eate flesh. And although by our Lawes, the bearing and wearing of hag-buts, and pistolets be forbidden, yet no man can find any fault in the King, for causing his traine vse them in any raide vpon the Borderers, or other malefactours or rebellious subiects. So as I haue alreadie said, a good King, although hee be aboue the Law, will subiect and frame his actions thereto, for examples sake to his subiects, and of his owne free-will, but not as subiect or bound thereto.

Since I haue so clearly prooued then out of the fundamentall lawes and practise of this country, what right & power a king hath ouer his land and subiects, it is easie to be vnderstood, what allegeance & obedience his lieges owe vnto him; I meane alwaies of such free Monarchies as our king is, and not of electiue kings, and much lesse of such sort of gouernors, as the dukes of *Venice* are, whose Aristocratick and limited gouernment, is nothing like to free Monarchies; although the malice of some writers hath not beene ashamed to mis-know any difference to be betwixt them. And if it be not lawfull to any particular Lordes tenants or vassals, vpon whatsoeuer pretext, to controll and displace their Master, and ouer-lord (as is clearer nor the Sunne by all Lawes of the world) how much lesse may the subiects and vassals of the great ouer-lord the KING controll or displace him? And since in all inferiour iudgements in the land, the people may not vpon any respects displace their Magistrates, although but subaltern: for the people of a borough, cannot displace their Prouost before the time of their election: nor in Ecclesiasticall policie the flocke can vpon any pretence displace the Pastor, nor iudge of him: yea euen the poore Schoolemaster cannot be displaced by his schollers: If these, I say (whereof some are but inferiour, subaltern, and temporall Magistrates, and none of them equall in any sort to the dignitie of a King) cannot be displaced for any occasion or pretext by them that are ruled by them: how much lesse is it lawfull vpon any pretext to controll or displace the great Prouost, and great Schoole-master of the whole land: except by inuerting the order of all Law and reason, the commanded may be made to command their commander, the iudged to iudge their Iudge, and they that are gouerned, to gouerne their time about their Lord and gouernour.

And the agreement of the Law of nature in this our ground with the Lawes and constitutions of God, and man, already alledged, will by two similitudes easily appeare. The King towards his people is rightly compared to a father of children, and to a head of a body composed of diuers members: For as fathers, the good Princes, and Magistrates of the people of God acknowledged themselues to their subiects. And for all other well ruled Common-wealths, the stile of *Pater patriæ* was euer, and is commonly vsed to Kings. And the proper office of a King towards his Subiects, agrees very wel with the office of the head towards the body, and all members thereof: For from the head, being the seate of Iudgement, proceedeth the care and foresight of guiding, and preuenting all euill that may come to the body or any part thereof. The head cares for the body, so doeth the King for his people. As the discourse and direction flowes from the head, and the execution according thereunto belongs to the rest of the members, euery one according to their office: so it is betwixt a wise Prince, and his people. As the iudgement comming from the head may not onely imploy the members, euery one in their owne office, as long as they are able for it; but likewise in case any of them be affected with any infirmitie must care and prouide for their remedy, in-case it be curable, and if otherwise, gar cut them off for feare of infecting of the rest: euen so is it betwixt the Prince, and his people. And as there is euer hope of curing any diseased member by the direction of the head, as long as it is whole; but by the contrary, if it be troubled, all the members are partakers of that paine, so is it betwixt the Prince and his people.

And now first for the fathers part (whose naturall loue to his children I described in the first part of this my discourse, speaking of the dutie that Kings owe to their Subiects) consider, I pray you what duetie his children owe to him, & whether vpon any pretext whatsoeuer, it wil not be thought monstrous and vnnaturall to his sons, to rise vp against him, to control him at their appetite, and when they thinke good to sley him, or to cut him off, and adopt to themselues any other they please in his roome: Or can any pretence of wickednes or rigor on his part be a iust excuse for his children to put hand into him? And although wee see by the course of nature, that loue vseth to descend more then to ascend, in case it were trew, that the father hated and wronged the children neuer so much, will any man, endued with the least sponke of reason, thinke it lawfull for them to meet him with the line? Yea, suppose the father were furiously following his sonnes with a drawen sword, is it lawfull for them to turne and strike againe, or make any resistance but by flight? I thinke surely, if there were no more but the example of bruit beasts & vnreasonable creatures, it may serue well enough to qualifie and proue this my argument. We reade often the pietie that the Storkes haue to their olde and decayed parents: And generally wee know, that there are many sorts of beasts and fowles, that with violence and many bloody strokes will beat and banish their yong ones from them, how soone they perceiue them to be able to fend themselues; but wee neuer read or heard of any resistance on their part, except among the vipers; which prooues such persons, as ought to be reasonable creatures, and yet vnnaturally follow this example, to be endued with their viperous nature.

And for the similitude of the head and the body, it may very well fall out that the head will be forced to garre cut off some rotten members (as I haue already said) to keep the rest of the body in integritie: but what state the body can be in, if the head, for any infirmitie that can fall to it, be cut off, I leaue it to the readers iudgement.

So as (to conclude this part) if the children may vpon any pretext that can be imagined, lawfully rise vp against their Father, cut him off, & choose any other whom they please in his roome; and if the body for the weale of it, may for any infirmitie that can be in the head, strike it off, then I cannot deny that the people may rebell, controll, and displace, or cut off their king at their owne pleasure, and vpon respects moouing them. And whether these similitudes represent better the office of a King, or the offices of Masters or Deacons of crafts, or Doctors in Physicke (which iolly comparisons are vsed by such writers as maintaine the contrary proposition) I leaue it also to the readers discretion.

And in case any doubts might arise in any part of this treatise, I wil (according to my promise) with the solution of foure principall and most weightie doubts, that the aduersaries may obiect, conclude this discourse. And first it is casten vp by diuers, that employ their pennes vpon Apologies for rebellions and treasons, that euery man is borne to carry such a naturall zeale and duety to his common-wealth, as to his mother; that seeing it so rent and deadly wounded, as whiles it will be by wicked and tyrannous Kings, good Citizens will be forced, for the naturall zeale and duety they owe to their owne natiue countrey, to put their hand to worke for freeing their common-wealth from such a pest.

Whereunto I giue two answeres: First, it is a sure Axiome in *Theologie*, that euill should not be done, that good may come of it: The wickednesse therefore of the King can neuer make them that are ordained to be iudged by him, to become his Iudges. And if it be not lawfull to a priuate man to reuenge his priuate iniury vpon his priuate aduersary (since God hath onely giuen the sword to the Magistrate) how much lesse is it lawfull to the people, or any part of them (who all are but priuate men, the authoritie being alwayes with the Magistrate, as I haue already proued) to take vpon them the vse of the sword, whom to it belongs not, against the publicke Magistrate, whom to onely it belongeth.

Next, in place of relieuing the common-wealth out of distresse (which is their onely excuse and colour) they shall heape double distresse and desolation vpon it; and so their rebellion shall procure the contrary effects that they pretend it for: For a king cannot be imagined to be so vnruly and tyrannous, but the common-wealth will be kept in better order, notwithstanding thereof, by him, then it can be by his way-taking. For first, all sudden mutations are perillous in common-wealths, hope being thereby giuen to all bare men to set vp themselues, and flie with other mens feathers, the reines being loosed to all the insolencies that disordered people can commit by hope of impunitie, because of the loosenesse of all things.

And next, it is certaine that a king can neuer be so monstrously vicious, but hee will generally fauour iustice, and maintaine some order, except in the particulars, wherein his inordinate lustes and passions cary him away; where by the contrary, no King being, nothing is vnlawfull to none: And so the olde opinion of the Philosophers prooues trew, That better it is to liue in a Common-wealth, where nothing is lawfull, then where all things are lawfull to all men; the Common-wealth at that time resembling an vndanted young horse that hath casten his rider: For as the diuine Poet Dv BARTAS sayth, *Better it were to suffer some disorder in the estate, and some spots in the Common-wealth, then in pretending to reforme, vtterly to ouerthrow the Republicke.*

The second obiection they ground vpon the curse that hangs ouer the common-wealth, where a wicked king reigneth: and, say they, there cannot be a more acceptable deed in the sight of God, nor more dutiful to their common-weale, then to free the countrey of such a curse, and vindicate to them their libertie, which is naturall to all creatures to craue.

Whereunto for answere, I grant indeed, that a wicked king is sent by God for a curse to his people, and a plague for their sinnes: but that it is lawfull to them to shake off that curse at their owne hand, which God hath laid on them, that I deny, and may so do iustly. Will any deny that the king of *Babel* was a curse to the people of God, as was plainly fore-spoken and threatned vnto them in the prophecie of their captiutie? And what was *Nero* to the Christian Church in his time? And yet *Ieremy* and *Paul* (as yee haue else heard) commanded them not onely to obey them, but heartily to pray for their welfare.

It is certaine then (as I haue already by the Law of God sufficiently proued) that patience, earnest prayers to God, and amendment of their liues, are the onely lawful means to moue God to relieue them of that heauie curse. As for vindicating to themselues their owne libertie, what lawfull power haue they to reuoke to themselues againe those priuiledges, which by their owne consent before were so fully put out of their hands? for if a Prince cannot iustly bring backe againe to himself the priuiledges once bestowed by him or his predecessors vpon any state or ranke of his subiects; how much lesse may the subiects reaue out of the princes hand that superioritie, which he and his Predecessors haue so long brooked ouer them?

But the vnhappy iniquitie of the time, which hath oft times giuen ouer good successe to their treasonable attempts, furnisheth them the ground of their third obiection: For, say they, the fortunate successe that God hath so oft giuen to such enterprises, prooueth plainely by the practise, that God fauoured the iustnesse of their quarrell.

To the which I answere, that it is trew indeed, that all the successe of battels, as well as other wordly things, lyeth onely in Gods hand: And therefore it is that in the Scripture he takes to himselfe the style of God of Hosts. But vpon that generall to conclude, that hee euer giues victory to the iust quarrell, would prooue the *Philistims*, and diuers other neighbour enemies of the people of God to haue oft times had the iust quarrel against the people of God, in respect of the many victories they obtained against them. And by that same argument they had also iust quarrell against the Arke of God: For they wan it in the field, and kept it long prisoner in their countrey. As likewise by all good Writers, as well Theologues, as other, the Duels and singular combats are disallowed; which are onely made vpon pretence, that GOD will kith thereby the iustice of the quarrell: For wee must consider that the innocent partie is not innocent before God: And therefore God will make oft times them that haue the wrong side reuenge iustly his quarrell; and when he hath done, cast his scourge in the fire; as he oft times did to his owne people, stirring vp and strengthening their enemies, while they were humbled in his sight, and then deliuered them in their hands. So God, as the great Iudge may iustly punish his Deputie, and for his rebellion against him stir vp his rebels to meet him with the like: And when it is done, the part of the instrument is no better then the diuels part is in tempting and torturing such as God committeth to him as his hangman to doe: Therefore, as I said in the beginning, it is oft times a very deceiueable argument, to iudge of the cause by the euent.

And the last obiection is grounded vpon the mutuall paction and adstipulation (as they call it) betwixt the King and his people, at the time of his coronation: For there, say they, there is a mutuall paction, and contract bound vp, and sworne betwixt the king, and the people: Whereupon it followeth, that if the one part of the contract or the Indent bee broken vpon the Kings side, the people are no longer bound to keep their part of it, but are thereby freed of their oath: For (say they) a contract betwixt two parties, of all Law frees the one partie, if the other breake vnto him.

As to this contract alledged made at the coronation of a King, although I deny any such contract to bee made then, especially containing such a clause irritant as they alledge; yet I confesse, that a king at his coronation, or at the entry to his kingdome, willingly promiseth to his people, to discharge honorably and trewly the office giuen him by God ouer them: But presuming that thereafter he breaks his promise vnto them neuer so inexcusable; the question is, who should bee iudge of the breake, giuing vnto them, this contract were made vnto them neuer so sicker, according to their alleageance. I thinke no man that hath but the smallest entrance into the ciuill Law, will doubt that of all Law, either ciuil or municipal of any nation, a contract cannot be thought broken by the one partie, and so the other likewise to be freed therefro, except that first a lawfull triall and cognition be had by the ordinary Iudge of the breakers thereof: Or else euery man may be both party and Iudge in his owne cause; which is absurd once to be thought. Now in this contract (I say) betwixt the king and his people, God is doubtles the only Iudge, both because to him onely the king must make count of his administration (as is oft said before) as likewise by the oath in the coronation, God is made iudge and reuenger of the breakers: For in his presence, as only iudge of oaths, all oaths ought to be made. Then since God is the onely Iudge betwixt the two parties contractors, the cognition and reuenge must onely appertaine to him: It followes therefore of necessitie, that God must

first giue sentence vpon the King that breaketh, before the people can thinke themselues
freed of their oath. What iustice then is it, that the partie shall be both iudge and partie,
vsurping vpon himselfe the office of God, may by this argument easily appeare: And shall
it lie in the hands of headlesse multitude, when they please to weary off subiection, to
cast off the yoake of gouernement that God hath laid vpon them, to iudge and punish him,
whom-by they should be iudged and punished, and in that case, wherein by their violence
they kythe themselues to be most passionate parties, to vse the office of an vngracious
Iudge or Arbiter? Nay, to speak trewly of that case, as it stands betwixt the king and his
people, none of them ought to iudge of the others break: For considering rightly the two
parties at the time of their mutuall promise, the king is the one party, and the whole
people in one body are the other party. And therfore since it is certaine, that a king, in
case so it should fal out, that his people in one body had rebelled against him, hee should
not in that case, as thinking himselfe free of his promise and oath, become an vtter
enemy, and practise the wreake of his whole people and natiue country: although he
ought iustly to punish the principall authours and bellowes of that vniuersall rebellion:
how much lesse then ought the people (that are alwaies subiect vnto him, and naked of all
authoritie on their part) presse to iudge and ouer-throw him? otherwise the people, as the
one partie contracters, shall no sooner challenge the king as breaker, but hee assoone shall
iudge them as breakers: so as the victors making the tyners the traitors (as our prouerbe
is) the partie shall aye become both iudge and partie in his owne particular, as I haue
alreadie said.

And it is here likewise to be noted, that the duty and alleageance, which the people
sweareth to their prince, is not only bound to themselues, but likewise to their lawfull
heires and posterity, the lineall succession of crowns being begun among the people of
God, and happily continued in diuers christian common-wealths: So as no obiection
either of heresie, or whatsoever priuate statute or law may free the people from their oath-
giuing to their king, and his succession, established by the old fundamentall lawes of the
kingdome: For, as hee is their heritable ouer-lord, and so by birth, not by any right in the
coronation, commeth to his crowne; it is a like vnlawful (the crowne euer standing full) to
displace him that succeedeth thereto, as to eiect the former: For at the very moment of the
expiring of the king reigning, the nearest and lawful heire entreth in his place: And so to
refuse him, or intrude another, is not to holde out vncomming in, but to expell and put out
their righteous King. And I trust at this time whole *France* acknowledgeth the
superstitious rebellion of the liguers, who vpon pretence of heresie, by force of armes
held so long out, to the great desolation of their whole countrey, their natiue and righteous
king from possessing of his owne crowne and naturall kingdome.

Not that by all this former discourse of mine, and Apologie for kings, I meane that
whatsoeuer errors and intollerable abominations a souereigne prince commit, hee ought to
escape all punishment, as if thereby the world were only ordained for kings, & they
without controlment to turne it vpside down at their pleasure: but by the contrary, by
remitting them to God (who is their onely ordinary Iudge) I remit them to the sorest and
sharpest schoolemaster that can be deuised for them: for the further a king is preferred by
God aboue all other ranks & degrees of men, and the higher that his seat is aboue theirs,
the greater is his obligation to his maker. And therfore in case he forget himselfe (his
vnthankfulnes being in the same measure of height) the sadder and sharper will his
correction be; and according to the greatnes of the height he is in, the weight of his fall

wil recompense the same: for the further that any person is obliged to God, his offence becomes and growes so much the greater, then it would be in any other. *Ioues* thunderclaps light oftner and sorer vpon the high & stately oakes, then on the low and supple willow trees: and the highest bench is sliddriest to sit vpon. Neither is it euer heard that any king forgets himselfe towards God, or in his vocation; but God with the greatnesse of the plague reuengeth the greatnes of his ingratitude: Neither thinke I by the force and argument of this my discourse so to perswade the people, that none will hereafter be raised vp, and rebell against wicked Princes. But remitting to the iustice and prouidence of God to stirre vp such scourges as pleaseth him, for punishment of wicked kings (who made the very vermine and filthy dust of the earth to bridle the insolencie of proud *Pharaoh*) my onely purpose and intention in this treatise is to perswade, as farre as lieth in me, by these sure and infallible grounds, all such good Christian readers, as beare not onely the naked name of a Christian, but kith the fruites thereof in their daily forme of life, to keep their hearts and hands free from such monstrous and vnnaturall rebellions, whensoeuer the wickednesse of a Prince shall procure the same at Gods hands: that, when it shall please God to cast such scourges of princes, and instruments of his fury in the fire, ye may stand vp with cleane handes, and unspotted consciences, hauing prooued your selues in all your actions trew Christians toward God, and dutifull subiects towards your King, hauing remitted the judgement and punishment of all his wrongs to him, whom to onely of right it appertaineth.

But crauing at God, and hoping that God shall continue his blessing with vs, in not sending such fearefull desolation, I heartily wish our kings behauiour so to be, and continue among vs, as our God in earth, and louing Father, endued with such properties as I described a King in the first part of this Treatise. And that ye (my deare countreymen, and charitable readers) may presse by all means to procure the prosperitie and welfare of your King; that as hee must on the one part thinke all his earthly felicitie and happinesse grounded vpon your weale, caring more for himselfe for your sake then for his owne, thinking himselfe onely ordained for your weale; such holy and happy emulation may arise betwixt him and you, as his care for your quietnes, and your care for his honour and preseruation, may in all your actions daily striue together, that the Land may thinke themselues blessed with such a King, and the king may thinke himselfe most happy in ruling ouer so louing and obedient subiects.

FINIS.

Notes

[1] Psal. 82. 6.

[2] Psal. 101.

[3] Psal. 101.

[4] 2. King. 18.

[5] 2. Chron. 29; 2. King. 22; and 23. 2; chro. 34, & 35.

[6] Psal. 72.

[7] 1. King. 3.
[8] Rom. 13.
[9] 1. Sam. 8.
[10] Ierem. 29.
[11] 1. Sam. 15.
[12] 1. Sam. 24.
[13] 2. Sam. 1.
[14] Ier. 27.
[15] Iere. 29.
[16] Iere. 13.

17. An Agreement of the People[*]

Levellers

An Agreement of the People, for a firme and present Peace, upon grounds of Common-Right.

Having by our late labours and hazards made it appeare to the world at how high a rate wee value our just freedome, and God having so far owned our cause, as to deliver the Enemies thereof into our hands: We do now hold our selves bound in mutual duty to each other, to take the best care we can for the future, to avoid both the danger of returning into a slavish condition, and the chargable remedy of another war: for as it cannot be imagined that so many of our Country-men would have opposed us in this quarrel, if they had understood their owne good; so may we safely promise to our selves, that when our Common Rights and liberties shall be cleared, their endeavours will be disappointed, that seek to make themselves our Masters: since therefore our former oppressions, and scarce yet ended troubles have beene occasioned, either by want of frequent Nationall meetings in Councell, or by rendring those meetings ineffectuall; We are fully agreed and resolved, to provide that hereafter our Representatives be neither left to an uncertainty for the time, nor made uselesse to the ends for which they are intended: In order whereunto we declare,

I. That the People of England being at this day very unequally distributed by Counties, Cities, & Burroughs, for the election of their Deputies in Parliament, ought to be more indifferently proportioned, according to the number of the Inhabitants: the circumstances whereof, for number, place, and manner, are to be set down before the end of this present Parliament.

[*] The Levellers probably wrote this agreement in October 1647, and it first appeared in pamphlet form on November 3, 1647. This particular excerpt was taken from *Leveller Manifestoes of the Puritan Revolution*, edited by Don M. Wolfe (New York: Humanities Press, 1967), 226–228.

2.

The parliament must be replaced with new representatives rather than the people who are who are in office continuously

II. That to prevent the many inconveniences apparently arising from the long continuance of the same persons in authority, this present Parliament be dissolved upon the last day of September, which shall be in the year of our Lord, 1648.

III. That the People do of course chuse themselves a Parliament once in two yeares, viz. upon the first Thursday in every 2d. March, after the manner as shall be prescribed before the end of this Parliament, to begin to sit upon the first Thursday in Aprill following at Westminster, or such other place as shall bee appointed from time to time by the preceding Representatives; and to continue till the last day of September, then next ensuing, and no longer.

IV. That the power of this, and all future Representatives of this Nation, is inferiour only to theirs who chuse them, and doth extend, without the consent or concurrence of any other person or persons; to the enacting, altering, and repealing of Lawes; to the erecting and abolishing of Offices and Courts; to the appointing, removing, and calling to account Magistrats, and Officers of all degrees; to the making War and peace, to the treating with forraign States: And generally, to whatsoever is not expresly, or implyedly reserved by the represented to themselves.

Which are as followeth,

1. That matters of Religion, and the wayes of Gods Worship, are not at all intrusted by us to any humane power, because therein wee cannot remit or exceed a tittle of what our Consciences dictate to be the mind of God, without wilfull sinne: neverthelesse the publike way of instructing the Nation (so it be not compulsive) is referred to their discretion.

2. That the matter of impresting and constraining any of us to serve in the warres, is against our freedome; and therefore we do not allow it in our Representatives; the rather, because money (the sinews of war) being alwayes at their disposall, they can never want numbers of men, apt enough to engage in any just cause.

3. That after the dissolution of this present Parliament, no person be at any time questioned for anything said or done, in reference to the late publike differences, otherwise then in execution of the Judgments of the present Representatives, or House of Commons.

4. That in all Laws made, or to be made, every person may be bound alike, and that no Tenure, Estate, Charter, Degree, Birth, or place, do confer any exemption from the ordinary Course of Legall proceedings, whereunto others are subjected.

5. That as the Laws ought to be equall, so they must be good, and not evidently destructive to the safety and well-being of the people.

These things we declare to be our native Rights, and therefore are agreed and resolved to maintain them with our utmost possibilities, against all opposition whatsoever, being compelled thereunto, not only by the examples of our Ancestors, whose bloud was often spent in vain for the recovery of their Freedomes, suffering themselves, through fradulent accommodations, to be still deluded of the fruit of their Victories, but also by our own

*wofull experience, who having long expected, & dearly earned the establishment of these
certain rules of Government are yet made to depend for the settlement of our Peace and
Freedome, upon him that intended our bondage, and brought a cruell Warre upon us....*

3. The people can begin voting on the parliament every 2 years

4. The people have more power over the parliament. Parliament oversees laws, offices + courts, war, + foreign policy

5. Religion and government are seperate

6) cannot draft men into war

7. Cant be tried or found quilty for any prior offenses to the end of the current parliament

8. Everyone, even nobles, must obey all law.

9. laws must be equal and good.
   For the well being of the people

18. Leviathan*

Thomas Hobbes

CHAP. XIII.

Of the NATURAL CONDITION *of Mankind, as concerning their Felicity, and Misery.*

Men by nature Equal.

Nature hath made men so equal, in the faculties of body, and mind; as that though there be found one man sometimes manifestly stronger in body, or of quicker mind than another; yet when all is reckoned together, the difference between man, and man, is not so considerable, as that one man can thereupon claim to himself any benefit, to which another may not pretend, as well as he. For as to the strength of body, the weakest has strength enough to kill the strongest, either by secret machination, or by confederacy with others, that are in the same danger with himself.

And as to the faculties of the mind, (setting aside the arts grounded upon words, and especially that skill of proceeding upon general, and infallible rules, called Science; which very few have, and but in few things; as being not a native faculty, born with us; nor attained, (as Prudence,) while we look after somewhat else,) I find yet a greater equality amongst men, than that of strength. For Prudence is but Experience; which equal time, equally bestows on all men, in those things they equally apply themselves unto. That which may perhaps make such equality incredible, is but a vain conceit of ones own wisdom, which almost all men think they have in a greater degree, than the Vulgar; that is, than all men but themselves, and a few others, whom by Fame, or for concurring with themselves, they approve. For such is the Nature of men, that howsoever they may acknowledge many others to be more witty, or more eloquent, or more learned; Yet they will hardly believe there be many so wise as themselves: For they see their own wit at hand, and other mens at a distance. But this proveth rather that men are in that point

* Thomas Hobbes first published *Leviathan* in 1651. This particular selection was taken from Hobbes, *Leviathan, or, The Matter, Form, and Power of a Common-wealth Ecclesiastical and Civil*, Chapters XIII, XIV, and XVII (London: Printed for Andrew Crooke, at the Green Dragon in St. Paul's Church-yard, 1651), 60–71, 85–88.

equal, than unequal. For there is not ordinarily a greater sign of the equal distribution of any thing, than that every man is contented with his share.

From this equality of ability, ariseth equality of hope in the attaining of our Ends. And therefore if any two men desire the same thing, which nevertheless they cannot both enjoy, they become enemies; and in the way to their End, (which is principally their own conservation, and sometimes their delectation only,) endeavour to destroy, or subdue one another. And from hence it comes to pass, that where an Invader hath no more to feare, than another mans single power; if one plant, sow, build, or possess a convenient Seat, other may probably be expected to come prepared with forces united, to dispossess, and deprive him, not only of the fruit of his labour, but also of his life, or liberty. And the Invader again is in the like danger of another. *From Equality proceeds Diffidence.*

And from this diffidence of one another, there is no way for any man to secure himself, so reasonable, as Anticipation; that is, by force, or wiles, to master the persons of all men he can, so long, till he see no other power great enough to endanger him: And this is no more than his own conservation requireth, and is generally allowed. Also because there be some, that taking pleasure in contemplating their own power in the acts of conquest, which they pursue farther than their security requires; if others, that otherwise would be glad to be at ease within modest bounds, should not by invasion increase their power, they would not be able, long time, by standing only on their defence, to subsist. And by consequence, such augmentation of dominion over men, being necessary to a mans conservation, it ought to be allowed him. *From Diffidence Warre.*

Again, men have no pleasure, (but on the contrary a great deal of grief) in keeping company, where there is no power able to over-awe them all. For every man looketh that his companion should value him, at the same rate he sets upon himself: And upon all signs of contempt, or undervaluing, naturally endeavours, as far as he dares (which amongst them that have no common power to keep them in quiet, is far enough to make them destroy each other,) to extort a greater value from his contemners, by dammage; and from others, by the example.

So that in the nature of man, we find three principal causes of quarrel. First, Competition; Secondly, Diffidence; Thirdly, Glory.

The first, maketh men invade for Gain; the second, for Safety; and the third, for Reputation. The first use Violence, to make themselves Masters of other mens persons, wives, children, and cattle; the second, to defend them; the third for trifles, as a word, a smile, a different opinion, and any other sign of undervalue, either direct in their Persons, or by reflection in their Kindred, their Friends, their Nation, their Profession, or their Name.

Hereby it is manifest, that during the time men live without a common Power to keep them all in awe, they are in that condition which is called Warre; and such a warre, as is of every man, against every man. For WARRE, consisteth not in Battel onely, or the act of fighting; but in a tract of time, wherein the Will to contend by Battel is sufficiently known: and therefore the notion of *Time*, is to be considered in the nature of Warre; as it is in the nature of Weather. For as the nature of Foul weather, lyeth not in a shower or two of rain; but in an inclination thereto of many days together: So the nature of War, consisteth not in actual fighting; but in the known disposition thereto, during all the time there is no assurance to the contrary. All other time is PEACE. *Out of Civil States, there is alwayes War of every one against every one.*

*The Incommo-
dities of such
a War.*

Whatsoever therefore is consequent to a time of Warre, where every man is Enemy to every man; the same is consequent to the time wherein men live without other security, than what their own strength, and their own invention shall furnish them withal. In such condition, there is no place for industry; because the fruit thereof is uncertain: and consequently no Culture of the Earth; no Navigations, nor use of the commodities that may be imported by Sea; no commodious Building; no Instruments of moving, and removing, such things as require much force; no Knowledge of the face of the Earth; no account of Time; no Arts; no Letters; no Society; and which is worst of all, continual fear, and danger of violent death; And the life of man, solitary, poor, nasty, brutish, and short.

It may seem strange to some man, that has not well weighed these things; that Nature should thus dissociate, and render men apt to invade, and destroy one another: and he may therefore, not trusting to this Inference, made from the Passions, desire perhaps to have the same confirmed by Experience. Let him therefore consider with himself, when taking a journey, he arms himself, and seeks to go well accompanied; when going to sleep, he locks his dores; when even in his house he locks his chests; and this when he knows there be Laws, and publick Officers, armed, to revenge all injuries shall be done him; what opinion he has of his fellow subjects, when he rides armed; of his fellow Citizens, when he locks his dores; and of his children, and servants, when he locks his chests. Does he not there as much accuse mankind by his actions, as I do by my words? But neither of us accuse mans nature in it. The Desires, and other Passions of man, are in themselves no Sin. No more are the Actions, that proceed from those Passions, till they know a Law that forbids them: which till Laws be made they cannot know: nor can any Law be made, till they have agreed upon the Persons that shall make it.

It may peradventure be thought, there was never such a time, nor condition of warre as this; and I believe it was never generally so, over all the world: but there are many places, where they live so now. For the savage people in many places of *America*, except the government of small Families, the concord whereof dependeth on natural lust, have no government at all; and live at this day in that brutish manner, as I said before. Howsoever, it may be perceived what manner of life there would be, where there were no common Power to feare; by the manner of life, which men that have formerly lived under a peaceful government, use to degenerate into, in a civil Warre.

But though there had never been any time, wherein particular men were in a condition of warre one against another; yet in all times, Kings, and persons of Sovereign authority, because of their Independency, are in continual jealousies, and in the state and posture of Gladiators; having their weapons pointing, and their eyes fixed on one another; that is, their Forts, Garrisons, and Guns upon the Frontiers of their Kingdomes; and continual Spyes upon their Neighbours; which is a posture of War. But because they uphold thereby, the Industry of their Subjects; there does not follow from it, that misery, which accompanies the Liberty of particular men.

*To such a War,
nothing is
Unjust.*

To this war of every man, against every man, this also is consequent; that nothing can be Unjust. The notions of Right and Wrong, Justice and Injustice have there no place. Where there is no common Power, there is no Law: where no Law, no Injustice. Force, and Fraud are in war the two Cardinal vertues. Justice, and Injustice are none of the Faculties neither of the Body, nor Mind. If they were, they might be in a man that were alone in the world, as well as his Senses, and Passions. They are Qualities, that relate to men in Society, not in Solitude. It is consequent also to the same condition, that there be no Propriety, no Dominion, no *Mine* and *Thine* distinct; but onely that to be every mans, that he can get; and for so long, as he can keep it. And thus much for the ill condition, which man by meer Nature is actually placed in; though with a possibility to come out of it, consisting partly in the Passions, partly in his Reason.

The Passions that encline men to Peace, are Fear of Death; Desire of such things as are necessary to commodious living; and a Hope by their Industry to obtain them. And reason suggesteth convenient Articles of Peace, upon which men may be drawn to agreement. These Articles, are they, which otherwise are called the Lawes of Nature: whereof I shall speak more particularly, in the two following Chapters.

The Passions that encline men to Peace.

[handwritten] Laws of nature

[handwritten] Death

CHAP. XIV.
Of the first and second NATURAL LAWS, and of CONTRACTS.

The RIGHT OF NATURE, which Writers commonly call *Jus Naturale*, is the Liberty each man hath, to use his own power, as he will himself, for the preservation of his own Nature; that is to say, of his own Life; and consequently of doing any thing, which in his own Judgement, and Reason, he shall conceive to be the aptest means thereunto.

Right of Nature what.

By LIBERTY, is understood, according to the proper signification of the word, the absence of external Impediments: which Impediments, may oft take away part of a mans power to do what he would; but cannot hinder him from using the power left him, according as his judgment, and reason shall dictate to him.

Liberty what.

A LAW OF NATURE, (*Lex Naturalis,*) is a Precept, or general Rule, found out by Reason, by which a man is forbidden to do, that, which is destructive of his life, or taketh away the means of preserving the same; and to omit, that, by which he thinketh it may be best preserved. For though they that speak of this Subject, use to confound *Jus*, and *Lex*, *Right* and *Law*: yet they ought to be distinguished; because RIGHT, consisteth in Liberty to do, or to forbear; Whereas LAW, determineth, and bindeth to one of them: so that Law, and Right, differ as much, as Obligation, and Liberty; which in one and the same matter are inconsistent.

A Law of Nature what.

Difference of Right and Law.

And because the condition of Man, (as hath been declared in the precedent Chapter) is a condition of War of every one against every one; in which case every one is governed by his own Reason; and there is nothing he can make use of, that may not be a help unto him, in preserving his life against his enemies; It followeth, that in such a condition, every man has a Right to every thing; even to one anothers body. And therefore, as long as this natural Right of every man to every thing endureth, there can be no security to any man, (how strong or wise soever he be,) of living out the time, which Nature ordinarily alloweth men to live. And consequently it is a Precept, or general rule of Reason, *That every man ought to endeavour Peace, as farre as he has hope of obtaining it; and when he cannot obtain it, that he may seek, and use all helps, and advantages of Warre.* The first branch of which Rule, containeth the first, and Fundamental Law of Nature; which is, *to seek Peace, and follow it.* The Second, the summe of the Right of Nature; which is, *By all means we can, to defend our selves.*

Naturally every man has Right to every thing.

The Fundamental Law of Nature.

*The second
Law of
Nature.*

From this Fundamental Law of Nature, by which men are commanded to endeavour Peace, is derived this second Law; *That a man be willing, when others are so too, as far-forth, as for Peace, and defence of himself he shall think it necessary, to lay down this right to all things; and be contented with so much liberty against other men, as he would allow other men against himself,* For as long as every man holdeth this Right, of doing anything he liketh; so long are all men in the condition of War. But if other men will not lay down their Right, as well as he; then there is no Reason for any one to devest himself of his: For that were to expose himself to Prey, (which no man is bound to) rather than to dispose himself to Peace. This is that Law of the Gospel; *Whatsoever you require that others should do to you, that do ye to them.* And that Law of all men, *Quod tibi fieri non vis, alteri ne feceris.*

*What it is to
lay down a
Right.*

To *lay down* a mans *Right* to any thing, is to *devest* himself of the *Liberty*, of hindring another of the benefit of his own Right to the same. For he that renounceth, or passeth away his Right, giveth not to any other man a Right which he had not before; because there is nothing to which every man had not Right by Nature: but only standeth out of his way, that he may enjoy his own original Right, without hindrance from him; not without hindrance from another. So that the effect which redoundeth to one man, by another mans defect of Right, is but so much diminution of impediments to the use of his own Right original.

*Renouncing a
Right, what it
is. Transferring
Right, what.
Obligation.*

*Duty.
Injustice.*

Right is laid aside, either by simply Renouncing it; or by Transferring it to another. By *Simply* RENOUNCING; when he cares not to whom the benefit thereof redoundeth. By TRANSFERRING; when he intendeth the benefit thereof to some certain person, or persons. And when a man hath in either manner abandoned, or granted away his Right; then he is said to be OBLIGED, or BOUND, not to hinder those, to whom such Right is granted, or abandoned, from the benefit of it: and that he *Ought*, and it is his DUTY, not to make void that voluntary act of his own: and that such hindrance is INJUSTICE, and INJURY, as being *Sine Jure*; the Right being before renounced, or transferred. So that *Injury*, or *Injustice*, in the controversies of the world, is somewhat like to that, which in the disputations of Scholars is called *Absurdity*. For as it is there called an Absurdity, to contradict what one maintained in the Beginning: so in the world, it is called Injustice, and Injury, voluntarily to undo that, which from the beginning he had voluntarily done. The way by which a man either simply Renounceth, or Transferreth his Right, is a Declaration, or Signification, by some voluntary and sufficient sign, or signs, that he doth so Renounce, or Transferre; or hath so renounced, or Transferred the same, to him that accepteth it. And these Signs are either Words onely, or Actions onely; or (as it happeneth most often) both Words, and Actions. And the same are the BONDS, by which men are bound, and obliged: Bonds, that have their strength, not from their own Nature, (for nothing is more easily broken then a mans word,) but from Fear of some evil consequence upon the rupture.

*Not all Rights
are alienable.*

Whensoever a man Transferreth his Right, or Renounceth it; it is either in consideration of some Right reciprocally transferred to himself; or for some other good he hopeth for thereby. For it is a voluntary act: and of the voluntary acts of every man, the object is some *Good to himself.* And therefore there be some Rights, which no man can be understood by any words, or other signs, to have abandoned, or transferred. As first a man cannot lay down the right of resisting them, that assault him by force, to take away his life; because he cannot be understood to aim thereby at any Good to himself. The same may be said of Wounds, and Chains, and Imprisonment; both because there is no benefit consequent to such patience; as there is to the patience of suffering another to be wounded, or imprisoned: as also because a man cannot tell, when he seeth men proceed against him by violence, whether they intend his death or not. And lastly the motive, and end for which this renouncing, and transferring of Right is introduced, is nothing else but the security of a mans person, in his life, and in the means of so preserving life, as not to be weary of it. And therefore if a man by words, or other signs, seem to dispoil himself of the End, for which those signs were intended; he is not to be understood as if he meant it, or that it was his will; but that he was ignorant of how such words and actions were to be interpreted.

The mutual transferring of Right, is that which men call CONTRACT.

Contract what.

There is difference between transferring of Right to the Thing; and transferring, or tradition, that is, delivery of the Thing it self. For the Thing may be delivered together with the Translation of the Right; as in buying and selling with ready money; or exchange of goods, or lands: and it may be delivered some time after.

Again, one of the Contractors, may deliver the thing contracted for on his part, and leave the other to perform his part at some determinate time after, and in the mean time be trusted; and then the Contract on his part, is called PACT, or COVENANT: Or both parts may contract now, to perform hereafter: in which cases, he that is to perform in time to come, being trusted, his performance is called *Keeping of Promise*, or Faith; and the failing of performance (if it be voluntary) *Violation of Faith*.

Covenant what.

When the transferring of Right, is not mutual; but one of the parties transferreth, in hope to gain thereby friendship, or service from another, or from his friends; or in hope to gain the reputation of Charity, or Magnanimity; or to deliver his mind from the pain of compassion; or in hope of reward in heaven; This is not Contract, but GIFT, FREE-GIFT, GRACE: which words signifie one and the same thing.

Free gift.

Signs of Contract, are either *Express*, or *by Inference*. Express, are words spoken with understanding of what they signifie: And such words are either of the time *Present*, or *Past*; as, *I Give, I Grant, I have Given, I have Granted, I will that this be yours*: Or of the future; as, *I will give, I will Grant*: which words of the future are called PROMISE.

Signs of Contract Express.

Signs by Inference, are sometimes the consequence of Words; sometimes the consequence of Silence; sometimes the consequence of Actions; sometimes the consequence of Forbearing an Action: and generally a sign by Inference, of any Contract, is whatsoever sufficiently argues the will of the Contractor.

Signs of Contract by Inference.

Words alone, if they be of the time to come, and contain a bare promise, are an insufficient sign of a Free-gift and therefore not obligatory. For if they be of the time to Come, as, *To morrow I will Give*, they are a sign I have not given yet, and consequently that my right is not transferred, but remaineth till I transfer it by some other Act. But if the words be of the time Present, or Past, as, *I have given, or do give to be delivered to morrow*, then is my to morrows Right given away to day; and that by the vertue of the words, though there were no other argument of my will. And there is a great difference in the signification of these words, *Volo hoc tuum esse cras*, and *Cras dabo*; that is, between *I will that this be thine to morrow*, and, *I will give it thee to morrow*: For the word *I will*, in the former manner of speech, signifies an act of the will Present; but in the later, it signifies a promise of an act of the will to Come: and therefore the former words, being of

Free gift passeth by words of the Present or Past.

the Present, transfer a future right; the later, that be of the Future, transfer nothing. But if there be other signs of the Will to transfer a Right, besides Words; then, though the gift be Free, yet may the right be understood to pass by words of the future: as if a man propound a Prize to him that comes first to the end of a race. The gift is Free; and though the words be of the Future, yet the Right passeth: for if he would not have his words so be understood, he should not have let them runne.

Signs of Con-
tract are words
both of the
Past, Present,
and Future.

In Contracts, the right passeth, not only where the words are of the time Present, or Past; but also where they are of the Future: because all Contract is mutual translation, or change of Right; and therefore he that promiseth onely, because he hath already received the benefit for which he promiseth, is to be understood as if he intended the Right should pass: for unless he had been content to have his words so understood, the other would not have performed his part first. And for that cause, in buying, and selling, and other acts of Contract, a Promise is equivalent to a Covenant; and therefore obligatory.

Merit what.

He that performeth first in the case of a Contract, is said to MERIT that which he is to receive by the performance of the other; and he hath it as *Due*. Also when a Prize is propounded to many, which is to be given to him only that winneth; or mony is thrown amongst many, to be enjoyed by them that catch it; though this be a Free-gift; yet so to Win, or so to Catch, is to *Merit*, and to have it as DUE. For the Right is transferred in the Propounding of the Prize, and in throwing down the mony; though it be not determined to whom, but by the Event of the contention. But there is between these two sorts of Merit, this difference, that in Contract, I Merit by vertue of my own power, and the Contractors need, but in this case of Free gift, I am enabled to Merit onely by the benignity of the Giver: In Contract, I merit at the Contractors hand that he should part with his right; In this case of Gift, I Merit not that the giver should part with his right; but that when he has parted with it, it should be mine, rather than anothers. And this I think to be the meaning of that distinction of the Schools, between *Meritum congrui*, and *Meritum condigni*. For God Almighty, having promised Paradise to those men (hoodwinkt with carnal desires) that can walk through this world according to the Precepts, and Limits prescribed by him; they say, he that shall so walk, shall Merit Paradise *ex congruo*. But because no man can demand a right to it, by his own Righteousness, or any other power in himself, but by the Free Grace of God only; they say, no man can Merit Paradise *ex condigno*. This I say, I think is the meaning of that distinction; but because Disputers do not agree upon the signification of their own termes of Art, longer than it serves their turn; I will not affirm any thing of their meaning: only this I say; when a gift is given indefinitely, as a Prize to be contended for, he that winneth Meriteth, and may claim the Prize as Due.

Covenants of
Mutual trust,
when Invalid.

If a Covenant be made, wherein neither of the parties perform presently, but trust one another; in the condition of meer Nature, (which is a condition of Warre of every man against every man,) upon any reasonable suspition, it is Void: But if there be a common Power set over them both, with right and force sufficient to compel performance; it is not Void. For he that performeth first, has no assurance the other will perform after; because the bonds of words are too weak to bridle mens ambition, avarice, anger, and other Passions, without the fear of some coercive Power; which in the condition of meer Nature, where all men are equal, and judges of the justness of their own fears, cannot possibly be supposed. And therefore he which performeth first, does but betray himself to his enemy; contrary to the Right (he can never abandon) of defending his life, and means of living.

must be common power

But in a civil estate, where there is a Power set up to constrain those that would otherwise violate their faith, that fear is no more reasonable; and for that cause, he which by the Covenant is to perform first, is obliged so to do.

The cause of fear, which maketh such a Covenant invalid, must be always something arising from the Covenant made; as some new fact, or other sign of the Will not to perform: else it cannot make the Covenant void. For that which could not hinder a man from promising, ought not to be admitted as a hindrance of performing.

He that transferreth any Right, transferreth the Means of enjoying it, as far as lyeth in his Power, As he that selleth Land, is understood to transfer the Herbage, and whatsoever grows upon it; Nor can he that sells a Mill turn away the Stream that drives it. And they that give to a man the Right of government in Soveraignty, are understood to give him the right of levying mony to maintain Soldiers; and of appointing Magistrates for the administration of Justice.

Right to the End, Contain-eth Right to the Means.

To make Covenants with brute Beasts, is impossible; because not understanding our speech, they understand not, nor accept of any Translation of Right; nor can translate any Right to another: and without mutual acceptation, there is no Covenant.

No Covenant with Beasts.

To make Covenant with God, is impossible, but by Mediation of such as God speaketh to, either by Revelation supernatural, or by his Lieutenants that govern under him, and in his Name: For otherwise we know not whether our Covenants be accepted, or not. And therefore they that Vow any thing contrary to any law of Nature, Vow in vain; as being a thing unjust to pay such Vow. And if it be a thing commanded by the Law of Nature, it is not the Vow, but the Law that binds them.

Nor with God; without special Revelation.

The matter, or subject of a Covenant, is always something that falleth under deliberation; (For to Covenant, is an act of the Will; that is to say an act, and the last act, of deliberation;) and is therefore always understood to be something to come; and which is judged Possible for him that Covenanteth, to perform.

No Covenant, but of Possible and Future.

And therefore, to promise that which is known to be Impossible, is no Covenant. But if that prove impossible afterwards, which before was thought possible, the Covenant is valid, and bindeth, (though not to the thing it self,) yet to the value; or, if that also be impossible, to the unfeigned endeavour of performing as much as is possible: for to more no man can be obliged.

Covenants, how made void.

Men are freed of their Covenants two ways; by Performing; or by being Forgiven. For Performance, is the natural end of obligation, and Forgiveness, the restitution of liberty; as being a re-transferring of that Right, in which the obligation consisteth.

Covenants entered into by fear, in the condition of meer Nature, are obligatory. For example, if I Covenant to pay a ransome, or service for my life, to an enemy; I am bound by it. For it is a Contract, wherein one receiveth the benefit of life; the other is to receive money, or service for it; and consequently, where no other Law (as in the condition, of meer Nature) forbiddeth the performance, the Covenant is valid. Therefore Prisoners of warre, if trusted with the payment of their Ransome, are obliged to pay it: And if a weaker Prince, make a disadvantageous peace with a stronger, for fear; he is bound to keep it; unless (as hath been said before) there ariseth some new, and just cause of fear, to renew the war. And even in Common-wealths, if I be forced to redeem my self from a Thief by promising him mony, I am bound to pay it, till the Civil Law discharge me. For whatsoever I may lawfully do without Obligation, the same I may lawfully Covenant to

Covenants extorted by fear are valid.

do through fear: and what I lawfully Covenant, I cannot lawfully break.

The former Covenant to one, makes void the later to another.

A former Covenant makes void a later. For a man that hath passed away his Right to one man to day, hath it not to pass to morrow to another: and therefore the later promise passeth no Right, but is null.

A mans Covenant not to defend himself, is void.

A Covenant not to defend my selfe from force, by force, is always void. For (as I have shewed before) no man can transferre, or lay down his Right to save himself from Death, Wounds, and Imprisonment, (the avoiding whereof is the onely End of laying down any Right,) and therefore the promise of not resisting force, in no Covenant transferreth any right; nor is obliging. For though a man may covenant thus, *Unless I do so, or so, kill me*; he cannot Covenant thus, *Unless I do so, or so, I will not resist you, when you come to kill me*. For man by nature choosèth the lesser evil, which is danger of death in resisting; rather than the greater, which is certain and present death in not resisting. And this is granted to be true by all men, in that they lead Criminals to Execution, and Prison, with armed men, notwithstanding that such Criminals have consented to the Law, by which they are condemned.

No man obliged to accuse himself.

A Covenant to accuse ones self, without assurance of pardon, is likewise invalide. For in the condition of Nature, where every man is Judge, there is no place for Accusation: and in the Civil State, the Accusation is followed with Punishment; which being Force, a man is not obliged not to resist. The same is also true, of the Accusation of those, by whose Condemnation a man falls into misery; as of a Father, Wife, or Benefactor. For the Testimony of such an Accuser, if it be not willingly given, is præsumed to be corrupted by Nature; and therefore not to be received: and where a mans Testimony is not to be credited, he is not bound to give it. Also Accusations upon Torture, are not to be reputed as Testimonies. For Torture is to be used but as means of conjecture, and light, in the further examination, and search of truth: and what is in that case confessed, tendeth to the ease of him that is Tortured; not to the informing of the Torturers: and therefore ought not to have the credit of a sufficient Testimony: for whether he delivers himself by true, or false Accusation, he does it by the Right of preserving his own life.

The End of an Oath.

The force of Words, being (as I have formerly noted) too weak to hold men to the performance of their Covenants; there are in mans nature, but two imaginable helps to strengthen it. And those are either a Fear of the consequence of breaking their word; or a Glory, or Pride in appearing not too need to break it. This later is a Generosity too rarely found to be presumed on, especially in the pursuers of Wealth, Command, or sensual Pleasure; which are the greatest part of Mankind. The Passion to be reckoned upon, is Fear; whereof there be two very general Objects: one, The Power of Spirits Invisible; the other, The Power of those men they shall therein Offend. Of these two, though the former be the greater Power, yet the fear of the latter is commonly the greater Fear. The Feare of the former is in every man, his own Religion: which hath place in the nature of man before Civil Society. The latter hath not so; at least not place enough, to keep men to their promises; because in the condition of meer Nature, the inequality of Power is not discerned, but by the event of Battel. So that before the time of Civil Society, or in the interruption thereof by Warre, there is nothing can strengthen a Covenant of Peace agreed on, against the temptations of Avarice, Ambition, Lust, or other strong desire, but the fear of that Invisible Power, which they every one Worship as God; and Fear as a Revenger of their perfidy. All therefore that can be done between two men not subject to Civil Power, is to put one another to swear by the God he feareth: Which *Swearing*, or OATH, is a *Forme of Speech, added to a Promise; by which he that promiseth, signifieth, that unlesse he performe, he renounceth the mercy of his God, or calleth to him for vengeance on himself.* Such was the Heathen Form, *Let Jupiter kill me else, as I kill this Beast.* So is our Forme, *I shall do thus, and thus, so help me God.* And this, with the Rites and Ceremonies, which every one useth in his own Religion, that the fear of breaking faith might be the greater.

The forme of an Oath.

By this it appears, that an Oath taken according to any other Forme, or Rite, then his, that sweareth, is in vain; and no Oath: And that there is no Swearing by any thing which the Swearer thinks not God. For though men have sometimes used to swear by their Kings, for fear, or flattery; yet they would have it thereby understood, they attributed to them divine honour. And that Swearing unnecessarily by God, is but prophaning of his name: and Swearing by other things, as men do in common discourse, is not Swearing, but an impious Custom, gotten by too much vehemence of talking.

No Oath, but by God.

It appears also, that the Oath adds nothing to the Obligation. For a Covenant, if lawful, binds in the sight of God, without the Oath, as much as with it: if unlawful, bindeth not at all; though it be confirmed with an Oath....

An Oath adds nothing to the Obligation.

CHAP. XVII.
Of the Causes, Generation, and Definition of a COMMON-WEALTH.

The final Cause, End, or Design of men, (who naturally love Liberty, and Dominion over others,) in the introduction of that restraint upon themselves, (in which we see them live in Common-wealths,) is the foresight of their own preservation, and of a more contented life thereby; that is to say, of getting themselves out from that miserable conditon of War, which is necessarily consequent (as hath been shewn) to the natural Passions of men, when there is no visible Power to keep them in awe, and tye them by fear of punishment to the performance of their Covenants, and observation of those Laws of Nature set down in the 14th. and 15th. Chapters.

The End of Common-wealth, particular Security:

Chap. 13.

For the Laws of Nature (as *Justice*, *Equity*, *Modesty*, *Mercy*, and (in summe) *doing to others, as we would be done to*,) of themselves, without the terrour of some Power, to cause them to be observed, are contrary to our natural Passions, that carry us to Partiality, Pride, Revenge, and the like. And Covenants without the Sword, are but Words, and of no strength to secure a man at all. Therefore notwithstanding the Laws of Nature, (which every one hath then kept, when he has the will to keep them, when he can do it safely,) if there be no Power erected, or not great enough for our security; every man will, and may lawfully rely on his own strength and art, for caution against all other men. And in all places, where men have lived by small Families, to rob and spoil one another, has been a Trade, and so far from being reputed against the Laws of Nature, that the greater spoils they gained, the greater was their honour; and men observed no other Laws therein, but the Laws of Honour; that is, to abstain from cruelty, leaving to men their lives, and instruments of husbandry. And as small Families did then; so now do Cities, and Kingdoms which are but greater Families (for their own security) enlarge their

Which is not to be had from the Law of Nature:

Dominions, upon all pretences of danger, and fear of Invasion, or assistance that may be given to Invaders, endeavour as much as they can, to subdue, or weaken their neighbours, by open force, and secret arts, for want of other Caution, justly; and are remembered for it in after ages with honour.

Nor from the conjunction of a few men or families:

Nor is it the joining together of a small number of men, that gives them this security; because in small numbers, small additions on the one side or the other, make the advantage of strength so great, as is sufficient to carry the Victory; and therefore gives encouragement to an Invasion. The multitude sufficient to confide in for our Security, is not determined by any certain number, but by comparison with the Enemy we fear; and is then sufficient when the odds of the Enemy is not of so visible and conspicuous moment, to determine the event of War, as to move him to attempt.

Nor from a great Multitude, unless directed by one judgment:

And be there never so great a Multitude; yet if their actions be directed according to their particular judgments, and particular appetites, they can expect thereby no defence, nor protection, neither against a Common enemy, nor against the injuries of one another. For being distracted in opinions concerning the best use and application of their strength, they do not help, but hinder one another; and reduce their strength by mutual opposition to nothing: whereby they are easily, not only subdued by a very few that agree together; but also when there is no Common enemy, they make War upon each other, for their particular interests. For if we could suppose a great Multitude of men to consent in the observation of Justice, and other Laws of Nature, without a common Power to keep them all in awe; we might as well suppose all Man-kind to do the same; and then there neither would be, nor need to be any Civil Government, or Common-wealth at all; because there would be Peace without subjection.

And that continually.

Nor is it enough for the security, which men desire should last all the time of their life, that they be governed, and directed by one judgment, for a limited time; as in one Battle, or one War. For though they obtain a Victory by their unanimous endeavour against a forreign enemy; yet afterwards, when either they have no Common enemy, or he that by one part is held for an enemy, is by another part held for a friend, they must needs by the difference of their interests dissolve, and fall again into a War amongst themselves.

Why certain creatures without reason, or speech, do nevertheless live in Society, without any coercive Power.

It is true, that certain living creatures, as Bees, and Ants, live sociably one with another, (which are therefore by *Aristotle* numbred amongst Political creatures;) and yet have no other direction, than their particular judgments and appetites; nor speech, whereby one of them can signifie to another, what he thinks expedient for the common benefit: and therefore some man may perhaps desire to know, why Man-kind cannot do the same. To which I answer,

First, that men are continually in competition for Honour and Dignity, which these creatures are not; and consequently amongst men there ariseth on that ground, Envy and Hatred and finally War; but amongst these not so.

Secondly, that amongst these creatures, the Common good differeth not from the Private; and being by nature inclined to their private, they procure thereby the common benefit. But man, whose Joy consisteth in comparing himself with other men, can relish nothing but what is eminent.

Thirdly, that these creatures, having not (as man) the use of reason, do not see, nor think they see any fault, in the administration of their common business: whereas amongst men, there are very many that think themselves wiser, and abler to govern the

Publique, better than the rest; and these strive to reform and innovate, one this way, another that way; and thereby bring it into Distraction and Civil War.

Fourthly, that these creatures, though they have some use of voice, in making known to one another their desires, and other affections; yet they want that art of words, by which some men can represent to others, that which is Good, in the likeness of Evil; and Evil, in the likeness of Good; and augment, or diminish the apparent greatness of Good and Evil; discontenting men, and troubling their Peace at their pleasure.

Fifthly, irrational creatures cannot distinguish between *Injury* and *Dammage*; and therefore as long as they be at ease, they are not offended with their fellows: whereas Man is then most troublesome, when he is most at ease: for then it is that he loves to shew his Wisdom, and controul the Actions of them that govern the Common-wealth.

Lastly, the agreement of these creatures is Natural; that of men, is by Covenant only, which is Artificial: and therefore it is no wonder if there be somewhat else required (besides Covenant) to make their Agreement constant and lasting; which is a Common Power, to keep them in awe, and to direct their actions to the Common Benefit.

The only way to erect such a Common Power, as may be able to defend them from the invasion of Forreigners, and the injuries of one another, and thereby to secure them in such sort, as that by their own industry, and by the fruits of the Earth, they may nourish themselves and live contentedly; is, to confer all their power and strength upon one Man, or upon one Assembly of men, that may reduce all their Wills, by plurality of voices, unto one Will: which is as much as to say, to appoint one Man, or Assembly of men, to bear their Person; and every one to own, and acknowledge himself to be Author of whatsoever he that so beareth their Person, shall Act, or cause to be Acted, in those things which concern the Common Peace and Safety; and therein to submit their Will, every one to his Will, and their Judgments, to his Judgment. This is more than Consent, or Concord: it is a real Unity of them all, in one and the same Person, made by Covenant of every man with every man, in such manner, as if every man should say to every man, *I Authorize and give up my Right of Governing my self, to this Man, or to this Assembly of men, on this condition, that thou give up thy Right to him, and Authorize all his Actions in like manner.* This done, the Multitude so united in one Person is called a COMMON-WEALTH, in Latine CIVITAS. This is the Generation of that great LEVIATHAN, or rather (to speak more reverently) of that *Mortal God*, to which we owe under the *Immortal God*, our peace and defence. For by this Authority, given him by every particular man in the Common-wealth, he hath the use of so much Power and Strength conferred on him, that by terrour thereof, he is enabled to perform the wills of them all, to Peace at home, and mutual aid against their enemies abroad. And in him consisteth the Essence of the Common-wealth; which (to define it,) is *One Person, of whose Acts a great Multitude, by mutual Covenants one with another, have made themselves every one the Author, to the end he may use the strength and means of them all, as he shall think expedient, for their Peace and Common Defence.*

And he that carrieth this Person, is called SOVERAIGN, and said to have *Soveraign Power*; and every one besides, his SUBJECT.

The attaining to this Soveraign Power, is by two ways. One, by Natural force; as when a man maketh his children to submit themselves, and their children to his government, as being able to destroy them if they refuse; or by War subdueth his enemies to his will,

The Genera-tion of a Common-wealth.

The Definition of a Common-wealth.

Soveraign, and Subject, what.

giving them their lives on that condition. The other, is when men agree amongst themselves, to submit to some Man, or Assembly of men, voluntarily, on confidence to be protected by him against all others. This latter may be called a Political Common-wealth, or Common-wealth by *Institution*; and the former a Common-wealth by *Acquisition*. And first, I shall speak of a Common-wealth by Institution.

19. Two Treatises of Government[*]

John Locke

CHAPTER VIII.
Of the Beginning of Political Societies.

95. Men being, as has been said, by nature all free, equal, and independent, no one can be put out of this estate and subjected to the political power of another without his own consent, which is done by agreeing with other men, to join and unite into a community for their comfortable, safe, and peaceable living, one amongst another, in a secure enjoyment of their properties, and a greater security against any that are not of it. This any number of men may do, because it injures not the freedom of the rest; they are left, as they were, in the liberty of the state of Nature. When any number of men have so consented to make one community or government, they are thereby presently incorporated, and make one body politic, wherein the majority have a right to act and conclude the rest.

96. For, when any number of men have, by the consent of every individual, made a community, they have thereby made that community one body, with a power to act as one body, which is only by the will and determination of the majority. For that which acts any community, being only the consent of the individuals of it, and it being one body, must move one way, it is necessary the body should move that way whither the greater force carries it, which is the consent of the majority, or else it is impossible it should act or continue one body, one community, which the consent of every individual that united into

[*] John Locke published his *Two Treatises of Government: In the Former, The False Principles and Foundation of Sir Robert Filmer, and His Followers, Are Detected and Overthrown. The Latter Is an Essay Concerning the True Original, Extent, and End of Civil-Government* circa 1690 in London. This particular selection was taken from Locke, *Two Treatises on Civil Government*, Book II, Chapters VIII–XI, with an introduction by Henry Morley (London: George Routledge and Sons Limited, 1884), 240–267.

it agreed that it should; and so every one is bound by that consent to be concluded by the majority. And therefore we see that in assemblies empowered to act by positive laws where no number is set by that positive law which empowers them, the act of the majority passes for the act of the whole, and of course determines as having, by the law of Nature and reason, the power of the whole.

97. And thus every man, by consenting with others to make one body politic under one government, puts himself under an obligation to every one of that society to submit to the determination of the majority, and to be concluded by it; or else this original compact, whereby he with others incorporates into one society, would signify nothing, and be no compact if he be left free and under no other ties than he was in before in the state of Nature. For what appearance would there be of any compact? What new engagement if he were no farther tied by any decrees of the society than he himself thought fit and did actually consent to? This would be still as great a liberty as he himself had before his compact, or any one else in the state of Nature, who may submit himself and consent to any acts of it if he thinks fit.

98. For if the consent of the majority shall not in reason be received as the act of the whole, and conclude every individual; nothing but the consent of every individual can make anything to be the act of the whole, which, considering the infirmities of health and avocations of business, which in a number though much less than that of a commonwealth, will necessarily keep many away from the public assembly; and the variety of opinions and contrariety of interests which unavoidably happen in all collections of men, it is next impossible ever to be had. And, therefore, if coming into society be upon such terms, it will be only like Cato's coming into the theatre, *tantum ut exiret*. Such a constitution as this would make the mighty leviathan of a shorter duration than the feeblest creatures, and not let it outlast the day it was born in, which cannot be supposed till we can think that rational creatures should desire and constitute societies only to be dissolved. For where the majority cannot conclude the rest, there they cannot act as one body, and consequently will be immediately dissolved again.

99. Whosoever, therefore, out of a state of Nature unite into a community, must be understood to give up all the power necessary to the ends for which they unite into society to the majority of the community, unless they expressly agreed in any number greater than the majority. And this is done by barely agreeing to unite into one political society, which is all the compact that is, or needs be, between the individuals that enter into or make up a commonwealth. And thus, that which begins and actually constitutes any political society is nothing but the consent of any number of freemen capable of majority, to unite and incorporate into such a society. And this is that, and that only, which did or could give beginning to any lawful government in the world.

100. To this I find two objections made: 1. That there are no instances to be found in story of a company of men, independent and equal one amongst another, that met together, and in this way began and set up a government. 2. It is impossible of right that men should do so, because all men, being born under government, they are to submit to that, and are not at liberty to begin a new one.

101. To the first there is this to answer: That it is not at all to be wondered that history gives us but a very little account of men that lived together in the state of Nature. The inconveniencies of that condition, and the love and want of society, no sooner brought

any number of them together, but they presently united and incorporated if they designed to continue together. And if we may not suppose men ever to have been in the state of Nature, because we hear not much of them in such a state, we may as well suppose the armies of Salmanasser or Xerxes were never children, because we hear little of them till they were men and embodied in armies. Government is everywhere antecedent to records, and letters seldom come in amongst a people till a long continuation of civil society has, by other more necessary arts, provided for their safety, ease, and plenty. And then they begin to look after the history of their founders, and search into their original when they have outlived the memory of it. For it is with commonwealths as with particular persons, they are commonly ignorant of their own births and infancies; and if they know anything of it, they are beholding for it to the accidental records that others have kept of it. And those that we have of the beginning of any polities in the world, excepting that of the Jews, where God Himself immediately interposed, and which favours not at all paternal dominion; are all either plain instances of such a beginning as I have mentioned, or at least have manifest footsteps of it.

102. He must show a strange inclination to deny evident matter of fact, when it agrees not with his hypothesis, who will not allow that the beginning of Rome and Venice were by the uniting together of several men, free and independent one of another, amongst whom there was no natural superiority or subjection. And if Josephus Acosta's word may be taken, he tells us that in many parts of America there was no government at all. "There are great and apparent conjectures," says he, "that these men (speaking of those of Peru) for a long time had neither kings nor commonwealths, but lived in troops, as they do this day in Florida — the Cheriquanas, those of Brazil, and many other nations, which have no certain kings, but, as occasion is offered in peace or war, they choose their captains as they please" (lib. i. cap. 25). If it be said, that every man there was born subject to his father, or the head of his family, that the subjection due from a child to a father took not away his freedom of uniting into what political society he thought fit, has been already proved; but be that as it will, these men, it is evident, were actually free; and whatever superiority some politicians now would place in any of them, they themselves claimed it not; but, by consent, were all equal, till, by the same consent, they set rulers over themselves. So that their politic societies all began from a voluntary union, and the mutual agreement of men freely acting in the choice of their governors and forms of government.

103. And I hope those who went away from Sparta, with Palantus, mentioned by Justin, will be allowed to have been freemen independent one of another, and to have set up a government over themselves by their own consent. Thus I have given several examples out of history of people, free and in the state of Nature, that, being met together, incorporated and began a commonwealth. And if the want of such instances be an argument to prove that government were not nor could not be so begun, I suppose the contenders for paternal empire were better let it alone than urge it against natural liberty; for if they can give so many instances out of history of governments began upon paternal right, I think (though at least an argument from what has been to what should of right be of no great force) one might, without any great danger, yield them the cause. But if I might advise them in the case, they would do well not to search too much into the original of governments as they have begun *de facto*, lest they should find at the foundation of most of them something very little favourable to the design they promote, and such a

power as they contend for.

104. But, to conclude: reason being plain on our side that men are naturally free; and the examples of history showing that the governments of the world, that were begun in peace, had their beginning laid on that foundation, and were made by the consent of the people; there can be little room for doubt, either where the right is, or what has been the opinion or practice of mankind about the first erecting of governments.

105. I will not deny that if we look back, as far as history will direct us, towards the original of commonwealths, we shall generally find them under the government and administration of one man. And I am also apt to believe that where a family was numerous enough to subsist by itself, and continued entire together, without mixing with others, as it often happens, where there is much land and few people, the government commonly began in the father. For the father having, by the law of Nature, the same power, with every man else, to punish, as he thought fit, any offences against that law, might thereby punish his transgressing children, even when they were men, and out of their pupilage; and they were very likely to submit to his punishment, and all join with him against the offender in their turns, giving him thereby power to execute his sentence against any transgression, and so, in effect, make him the law-maker and governor over all that remained in conjunction with his family. He was fittest to be trusted; paternal affection secured their property and interest under his care, and the custom of obeying him in their childhood made it easier to submit to him rather than any other. If, therefore, they must have one to rule them, as government is hardly to be avoided amongst men that live together, who so likely to be the man as he that was their common father, unless negligence, cruelty, or any other defect of mind or body, made him unfit for it. But when either the father died, and left his next heir — for want of age, wisdom, courage, or any other qualities — less fit for rule, or where several families met and consented to continue together, there, it is not to be doubted, but they used their natural freedom to set up him whom they judged the ablest and most likely to rule well over them. Conformable hereunto we find the people of America, who — living out of the reach of the conquering swords and spreading domination of the two great empires of Peru and Mexico — enjoyed their own natural freedom, though, *cæteris paribus*, they commonly prefer the heir of their deceased king; yet, if they find him any way weak or incapable, they pass him by, and set up the stoutest and bravest man for their ruler.

106. Thus, though looking back as far as records give us any account of peopling the world, and the history of nations, we commonly find the government to be in one hand, yet it destroys not that which I affirm — viz., that the beginning of politic society depends upon the consent of the individuals to join into and make one society, who, when they are thus incorporated, might set up what form of government they thought fit. But this having given occasion to men to mistake and think that, by Nature, government was monarchical, and belonged to the father, it may not be amiss here to consider why people, in the beginning, generally pitched upon this form, which, though perhaps the father's pre-eminency might, in the first institution of some commonwealths, give a rise to and place in the beginning the power in one hand; yet it is plain that the reason that continued the form of government in a single person was not any regard or respect to paternal authority, since all petty monarchies — that is, almost all monarchies, near their original, have been commonly, at least upon occasion, elective.

107. First, then, in the beginning of things, the father's government of the childhood of those sprung from him having accustomed them to the rule of one man, and taught them that where it was exercised with care and skill, with affection and love to those under it, it was sufficient to procure and preserve men (all the political happiness they sought for in society), it was no wonder that they should pitch upon and naturally run into that form of government which, from their infancy, they had been all accustomed to, and which, by experience, they had found both easy and safe. To which, if we add, that monarchy being simple and most obvious to men, whom neither experience had instructed in forms of government, nor the ambition or insolence of empire had taught to beware of the encroachments of prerogative or the inconveniencies of absolute power, which monarchy, in succession, was apt to lay claim to and bring upon them; it was not at all strange that they should not much trouble themselves to think of methods of restraining any exorbitances of those to whom they had given the authority over them, and of balancing the power of government by placing several parts of it in different hands. They had neither felt the oppression of tyrannical dominion, nor did the fashion of the age, nor their possessions or way of living, which afforded little matter for covetousness or ambition, give them any reason to apprehend or provide against it; and, therefore, it is no wonder they put themselves into such a frame of government as was not only, as I said, most obvious and simple, but also best suited to their present state and condition, which stood more in need of defence against foreign invasions and injuries than of multiplicity of laws where there was but very little property, and wanted not variety of rulers and abundance of officers to direct and look after their execution where there were but few trespasses and few offenders. Since, then, those who liked one another so well as to join into society cannot but be supposed to have some acquaintance and friendship together, and some trust one in another, they could not but have greater apprehensions of others than of one another; and, therefore, their first care and thought cannot but be supposed to be, how to secure themselves against foreign force. It was natural for them to put themselves under a frame of government which might best serve to that end, and choose the wisest and bravest man to conduct them in their wars and lead them out against their enemies, and in this chiefly be their ruler.

108. Thus we see that the kings of the Indians, in America, which is still a pattern of the first ages in Asia and Europe, whilst the inhabitants were too few for the country, and want of people and money gave men no temptation to enlarge their possessions of land or contest for wider extent of ground, are little more than generals of their armies; and though they command absolutely in war, yet at home, and in time of peace, they exercise very little dominion, and have but a very moderate sovereignty, the resolutions of peace and war being ordinarily either in the people or in a council, though the war itself, which admits not of pluralities of governors, naturally devolves the command into the king's sole authority.

109. And thus, in Israel itself, the chief business of their judges and first kings seems to have been to be captains in war and leaders of their armies, which (besides what is signified by "going out and in before the people," which was, to march forth to war and home again in the heads of their forces), appears plainly in the story of Jephtha. The Ammonites making war upon Israel, the Gileadites, in fear, send to Jephtha, a bastard of their family, whom they had cast off, and article with him, if he will assist them against the Ammonites, to make him their ruler, which they do in these words: "And the people

made him head and captain over them" (Judges xi. 11), which was, as it seems, all one as to be judge. "And he judged Israel" (Judges xii. 7) — that is, was their captain-general — "six years." So when Jotham upbraids the Shechemites with the obligation they had to Gideon, who had been their judge and ruler, he tells them: "He fought for you, and adventured his life for, and delivered you out of the hands of Midian" (Judges ix. 17). Nothing mentioned of him but what he did as a general, and, indeed, that is all is found in his history, or in any of the rest of the judges. And Abimelech particularly is called king, though at most he was but their general. And when, being weary of the ill-conduct of Samuel's sons, the children of Israel desired a king, "like all the nations, to judge them, and to go out before them, and to fight their battles" (I Sam. viii. 20), God, granting their desire, says to Samuel, "I will send thee a man, and thou shalt anoint him to be captain over my people Israel, that he may save my people out of the hands of the Philistines" (ix. 16). As if the only business of a king had been to lead out their armies and fight in their defence; and, accordingly, at his inauguration, pouring a vial of oil upon him, declares to Saul that "the Lord had anointed him to be captain over his inheritance" (x. 1). And therefore those who, after Saul's being solemnly chosen and saluted king by the tribes at Mispah, were unwilling to have him their king, make no other objection but this, "How shall this man save us?" (v. 27), as if they should have said: "This man is unfit to be our king, not having skill and conduct enough in war to be able to defend us." And when God resolved to transfer the government to David, it is in these words: "But now thy kingdom shall not continue: the Lord hath sought him a man after His own heart, and the Lord hath commanded him to be captain over His people" (xiii. 14). As if the whole kingly authority were nothing else but to be their general; and therefore the tribes who had stuck to Saul's family, and opposed David's reign, when they came to Hebron with terms of submission to him, they tell him, amongst other arguments, they had to submit to him as to their king, that he was, in effect, their king in Saul's time, and therefore they had no reason but to receive him as their king now. "Also," say they, "in time past, when Saul was king over us, thou wast he that leddest out and broughtest in Israel, and the Lord said unto thee, Thou shalt feed my people Israel, and thou shalt be a captain over Israel."

110. Thus, whether a family, by degrees, grew up into a commonwealth, and the fatherly authority being continued on to the elder son, every one in his turn growing up under it tacitly submitted to it, and the easiness and equality of it not offending any one, every one acquiesced till time seemed to have confirmed it and settled a right of succession by prescription; or whether several families, or the descendants of several families, whom chance, neighbourhood, or business brought together, united into society; the need of a general whose conduct might defend them against their enemies in war, and the great confidence the innocence and sincerity of that poor but virtuous age, such as are almost all those which begin governments that ever come to last in the world, gave men one of another, made the first beginners of commonwealths generally put the rule into one man's hand, without any other express limitation or restraint but what the nature of the thing and the end of government required. It was given them for the public good and safety, and to those ends, in the infancies of commonwealths, they commonly used it; and unless they had done so, young societies could not have subsisted. Without such nursing fathers, without this care of the governors, all governments would have sunk under the weakness and infirmities of their infancy, the prince and the people had soon perished together.

111. But the golden age (though before vain ambition, and *amor sceleratus habendi*, evil concupiscence had corrupted men's minds into a mistake of true power and honour) had more virtue, and consequently better governors, as well as less vicious subjects; and there was then no stretching prerogative on the one side to oppress the people, nor, consequently, on the other, any dispute about privilege, to lessen or restrain the power of the magistrate; and so no contest betwixt rulers and people about governors or government.¹ Yet, when ambition and luxury, in future ages, would retain and increase the power, without doing the business for which it was given, and aided by flattery, taught princes to have distinct and separate interests from their people, men found it necessary to examine more carefully the original and rights of government, and to find out ways to restrain the exorbitances and prevent the abuses of that power, which they having entrusted in another's hands, only for their own good, they found was made use of to hurt them.

112. Thus we may see how probable it is that people that were naturally free, and, by their own consent, either submitted to the government of their father, or united together, out of different families, to make a government, should generally put the rule into one man's hands, and choose to be under the conduct of a single person, without so much, as by express conditions, limiting or regulating his power, which they thought safe enough in his honesty and prudence; though they never dreamed of monarchy being *jure Divino*, which we never heard of among mankind till it was revealed to us by the divinity of this last age, nor ever allowed paternal power to have a right to dominion or to be the foundation of all government. And thus much may suffice to show that, as far as we have any light from history, we have reason to conclude that all peaceful beginnings of government have been laid in the consent of the people. I say "peaceful," because I shall have occasion, in another place, to speak of conquest, which some esteem a way of beginning of governments.

The other objection, I find, urged against the beginning of polities, in the way I have mentioned, is this, viz.: —

113. "That all men being born under government, some or other, it is impossible any of them should ever be free and at liberty to unite together and begin a new one, or ever be able to erect a lawful government." If this argument be good, I ask, How came so many lawful monarchies into the world? For if anybody, upon this supposition, can show me any one man, in any age of the world, free to begin a lawful monarchy, I will be bound to show him ten other free men at liberty, at the same time, to unite and begin a new government under a regal or any other form. It being demonstration that if any one born under the dominion of another may be so free as to have a right to command others in a new and distinct empire, every one that is born under the dominion of another may be so free too, and may become a ruler or subject of a distinct separate government. And so, by this their own principle, either all men, however born, are free, or else there is but one lawful prince, one lawful government in the world; and then they have nothing to do but barely to show us which that is, which, when they have done, I doubt not but all mankind will easily agree to pay obedience to him.

114. Though it be a sufficient answer to their objection to show that it involves them in the same difficulties that it doth those they use it against, yet I shall endeavour to discover the weakness of this argument a little farther.

"All men," say they, "are born under government, and therefore they cannot be at liberty to begin a new one. Every one is born a subject to his father or his prince, and is therefore under the perpetual tie of subjection and allegiance." It is plain mankind never owned nor considered any such natural subjection that they were born in, to one or to the other, that tied them, without their own consents, to a subjection to them and their heirs.

115. For there are no examples so frequent in history, both sacred and profane, as those of men withdrawing themselves and their obedience from the jurisdiction they were born under, and the family or community they were bred up in, and setting up new governments in other places, from whence sprang all that number of petty commonwealths in the beginning of ages, and which always multiplied as long as there was room enough, till the stronger or more fortunate swallowed the weaker; and those great ones, again breaking to pieces, dissolved into lesser dominions; all which are so many testimonies against paternal sovereignty, and plainly prove that it was not the natural right of the father descending to his heirs that made governments in the beginning; since it was impossible, upon that ground, there should have been so many little kingdoms but only one universal monarchy if men had not been at liberty to separate themselves from their families and their government, be it what it will that was set up in it, and go and make distinct commonwealths and other governments as they thought fit.

116. This has been the practice of the world from its first beginning to this day; nor is it now any more hindrance to the freedom of mankind, that they are born under constituted and ancient polities that have established laws and set forms of government, than if they were born in the woods amongst the unconfined inhabitants that run loose in them. For those who would persuade us that by being born under any government we are naturally subjects to it, and have no more any title or pretence to the freedom of the state of Nature, have no other reason (bating that of paternal power, which we have already answered) to produce for it, but only because our fathers or progenitors passed away their natural liberty, and thereby bound up themselves and their posterity to a perpetual subjection to the government which they themselves submitted to. It is true that whatever engagements or promises any one made for himself, he is under the obligation of them, but cannot by any compact whatsoever bind his children or posterity. For his son, when a man, being altogether as free as the father, any act of the father can no more give away the liberty of the son than it can of anybody else. He may, indeed, annex such conditions to the land he enjoyed, as a subject of any commonwealth, as may oblige his son to be of that community, if he will enjoy those possessions which were his father's, because that estate being his father's property, he may dispose or settle it as he pleases.

117. And this has generally given the occasion to the mistake in this matter; because commonwealths not permitting any part of their dominions to be dismembered, nor to be enjoyed by any but those of their community, the son cannot ordinarily enjoy the possessions of his father but under the same terms his father did, by becoming a member of the society, whereby he puts himself presently under the government he finds there established, as much as any other subject of that commonweal. And thus the consent of free men, born under government, which only makes them members of it, being given separately in their turns, as each comes to be of age, and not in a multitude together, people take no notice of it, and thinking it not done at all, or not necessary, conclude they are naturally subjects as they are men.

118. But it is plain governments themselves understand it otherwise; they claim no power over the son, because of that they had over the father; nor look on children as being their subjects, by their fathers being so. If a subject of England have a child by an Englishwoman in France, whose subject is he? Not the King of England's; for he must have leave to be admitted to the privileges of it. Nor the King of France's, for how then has his father a liberty to bring him away, and breed him as he pleases; and whoever was judged as a traitor or deserter, if he left, or warred against a country, for being barely born in it of parents that were aliens there? It is plain, then, by the practice of governments themselves, as well as by the law of right reason, that a child is born a subject of no country nor government. He is under his father's tuition and authority till he come to age of discretion, and then he is a free man, at liberty what government he will put himself under, what body politic he will unite himself to. For if an Englishman's son born in France be at liberty, and may do so, it is evident there is no tie upon him by his father being a subject of that kingdom, nor is he bound up by any compact of his ancestors; and why then hath not his son, by the same reason, the same liberty, though he be born anywhere else? Since the power that a father hath naturally over his children is the same wherever they be born, and the ties of natural obligations are not bounded by the positive limits of kingdoms and commonwealths.

119. Every man being, as has been showed, naturally free, and nothing being able to put him into subjection to any earthly power, but only his own consent, it is to be considered what shall be understood to be a sufficient declaration of a man's consent to make him subject to the laws of any government. There is a common distinction of an express and a tacit consent, which will concern our present case. Nobody doubts but an express consent of any man, entering into any society, makes him a perfect member of that society, a subject of that government. The difficulty is, what ought to be looked upon as a tacit consent, and how far it binds — *i.e.*, how far any one shall be looked on to have consented, and thereby submitted to any government, where he has made no expressions of it at all. And to this I say, that every man that hath any possession or enjoyment of any part of the dominions of any government doth hereby give his tacit consent, and is as far forth obliged to obedience to the laws of that government, during such enjoyment, as any one under it, whether this his possession be of land to him and his heirs for ever, or a lodging only for a week; or whether it be barely travelling freely on the highway; and, in effect, it reaches as far as the very being of any one within the territories of that government.

120. To understand this the better, it is fit to consider that every man when he at first incorporates himself into any commonwealth, he, by his uniting himself thereunto, annexed also, and submits to the community those possessions which he has, or shall acquire, that do not already belong to any other government. For it would be a direct contradiction for any one to enter into society with others for the securing and regulating of property, and yet to suppose his land, whose property is to be regulated by the laws of the society, should be exempt from the jurisdiction of that government to which he himself, and the property of the land, is a subject. By the same act, therefore, whereby any one unites his person, which was before free, to any commonwealth, by the same he unites his possessions, which were before free, to it also; and they become, both of them, person and possession, subject to the government and dominion of that commonwealth as long as it hath a being. Whoever therefore, from thenceforth, by inheritance, purchases

permission, or otherwise enjoys any part of the land so annexed to, and under the government of that commonweal, must take it with the condition it is under — that is, of submitting to the government of the commonwealth, under whose jurisdiction it is, as far forth as any subject of it.

121. But since the government has a direct jurisdiction only over the land and reaches the possessor of it (before he has actually incorporated himself in the society) only as he dwells upon and enjoys that, the obligation any one is under by virtue of such enjoyment to submit to the government begins and ends with the enjoyment; so that whenever the owner, who has given nothing but such a tacit consent to the government will, by donation, sale or otherwise, quit the said possession. He is at liberty to go and incorporate himself into any other commonwealth, or agree with others to begin a new one *in vacuis locis*, in any part of the world they can find free and unpossessed; whereas he that has once, by actual agreement and any express declaration, given his consent to be of any commonweal, is perpetually and indispensably obliged to be, and remain unalterably a subject to it, and can never be again in the liberty of the state of Nature, unless by any calamity the government he was under comes to be dissolved.

122. But submitting to the laws of any country, living quietly and enjoying privileges and protection under them, makes not a man a member of that society; it is only a local protection and homage due to and from all those who, not being in a state of war, come within the territories belonging to any government, to all parts whereof the force of its law extends. But this no more makes a man a member of that society, a perpetual subject of that commonwealth, than it would make a man a subject to another in whose family he found it convenient to abide for some time, though, whilst he continued in it, he were obliged to comply with the laws and submit to the government he found there. And thus we see that foreigners, by living all their lives under another government, and enjoying the privileges and protection of it, though they are bound, even in conscience, to submit to its administration as far forth as any denizen, yet do not thereby come to be subjects or members of that commonwealth. Nothing can make any man so, but his actually entering into it by positive engagement and express promise and compact. This is that which, I think, concerning the beginning of political societies, and that consent which makes any one a member of any commonwealth.

CHAPTER IX.
Of the Ends of Political Society and Government.

123. If man in the state of Nature be so free as has been said, if he be absolute lord of his own person and possessions, equal to the greatest and subject to nobody, why will he part with his freedom, this empire, and subject himself to the dominion and control of any other power? To which it is obvious to answer, that though in the state of Nature he hath such a right, yet the enjoyment of it is very uncertain and constantly exposed to the invasion of others; for all being kings as much as he, every man his equal, and the greater part no strict observers of equity and justice, the enjoyment of the property he has in this state is very unsafe, very insecure. This makes him willing to quit this condition which, however free, is full of fears and continual dangers; and it is not without reason that he

seeks out and is willing to join in society with others who are already united, or have a mind to unite for the mutual preservation of their lives, liberties and estates, which I call by the general name — property.

124. The great and chief end, therefore, of men uniting into commonwealths, and putting themselves under government, is the preservation of their property; to which in the state of Nature there are many things wanting.

Firstly, There wants an established, settled, known law, received and allowed by common consent to be the standard of right and wrong, and the common measure to decide all controversies between them. For though the law of Nature be plain and intelligible to all rational creatures, yet men, being biased by their interest, as well as ignorant for want of study of it, are not apt to allow of it as a law binding to them in the application of it to their particular cases.

125. Secondly: in the state of Nature there wants a known and indifferent judge, with authority to determine all differences according to the established law. For every one in that state being both judge and executioner of the law of Nature, men being partial to themselves, passion and revenge is very apt to carry them too far, and with too much heat in their own cases, as well as negligence and unconcernedness, make them too remiss in other men's.

126. Thirdly: in the state of Nature there often wants power to back and support the sentence when right, and to give it due execution. They who by any injustice offended will seldom fail where they are able by force to make good their injustice. Such resistance many times makes the punishment dangerous, and frequently destructive to those who attempt it.

127. Thus mankind, notwithstanding all the privileges of the state of Nature, being but in an ill condition while they remain in it are quickly driven into society. Hence it comes to pass, that we seldom find any number of men live any time together in this state. The inconveniencies that they are therein exposed to by the irregular and uncertain exercise of the power every man has of punishing the transgressions of others, make them take sanctuary under the established laws of government, and therein seek the preservation of their property. It is this makes them so willingly give up every one his single power of punishing to be exercised by such alone as shall be appointed to it amongst them, and by such rules as the community, or those authorized by them to that purpose, shall agree on. And in this we have the original right and rise of both the legislative and executive power as well as of the governments and societies themselves.

128. For in the state of Nature to omit the liberty he has of innocent delights, a man has two powers. The first is to do whatsoever he thinks fit for the preservation of himself and others within the permission of the law of Nature; by which law, common to them all, he and all the rest of mankind are one community, make up one society distinct from all other creatures, and were it not for the corruption and viciousness of degenerate men, there would be no need of any other, no necessity that men should separate from this great and natural community, and associate into lesser combinations. The other power a man has in the state of Nature is the power to punish the crimes committed against that law. Both these he gives up when he joins in a private, if I may so call it, or particular political society, and incorporates into any commonwealth separate from the rest of mankind.

129. The first power — viz., of doing whatsoever he thought fit for the preservation of himself and the rest of mankind, he gives up to be regulated by laws made by the society, so far forth as the preservation of himself and the rest of that society shall require; which laws of the society in many things confine the liberty he had by the law of Nature.

130. Secondly. The power of punishing he wholly gives up, and engages his natural force, which he might before employ in the execution of the law of Nature, by his own single authority, as he thought fit, to assist the executive power of the society as the law thereof shall require. For being now in a new state, wherein he is to enjoy many conveniencies from the labour, assistance, and society of others in the same community, as well as protection from its whole strength, he is to part also with as much of his natural liberty, in providing for himself, as the good, prosperity, and safety of the society shall require, which is not only necessary but just, since the other members of the society do the like.

131. But though men when they enter into society give up the equality, liberty, and executive power they had in the state of Nature into the hands of the society, to be so far disposed of by the legislative as the good of the society shall require, yet it being only with an intention in every one the better to preserve himself, his liberty and property (for no rational creature can be supposed to change his condition with an intention to be worse), the power of the society or legislative constituted by them can never be supposed to extend farther than the common good, but is obliged to secure every one's property by providing against those three defects above mentioned that made the state of Nature so unsafe and uneasy. And so, whoever has the legislative or supreme power of any commonwealth, is bound to govern by established standing laws, promulgated and known to the people, and not by extemporary decrees, by indifferent and upright judges, who are to decide controversies by those laws; and to employ the force of the community at home only in the execution of such laws, or abroad to prevent or redress foreign injuries and secure the community from inroads and invasion. And all this to be directed to no other end but the peace, safety, and public good of the people.

CHAPTER X.
Of the Forms of a Commonwealth.

132. The majority having, as has been showed, upon men's first uniting into society, the whole power of the community naturally in them, may employ all that power in making laws for the community from time to time, and executing those laws by officers of their own appointing, and then the form of the government is a perfect democracy; or else may put the power of making laws into the hands of a few select men, and their heirs or successors, and then it is an oligarchy; or else into the hands of one man, and then it is a monarchy; if to him and his heirs, it is a hereditary monarchy; if to him only for life, but upon his death the power only of nominating a successor, to return to them, an elective monarchy. And so accordingly of these make compounded and mixed forms of government, as they think good. And if the legislative power be at first given by the majority to one or more persons only for their lives, or any limited time, and then the supreme power to revert to them again, when it is so reverted the community may dispose

of it again anew into what hands they please, and so constitute a new form of government; for the form of government depending upon the placing the supreme power, which is the legislative, it being impossible to conceive that an inferior power should prescribe to a superior, or any but the supreme make laws, according as the power of making laws is placed, such is the form of the commonwealth.

133. By "commonwealth" I must be understood all along to mean not a democracy, or any form of government, but any independent community which the Latins signified by the word *civitas*, to which the word which best answers in our language is "commonwealth," and most properly expresses such a society of men which "community" does not (for there may be subordinate communities in a government), and "city" much less. And therefore, to avoid ambiguity, I crave leave to use the word "commonwealth" in that sense, in which sense I find the word used by King James himself, which I think to be its genuine signification, which, if anybody dislike, I consent with him to change it for a better.

CHAPTER XI.
Of the Extent of the Legislative Power.

134. The great end of men's entering into society being the enjoyment of their properties in peace and safety, and the great instrument and means of that being the laws established in that society, the first and fundamental positive law of all commonwealths is the establishing of the legislative power, as the first and fundamental natural law which is to govern even the legislative itself, is the preservation of the society and (as far as will consist with the public good) of every person in it. This legislative is not only the supreme power of the commonwealth, but sacred and unalterable in the hands where the community have once placed it. Nor can any edict of anybody else, in what form soever conceived, or by what power soever backed, have the force and obligation of a law which has not its sanction from that legislative which the public has chosen and appointed; for without this the law could not have that which is absolutely necessary to its being a law, the consent of the society, over whom nobody can have a power to make laws^2 but by their own consent and by authority received from them; and therefore all the obedience, which by the most solemn ties any one can be obliged to pay, ultimately terminates in this supreme power, and is directed by those laws which it enacts. Nor can any oaths to any foreign power whatsoever, or any domestic subordinate power, discharge any member of the society from his obedience to the legislative, acting pursuant to their trust, nor oblige him to any obedience contrary to the laws so enacted or farther than they do allow, it being ridiculous to imagine one can be tied ultimately to obey any power in the society which is not the supreme.

135. Though the legislative, whether placed in one or more, whether it be always in being or only by intervals, though it be the supreme power in every commonwealth; yet, first, it is not, nor can possibly be, absolutely arbitrary over the lives and fortunes of the people. For it being but the joint power of every member of the society given up to that person or assembly which is legislator, it can be no more than those persons had in a state of Nature before they entered into society, and gave it up to the community. For nobody

can transfer to another more power than he has in himself, and nobody has an absolute arbitrary power over himself, or over any other, to destroy his own life, or take away the life or property of another. A man, as has been proved, cannot subject himself to the arbitrary power of another; and having, in the state of Nature, no arbitrary power over the life, liberty, or possession of another, but only so much as the law of Nature gave him for the preservation of himself and the rest of mankind, this is all he doth, or can give up to the commonwealth, and by it to the legislative power, so that the legislative can have no more than this. Their power in the utmost bounds of it is limited to the public good of the society.[3] It is a power that hath no other end but preservation, and therefore can never have a right to destroy, enslave, or designedly to impoverish the subjects; the obligations of the law of Nature cease not in society, but only in many cases are drawn closer, and have, by human laws, known penalties annexed to them to enforce their observation. Thus the law of Nature stands as an eternal rule to all men, legislators as well as others. The rules that they make for other men's actions must, as well as their own and other men's actions, be conformable to the law of Nature — *i.e.*, to the will of God, of which that is a declaration, and the fundamental law of Nature being the preservation of mankind, no human sanction can be good or valid against it.

136. Secondly, the legislative or supreme authority cannot assume to itself a power to rule by extemporary arbitrary decrees, but is bound to dispense justice and decide the rights of the subject by promulgated standing laws,[4] and known authorized judges. For the law of Nature being unwritten, and so nowhere to be found but in the minds of men, they who, through passion or interest, shall miscite or misapply it, cannot so easily be convinced of their mistake where there is no established judge; and so it serves not as it ought, to determine the rights and fence the properties of those that live under it, especially where every one is judge, interpreter, and executioner of it too, and that in his own case; and he that has right on his side, having ordinarily but his own single strength, hath not force enough to defend himself from injuries or punish delinquents. To avoid these inconveniencies which disorder men's properties in the state of Nature, men unite into societies that they may have the united strength of the whole society to secure and defend their properties, and may have standing rules to bound it by which every one may know what is his. To this end it is that men give up all their natural power to the society they enter into, and the community put the legislative power into such hands as they think fit, with this trust, that they shall be governed by declared laws, or else their peace, quiet, and property will still be at the same uncertainty as it was in the state of Nature.

137. Absolute arbitrary power, or governing without settled standing laws, can neither of them consist with the ends of society and government, which men would not quit the freedom of the state of Nature for, and tie themselves up under were it not to preserve their lives, liberties, and fortunes; and by stated rules of right and property to secure their peace and quiet. It cannot be supposed that they should intend, had they a power so to do, to give any one or more an absolute arbitrary power over their persons and estates, and put a force into the magistrate's hand to execute his unlimited will arbitrarily upon them; this were to put themselves into a worse condition than the state of Nature, wherein they had a liberty to defend their right against the injuries of others, and were upon equal terms of force to maintain it, whether invaded by a single man or many in combination. Whereas by supposing they have given up themselves to the absolute arbitrary power and will of a legislator, they have disarmed themselves, and armed him to make a prey of

them when he pleases; he being in a much worse condition that is exposed to the arbitrary power of one man who has the command of a hundred thousand than he that is exposed to the arbitrary power of a hundred thousand single men, nobody being secure, that his will who has such a command is better than that of other men, though his force be a hundred thousand times stronger. And, therefore, whatever form the commonwealth is under, the ruling power ought to govern by declared and received laws, and not by extemporary dictates and undetermined resolutions, for then mankind will be in a far worse condition than in the state of Nature if they shall have armed one or a few men with the joint power of a multitude, to force them to obey at pleasure the exorbitant and unlimited decrees of their sudden thoughts, or unrestrained, and till that moment, unknown wills, without having any measures set down which may guide and justify their actions. For all the power the government has, being only for the good of the society, as it ought not to be arbitrary and at pleasure, so it ought to be exercised by established and promulgated laws, that both the people may know their duty, and be safe and secure within the limits of the law, and the rulers, too, kept within their due bounds, and not be tempted by the power they have in their hands to employ it to purposes, and by such measures as they would not have known, and own not willingly.

138. Thirdly, the supreme power cannot take from any man any part of his property without his own consent. For the preservation of property being the end of government, and that for which men enter into society, it necessarily supposes and requires that the people should have property, without which they must be supposed to lose that by entering into society, which was the end for which they entered into it; too gross an absurdity for any man to own. Men, therefore, in society having property, they have such a right to the goods, which by the law of the community are theirs, that nobody hath a right to take them, or any part of them, from them without their own consent; without this they have no property at all. For I have truly no property in that which another can by right take from me when he pleases against my consent. Hence it is a mistake to think that the supreme or legislative power of any commonwealth can do what it will, and dispose of the estates of the subject arbitrarily, or take any part of them at pleasure. This is not much to be feared in governments where the legislative consists wholly or in part in assemblies which are variable, whose members upon the dissolution of the assembly are subjects under the common laws of their country, equally with the rest. But in governments where the legislative is in one lasting assembly, always in being or in one man as in absolute monarchies, there is danger still, that they will think themselves to have a distinct interest from the rest of the community, and so will be apt to increase their own riches and power by taking what they think fit from the people. For a man's property is not at all secure, though there be good and equitable laws to set the bounds of it between him and his fellow subjects, if he who commands those subjects have power to take from any private man what part he pleases of his property, and use and dispose of it as he thinks good.

139. But government into whosesoever hands it is put, being as I have before showed, entrusted with this condition, and for this end, that men might have and secure their properties, the prince or senate, however it may have power to make laws for the regulating of property between the subjects one amongst another, yet can never have a power to take to themselves the whole, or any part of the subjects' property, without their own consent; for this would be in effect to leave them no property at all. And to let us see

that even absolute power, where it is necessary, is not arbitrary by being absolute, but is still limited by that reason, and confined to those ends which required it in some cases to be absolute, we need look no farther than the common practice of martial discipline. For the preservation of the army, and in it of the whole commonwealth, requires an absolute obedience to the command of every superior officer, and it is justly death to disobey or dispute the most dangerous or unreasonable of them; but yet we see that neither the serjeant that could command a soldier to march up to the mouth of a cannon, or stand in a breach where he is almost sure to perish, can command that soldier to give him one penny of his money; nor the general that can condemn him to death for deserting his post, or not obeying the most desperate orders, cannot yet with all his absolute power of life and death dispose of one farthing of that soldier's estate, or seize one jot of his goods; whom yet he can command anything, and hang for the least disobedience. Because such a blind obedience is necessary to that end for which the commander has his power — viz., the preservation of the rest, but the disposing of his goods has nothing to do with it.

140. It is true governments cannot be supported without great charge, and it is fit every one who enjoys his share of the protection should pay out of his estate his proportion for the maintenance of it. But still it must be with his own consent — *i.e.*, the consent of the majority, giving it either by themselves or their representatives chosen by them; for if any one shall claim a power to lay and levy taxes on the people by his own authority, and without such consent of the people, he thereby invades the fundamental law of property, and subverts the end of government. For what property have I in that which another may by right take when he pleases to himself?

141. Fourthly. The legislative cannot transfer the power of making laws to any other hands, for it being but a delegated power from the people, they who have it cannot pass it over to others. The people alone can appoint the form of the commonwealth, which is by constituting the legislative, and appointing in whose hands that shall be. And when the people have said, "We will submit, and be governed by laws made by such men, and in such forms," nobody else can say other men shall make laws for them; nor can they be bound by any laws but such as are enacted by those whom they have chosen and authorized to make laws for them.

142. These are the bounds which the trust that is put in them by the society and the law of God and Nature have set to the legislative power of every commonwealth, in all forms of government. First: They are to govern by promulgated established laws, not to be varied in particular cases, but to have one rule for rich and poor, for the favourite at Court, and the countryman at plough. Secondly: These laws also ought to be designed for no other end ultimately but the good of the people. Thirdly: They must not raise taxes on the property of the people without the consent of the people given by themselves or their deputies. And this properly concerns only such governments where the legislative is always in being, or at least where the people have not reserved any part of the legislative to deputies, to be from time to time chosen by themselves. Fourthly: Legislative neither must nor can transfer the power of making laws to anybody else, or place it anywhere but where the people have.

Notes

[1] "At first, when some certain kind of regimen was once approved, it may be nothing was then further thought upon for the manner of governing, but all permitted unto their wisdom and discretion, which were to rule till, by experience, they found this for all parts very inconvenient, so as the thing which they had devised for a remedy did indeed but increase the sore which it should have cured. They saw that to live by one man's will became the cause of all men's misery. This constrained them to come unto laws wherein all men might see their duty beforehand, and know the penalties of transgressing them." — Hooker, Eccl. Pol. lib. i. sect. 10.

[2] "The lawful power of making laws to command whole politic societies of men, belonging so properly unto the same entire societies, that for any prince or potentate of what kind soever upon earth, to exercise the same of himself, and not by express commission immediately and personally received from God, or else by authority derived at the first from their consent, upon whose persons they impose laws, it is no better than mere tyranny. Laws they are not, therefore, which public approbation hath not made so." — Hooker, Eccl. Pol., lib. i., sect. 10. "Of this point, therefore, we are to note that such men naturally have no full and perfect power to command whole politic multitudes of men, therefore utterly without our consent we could in such sort be at no man's commandment living. And to be commanded, we do consent when that society, whereof we be a part, hath at any time before consented, without revoking the same after by the like universal agreement.

"Laws therefore human, of what kind soever, are available by consent." — *Hooker Eccl. Pol.*

[3] "Two foundations there are which bear up public societies; the one a natural inclination whereby all men desire sociable life and fellowship; the other an order, expressly or secretly agreed upon, touching the manner of their union in living together. The latter is that which we call the law of a commonweal, the very soul of a politic body, the parts whereof are by law animated, held together, and set on work in such actions as the common good requireth. Laws politic, ordained for external order and regimen amongst men, are never framed as they should be, unless presuming the will of man to be inwardly obstinate, rebellious, and averse from all obedience to the sacred laws of his nature; in a word, unless presuming man to be in regard of his depraved mind, little better than a wild beast, they do accordingly provide notwithstanding, so to frame his outward actions, that they be no hindrance unto the common good, for which societies are instituted. Unless they do this they are not perfect." — Hooker, Eccl. Pol., lib. i., sect. 10.

[4] "Human laws are measures in respect of men whose actions they must direct, howbeit such measures they are as have also their higher rules to be measured by, which rules are two — the law of God and the law of Nature; so that laws human must be made according to the general laws of Nature, and without contradiction to any positive law of Scripture, otherwise they are ill made." — *Ibid.*, lib. iii., sect. 9.

"To constrain men to anything inconvenient doth seem unreasonable." — *Ibid.*, lib. i., sect. 10.

20. Essays: Moral and Political[*]

David Hume

Essay XII.
Of the Original Contract.

As no party, in the present age, can well support itself, without a philosophical or speculative system of principles, annexed to its political or practical one; we accordingly find, that each of the factions, into which this nation is divided, has reared up a fabric of the former kind, in order to protect and cover that scheme of actions, which it pursues. The people being commonly very rude builders, especially in this speculative way, and more especially still, when actuated by party-zeal; it is natural to imagine, that their workmanship must be a little unshapely, and discover evident marks of that violence and hurry, in which it was raised. The one party, by tracing up Government to the DEITY, endeavour to render it so sacred and inviolate, that it must be little less than sacrilege, however tyrannical it may become, to touch or invade it, in the smallest article. The other party, by founding government altogether on the consent of the PEOPLE, suppose that there is a kind of *original contract*, by which the subjects have tacitly reserved the power of resisting their sovereign, whenever they find themselves aggrieved by that authority, with which they have, for certain purposes, voluntarily entrusted him. These are the speculative principles of the two parties; and these too are the practical consequences deduced from them.

I shall venture to affirm, *That both these systems of speculative principles are just; though not in the sense, intended by the parties:* And, *That both the schemes of practical consequences are prudent; though not in the extremes, to which each party, in opposition*

[*] David Hume published *Essays: Moral and Political* in 1748. This particular selection was taken from Hume, *Essays: Moral, Political, and Literary*, Volume I, Essay XII, edited by T.H. Green and T.H. Grose (London: Longmans, Green, and Co., 1882), 443–460.

to the other, has commonly endeavoured to carry them.

That the DEITY is the ultimate author of all government, will never be denied by any, who admit a general providence, and allow, that all events in the universe are conducted by an uniform plan, and directed to wise purposes. As it is impossible for the human race to subsist, at least in any comfortable or secure state, without the protection of government; this institution must certainly have been intended by that beneficent Being, who means the good of all his creatures: And as it has universally, in fact, taken place, in all countries, and all ages; we may conclude, with still greater certainty, that it was intended by that omniscient Being, who can never be deceived by any event or operation. But since he gave rise to it, not by any particular or miraculous interposition, but by his concealed and universal efficacy; a sovereign cannot, properly speaking, be called his vice-gerent, in any other sense than every power or force, being derived from him, may be said to act by his commission. Whatever actually happens is comprehended in the general plan or intention of providence; nor has the greatest and most lawful prince any more reason, upon that account, to plead a peculiar sacredness or inviolable authority, than an inferior magistrate, or even an usurper, or even a robber and a pyrate. The same divine superintendant, who, for wise purposes, invested [1]a TITUS or a TRAJAN with authority, did also, for purposes, no doubt, equally wise, though unknown, bestow power on a BORGIA or an ANGRIA. The same causes, which gave rise to the sovereign power in every state, established likewise every petty jurisdiction in it, and every limited authority. A constable, therefore, no less than a king, acts by a divine commission, and possesses an indefeasible right.

When we consider how nearly equal all men are in their bodily force, and even in their mental powers and faculties, till cultivated by education; we must necessarily allow, that nothing but their own consent could, at first, associate them together, and subject them to any authority. The people, if we trace government to its first origin in the woods and desarts, are the source of all power and jurisdiction, amid voluntarily, for the sake of peace and order, abandoned their native liberty, and received laws from their equal and companion. The conditions, upon which they were willing to submit, were either expressed, or were so clear and obvious, that it might well be esteemed superfluous to express them. If this, then, be meant by the *original contract*, it cannot be denied, that all government is, at first, founded on a contract, and that the most ancient rude combinations of mankind were formed chiefly by that principle. In vain, are we asked in what records this charter of our liberties is registered. It was not written on parchment, nor yet on leaves or barks of trees. It preceded the use of writing and all the other civilized arts of life. But we trace it plainly in the nature of man, and in the equality, [2]or something approaching equality, which we find in all the individuals of that species. The force, which now prevails, and which is founded on fleets and armies, is plainly political, and derived from authority, the effect of established government. A man's natural force consists only in the vigour of his limbs, and the firmness of his courage; which could never subject multitudes to the command of one. Nothing but their own consent, and their sense of the advantages resulting from peace and order, could have had that influence.

[3]Yet even this consent was long very imperfect, and could not be the basis of a regular administration. The chieftain, who had probably acquired his influence during the continuance of war, ruled more by persuasion than command; and till he could employ force to reduce the refractory and disobedient, the society could scarcely be said to have

attained a state of civil government. No compact or agreement, it is evident, was expressly formed for general submission; an idea far beyond the comprehension of savages: Each exertion of authority in the chieftain must have been particular, and called forth by the present exigencies of the case: The sensible utility, resulting from his interposition, made these exertions become daily more frequent; and their frequency gradually produced an habitual, and, if you please to call it so, a voluntary, and therefore precarious, acquiescence in the people.

But philosophers, who have embraced a party (if that be not a contradiction in terms) are not contented with these concessions. They assert, not only that government in its earliest infancy arose from consent or rather the voluntary acquiescence of the people; but also, that, even at present, when it has attained its full maturity, it rests on no other foundation. They affirm, that all men are still born equal, and owe allegiance to no prince or government, unless bound by the obligation and sanction of a *promise*. And as no man, without some equivalent, would forego the advantages of his native liberty, and subject himself to the will of another; this promise is always understood to be conditional, and imposes on him no obligation, unless he meet with justice and protection from his sovereign. These advantages the sovereign promises him in return; and if he fail in the execution, he has broken, on his part, the articles of engagement, and has thereby freed his subject from all obligations to allegiance. Such, according to these philosophers, is the foundation of authority in every government; and such the right of resistance, possessed by every subject.

But would these reasoners look abroad into the world, they would meet with nothing that, in the least, corresponds to their ideas, or can warrant so refined and philosophical a system. On the contrary, we find, every where, princes, who claim their subjects as their property, and assert their independent right of sovereignty, from conquest or succession. We find also, every where, subjects, who acknowledge this right in their prince, and suppose themselves born under obligations of obedience to a certain sovereign, as much as under the ties of reverence and duty to certain parents. These connexions are always conceived to be equally independent of our consent, in PERSIA and CHINA; in FRANCE and SPAIN; and even in HOLLAND and ENGLAND, wherever the doctrines above-mentioned have not been carefully inculcated. Obedience or subjection becomes so familiar, that most men never make any enquiry about its origin or cause, more than about the principle of gravity, resistance, or the most universal laws of nature. Or if curiosity ever move them; as soon as they learn, that they themselves and their ancestors have, for several ages, or from time immemorial, been subject to such a form of government or such a family; they immediately acquiesce, and acknowledge their obligation to allegiance. Were you to preach, in most parts of the world, that political connexions are founded altogether on voluntary consent or a mutual promise, the magistrate would soon imprison you, as seditious, for loosening the ties of obedience; if your friends did not before shut you up as delirious, for advancing such absurdities. It is strange, that an act of the mind, which every individual is supposed to have formed, and after he came to the use of reason too, otherwise it could have no authority; that this act, I say, should be so much unknown to all of them, that, over the face of the whole earth, there scarcely remain any traces or memory of it.

But the contract, on which government is founded, is said to be the *original contract*; and consequently may be supposed too old to fall under the knowledge of the present generation. If the agreement, by which savage men first associated and conjoined their force, be here meant, this is acknowledged to be real; but being so ancient, and being obliterated by a thousand changes of government and princes, it cannot now be supposed to retain any authority. If we would say any thing to the purpose, we must assert, that every particular government, which is lawful, and which imposes any duty of allegiance on the subject, was, at first, founded on consent and a voluntary compact. But besides that this supposes the consent of the fathers to bind the children, even to the most remote generations, (which republican writers will never allow) besides this, I say, it is not justified by history or experience, in any age or country of the world.

Almost all the governments, which exist at present, or of which there remains any record in story, have been founded originally, either on usurpation or conquest, or both, without any pretence of a fair consent, or voluntary subjection of the people. When an artful and bold man is placed at the head of an army or faction, it is often easy for him, by employing, sometimes violence, sometimes false pretences, to establish his dominion over a people a hundred times more numerous than his partizans. He allows no such open communication, that his enemies can know, with certainty, their number or force. He gives them no leisure to assemble together in a body to oppose him. Even all those, who are the instruments of his usurpation, may wish his fall; but their ignorance of each other's intention keeps them in awe, and is the sole cause of his security. By such arts as these, many governments have been established; and this is all the *original contract*, which they have to boast of.

The face of the earth is continually changing, by the encrease of small kingdoms into great empires, by the dissolution of great empires into smaller kingdoms, by the planting of colonies, by the migration of tribes. Is there any thing discoverable in all these events, but force and violence? Where is the mutual agreement or voluntary association so much talked of?

Even the smoothest way, by which a nation may receive a foreign master, by marriage or a will, is not extremely honourable for the people; but supposes them to be disposed of, like a dowry or a legacy, according to the pleasure or interest of their rulers.

But where no force interposes, and election takes place; what is this election so highly vaunted? It is either the combination of a few great men, who decide for the whole, and will allow of no opposition: Or it is the fury of a multitude, that follow a seditious ringleader, who is not known, perhaps, to a dozen among them, and who owes his advancement merely to his own impudence, or to the momentary caprice of his fellows.

Are these disorderly elections, which are rare too, of such mighty authority, as to be the only lawful foundation of all government and allegiance?

In reality, there is not a more terrible event, than a total dissolution of government, which gives liberty to the multitude, and makes the determination or choice of a new establishment depend upon a number, which nearly approaches to that of the body of the people: For it never comes entirely to the whole body of them. Every wise man, then, wishes to see, at the head of a powerful and obedient army, a general, who may speedily seize the prize, and give to the people a master, which they are so unfit to chuse for themselves. So little correspondent is fact and reality to those philosophical notions.

Let not the establishment at the *Revolution* deceive us, or make us so much in love with a philosophical origin to government, as to imagine all others monstrous and irregular.

Even that event was far from corresponding to these refined ideas. It was only the succession, and that only in the regal part of the government, which was then changed: And it was only the majority of seven hundred, who determined that change for near ten millions. I doubt not, indeed, but the bulk of those ten millions acquiesced willingly in the determination: But was the matter left, in the least, to their choice? Was it not justly supposed to be, from that moment, decided, and every man punished, who refused to submit to the new sovereign? How otherwise could the matter have ever been brought to any issue or conclusion?

The republic of ATHENS was, I believe, the most extensive democracy, that we read of in history: Yet if we make the requisite allowances for the women, the slaves, and the strangers, we shall find, that that establishment was not, at first, made, nor any law ever voted, by a tenth part of those who were bound to pay obedience to it: Not to mention the islands and foreign dominions, which the ATHENIANS claimed as theirs by right of conquest. And as it is well known, that popular assemblies in that city were always full of licence and disorder, notwithstanding the institutions and laws by which they were checked: How much more disorderly must they prove, where they form not the established constitution, but meet tumultuously on the dissolution of the ancient government, in order to give rise to a new one? How chimerical must it be to talk of a choice in such circumstances?

[4]The ACHÆANS enjoyed the freest and most perfect democracy of all antiquity; yet they employed force to oblige some cities to enter into their league, as we learn from POLYBIUS.[5]

HARRY the IVth and HARRY the VIIth of ENGLAND, had really no title to the throne but a parliamentary election; yet they never would acknowledge it, lest they should thereby weaken their authority. Strange, if the only real foundation of all authority be consent and promise!

It is in vain to say, that all governments are or should be, at first, founded on popular consent, as much as the necessity of human affairs will admit. This favours entirely my pretension. I maintain, that human affairs will never admit of this consent; seldom of the appearance of it. But that conquest or usurpation, that is, in plain terms, force, by dissolving the ancient governments, is the origin of almost all the new ones, which were ever established in the world. And that in the few cases, where consent may seem to have taken place, it was commonly so irregular, so confined, or so much intermixed either with fraud or violence, that it cannot have any great authority.

[6]My intention here is not to exclude the consent of the people from being one just foundation of government where it has place. It is surely the best and most sacred of any. I only pretend, that it has very seldom had place in any degree, and never almost in its full extent. And that therefore some other foundation of government must also be admitted.

Were all men possessed of so inflexible a regard to justice, that, of themselves, they would totally abstain from the properties of others; they had for ever remained in a state of absolute liberty, without subjection to any magistrate or political society: But this is a state of perfection, of which human nature is justly deemed incapable. Again; were all men possessed of so perfect an understanding, as always to know their own interests, no form of government had ever been submitted to, but what was established on consent, and was fully canvassed by every member of the society: But this state of perfection is likewise much superior to human nature. Reason, history, and experience shew us, that all political societies have had an origin much lest accurate and regular; and were one to choose a period of time, when the people's consent was the least regarded in public transactions, it would be precisely on the establishment of a new government. In a settled constitution, their inclinations are often consulted; but during the fury of revolutions, conquests, and public convulsions, military force or political craft usually decides the controversy.

When a new government is established, by whatever means, the people are commonly dissatisfied with it, and pay obedience more from fear and necessity, than from any idea of allegiance or of moral obligation. The prince is watchful and jealous, and must carefully guard against every beginning or appearance of insurrection. Time, by degrees, removes all these difficulties, and accustoms the nation to regard, as their lawful or native princes, that family, which, at first, they considered as usurpers or foreign conquerors. In order to found this opinion, they have no recourse to any notion of voluntary consent or promise, which, they know, never was, in this case, either expected or demanded. The original establishment was formed by violence, and submitted to from necessity. The subsequent administration is also supported by power, and acquiesced in by the people, not as a matter of choice, but of obligation. They imagine not that their consent gives their prince a title: But they willingly consent, because they think, that, from long possession, he has acquired a title, independent of their choice or inclination.

Should it be said, that, by living under the dominion of a prince, which one might leave, every individual has given a *tacit* consent to his authority, and promised him obedience; it may be answered, that such an implied consent can only have place, where a man imagines, that the matter depends on his choice. But where he thinks (as all mankind do who are born under established governments) that by his birth he owes allegiance to a certain prince or certain form of government; it would be absurd to infer a consent or choice, which he expressly, in this case, renounces and disclaims.

Can we seriously say, that a poor peasant or artizan has a free choice to leave his country, when he knows no foreign language or manners, and lives from day to day, by the small wages which he acquires? We may as well assert, that a man, by remaining in a vessel, freely consents to the dominion of the master; though he was carried on board while asleep, and must leap into the ocean, and perish, the moment he leaves her.

What if the prince forbid his subjects to quit his dominions; as in TIBERIUS's time, it was regarded as a crime in a ROMAN knight that he had attempted to fly to the PARTHIANS, in order to escape the tyranny of that emperor?[7] Or as the ancient MUSCOVITES prohibited all travelling under pain of death? And did a prince observe, that many of his subjects were seized with the frenzy of migrating to foreign countries, he would doubtless, with great reason and justice, restrain them, in order to prevent the depopulation of his own kingdom. Would he forfeit the allegiance of all his subjects, by so wise and reasonable a law? Yet the freedom of their choice is surely, in that case, ravished from them.

A company of men, who should leave their native country, in order to people some uninhabited region, might dream of recovering their native freedom; but they would soon find, that their prince still laid claim to them, and called them his subjects, even in their new settlement. And in this he would but act conformably to the common ideas of mankind.

The truest *tacit* consent of this kind, that is ever observed, is when a foreigner settles in any country, and is beforehand acquainted with the prince, and government, and laws, to which he must submit: Yet is his allegiance, though more voluntary, much less expected or depended on, than that of a natural born subject. On the contrary, his native prince still asserts a claim to him. And if he punish not the renegade, when he seizes him in war with his new prince's commission; this clemency is not founded on the municipal law, which in all countries condemns the prisoner; but on the consent of princes, who have agreed to this indulgence, in order to prevent reprisals.

[8]Did one generation of men go off the stage at once, and another succeed, as is the case with silk-worms and butterflies, the new race, if they had sense enough to choose their government, which surely is never the case with men, might voluntarily, and by general consent, establish their own form of civil polity, without any regard to the laws or precedents, which prevailed among their ancestors. But as human society is in perpetual flux, one man every hour going out of the world, another coming into it, it is necessary, in order to preserve stability in government, that the new brood should conform themselves to the established constitution, and nearly follow the path which their fathers, treading in the footsteps of theirs, had marked out to them. Some innovations must necessarily have place in every human institution, and it is happy where the enlightened genius of the age gives these a direction to the side of reason, liberty, and justice: but violent innovations no individual is entitled to make: they are even dangerous to be attempted by the legislature: more ill than good is ever to be expected from them: and if history affords examples to the contrary, they are not to be drawn into precedent, and are only to be regarded as proofs, that the science of politics affords few rules, which will not admit of some exception, and which may not sometimes be controuled by fortune and accident. The violent innovations in the reign of HENRY VIII. proceeded from an imperious monarch, seconded by the appearance of legislative authority: Those in the reign of CHARLES I. were derived from faction and fanaticism, and both of them have proved happy in the issue: But even the former were long the source of many disorders, and still more dangers; and if the measures of allegiance were to be taken from the latter, a total anarchy must have place in human society, and a final period at once be put to every government.

Suppose, that an usurper, after having banished his lawful prince and royal family, should establish his dominion for ten or a dozen years in any country, and should preserve so exact a discipline in his troops, and so regular a disposition in his garrisons, that no insurrection had ever been raised, or even murmur heard, against his administration: Can it be asserted, that the people, who in their hearts abhor his treason, have tacitly consented to his authority, and promised him allegiance, merely because, from necessity, they live under his dominion? Suppose again their native prince restored, by means of an army, which he levies in foreign countries: They receive him with joy and exultation, and shew plainly with what reluctance they had submitted to any other yoke. I may now ask, upon what foundation the prince's title stands? Not on popular consent surely: For though the people willingly acquiesce in his authority, they never imagine, that their consent made him sovereign. They consent; because they apprehend him to be already, by birth, their lawful sovereign. And as to that tacit consent, which may now be inferred from their living under his dominion, this is no more than what they formerly gave to the tyrant and usurper.

When we assert, that all lawful government arises from the consent of the people, we certainly do them a great deal more honour than they deserve, or even expect and desire from us. After the ROMAN dominions became too unwieldly for the republic to govern them, the people, over the whole known world, were extremely grateful to AUGUSTUS for that authority, which, by violence, he had established over them; and they showed an equal disposition to submit to the successor, whom he left them, by his last will and testament. It was afterwards their misfortune, that there never was, in one family, any long regular succession; but that their line of princes was continually broken, either by private assassinations or public rebellions. The *prætorian* bands, on the failure of every family, set up one emperor; the legions in the East a second; those in GERMANY, perhaps, a third: And the sword alone could decide the controversy. The condition of the people, in that mighty monarchy, was to be lamented, not because the choice of the emperor was never left to them; for that was impracticable: But because they never fell under any succession of masters, who might regularly follow each other. As to the violence and wars and bloodshed, occasioned by every new settlement; these were not blameable, because they were inevitable.

The house of LANCASTER ruled in this island about sixty years;[9] yet the partizans of the white rose seemed daily to multiply in ENGLAND. The present establishment has taken place during a still longer period. Have all views of right in another family been utterly extinguished; even though scarce any man now alive had arrived at years of discretion, when it was expelled, or could have consented to its dominion, or have promised it allegiance? A sufficient indication surely of the general sentiment of mankind on this head. For we blame not the partizans of the abdicated family, merely on account of the long time, during which they have preserved their imaginary loyalty. We blame them for adhering to a family, which, we affirm, has been justly expelled, and which, from the moment the new settlement took place, had forfeited all title to authority.

But would we have a more regular, at least a more philosophical, refutation of this principle of an original contract or popular consent; perhaps, the following observations may suffice.

All *moral* duties may be divided into two kinds. The *first* are those, to which men are impelled by a natural instinct or immediate propensity, which operates on them, independent of all ideas of obligation, and of all views, either to public or private utility. Of this nature are, love of children, gratitude to benefactors, pity to the unfortunate. When we reflect on the advantage, which results to society from such humane instincts, we pay them the just tribute of moral approbation and esteem: But the person, actuated by them, feels their power and influence, antecedent to any such reflection.

The *second* kind of moral duties are such as are not supported by any original instinct of nature, but are performed entirely from a sense of obligation, when we consider the necessities of human society, and the impossibility of supporting it, if these duties were neglected. It is thus *justice* or a regard to the property of others, *fidelity* or the observance of promises, become obligatory, and acquire an authority over mankind. For as it is evident, that every man loves himself better than any other person, he is naturally impelled to extend his acquisitions as much as possible; and nothing can restrain him in this propensity, but reflection and experience, by which he learns the pernicious effects of that licence, and the total dissolution of society which must ensue from it. His original inclination, therefore, or instinct, is here checked and restrained by a subsequent judgment or observation.

The case is precisely the same with the political or civil duty of *allegiance*, as with the natural duties of justice and fidelity. Our primary instincts lead us, either to indulge ourselves in unlimited freedom, or to seek dominion over others: And it is reflection only, which engages us to sacrifice such strong passions to the interests of peace and public order. A small degree of experience and observation suffices to teach us, that society cannot possibly be maintained without the authority of magistrates, and that this authority must soon fall into contempt, where exact obedience is not paid to it. The observation of these general and obvious interests is the source of all allegiance, and of that moral obligation, which we attribute to it.

What necessity, therefore, is there to found the duty of *allegiance* or obedience to magistrates on that of *fidelity* or a regard to promises, and to suppose, that it is the consent of each individual, which subjects him to government; when it appears, that both allegiance and fidelity stand precisely on the same foundation, and are both submitted to by mankind, on account of the apparent interests and necessities of human society? We are bound to obey our sovereign, it is said; because we have given a tacit promise to that purpose. But why are we bound to observe our promise? It must here be asserted, that the commerce and intercourse of mankind, which are of such mighty advantage, can have no security where men pay no regard to their engagements. In like manner, may it be said, that men could not live at all in society, at least in a civilized society, without laws and magistrates and judges, to prevent the encroachments of the strong upon the weak, of the violent upon the just and equitable. The obligation to allegiance being of like force and authority with the obligation to fidelity, we gain nothing by resolving the one into the other. The general interests or necessities of society are sufficient to establish both.

If the reason be asked of that obedience, which we are bound to pay to government, I readily answer, *because society could not otherwise subsist*: And this answer is clear and intelligible to all mankind. Your answer is, *because we should keep our word*. But besides, that no body, till trained in a philosophical system, can either comprehend or relish this answer: Besides this, I say, you find yourself embarrassed, when it is asked, *why we are bound to keep our word?* Nor can you give any answer, but what would, immediately, without any circuit, have accounted for our obligation to allegiance.

But *to whom is allegiance due? And who is our lawful sovereign?* This question is often the most difficult of any, and liable to infinite discussions. When people are so happy, that they can answer, *Our present sovereign, who inherits, in a direct line, from ancestors, that have governed us for many ages;* this answer admits of no reply; even though historians, in tracing up to the remotest antiquity, the origin of that royal family, may find, as commonly happens, that its first authority was derived from usurpation and violence. It is confessed, that private justice, or the abstinence from the properties of others, is a most cardinal virtue: Yet reason tells us, that there is no property in durable objects, such as lands or houses, when carefully examined in passing from hand to hand, but must, in some period, have been founded on fraud and injustice. The necessities of human society, neither in private nor public life, will allow of such an accurate enquiry: And there is no virtue or moral duty, but what may, with facility, be refined away, if we indulge a false philosophy, in sifting and scrutinizing it, by every captious rule of logic, in every light or position, in which it may be placed.

The questions with regard to private property have filled infinite volumes of law and philosophy, if in both we add the commentators to the original text; and in the end, we may safely pronounce, that many of the rules, there established, are uncertain, ambiguous, and arbitrary. The like opinion may be formed with regard to the succession and rights of princes and forms of government.[10] Several cases, no doubt, occur, especially in the infancy of any constitution, which admit of no determination from the laws of justice and equity: And our historian RAPIN [11]pretends, that the controversy between EDWARD the THIRD and PHILIP DE VALOIS was of this nature, and could be decided only by an appeal to heaven, that is, by war and violence.

Who shall tell me, whether GERMANICUS or DRUSUS ought to have succeeded to TIBERIUS, had he died, while they were both alive, without naming any of them for his successor? Ought the right of adoption to be received as equivalent to that of blood, in a nation, where it had the same effect in private families, and had already, in two instances, taken place in the public? Ought GERMANICUS to be esteemed the elder son because he was born before DRUSUS; or the younger, because he was adopted after the birth of his brother? Ought the right of the elder to be regarded in a nation, where he had no advantage in the succession of private families? Ought the ROMAN empire at that time to be deemed hereditary, because of two examples; or ought it, even so early, to be regarded as belonging to the stronger or to the present possessor, as being founded on so recent an usurpation?

COMMODUS mounted the throne after a pretty long succession of excellent emperors, who had acquired their title, not by birth, or public election, but by the fictitious rite of adoption. That bloody debauchee being murdered by a conspiracy suddenly formed between his wench and her gallant, who happened at that time to be *Prætorian Præfect*; these immediately deliberated about choosing a master to human kind, to speak in the style of those ages; and they cast their eyes on PERTINAX. Before the tyrant's death was known, the *Præfect* went secretly to that senator, who, on the appearance of the soldiers, imagined that his execution had been ordered by COMMODUS. He was immediately saluted emperor by the officer and his attendants; chearfully proclaimed by the populace; unwillingly submitted to by the guards; formally recognized by the senate; and passively received by the provinces and armies of the empire.

The discontent of the *Prætorian* bands broke out in a sudden sedition, which occasioned the murder of that excellent prince: And the world being now without a master and without government, the guards thought proper to set the empire formally to sale. JULIAN, the purchaser, was proclaimed by the soldiers, recognized by the senate, and submitted to by the people; and must also have been submitted to by the provinces, had not the envy of the legions begotten opposition and resistance. PESCENNIUS NIGER in SYRIA elected himself emperor, gained the tumultuary consent of his army, and was attended with the secret good-will of the senate and people of ROME. ALBINUS in BRITAIN found an equal right to set up his claim; but SEVERUS, who governed PANNONIA, prevailed in the end above both of them. That able politician and warrior, finding his own birth and dignity too much inferior to the imperial crown, professed, at first, an intention only of revenging the death of PERTINAX. He marched as general into

ITALY; defeated JULIAN; and without our being able to fix any precise commencement even of the soldiers' consent, he was from necessity acknowledged emperor by the senate and people; and fully established in his violent authority by subduing NIGER and ALBINUS.[12]

Inter hœc Gordianus CÆSAR (says CAPITOLINUS, speaking of another period) *sublatus a militibus,* Imperator *est appellatus, quia non erat alius in præsenti,* It is to be remarked, that GORDIAN was a boy of fourteen years of age.

Frequent instances of a like nature occur in the history of the emperors; in that of ALEXANDER's successors; and of many other countries: Nor can anything be more unhappy than a despotic government of this kind; where the succession is disjoined and irregular, and must be determined, on every vacancy, by force or election. In a free government, the matter is often unavoidable, and is also much less dangerous. The interests of liberty may there frequently lead the people, in their own defence, to alter the succession of the crown. And the constitution, being compounded of parts, may still maintain a sufficient stability, by resting on the aristocratical or democratical members, though the monarchical be altered, from time to time, in order to accommodate it to the former.

In an absolute government, when there is no legal prince, who has a title to the throne, it may safely be determined to belong to the first occupant. Instances of this kind are but too frequent, especially in the eastern monarchies. [13]When any race of princes expires, the will or destination of the last sovereign will be regarded as a title. Thus the edict of LEWIS the XIVth, who called the bastard princes to the succession in case of the failure of all the legitimate princes, would, in such an event, have some authority.[14] [15]Thus the will of CHARLES the Second disposed of the whole SPANISH monarchy. The cession of the ancient proprietor, especially when joined to conquest, is likewise deemed a good title. The general obligation, which binds us to government, is the interest and necessities of society; and this obligation is very strong. The determination of it to this or that particular prince or form of government is frequently more uncertain and dubious. Present possession has considerable authority in these cases, and greater than in private property; because of the disorders which attend all revolutions and changes of government.[16]

We shall only observe, before we conclude, that, though an appeal to general opinion may justly, in the speculative sciences of metaphysics, natural philosophy, or astronomy, be deemed unfair and inconclusive, yet in all questions with regard to morals, as well as criticism, there is really no other standard, by which any controversy can ever be decided. And nothing is a clearer proof, that a theory of this kind is erroneous, than to find, that it leads to paradoxes, repugnant to the common sentiments of mankind, and to the practice and opinion of all nations and all ages. The doctrine, which founds all lawful government on an *original contract,* or consent of the people, is plainly of this kind; nor has the most noted of its partizans, in prosecution of it, scrupled to affirm, *that absolute monarchy is inconsistent with civil society, and so can be no form of civil government at all,*[17] and *that the supreme power in a state cannot take from any man, by taxes and impositions, any part of his property, without his own consent or that of his representatives.*[18] What authority any moral reasoning can have, which leads into opinions so wide of the general practice of mankind, in every place but this single kingdom, it is easy to determine.[19]

The only passage I meet with in antiquity, where the obligation of obedience to government is ascribed to a promise, is in PLATO's *Crito*: where SOCRATES refuses to escape from prison, because he had tacitly promised to obey the laws. Thus he builds a *tory* consequence of passive obedience, on a *whig* foundation of the original contract.

New discoveries are not to be expected in these matters. If scarce any man, till very lately, ever imagined that government was founded on compact, it is certain that it cannot, in general, have any such foundation.

The crime of rebellion among the ancients was commonly expressed by the terms νεωτερίζειν, *novas res moliri*.

Notes

[1] [An Elizabeth or a Henry the 4th of France: Editions D to P.]

[2] [Or equality: added in Editions Q.]

[3] [This paragraph was added in Edition R.]

[4] [The two following paragraphs were added in Edition K.]

[5] Lib. ii. cap. 38.

[6] [This paragraph and the next were added in Edition K.]

[7] TACIT. Ann. vi. cap. 14.

[8] [This paragraph was added in Edition R.]

[9] [The latter half of this sentence was added in Edition K.]

[10] [Edition D omits from this sentence down to 'monarchies' on page 214: and substitutes as follows — The Discussion of these Matters would lead us entirely beyond the Compass of these Essays. 'Tis sufficient for our present Purpose, if we have been able to determine, in general, the Foundation of that Allegiance, which is due to the established Government, in every Kingdom and Commonwealth. When there is no legal Prince, who has a Title to a Throne, I believe it may safely be determined to belong to the first Occupier. This was frequently the Case with the ROMAN Empire.]

[11] [Allows: Editions K to P.]

[12] HERODIAN, lib. ii.

[13] [In Edition D the remainder of this paragraph is given in continuation of the following note.]

[14] It is remarkable, that, in the remonstrance of the duke of BOURBON and the legitimate princes, against this destination of LOUIS the XIVth, the doctrine of the *original contract* is insisted on, even in that absolute government. The FRENCH nation, say they, chusing HUGH CAPET and his posterity to rule over them and their posterity, where the former line fails, there is a tacit right reserved to choose a new royal family; and this right is invaded by calling the bastard princes to the throne, without the consent of the nation. But the Comte de BOULAINVILLIERS, who wrote in defence of the bastard princes, ridicules this notion of an original contract, especially when applied to HUGH CAPET; who mounted the throne, says he, by the same arts, which have ever been employed by all conquerors and usurpers. He got his title, indeed, recognized by the states after he had put himself in possession: But is this a choice or a contract? The Comte de BOULAINVILLIERS, we may observe, was a noted republican; but being a man of learning, and very conversant in history, he knew that the people were never almost consulted in these revolutions and new establishments, and that time alone bestowed right and authority on what was commonly at first founded on force and violence. See *Etat de la France*, Vol. III.

[15] [This sentence was added in Edition M.]

[16] [Here Editions K to P subjoin in a note what is now the concluding paragraph of the Essay.]

[17] See LOCKE on Government, chap. vii. § 90.

[18] Id. chap. xi. § 138, 139, 140.

[19] [At this point editions D to P stop. Editions K to P give the next two paragraphs as a note; they have already given the concluding one as a note on another page.]

Part IV
The Status of Followers

21. Discourses on Livy*

Niccolo Machiavelli

Chapter LVIII.
The People Are Wiser and More Constant Than Princes.

Titus Livius as well as all other historians affirm that nothing is more uncertain and inconstant than the multitude; for it appears from what he relates of the actions of men, that in many instances the multitude, after having condemned a man to death, bitterly lamented it, and most earnestly wished him back. This was the case with the Roman people and Manlius Capitolinus, whom they had condemned to death and afterwards most earnestly desired him back, as our author says in the following words: "No sooner had they found out that they had nothing to fear from him, than they began to regret and to wish him back." And elsewhere, when he relates the events that occurred in Syracuse after the death of Hieronymus, nephew of Hiero, he says: "It is the nature of the multitude either humbly to serve or insolently to dominate." I know not whether, in undertaking to defend a cause against the accusations of all writers, I do not assume a task so hard and so beset with difficulties as to oblige me to abandon it with shame, or to go on with it at the risk of being weighed down by it. Be that as it may, however, I think, and ever shall think, that it cannot be wrong to defend one's opinions with arguments founded upon reason, without employing force or authority.

I say, then, that individual men, and especially princes, may be charged with the same defects of which writers accuse the people; for whoever is not controlled by laws will commit the same errors as an unbridled multitude. This may easily be verified, for there have been and still are plenty of princes, and a few good and wise ones, such, I mean, as needed not the curb that controlled them. Amongst these, however, are not to be counted either the kings that lived in Egypt at that ancient period when that country was governed

---

* Niccolo Machiavelli finished writing *Discorsi sopra la Prima Deca di Tito Livio* (*Discourses on the First Decade of Titus Livius*) between 1513 and 1517; it was published posthumously in the year 1531. This particular selection was taken from Machiavelli, *The Historical, Political, and Diplomatic Writings of Niccolo Machiavelli*, Volume II, Book I, Chapter LVIII, translated by Christian E. Detmold (Boston: James R. Osgood and Company, 1882), 214–219.

by laws, or those that arose in Sparta; neither such as are born in our day in France, for that country is more thoroughly regulated by laws than any other of which we have any knowledge in modern times. And those kings that arise under such constitutions are not to be classed amongst the number of those whose individual nature we have to consider, and see whether it resembles that of the people; but they should be compared with a people equally controlled by law as those kings were, and then we shall find in that multitude the same good qualities as in those kings, and we shall see that such a people neither obey with servility nor command with insolence. Such were the people of Rome, who, so long as that republic remained uncorrupted, neither obeyed basely nor ruled insolently, but rather held its rank honorably, supporting the laws and their magistrates. And when the unrighteous ambition of some noble made it necessary for them to rise up in self-defence, they did so, as in the case of Manlius, the Decemvirs, and others who attempted to oppress them; and so when the public good required them to obey the Dictators and Consuls, they promptly yielded obedience. And if the Roman people regretted Manlius Capitolinus after his death, it is not to be wondered at; for they regretted his virtues, which had been such that the remembrance of them filled every one with pity, and would have had the power to produce the same effect upon any prince; for all writers agree that virtue is to be admired and praised, even in one's enemies. And if intense desire could have restored Manlius to life, the Roman people would nevertheless have pronounced the same judgment against him as they did the first time, when they took him from prison and condemned him to death. And so we have seen princes that were esteemed wise, who have caused persons to be put to death and afterwards regretted it deeply; such as Alexander the Great with regard to Clitus and other friends, and Herod with his wife Mariamne. But what our historian says of the character of the multitude does not apply to a people regulated by laws, as the Romans were, but to an unbridled multitude, such as the Syracusans; who committed all the excesses to which infuriated and unbridled men abandon themselves, as did Alexander the Great and Herod in the above-mentioned cases.

Therefore, the character of the people is not to be blamed any more than that of princes, for both alike are liable to err when they are without any control. Besides the examples already given, I could adduce numerous others from amongst the Roman Emperors and other tyrants and princes, who have displayed as much inconstancy and recklessness as any populace ever did. Contrary to the general opinion, then, which maintains that the people, when they govern, are inconsistent, unstable, and ungrateful, I conclude and affirm that these defects are not more natural to the people than they are to princes. To charge the people and princes equally with them may be the truth, but to except princes from them would be a great mistake. For a people that governs and is well regulated by laws will be stable, prudent, and grateful, as much so, and even more, according to my opinion, than a prince, although he be esteemed wise; and, on the other hand, a prince, freed from the restraints of the law, will be more ungrateful, inconstant, and imprudent than a people similarly situated. The difference in their conduct is not due to any difference in their nature (for that is the same, and if there be any difference for good, it is on the side of the people); but to the greater or less respect they have for the laws under which they respectively live. And whoever studies the Roman people will see that for four hundred years they have been haters of royalty, and lovers of the glory and common good of their country; and he will find any number of examples that will prove both the one and the other. And should any one allege the ingratitude which the Roman people displayed towards Scipio, I shall reply the same as I have said in another place on this subject, where I have demonstrated that the people are less ungrateful than princes. But as regards prudence and stability, I say that the people are more prudent and stable, and have better judgment than a prince; and it is not without good reason that it is said, "The voice of the people is the voice of God"; for we see popular opinion prognosticate events in such a wonderful manner that it would almost seem as if the people had some occult virtue, which enables them to foresee the good and the evil. As to the people's capacity of judging of things, it is exceedingly rare that, when they hear two orators of equal talents advocate different measures, they do not decide in favor of the best of the two; which proves their ability to discern the truth of what they hear. And if occasionally they are misled in matters involving questions of courage or seeming utility, (as has been said above,) so is a prince also many times misled by his own passions, which are much greater than those of the people. We also see that in the election of their magistrates they make far better choice than princes; and no people will ever be persuaded to elect a man of infamous character and corrupt habits to any post of dignity, to which a prince is easily influenced in a thousand different ways. When we see a people take an aversion to anything, they persist in it for many centuries, which we never find to be the case with princes. Upon both these points the Roman people shall serve me as a proof, who in the many elections of Consuls and Tribunes had to regret only four times the choice they had made. The Roman people held the name of king in such detestation, as we have said, that no extent of services rendered by any of its citizens who attempted to usurp that title could save him from his merited punishment. We furthermore see the cities where the people are masters make the greatest progress in the least possible time, and much greater than such as have always been governed by princes; as was the case with Rome after the expulsion of the kings, and with Athens after they rid themselves of Pisistratus; and this can be attributed to no other cause than that the governments of the people are better than those of princes.

It would be useless to object to my opinion by referring to what our historian has said in the passages quoted above, and elsewhere; for if we compare the faults of a people with those of princes, as well as their respective good qualities, we shall find the people vastly superior in all that is good and glorious. And if princes show themselves superior in the making of laws, and in the forming of civil institutions and new statutes and ordinances, the people are superior in maintaining those institutions, laws, and ordinances, which certainly places them on a par with those who established them.

And finally to sum up this matter, I say that both governments of princes and of the people have lasted a long time, but both required to be regulated by laws. For a prince who knows no other control but his own will is like a madman, and a people that can do as it pleases will hardly be wise. If now we compare a prince who is controlled by laws, and a people that is untrammelled by them, we shall find more virtue in the people than in the prince; and if we compare them when both are freed from such control, we shall see that the people are guilty of fewer excesses than the prince, and that the errors of the people are of less importance, and therefore more easily remedied. For a licentious and mutinous people may easily be brought back to good conduct by the influence and persuasion of a good man, but an evil-minded prince is not amenable to such influences, and therefore there is no other remedy against him but cold steel. We may judge then from this of the relative defects of the one and the other; if words suffice to correct those of the people, whilst those of the prince can only be remedied by violence, no one can fail to see that where the greater remedy is required, there also the defects must be greater. The follies which a people commits at the moment of its greatest license are not what is most to be feared; it is not the immediate evil that may result from them that inspires apprehension, but the fact that such general confusion might afford the opportunity for a tyrant to seize the government. But with evil-disposed princes the contrary is the case; it is the immediate present that causes fear, and there is hope only in the future; for men will persuade themselves that the termination of his wicked life may give them a chance of liberty. Thus we see the difference between the one and the other to be, that the one touches the present and the other the future. The excesses of the people are directed against those whom they suspect of interfering with the public good; whilst those of princes are against apprehended interference with their individual interests. The general prejudice against the people results from the fact that everybody can freely and fearlessly speak ill of them in mass, even whilst they are at the height of their power; but a prince can only be spoken of with the greatest circumspection and apprehension. And as the subject leads me to it, I deem it not amiss to examine in the following chapter whether alliances with a republic or with a prince are most to be trusted.

22. The Phenomenology of Mind[*]

Georg Wilhelm Friedrich Hegel

A

Independence and Dependence of Self-Consciousness
Lordship and Bondage

[*Translator's note*: The selves conscious of self in another self are, of course, distinct and separate from each other. The difference is, in the first instance, a question of degree of self-assertion and self-maintenance: one is stronger, higher, more independent than another, and capable of asserting this at the expense of the other. Still, even this distinction of primary and secondary rests ultimately on their identity of constitution; and the course of the analysis here gradually brings out this essential identity as the true fact. The equality of the selves is the truth, or completer realisation, of self in another self; the affinity is higher and more ultimate than the disparity. Still, the struggle and conflict of selves must be gone through in order to bring out this result. Hence the present section.

The background of Hegel's thought is the remarkable human phenomenon of the subordination of one self to another which we have in all forms of servitude — whether slavery, serfdom, or voluntary service. Servitude is not only a phase of human history, it is in principle a condition of the development and maintenance of the consciousness of self as a fact of experience.]

Self-consciousness exists in itself and for itself, in that, and by the fact that it exists for another self-consciousness; that is to say, it *is* only by being acknowledged or

[*] Georg Wilhelm Friedrich Hegel published *The Phenomenology of Mind* in 1807. This particular selection was taken from Hegel, *The Phenomenology of Mind,* translated with an introduction and notes by J.B. Baillie (London: Swan Sonnenschein & Co., Limited, 1910), 175–188.

"recognised." The conception of this its unity in its duplication, of infinitude realising itself in self-consciousness, has many sides to it and encloses within it elements of varied significance. Thus its moments must on the one hand be strictly kept apart in detailed distinctiveness, and, on the other, in this distinction must, at the same time, also be taken as not distinguished, or must always be accepted and understood in their opposite sense. This double meaning of what is distinguished lies in the nature of selfconsciousness: — of its being infinite, or directly the opposite of the determinateness in which it is fixed. The detailed exposition of the notion of this spiritual unity in its duplication will bring before us the process of Recognition.

Self-consciousness has before it another self-consciousness; it has come outside itself. This has a double significance. First it has lost its own self, since it finds itself as an *other* being; secondly, it has thereby sublated that other, for it does not regard the other as essentially real, but sees its own self in the other.

It must cancel this its other. To do so is the sublation of that first double meaning, and is therefore a second double meaning. First, it must set itself to sublate the other independent being, in order thereby to become certain of itself as true being, secondly, it thereupon proceeds to sublate its own self, for this other is itself.

This sublation in a double sense of its otherness in a double sense is at the same time a return in a double sense into its self. For, firstly, through sublation, it gets back itself, because it becomes one with itself again through the cancelling of *its* otherness; but secondly, it likewise gives otherness back again to the other self-consciousness, for it was aware of being in the other, it cancels this its own being in the other and thus lets the other again go free.

This process of self-consciousness in relation to another self-consciousness has in this manner been represented as the action of one alone. But this action on the part of the one has itself the double significance of being at once its own action and the action of that other as well. For the other is likewise independent, shut up within itself, and there is nothing in it which is not there through itself. The first does not have the object before it in the way that object primarily exists for desire, but as an object existing independently for itself, over which therefore it has no power to do anything for its own behoof, if that object does not *per se* do what the first does to it. The process then is absolutely the double process of both self-consciousnesses. Each sees the other do the same as itself; each itself does what it demands on the part of the other, and for that reason does what it does, only so far as the other does the same. Action from one side only would be useless, because what is to happen can only be brought about by means of both.

The action has then a *double entente* not only in the sense that it is an act done to itself as well as to the other, but also inasmuch as it is in its undivided entirety the act of the one as well as of the other.

In this movement we see the process repeated which came before us as the play of forces; in the present case, however, it is found in consciousness. What in the former had effect only for us [contemplating experience], holds here for the terms themselves. The middle term is self-consciousness which breaks itself up into the extremes; and each extreme is this interchange of its own determinateness, and complete transition into the opposite. While *qua* consciousness, it no doubt comes outside itself, still, in being outside itself it is at the same time restrained within itself, it exists for itself, and its self-externalisation is for consciousness. *Consciousness* finds that it immediately is and is not another consciousness, as also that this other is for itself only when it cancels itself as existing for itself, and has self-existence only in the self-existence of the other. Each is the mediating term to the other, through which each mediates and unites itself with itself; and each is to itself and to the other an immediate self-existing reality, which, at the same time, exists thus for itself only through this mediation. They recognise themselves as mutually recognising one another.

This pure conception of recognition, of duplication of self-consciousness within its unity, we must now consider in the way its process appears for self-consciousness. It will, in the first place, present the aspect of the disparity of the two, or the break-up of the middle term into the extremes, which, *qua* extremes, are opposed to one another, and of which one is merely recognised, while the other only recognises.

Self-consciousness is primarily simple existence for self, self-identity by exclusion of every other from itself. It takes its essential nature and absolute object to be Ego; and in this immediacy, in this bare fact of its self-existence, it is individual. That which for it is other stands as unessential object, as object with the impress and character of negation. But the other is also a self-consciousness; an individual makes its appearance in antithesis to an individual. Appearing thus in their immediacy, they are for each other in the manner of ordinary objects. They are independent individual forms, modes of consciousness that have not risen above the bare level of life (for the existent object here has been determined as life). They are, moreover, forms of consciousness which have not yet accomplished for one another the process of absolute abstraction, of uprooting all immediate existence, and of being merely the bare, negative fact of self-identical consciousness; or, in other words, have not yet revealed themselves to each other as existing purely for themselves, i.e. as self-consciousness. Each is indeed certain of its own self, but not of the other, and hence its own certainty of itself is still without truth. For its truth would be merely that its own individual existence for itself would be shown to it to be an independent object, or, which is the same thing, that the object would be exhibited as this pure certainty of itself. By the notion of recognition, however, this is not possible, except in the form that as the other is for it, so it is for the other; each in its self through its own action and again through the action of the other achieves this pure abstraction of existence for self.

The presentation of itself, however, as pure abstraction of self-consciousness consists in showing itself as a pure negation of its objective form, or in showing that it is fettered to no determinate existence, that it is not bound at all by the particularity everywhere characteristic of existence as such, and is *not* tied up with life. The process of bringing all this out involves a twofold action — action on the part of the other, and action on the part of itself. In so far as it is the other's action, each aims at the destruction and death of the other. But in this there is implicated also the second kind of action, self-activity; for each implies that it risks its own life. The relation of both self-consciousnesses is in this way so constituted that they prove themselves and each other through a life-and-death struggle. They must enter into this struggle, for they must bring their certainty of themselves, the certainty of being for themselves, to the level of objective truth, and make this a fact both in the case of the other and in their own case as well. And it is solely by risking life, that freedom is obtained; only thus is it tried and proved that the essential nature of self-consciousness is not bare existence, is not the merely immediate form in which it at first makes its appearance, is not its mere absorption in the expanse of life. Rather it is thereby guaranteed that there is nothing present but what might be taken as a vanishing moment — that self-consciousness is merely pure self-existence, being-for-self. The individual, who has not staked his life, may, no doubt, be recognised as a Person; but he has not attained the truth of this recognition as an independent self-consciousness. In the same way each must aim at the death of the other, as it risks its own life thereby; for that other is to it of no more worth than itself; the other's reality is presented to the former as an external other, as outside itself; it must cancel that externality. The other is a purely existent consciousness and entangled in manifold ways; it must regard its otherness as pure existence for itself or as absolute negation.

This trying and testing, however, by a struggle to the death, cancels both the truth which was to result from it, and therewith the certainty of self altogether. For just as life is the natural "position" of consciousness, independence without absolute negativity, so death is the natural "negation" of consciousness, negation without independence, which thus remains without the requisite significance of actual recognition. Through death, doubtless, there has arisen the certainty that both did stake their life, and held it lightly both in their own case and in the case of the other; but that is not for those who underwent this struggle. They cancel their consciousness which had its place in this alien element of natural existence; in other words, they cancel themselves and are sublated, as terms or extremes seeking to have existence on their own account. But along with this there vanishes from the play of change, the essential moment, viz. that of breaking up into extremes with opposite characteristics; and the middle term collapses into a lifeless unity which is broken up into lifeless extremes, merely existent and not opposed. And the two do not mutually give and receive one another back from each other through consciousness; they let one another go quite indifferently, like things. Their act is abstract negation, not the negation characteristic of consciousness, which cancels in such a way that it preserves and maintains what is sublated, and thereby survives its being sublated.

In this experience self-consciousness becomes aware that *life* is as essential to it as pure self-consciousness. In immediate self-consciousness the simple ego is absolute object, which, however, is for us or in itself absolute mediation, and has as its essential moment substantial and solid independence. The dissolution of that simple unity is the result of the first experience; through this there is posited a pure self-consciousness, and a consciousness which is not purely for itself, but for another, i.e. as an existent consciousness, consciousness in the form and shape of thinghood. Both moments are essential, since, in the first instance, they are unlike and opposed, and their reflexion into unity has not yet come to light, they stand as two opposed forms or modes of consciousness. The one is independent whose essential nature is to be for itself, the other is dependent whose essence is life or existence for another. The former is the Master, or Lord, the latter the Bondsman.

The master is the consciousness that exists *for itself*; but no longer merely the general notion of existence for self. Rather, it is consciousness which, while existing on its own account, is mediated with itself through an other consciousness, viz. bound up with an independent being or with thinghood in general. The master brings himself into relation to both these moments, to a thing as such, the object of desire, and to the consciousness whose essential character is thinghood, and since the master, *qua* notion of self-consciousness, is (*a*) an immediate relation of self-existence, but is now moreover at the same time (*b*) mediation, or a being-for-self which is for itself only through an other — he [the master] stands in relation (*a*) immediately to both (*b*) mediately to each through the other. The master relates himself to the bondsman mediately through independent existence, for that is precisely what keeps the bondsman in thrall; it is his chain, from which he could not in the struggle get away, and for that reason he proves himself dependent, shows that his independence consists in being a thing. The master, however, is the power controlling this state of existence, for he has shown in the struggle that he holds existence to be merely something negative. Since he is the power dominating the negative nature of existence, while this existence again is the power controlling the other [the bondsman], the master holds, *par consequence*, this other in subordination. In the same way the master relates himself to the thing mediately through the bondsman. The bondsman being a self-consciousness in the broad sense, also takes up a negative attitude to things and cancels them; but the thing is, at the same time, independent for him, and, in consequence, he cannot, with all his negating, get so far as to annihilate it outright and be done with it; that is to say, he merely works on it. To the master, on the other hand, by means of this mediating process, belongs the immediate relation, in the sense of the pure negation of it, in other words he gets the enjoyment. What mere desire did not attain, he now succeeds in attaining, viz. to have done with the thing, and find satisfaction in enjoyment. Desire alone did not get the length of this, because of the independence of the thing. The master, however, who has interposed the bondsman between it and himself, thereby relates himself merely to the dependence of the thing, and enjoys it without qualification and without reserve. The aspect of its independence he leaves to the bondsman, who labours upon it.

In these two moments, the master gets his recognition through an other consciousness, for in them the latter affirms itself as unessential, both by working upon the thing, and, on the other hand, by the fact of being dependent on a determinate existence; in neither case can this other get the mastery over existence, and succeed in absolutely negating it. We have thus here this moment of recognition, viz. that the other consciousness cancels itself as self-existent, and, *ipso facto*, itself does what the first does to it. In the same way we have the other moment, that this action on the part of the second is the action proper of the first; for what is done by the bondsman is properly an action on the part of the master. The latter exists only for himself, that is his essential nature; he is the negative power without qualification, a power to which the thing is naught, and his is thus the absolutely essential action in this situation, while the bondsman's is not so, his is an unessential activity. But for recognition proper there is needed the moment that what the master does to the other he should also do to himself, and what the bondsman does to himself, he should do to the other also. On that account a form of recognition has arisen that is one-sided and unequal.

In all this, the unessential consciousness is, for the master, the object which embodies the truth of his certainty of himself. But it is evident that this object does not correspond to its notion; for, just where the master has effectively achieved lordship, he really finds that something has come about quite different from an independent consciousness. It is not an independent, but rather a dependent consciousness that he has achieved. He is thus not assured of self-existence as his truth; he finds that his truth is rather the unessential consciousness, and the fortuitous unessential action of that consciousness.

The truth of the independent consciousness is accordingly the consciousness of the bondsman. This doubtless appears in the first instance outside it, and not as the truth of self-consciousness. But just as lordship showed its essential nature to be the reverse of what it wants to be, so, too, bondage will, when completed, pass into the opposite of what it immediately is: being a consciousness repressed within itself, it will enter into itself, and change round into real and true independence.

We have seen what bondage is only in relation to lordship. But it is a self-consciousness, and we have now to consider what it is, in this regard, in and for itself. In the first instance, the master is taken to be the essential reality for the state of bondage; hence, for it, the truth is the independent consciousness existing for itself, although this truth is not yet taken as inherent in bondage itself. Still, it does in fact contain within itself this truth of pure negativity and self-existence, because it has experienced this reality within it. For this self-consciousness was not in peril and fear for this element or that, nor for this or that moment of time, it was afraid for its entire being; it felt the fear of death, it was in mortal terror of its sovereign master. It has been in that experience melted to its inmost soul, has trembled throughout its every fibre, the stable foundations of its whole being have quaked within it. This complete perturbation of its entire substance, this absolute dissolution of all its stability into fluent continuity, is, however, the simple, ultimate nature of self-consciousness, absolute negativity, pure self-referrent existence, which consequently is involved in this type of consciousness. This moment of pure self-existence is moreover a fact for it; for in the master this moment is consciously his object. Further, this bondsman's consciousness is not only this total dissolution in a general way; in serving and toiling, the bondsman actually carries this out. By serving he cancels in every particular moment his dependence on and attachment to natural existence, and by his work removes this existence away.

The feeling of absolute power, however, realised both in general and in the particular form of service, is only dissolution implicitly, and albeit the fear of his lord is the beginning of wisdom, consciousness is not therein aware of being self-existent. Through work and labour, however, this consciousness of the bondsman comes to itself. In the moment which corresponds to desire in the case of the master's consciousness, the aspect of the non-essential relation to the thing seemed to fall to the lot of the servant, since the thing there retained its independence. Desire has reserved to itself the pure negating of the object and thereby unalloyed feeling of self. This satisfaction, however, just for that reason is itself only a state of evanescence, for it lacks objectivity or subsistence. Labour, on the other hand, is desire restrained and checked, evanescence delayed and postponed; in other words, labour shapes and fashions the thing. The negative relation to the object passes into the *form* of the object, into something that is permanent and remains; because it is just for the labourer that the object has independence. This negative mediating agency, this activity giving shape and form, is at the same time the individual existence, the pure self-existence of that consciousness, which now in the work it does is externalised and passes into the condition of permanence. The consciousness that toils and serves accordingly comes by this means to view that independent being as its self.

But again, shaping or forming the object has not only the positive significance that the bondsman becomes thereby aware of himself as factually and objectively self-existent; this type of consciousness has also a negative import, in contrast with its first moment, the element of fear. For in shaping the thing it only becomes aware of its own proper negativity, its existence on its own account, as an object, through the fact that it cancels the actual form confronting it. But this objective negative element is precisely the alien, external reality, before which it trembled. Now, however, it destroys this extraneous alien negative, affirms and sets itself up as a negative in the element of permanence, and thereby becomes aware of being objectively for itself. In the master, this self-existence is felt to be an other, is only external; in fear, the self-existence is present implicitly; in fashioning the thing, self-existence comes to be felt explicitly as its own proper being, and it attains the consciousness that itself exists in its own right and on its own account (*an und für sich*). By the fact that the form is objectified, it does not become something other than the consciousness moulding the thing through work; for just that form is his pure self-existence, which therein becomes truly realised. Thus precisely in labour where there seemed to be merely some outsider's mind and ideas involved, the bondsman becomes aware, through this re-discovery of himself by himself, of having and being a "mind of his own."

For this reflexion of self into self the two moments, fear and service in general, as also that of formative activity, are necessary: and at the same time both must exist in a universal manner. Without the discipline of service and obedience, fear remains formal and does not spread over the whole known reality of existence. Without the formative activity shaping the thing, fear remains inward and mute, and consciousness does not become objective for itself. Should consciousness shape and form the thing without the initial state of absolute fear, then it has merely a vain and futile "mind of its own"; for its form or negativity is not negativity *per se*, and hence its formative activity cannot furnish the consciousness of itself as essentially real. If it has endured not absolute fear, but merely some slight anxiety, the negative reality has remained external to it, its substance has not been through and through infected thereby. Since the entire content of its natural consciousness has not tottered and shaken, it is still inherently a determinate mode of being; having a "mind of its own" (*der eigen Sinn*) is simply stubbornness (*Eigensinn*), a type of freedom which does not get beyond the attitude of bondage. The less the pure form can become its essential nature, the less is that form, as overspreading and controlling particulars, a universal formative activity, an absolute notion; it is rather a piece of cleverness which has mastery within a certain range, but does not wield universal power and dominate the entire objective reality.

23. A Vindication of the Rights of Woman[*]

Mary Wollstonecraft

Chap. IV.

Observations on the State of Degradation to Which Woman Is Reduced by Various Causes.

That woman is naturally weak, or degraded by a concurrence of circumstances, is, I think, clear. But this position I shall simply contrast with a conclusion, which I have frequently heard fall from sensible men in favour of an aristocracy: that the mass of mankind cannot be any thing, or the obsequious slaves, who patiently allow themselves to be penned up, would feel their own consequence, and spurn their chains. Men, they further observe, submit every where to oppression, when they have only to lift up their heads to throw off the yoke; yet, instead of asserting their birthright, they quietly lick the dust, and say, let us eat and drink, for to-morrow we die. Women, I argue from analogy, are degraded by the same propensity to enjoy the present moment; and, at last, despise the freedom which they have not sufficient virtue to struggle to attain. But I must be more explicit.

With respect to the culture of the heart, it is unanimously allowed that sex is out of the question; but the line of subordination in the mental powers is never to be passed over.[1] Only 'absolute in loveliness,' the portion of rationality granted to woman, is indeed very scanty; for, denying her genius and judgment, it is scarcely possible to divine what remains to characterize intellect.

The stamina of immortality, if I may be allowed the phrase, is the perfectibility of human reason: for, was man created perfect, or did a flood of knowledge break in upon

[*] Mary Wollstonecraft's first edition of *A Vindication of the Rights of Woman* appeared in print in early 1792, and a second edition was released later the same year. This particular selection was taken from Wollstonecraft, *A Vindication of the Rights of Woman: With Strictures on Political and Moral Subjects*, 2d ed., Chapter IV (Boston: printed by Peter Edes for Thomas and Andrews, 1792), 94–121.

him, when he arrived at maturity, that precluded error, I should doubt whether his existence would be continued after the dissolution of the body. But, in the present state of things, every difficulty in morals that escapes from human discussion, and equally baffles the investigation of profound thinking, and the lightning glance of genius, is an argument on which I build my belief of the immortality of the soul. Reason is, consequentially, the simple power of improvement; or, more properly speaking, of discerning truth. Every individual is in this respect a world in itself. More or less may be conspicuous in one being than another; but the nature of reason must be the same in all, if it be an emanation of divinity, the tie that connects the creature with the Creator; for, can that soul be stamped with the heavenly image, that is not perfected by the exercise of its own reason?[2] Yet outwardly ornamented with elaborate care, and so adorned to delight man, 'that with honour he may love,'[3] the soul of woman is not allowed to have this distinction, and man, ever placed between her and reason, she is always represented as only created to see through a gross medium, and to take things on trust. But, dismissing these fanciful theories, and considering woman as a whole; let it be what it will, instead of a part of man, the inquiry is whether she has reason or not. If she has, which, for a moment, I will take for granted, she was not created merely to be the solace of man, and the sexual should not destroy the human character.

Into this error men have, probably, been led by viewing education in a false light; not considering it as the first step to form a being advancing gradually towards perfection;[4] but only as a preparation for life. On this sensual error, for I must call it so, has the false system of female manners been reared, which robs the whole sex of its dignity, and classes the brown and fair with the smiling flowers that only adorns the land. This has ever been the language of men, and the fear of departing from a supposed sexual character, has made even women of superior sense adopt the same sentiments.[5] Thus understanding, strictly speaking, has been denied to woman; and instinct, sublimated into wit and cunning, for the purposes of life, has been substituted in its stead.

The power of generalizing ideas, of drawing comprehensive conclusions from individual observations, is the only acquirement, for an immortal being, that really deserves the name of knowledge. Merely to observe, without endeavouring to account for any thing, may (in a very incomplete manner) serve as the common sense of life; but where is the store laid up that is to clothe the soul when it leaves the body?

This power has not only been denied to women; but writers have insisted that it is inconsistent, with a few exceptions, with their sexual character. Let men prove this, and I shall grant that woman only exists for man. I must, however, previously remark, that the power of generalizing ideas, to any great extent, is not very common amongst men or women. But this exercise is the true cultivation of the understanding; and every thing conspires to render the cultivation of the understanding more difficult in the female than the male world.

I am naturally led by this assertion to the main subject of the present chapter, and shall now attempt to point out some of the causes that degrade the sex, and prevent women from generalizing their observations.

I shall not go back to the remote annals of antiquity to trace the history of woman; it is sufficient to allow that she has always been either a slave, or a despot, and to remark, that each of these situations equally retards the progress of reason. The grand source of female folly and vice has ever appeared to me to arise from narrowness of mind; and the very constitution of civil governments has put almost insuperable obstacles in the way to prevent the cultivation of the female understanding: — yet virtue can be built on no other foundation! The same obstacles are thrown in the way of the rich, and the same consequences ensue.

Necessity has been proverbially termed the mother of invention — the aphorism may be extended to virtue. It is an acquirement, and an acquirement to which pleasure must be sacrificed — and who sacrifices pleasure when it is within the grasp, whose mind has not been opened and strengthened by adversity, or the pursuit of knowledge goaded on by necessity? — Happy is it when people have the cares of life to struggle with; for these struggles prevent their becoming a prey to enervating vices, merely from idleness! But, if from their birth men and women are placed in a torrid zone, with the meridian sun of pleasure darting directly upon them, how can they sufficiently brace their minds to discharge the duties of life, or even to relish the affections that carry them out of themselves?

Pleasure is the business of woman's life, according to the present modification of society, and while it continues to be so, little can be expected from such weak beings. Inheriting, in a lineal descent from the first fair defect in nature, the sovereignty of beauty, they have, to maintain their power, resigned the natural rights, which the exercise of reason might have procured them, and chosen rather to be short-lived queens than labour to obtain the sober pleasures that arise from equality. Exalted by their inferiority (this sounds like a contradiction) they constantly demand homage as women, though experience should teach them that the men who pride themselves upon paying this arbitrary insolent respect to the sex, with the most scrupulous exactness, are most inclined to tyrannize over, and despise, the very weakness they cherish. Often do they repeat Mr. Hume's sentiments; when, comparing the French and Athenian character, he alludes to women. 'But what is more singular in this whimsical nation, say I to the Athenians, is, that a frolic of yours during the Saturnalia, when the slaves are served by their masters, is, seriously, continued by them through the whole year, and through the whole course of their lives; accompanied too with some circumstances, which still further augment the absurdity and ridicule. Your sport only elevates for a few days those whom fortune has thrown down, and whom she too, in sport, may really elevate for ever above you. But this nation gravely exalts those, whom nature has subjected to them, and whose inferiority and infirmities are absolutely incurable. The women, though without virtue, are their masters and sovereigns.'

Ah! why do women, I write with affectionate solicitude, condescend to receive a degree of attention and respect from strangers, different from that reciprocation of civility which the dictates of humanity and the politeness of civilization authorise between man and man? And, why do they not discover, when 'in the noon of beauty's power,' that they are treated like queens only to be deluded by hollow respect, till they are led to resign, or not assume, their natural prerogatives? Confined then in cages like the feathered race, they have nothing to do but to plume themselves, and stalk with mock majesty from perch to perch. It is true they are provided with food and raiment, for which they neither toil nor spin; but health, liberty, and virtue, are given in exchange. But, where, amongst mankind has been found sufficient strength of mind to enable a being to resign these adventitious prerogatives; one who, rising with the calm dignity of reason above opinion, dared to be proud of the privileges inherent in man? And it is vain to expect it whilst hereditary power chokes the affections and nips reason in the bud.

The passions of men have thus placed women on thrones, and, till mankind become more reasonable, it is to be feared that women will avail themselves of the power which they attain with the least exertion, and which is the most indisputable. They will smile, — yes, they will smile, though told that —

> 'In beauty's empire is no mean,
> 'And woman, either slave or queen,
> 'Is quickly scorn'd when not ador'd.'

But the adoration comes first, and the scorn is not anticipated.

Lewis the XIVth, in particular, spread factitious manners, and caught, in a specious way, the whole nation in his toils; for, establishing an artful chain of despotism, he made it the interest of the people at large, individually to respect his station and support his power. And women, whom he flattered by a puerile attention to the whole sex, obtained in his reign that prince-like distinction so fatal to reason and virtue.

A king is always a king — and a woman always a woman:[6] his authority and her sex, ever stand between them and rational converse. With a lover, I grant; she should be so, and her sensibility will naturally lead her to endeavour to excite emotion, not to gratify her vanity, but her heart. This I do not allow to be coquetry, it is the artless impulse of nature, I only exclaim against the sexual desire of conquest when the heart is out of the question.

This desire is not confined to women; 'I have endeavoured,' says Lord Chesterfield, 'to gain the hearts of twenty women, whose persons I would not have given a fig for.' The libertine, who, in a gust of passion, takes advantage of unsuspecting tenderness, is a saint when compared with this cold-hearted rascal; for I like to use significant words. Yet only taught to please, women are always on the watch to please, and with true heroic ardour endeavour to gain hearts merely to resign, or spurn them, when the victory is decided, and conspicuous.

I must descend to the minutiæ of the subject.

I lament that women are systematically degraded by receiving the trivial attentions, which men think it manly to pay to the sex, when, in fact, they are insultingly supporting their own superiority. It is not condescension to bow to an inferiour. So ludicrous, in fact, do these ceremonies appear to me, that I scarcely am able to govern my muscles, when I see a man start with eager, and serious solicitude to lift a handkerchief, or shut a door, when the *lady* could have done it herself, had she only moved a pace or two.

A wild wish has just flown from my heart to my head, and I will not stifle it though it may excite a horse-laugh. — I do earnestly wish to see the distinction of sex confounded in society, unless where love animates the behaviour. For this distinction is, I am firmly persuaded, the foundation of the weakness of character ascribed to woman; is the cause why the understanding is neglected, whilst accomplishments are acquired with sedulous care: and the same cause accounts for their preferring the graceful before the heroic virtues.

Mankind, including every description, wish to be loved and respected for *something*; and the common herd will always take the nearest road to the completion of their wishes. The respect paid to wealth and beauty is the most certain, and unequivocal; and, of course, will always attract the vulgar eye of common minds. Abilities and virtues are absolutely necessary to raise men from the middle rank of life into notice; and the natural consequence is notorious, the middle rank contains most virtue and abilities. Men have thus, in one station, at least, an opportunity of exerting themselves with dignity, and of rising by the exertions which really improve a rational creature; but the whole female sex are, till their character is formed, in the same condition as the rich: for they are born, I now speak of a state of civilization, with certain sexual privileges, and whilst they are gratuitously granted them, few will ever think of works of supererogation, to obtain the esteem of a small number of superior people.

When do we hear of women who, starting out of obscurity, boldly claim respect on account of their great abilities or daring virtues? Where are they to be found? — 'To be observed, to be attended to, to be taken notice of with sympathy, complacency, and approbation, are all the advantages which they seek.' — True! my male readers will probably exclaim; but let them, before they draw any conclusion, recollect that this was not written originally as descriptive of women, but of the rich. In Dr. Smith's Theory of Moral Sentiments, I have found a general character of people of rank and fortune, that, in my opinion, might with the greatest propriety be applied to the female sex. I refer the sagacious reader to the whole comparison; but must be allowed to quote a passage to enforce an argument that I mean to insist on, as the one most conclusive against a sexual character. For if, excepting warriors, no great men, of any denomination, have ever appeared amongst the nobility, may it not be fairly inferred that their local situation swallowed up the man, and produced a character similar to that of women, who are *localized*, if I may be allowed the word, by the rank they are placed in, by *courtesy*? Women, commonly called Ladies, are not to be contradicted in company, are not allowed to exert any manual strength; and from them the negative virtues only are expected, when any virtues are expected, patience, docility, good-humour, and flexibility; virtues incompatible with any vigorous exertion of intellect. Besides, by living more with each other, and being seldom absolutely alone, they are more under the influence of sentiments than passions. Solitude and reflection are necessary to give to wishes the force of passions, and to enable the imagination to enlarge the object, and make it the most desirable. The same may be said of the rich; they do not sufficiently deal in general ideas, collected by impassioned thinking, or calm investigation, to acquire that strength of character on which great resolves are built. But hear what an acute observer says of the great.

'Do the great seem insensible of the easy price at which they may acquire the publick admiration; or do they seem to imagine that to them, as to other men, it must be the purchase either of sweat or of blood? By what important accomplishments is the young nobleman instructed to support the dignity of his rank, and to render himself worthy of that superiority over his fellow-citizens, to which the virtue of his ancestors had raised them? Is it by knowledge, by industry, by patience, by self-denial, or by virtue of any kind? As all his words, as all his motions are attended to, he learns an habitual regard to every circumstance of ordinary behaviour, and studies to perform all those small duties with the most exact propriety. As he is conscious how much he is observed, and how much mankind are disposed to favour all his inclinations, he acts, upon the most indifferent occasions, with that freedom and elevation which the thought of this naturally inspires. His air, his manner, his deportment, all mark that elegant and graceful sense of his own superiority, which those who are born to inferiour station can hardly ever arrive at. These are the arts by which he proposes to make mankind more easily submit to his authority, and to govern their inclinations according to his own pleasure: and in this he is seldom disappointed. These arts, supported by rank and pre-eminence, are, upon ordinary occasions, sufficient to govern the world. Lewis XIV. during the greater part of his reign, was regarded, not only in France, but over all Europe, as the most perfect model of a great prince. But what were the talents and virtues by which he acquired this great reputation? Was it by the scrupulous and inflexible justice of all his undertakings, by the immense dangers and difficulties with which they were attended, or by the unwearied and unrelenting application with which he pursued them? Was it by his extensive knowledge, by his exquisite judgment, or by his heroic valour? It was by none of these qualities. But he was, first of all, the most powerful prince in Europe, and consequently held the highest rank among kings; and then, says his historian, "he surpassed all his courtiers in the gracefulness of his shape, and the majestic beauty of his features. The sound of his voice, noble and affecting, gained those hearts which his presence intimidated. He had a step and a deportment which could suit only him and his rank, and which would have been ridiculous in any other person. The embarrassment which he occasioned to those who spoke to him, flattered that secret satisfaction with which he felt his own superiority." 'These frivolous accomplishments, supported by his rank, and, no doubt too, by a degree of other talents and virtues, which seems, however, not to have been much above mediocrity, established this prince in the esteem of his own age, and have drawn, even from posterity, a good deal of respect for his memory. Compared with these, in his own times, and in his own presence, no other virtue, it seems, appeared to have any merit. Knowledge, industry, valour, and beneficence, trembled, were abashed, and lost all dignity before them.'

Woman also thus 'in herself complete,' by possessing all these *frivolous* accomplishments, so changes the nature of things

> — 'That what she wills to do or say
> 'Seems wisest, virtuousest, discreetest, best;
> 'All higher knowledge in *her presence* falls
> 'Degraded. Wisdom in discourse with her
> 'Loses discountenanc'd, and, like Folly, shows;
> 'Authority and Reason on her wait.' —

And all this is built on her loveliness!

In the middle rank of life, to continue the comparison, men, in their youth, are prepared for professions, and marriage is not considered as the grand feature in their lives; whilst women, on the contrary, have no other scheme to sharpen their faculties. It is not business, extensive plans, or any of the excursive flights of ambition, that engross their attention; no, their thoughts are not employed in rearing such noble structures. To rise in the world, and have the liberty of running from pleasure to pleasure, they must marry advantageously, and to this object their time is sacrificed, and their persons often legally prostituted. A man when he enters any profession has his eye steadily fixed on some future advantage (and the mind gains great strength by having all its efforts directed to one point) and, full of his business, pleasure is considered as mere relaxation; whilst women seek for pleasure as the main purpose of existence. In fact, from the education, which they receive from society, the love of pleasure may be said to govern them all; but does this prove that there is a sex in souls? It would be just as rational to declare that the courtiers in France, when a destructive system of despotism had formed their character, were not men, because liberty, virtue, and humanity, were sacrificed to pleasure and vanity. — Fatal passions, which have ever domineered over the *whole* race!

The same love of pleasure, fostered by the whole tendency of their education, gives a trifling turn to the conduct of women in most circumstances: for instance, they are ever anxious about secondary things; and on the watch for adventures; instead of being occupied by duties.

A man, when he undertakes a journey, has, in general, the end in view; a woman thinks more of the incidental occurrences, the strange things that may possibly occur on the road; the impression that she may make on her fellow-travellers; and, above all, she is anxiously intent on the care of the finery that she carries with her, which is more than ever a part of herself, when going to figure on a new scene; when, to use an apt French turn of expression, she is going to produce a sensation. — Can dignity of mind exist with such trivial cares?

In short, women, in general, as well as the rich of both sexes, have acquired all the follies and vices of civilization, and missed the useful fruit. It is not necessary for me always to premise, that I speak of the condition of the whole sex, leaving exceptions out of the question. Their senses are inflamed, and their understandings neglected, consequently they become the prey of their senses, delicately termed sensibility, and are blown about by every momentary gust of feeling. They are, therefore, in a much worse condition than they would be in were they in a state nearer to nature. Ever restless and anxious, their over exercised sensibility not only renders them uncomfortable themselves, but troublesome, to use a soft phrase, to others. All their thoughts turn on things calculated to excite emotion; and feeling, when they should reason, their conduct is unstable, and their opinions are wavering — not the wavering produced by deliberation or progressive views, but by contradictory emotions. By fits and starts they are warm in many pursuits; yet this warmth, never concentrated into perseverance, soon exhausts itself; exhaled by its own heat, or meeting with some other fleeting passion, to which reason has never given any specific gravity, neutrality ensues. Miserable, indeed, must be that being whose cultivation of mind has only tended to inflame its passions! A distinction should be made between inflaming and strengthening them. The passions thus pampered, whilst the judgment is left unformed, what can be expected to ensue? — Undoubtedly, a mixture of madness and folly!

This observation should not be confined to the *fair* sex; however, at present, I only mean to apply it to them.

Novels, music, poetry, and gallantry, all tend to make women the creatures of sensation, and their character is thus formed during the time they are acquiring accomplishments, the only improvement they are excited, by their station in society, to acquire. This overstretched sensibility naturally relaxes the other powers of the mind, and prevents intellect from attaining that sovereignty which it ought to attain to render a rational creature useful to others, and content with its own station: for the exercise of the understanding, as life advances, is the only method pointed out by nature to calm the passions.

Satiety has a very different effect, and I have often been forcibly struck by an emphatical description of damnation: — when the spirit is represented as continually hovering with abortive eagerness round the defiled body, unable to enjoy any thing without the organs of sense. Yet, to their senses, are women made slaves, because it is by their sensibility that they obtain present power.

And will moralists pretend to assert, that this is the condition in which one half of the human race should be encouraged to remain with listless inactivity and stupid acquiescence? Kind instructors! what were we created for? To remain, it may be said, innocent; they mean in a state of childhood. — We might as well never have been born, unless it were necessary that we should be created to enable man to acquire the noble privilege of reason, the power of discerning good from evil, whilst we lie down in the dust from whence we were taken, never to rise again. —

It would be an endless task to trace the variety of meannesses, cares, and sorrows, into which women are plunged by the prevailing opinion, that they were created rather to feel than reason, and that all the power they obtain, must be obtained by their charms and weakness:

'Fine by defect, and amiably weak!'

And, made by this amiable weakness entirely dependent, excepting what they gain by illicit sway, on man, not only for protection, but advice, is it surprising that, neglecting the duties that reason alone points out, and shrinking from trials calculated to strengthen their minds, they only exert themselves to give their defects a graceful covering, which may serve to heighten their charms in the eye of the voluptuary, though it sink them below the scale of moral excellence?

Fragile in every sense of the word, they are obliged to look up to man for every comfort. In the most trifling dangers they cling to their support, with parasitical tenacity, piteously demanding succour; and their *natural* protector extends his arm, or lifts up his voice, to guard the lovely trembler — from what? Perhaps the frown of an old cow, or the jump of a mouse; a rat, would be a serious danger. In the name of reason, and even common sense, what can save such beings from contempt; even though they be soft and fair?

These fears, when not affected, may be very petty; but they shew a degree of imbecility that degrades a rational creature in a way women are not aware of — for love and esteem are very distinct things.

I am fully persuaded that we should hear of none of these infantile airs, if girls were allowed to take sufficient exercise, and not confined in close rooms till their muscles are relaxed, and their powers of digestion destroyed. To carry the remark still further, if fear in girls, instead of being cherished, perhaps, created, was treated in the same manner as cowardice in boys, we should quickly see women with more dignified aspects. It is true, they could not then with equal propriety be termed the sweet flowers that smile in the walk of man; but they would be more respectable members of society, and discharge the important duties of life by the light of their own reason. 'Educate women like men,' says Rousseau, 'and the more they resemble our sex the less power will they have over us.' This is the very point I aim at. I do not wish them to have power over men; but over themselves.

In the same strain have I heard men argue against instructing the poor; for many are the forms that aristocracy assumes. 'Teach them to read and write,' say they, 'and you take them out of the station assigned them by nature.' An eloquent Frenchman has answered them, I will borrow his sentiments. But they know not, when they make man a brute, that they may expect every instant to see him transformed into a ferocious beast. Without knowledge there can be no morality!

Ignorance is a frail base for virtue! Yet, that is the condition for which woman was organized, has been insisted upon by the writers who have most vehemently argued in favour of the superiority of man; a superiority not in degree, but essence; though, to soften the argument, they have laboured to prove, with chivalrous generosity, that the sexes ought not to be compared; man was made to reason, woman to feel; and that together, flesh and spirit, they make the most perfect whole, by blending happily reason and sensibility into one character.

And what is sensibility? 'Quickness of sensation; quickness of perception; delicacy.' Thus is it defined by Dr. Johnson; and the definition gives me no other idea than of the most exquisitely polished instinct. I discern not a trace of the image of God in either sensation or matter. Refined seventy times seven, they are still material; intellect dwells not there; nor will fire ever make lead gold!

I come round to my old argument; if woman be allowed to have an immortal soul, she must have, as the employment of life, an understanding to improve. And when, to render the present state more complete, though every thing proves it to be but a fraction of a mighty sum, she is incited by present gratification to forget her grand destination, Nature is counteracted, or she was born only to procreate and die. Or, granting brutes, of every description, a soul, though not a reasonable one, the exercise of instinct and sensibility may be the step, which they are to take, in this life, towards the attainment of reason in the next; so that through all eternity they will lag behind man, who, why we cannot tell, had the power given him of attaining reason in his first mode of existence.

When I treat of the peculiar duties of women, as I should treat of the peculiar duties of a citizen or father, it will be found that I do not mean to insinuate that they should be taken out of their families, speaking of the majority. 'He that hath wife and children,' says Lord Bacon, 'hath given hostages to fortune; for they are impediments to great enterprises, either of virtue or mischief. Certainly the best works, and of greatest merit for the public, have proceeded from the unmarried or childless men.' I say the same of women. But, the welfare of society is not built on extraordinary exertions; and were it more reasonably organized, there would be still less need of great abilities, or heroic virtues.

In the regulation of a family, in the education of children, understanding, in an unsophisticated sense, is particularly required: strength both of body and mind; yet the men who, by their writings, have most earnestly laboured to domesticate women, have endeavoured, by arguments dictated by a gross appetite, that satiety had rendered fastidious, to weaken their bodies and cramp their minds. But, if even by these sinister methods they really *persuaded* women, by working on their feelings, to stay at home, and fulfil the duties of a mother and mistress of a family, I should cautiously oppose opinions that led women to right conduct, by prevailing on them to make the discharge of a duty the business of life, though reason were insulted. Yet, and I appeal to experience, if by neglecting the understanding they are as much, nay, more detached from these domestic duties, than they could be by the most serious intellectual pursuit, though it may be observed that the mass of mankind will never vigorously pursue an intellectual object,[7] I may be allowed to infer that reason is absolutely necessary to enable a woman to perform any duty properly, and I must again repeat, that sensibility is not reason.

The comparison with the rich still occurs to me; for, when men neglect the duties of humanity, women will do the same; a common stream hurries them both along with thoughtless celerity. Riches and honours prevent a man from enlarging his understanding, and enervate all his powers by reversing the order of nature, which has ever made true pleasure the reward of labour. Pleasure — enervating pleasure is, likewise, within women's reach without earning it. But, till hereditary possessions are spread abroad, how can we expect men to be proud of virtue? And, till they are, women will govern them by the most direct means, neglecting their dull domestic duties to catch the pleasure that is on the wing of time.

'The power of the woman,' says some author, 'is her sensibility;' and men, not aware of the consequence, do all they can to make this power swallow up every other. Those who constantly employ their sensibility will have most; for example; poets, painters, and composers.[8] Yet, when the sensibility is thus increased at the expense of reason, and even the imagination, why do philosophical men complain of their fickleness? The sexual attention of man particularly acts on female sensibility, and this sympathy has been exercised from their youth up. A husband cannot long pay those attentions with the passion necessary to excite lively emotions, and the heart, accustomed to lively emotions, turns to a new lover, or pines in secret, the prey of virtue or prudence. I mean when the heart has really been rendered susceptible, and the taste formed; for I am apt to conclude, from what I have seen in fashionable life, that vanity is oftener fostered than sensibility by the mode of education, and the intercourse between the sexes, which I have reprobated; and that coquetry more frequently proceeds from vanity than from that inconstancy, which overstrained sensibility naturally produces.

Another argument that has had a great weight with me, must, I think, have some force with every considerate, benevolent heart. Girls who have been thus weakly educated, are often cruelly left by their parents without any provision; and, of course, are dependent on, not only the reason, but the bounty of their brothers. These brothers are, to view the fairest side of the question, good sort of men, and give as a favour, what children of the same parents had an equal right to. In this equivocal humiliating situation, a docile female may remain some time, with a tolerable degree of comfort. But, when the brother marries, a probable circumstance, from being considered as the mistress of the family, she is viewed with averted looks as an intruder, an unnecessary burden on the benevolence of the master of the house, and his new partner.

Who can recount the misery, which many unfortunate beings, whose minds and bodies are equally weak, suffer in such situations — unable to work, and ashamed to beg? The wife, a cold-hearted, narrow-minded, woman, and this is not an unfair supposition; for the present mode of education does not tend to enlarge the heart any more than the understanding, is jealous of the little kindness which her husband shews to his relations; and her sensibility not rising to humanity, she is displeased at seeing the property of *her* children lavished on an helpless sister.

These are matters of fact, which have come under my eye, again and again. The consequence is obvious, the wife has recourse to cunning to undermine the habitual affection, which she is afraid openly to oppose; and neither tears nor caresses are spared till the spy is worked out of her home, and thrown on the world, unprepared for its difficulties; or sent, as a great effort of generosity, or from some regard to propriety, with a small stipend, and an uncultivated mind, into joyless solitude.

These two women may be much upon a par, with respect to reason and humanity; and changing situations might have acted just the same selfish part; but had they been differently educated, the case would also have been very different. The wife would not have had that sensibility, of which self is the centre, and reason might have taught her not to expect, and not even to be flattered, by the affection of her husband, if it led him to violate prior duties. She would wish not to love him merely because he loved her, but on account of his virtues; and the sister might have been able to struggle for herself instead of eating the bitter bread of dependence.

I am, indeed, persuaded that the heart, as well as the understanding, is opened by cultivation; and by, which may not appear so clear, strengthening the organs; I am not now talking of momentary flashes of sensibility, but of affections. And, perhaps, in the education of both sexes, the most difficult task is so to adjust instruction as not to narrow the understanding, whilst the heart is warmed by the generous juices of spring, just raised by the electric fermentation of the season; nor to dry up the feelings by employing the mind in investigations remote from life.

With respect to women, when they receive a careful education, they are either made fine ladies, brimful of sensibility, and teeming with capricious fancies; or mere notable women. The latter are often friendly, honest creatures, and have a shrewd kind of good sense joined with worldly prudence, that often render them more useful members of society than the fine sentimental lady, though they possess neither greatness of mind nor taste. The intellectual world is shut against them; take them out of their family or neighbourhood, and they stand still; the mind finding no employment, for literature affords a fund of amusement which they have never sought to relish, but frequently to despise. The sentiments and taste of more cultivated minds appear ridiculous, even in those whom chance and family connections have led them to love; but in mere acquaintance they think it all affectation.

A man of sense can only love such a woman on account of her sex, and respect her, because she is a trusty servant. He lets her, to preserve his own peace, scold the servants, and go to church in clothes made of the very best materials. A man of her own size of understanding would, probably, not agree so well with her; for he might wish to encroach on her prerogative, and manage some domestic concerns himself. Yet women, whose minds are not enlarged by cultivation, or the natural selfishness of sensibility expanded by reflection, are very unfit to manage a family; for, by an undue stretch of power, they are always tyrannizing to support a superiority that only rests on the arbitrary distinction of fortune. The evil is sometimes more serious, and domestics are deprived of innocent indulgences, and made to work beyond their strength, in order to enable the notable woman to keep a better table, and outshine her neighbours in finery and parade. If she attend to her children, it is, in general, to dress them in a costly manner — and, whether this attention arise from vanity or fondness, it is equally pernicious.

Besides, how many women of this description pass their days; or, at least, their evenings, discontentedly. Their husbands acknowledge that they are good managers, and chaste wives; but leave home to seek for more agreeable, may I be allowed to use a significant French word, *piquant* society; and the patient drudge, who fulfils her task, like a blind horse in a mill, is defrauded of her just reward; for the wages due to her are the caresses of her husband; and women who have so few resources in themselves, do not very patiently bear this privation of a natural right.

A fine lady, on the contrary, has been taught to look down with contempt on the vulgar employments of life; though she has only been incited to acquire accomplishments that rise a degree above sense; for even corporeal accomplishments cannot be acquired with any degree of precision unless the understanding has been strengthened by exercise. Without a foundation of principles taste is superficial; and grace must arise from something deeper than imitation. The imagination, however, is heated, and the feelings rendered fastidious, if not sophisticated; or, a counterpoise of judgment is not acquired, when the heart still remains artless, though it becomes too tender.

These women are often amiable; and their hearts are really more sensible to general benevolence, more alive to the sentiments that civilize life, than the square-elbowed family drudge; but, wanting a due proportion of reflection and self-government, they only inspire love; and are the mistresses of their husbands, whilst they have any hold on their affections; and the platonic friends of his male acquaintance. These are the fair defects in nature; the women who appear to be created not to enjoy the fellowship of man, but to save him from sinking into absolute brutality, by rubbing off the rough angles of his character; and by playful dalliance to give some dignity to the appetite that draws him to them. Gracious Creator of the whole human race! hast thou created such a being as woman, who can trace thy wisdom in thy works, and feel that thou alone art by thy nature, exalted above her, — for no better purpose? — Can she believe that she was only made to submit to man, her equal; a being, who, like her, was sent into the world to acquire virtue? — Can she consent to be occupied merely to please him; merely to adorn the earth, when her soul is capable of rising to thee? — And can she rest supinely dependent on man for reason, when she ought to mount with him the arduous steeps of knowledge? —

Yet, if love be the supreme good, let women be only educated to inspire it, and let every charm be polished to intoxicate the senses; but, if they are moral beings, let them have a chance to become intelligent; and let love to man be only a part of that glowing flame of universal love, which, after encircling humanity, mounts in grateful incense to God....

Notes

[1] Into what inconsistencies do men fall when they argue without the compass of principles. Women, weak women, are compared with angels; yet, a superior order of beings should be supposed to possess more intellect than man; or, in what does their superiority consist? In the same style, to drop the sneer, they are allowed to possess more goodness of heart, piety, and benevolence.—I doubt the fact, though it be courteously brought forward, unless ignorance be allowed to be the mother of devotion; for I am firmly persuaded that, on an average, the proportion between virtue and knowledge, is more upon a par than is commonly granted.

[2] 'The brutes,' says Lord Monboddo, 'remain in the state in which nature has placed them, except in so far as their natural instinct is improved by the culture *we* bestow upon them.'

[3] Vide Milton.

[4] This word is not strictly just, but I cannot find a better.

[5] 'Pleasure's the portion of th' *inferiour* kind;
    But glory, virtue, Heaven for *man* design'd.'

After writing these lines, how could Mrs. Barbauld write the following ignoble comparison?

> '*To a Lady, with some painted flowers.*'
> 'Flowers to the fair; to you these flowers I bring,
> 'And strive to greet you with an earlier spring.
> '*Flowers* SWEET, *and gay, and* DELICATE LIKE YOU;
> '*Emblems of innocence, and beauty too.*
> 'With flowers the Graces bind their yellow hair,
> 'And flowery wreaths consenting lovers wear.
> '*Flowers, the sole luxury which nature knew,*
> 'In Eden's pure and guiltless garden grew.
> '*To loftier forms are rougher tasks assign'd;*
> '*The sheltering oak resists the stormy wind,*
> '*The tougher yew repels invading foes,*
> '*And the tall pine for future navies grows;*
> '*But this soft family, to cares unknown,*
> '*Were born for pleasure and delight* ALONE.
> 'Gay without toil, and lovely without art,
> '*They spring to* CHEER *the sense, and* GLAD *the heart.*
> 'Nor blush, my fair, to own you copy these;
> '*Your* BEST, *your* SWEETEST *empire is—*TO PLEASE.'

So the men tell us; but virtue, says reason, must be acquired by *rough* toils, and useful struggles with worldly *cares*.

[6] And a wit, always a wit, might be added; for the vain foolery of wits and beauties to obtain attention, and make conquests, are much upon a par.

[7] The mass of mankind are rather the slaves of their appetites than of their passions.

[8]Men of these descriptions pour it into their compositions, to amalgamate the gross materials; and, moulding them with passion, give to the inert body a soul; but, in woman's imagination, love alone concentrates these ethereal beams.

24. Address to the American Equal Rights Association[*]

Elizabeth Cady Stanton

In considering the question of suffrage, there are two starting points: one, that this right is a gift of society, in which certain men, having inherited this privilege from some abstract body and abstract place, have now the right to secure it for themselves and their privileged order to the end of time. This principle leads logically to governing races, classes, families; and, in direct antagonism to our idea of self-government, takes us back to monarchies and despotisms, to an experiment that has been tried over and over again, 6,000 years, and uniformly failed. "I do not hold my liberties," says Gratz Brown in the Senate of the United States, "by any such tenure. On the contrary, I believe, whenever you establish that doctrine, whenever you crystalize that idea in the public mind of this country, you ring the death-knell of American liberties."

Ignoring this point of view as untenable and anti-republican, and taking the opposite, that suffrage is a natural right — as necessary to man under government, for the protection of person and property, as are air and motion to life — we hold the talisman by which to show the right of all classes to the ballot, to remove every obstacle, to answer every objection, to point out the tyranny of every qualification to the free exercise of this sacred right.

[*] Elizabeth Cady Stanton delivered this speech to the American Equal Rights Association in New York in May 1867 on the occasion of the organization's first anniversary. This particular selection represents the 'Address of Elizabeth Cady Stanton' in its entirety and was taken from the *Proceedings of the First Anniversary of the American Equal Rights Association, Held at the Church of the Puritans, New York, May 9 and 10, 1867*, phonographic report by H.M. Parkhurst (New York: printed by Robert J. Johnston, 1867), 7–17.

To discuss the question of suffrage for women and negroes, as women and negroes, and not as citizens of a republic, implies that there are some reasons for demanding this right for these classes that do not apply to "white males."

The obstinate persistence with which fallacious and absurd objections are pressed against their enfranchisement — as if they were anomalous beings, outside all human laws and necessities — is most humiliating and insulting to every black man and woman who has one particle of healthy, high-toned self-respect. There are no special claims to propose for women and negroes, no new arguments to make in their behalf. The same already made to extend suffrage to all the white men in this country, the same John Bright makes for the working men of England, the same made for the enfranchisement of 22,000,000 Russian serfs, are all we have to make for black men and women. As the greater includes the less, an argument for universal suffrage covers the whole question, the rights of all citizens. In thus relaying the foundations of government, we settle all these side issues of race, color and sex, end all class legislation, and remove forever the fruitful cause of all the jealousies, dissensions and revolutions of the past. This is the platform of the American Equal Rights Association. "We are masters of the situation." Here black men and women are buried in the citizen. As in the war, freedom was the key-note of victory, so now is universal suffrage the key-note of reconstruction.

"Negro suffrage" may answer as a party cry for an effete political organization through another Presidential campaign; but the people of this country have a broader work on hand to-day than to save the Republican party, or, with some abolitionists, to settle the rights of races. The battles of the ages have been fought for races, classes, parties, over and over again, and force always carried the day, and will until we settle the higher, the holier question of individual rights. This is our American idea, and on a wise settlement of this question rests the problem whether our nation shall live or perish.

The principle of inequality in government has been thoroughly tried, and every nation based on that idea that has not already perished, clearly shows the seeds of death in its dissensions and decline. Though it has never been tried, we know an experiment on the basis of equality would be safe; for the laws in the world of morals are as immutable as in the world of matter. As the Astronomer Le Verrier discovered the planet that bears his name by a process of reason and calculation through the variations of other planets from known laws, so can the true statesman, through the telescope of justice, see the genuine republic of the future amid the ruins of the mighty nations that have passed away. The opportunity now given us to make the experiment of self-government should be regarded by every American citizen as a solemn and a sacred trust. When we remember that a nation's life and growth and immortality depend on its legislation, can we exalt too highly the dignity and responsibility of the ballot, the science of political economy, the sphere of government? Statesmanship is, of all sciences, the most exalted and comprehensive, for it includes all others. Among men we find those who study the laws of national life more liberal and enlightened on all subjects than those who confine their researches in special directions. When we base nations on justice and equality, we lift government out of the mists of speculation into the dignity of a fixed science. Everything short of this is trick, legerdemain, sleight of hand. Magicians may make nations seem to live, but they do not. The Newtons of our day who should try to make apples stand in the air or men walk on the wall, would be no more puerile in their experiments than are they who build nations outside of law, on the basis of inequality.

What thinking man can talk of *coming down* into the arena of politics? If we need purity, honor, self-sacrifice and devotion anywhere, we need them in those who have in their keeping the life and prosperity of a nation. In the enfranchisement of woman, in lifting her up into this broader sphere, we see for her new honor and dignity, more liberal, exalted and enlightened views of life, its objects, ends and aims, and an entire revolution in the new world of interest and action where she is soon to play her part. And in saying this, I do not claim that woman is better than man, but that the sexes have a civilizing power on each other. The distinguished historian, Henry Thomas Buckle, says:

"The turn of thought of women, their habits of mind, their conversation, invariably extending over the whole surface of society, and frequently penetrating its intimate structure, have, more than all other things put together, tended to raise us into an ideal world, and lift us from the dust into which we are too prone to grovel.

And this will be her influence in exalting and purifying the world of politics. When woman understands the momentous interests that depend on the ballot, she will make it her first duty to educate every American boy and girl into the idea that to vote is the most sacred act of citizenship — a religious duty not to be discharged thoughtlessly, selfishly or corruptly; but conscientiously, remembering that, in a republican government, to every citizen is entrusted the interests of the nation. "Would you fully estimate the responsibility of the ballot, think of it as the great regulating power of a continent, of all our interests, political, commercial, religious, educational, social and sanitary!"

To many minds, this claim for the ballot suggests nothing more than a rough polling-booth where coarse, drunken men, elbowing each other, wade knee-deep in mud to drop a little piece of paper two inches long into a box — simply this and nothing more. The poet Wordsworth, showing the blank materialism of those who see only with their outward eyes, says of his Peter Bell:

> "A primrose on the river's brink
> A yellow primrose was to him,
> And it was nothing more."

So our political Peter Bells see the rough polling-booth, in this great right of citizenship, and nothing more. In this act, so lightly esteemed by the mere materialist, behold the realization of that great idea struggled for in the ages and proclaimed by the Fathers, the right of self-government. That little piece of paper dropped into a box is the symbol of equality, of citizenship, of wealth, virtue, education, self-protection, dignity, independence and power — the mightiest engine yet placed in the hand of man for the uprooting of ignorance, tyranny, superstition, the overturning of thrones, altars, kings, popes, despotisms, monarchies and empires. What phantom can the sons of the Pilgrims be chasing, when they make merchandise of a power like this? Judas Iscariot, selling his Master for thirty pieces of silver, is a fit type of those American citizens who sell their votes, and thus betray the right of self-government. Talk not of the "muddy pool of politics," as if such things must need be. Behold, with the coming of woman into this higher sphere of influence, the dawn of the new day, when politics, so called, are to be lifted into the world of morals and religion; when the polling-booth shall be a beautiful temple, surrounded by fountains and flowers and triumphal arches, through which young men and maidens shall go up in joyful procession to ballot for justice and freedom; and when our elections shall be like the holy feasts of the Jews at Jerusalem. Through the trials of this second revolution shall not our nation rise up, with new virtue and strength, to fulfil her mission in leading all the peoples of the earth to the only solid foundation of government, "equal rights to all?" What an inheritance is ours! What boundless resources for wealth, happiness and development! With every variety of climate and production, with our mighty lakes and rivers, majestic forests and inexhaustible mines, nothing can check our future prosperity but a lack of virtue in the people. Let us not, like the foolish prodigal, waste our substance in riotous living, and, through ease, luxury and corruption, check the onward march of this western civilization. Our danger lies, not in the direction of despotism, in the one-man power, in centralization; but in the corruption of the people. Is it not enough to fill any true patriot with apprehension, to read the accounts in our daily journals of the wholesale bribery that unblushingly shows itself everywhere? It is not the poor, unlettered foreigner alone who sells his vote; but native-born American citizens, congressmen, senators, judges, jurors, "white males" who own $250 worth of real estate and can read the Constitution. It is not in Wall street alone that men gamble in stocks; but our State and National Capitols — even our courts of justice — are made houses of merchandise. Women of the Republic, what say you for your sons? What say our legislators for themselves? — they who claim to represent their mothers, wives and daughters, to have their lives, liberty and happiness in their keeping. "There is something rotten in Denmark." Ralph Waldo Emerson says, "men are what their mothers made them." The fountain rises no higher than its source. The art, the stratagem, the duplicity, the sham of our social life is all repeated in our legislation. "Give a man a right over my subsistence," says Alexander Hamilton, "and he has a right over my whole moral being." When any class lives by favors, rather than honorable, profitable labor; when shelter, food and clothes are to be wheedled out of a privileged order, life is necessarily based on chicanery, degradation and dishonor. In woman's aimless, dependent education, her noblest aspirations, her holiest sentiments, are perverted or sacrificed. She has but one object in life, and that one is desecrated, compelled as she is, in ease and luxury, to marry for a position, a palace, equipage, silks and diamonds, or, in poverty and isolation, for bread and a home. With marriages of interest, convenience, necessity, the very fountains of life are poisoned. This first false step in our social life can only be remedied by making woman independent, and profitable labor honorable for all. Educate girls for all the avocations of life. Teach them to scorn, as the boy does, to live on the bounty of another. Virtue and independence go hand in hand. If you would have the future men of this nation do justice and walk uprightly, remove every barrier in the way of woman's elevation, that she, too, with honor and dignity on her brow, may stand self-poised, above fear, want or temptation.

Never, until woman is an independent, self-sustaining force in society, can she take her true, exalted position as the mother, the educator of the race. Never, as a dependent on his wish, his will, his bounty to be sheltered, fed and clothed, will man recognize in woman an equal moral power in the universe of mind. The same principle that governed plantation life, governs the home. The master could quote law and gospel for his authority over the slave, so can the husband still. You see man's idea of woman's true position in his codes and creeds. His commentaries on Blackstone and the Bible alike place her "*sub potestate viri;*" under the power of man. The mass of both men and women really believe this to be the Heaven-ordained status of a Christian wife. Hence we have, in the home as on the plantation, ruler and subject on one side, purse, power and rights on the other — favors or wrongs, according to the character of the "divinely-appointed head." But fair, equal-handed justice can never be found where the rights of one class are at the mercy of another. The black man, as a slave, was compelled to lie and cheat and steal. All he got was by his wits; he had no rights which any one was bound to respect. He had nothing to hope for, nothing to gain; hence food and clothes were more to him than principles. But that chain is broken; he is free, holds the ballot, lives on his own earnings. With responsibility come honesty, honor, dignity; and to-day Gov. Orr reasons with him as a man, and gives him dissertations *on the policy of fair-dealing with white men.* But, if a woman corners her husband in fair debate, shows him that her plan of action in any direction is better than his, he flies into a passion, declares "there is no reasoning with a woman," and, from sheer will, thwarts the end she desires. Thus she is driven to cunning and management to get what is denied as her right. Shut up to a life of folly, fashion and dependence, with no means of her own to gratify her taste or vanity, she would be a dull scholar not to learn the wisdom of having no opinion, will or wish opposed to him who carries the purse. She has no purse of her own, so she makes bills at the milliner's, the dress-maker's, the fancy store, the restaurant which she cannot pay. She staves off their claims as long as possible; but at last the awful moment comes, and the bills are sent to her husband. He raises a tempest at home, refuses to pay, is sued, and is laughed at in court as some malicious lawyer slowly reads over the articles of his wife's wardrobe and how many times she ate ice-cream or oysters in one week, all of which is published to the world the next day. And this is the beautiful, refined seclusion where the feminine element is supposed to be most favorably developed; from which the liberal pulpit even fears to transplant woman to the world of work, where she may become honest and independent. Under such circumstances, how can woman base her every-day life on principle? False to herself, how can she be true to others? So long as she is petty, servile, tricky, how can her sons be magnanimous, noble and just?

And this is the "home influence" of which we hear so much — the great normal-school of legislators, senators and presidents. Here are your boasted mothers, the women who govern the world, without enough force or dignity or principle to stand upright themselves. The family, that great conservator of national strength and morals — how can you cement its ties but by the virtue and independence of both man and woman? If one-half we hear of the bribery and corruption of our day be true, and we are responsible for this state of things, we must confess that woman has made a most lamentable failure in governing the world for the last six thousand years by the "magic power of influence." If this be indeed her work, and if, in fact, as all philosophers tell us, woman does govern the world, it behooves her now to demand a fitting education for so responsible a position, that she may understand the science of life, and make a new experiment in government with the direct power of the ballot-box; that, by an intelligent use of the franchise, she may so change the conditions of life as to lift the race on a higher platform than she could ever do by tact, cunning or management. The effect of concentrating all woman's thoughts and interests in home-life, intensifies her selfishness and narrows her ideas in every direction; hence she is arbitrary in her views of government, bigoted in religion, and exclusive in society. She is the ignorant, the conservative element, the staunch supporter everywhere of the aristocratic idea. Look at the long line of equipages and liveried servants in Fifth Avenue and Central Park, the pageant composed chiefly of women. Think of stalwart men, dressed up like monkeys, perched on the back seat of a carriage for ornament. A coat of arms and livery belong legitimately to countries that boast an order of nobility, an established church, a law of primogeniture — where families live through centuries; but here, where the tallow chandler of yesterday lives in a palace to-day, they are out of place. What a spectacle for us who proclaimed the glorious doctrine of equality a century ago, to be imitating the sham and tinsel of the effete civilizations of the Old World — degrading the dignity and majesty of the idea on which our government is based!

Now men in political life cannot afford to do these things. They always have the ballot-box, that great leveller, before their eyes. They keep their kid gloves in their pockets, shake hands all round, and act as if they believed all men equal, especially about election time. This practice they have in the right direction, does in time mould them anew into broader, more liberal views than the women by their side. When our fashionable, educated women vote, there will be an enthusiasm thrown round our republican idea such as we have never realized before. It is in vain to look for a genuine republic in this country until the women are baptized into the idea, until they understand the genius of our institutions, until they study the science of government, until they hold the ballot in their hands and have a direct voice in our legislation. What is the reason, with the argument in favor of the enfranchisement of women all on one side, without an opponent worthy of consideration — while British statesmen, even, are discussing this question — that Northern men are so dumb and dogged, manifesting a studied indifference to what they can neither answer nor prevent? What is the reason that even abolitionists who have fearlessly claimed political, religious and social equality for woman for the last twenty years, should now, with bated breath, give her but a passing word in their public speeches and editorial comments — as if her rights constituted but a side issue in this grave question of reconstruction? All must see that this claim for *male*-hood suffrage is but another experiment in class legislation, another violation of the republican idea. With the black man we have no new element in government; but with the education and elevation of woman we have a power that is to galvanize the Saxon race into a higher and nobler life, and thus, by the law of attraction, to lift all races to a more even platform than can ever be reached in the political isolation of the sexes. Why ignore 15,000,000 women in the reconstruction? The philosophy of this silence is plain enough. The black man crowned with the rights of citizenship, there are no political Ishmaelites left but the women. This is the last stronghold of aristocracy in the country. Sydney Smith says: "There always has been, and always will be, a class of men in the world so small that, if women were educated, there would be nothing left below them."

It is consolation to the "white male," to the popinjays in all our seminaries of learning, to the ignorant foreigner, the boot-black and barber, the idiot — for a "white male" may vote if he be not more than nine-tenths a fool — to look down on women of wealth and education, who write books, make speeches, and discuss principles with the savans of their age. It is a consolation for these classes to be able to say, well, if women can do these things, "they can't vote, after all." I heard some boys discoursing thus not long since. I told them they reminded me of a story I heard of two Irishmen the first time they saw a locomotive with a train of cars. As the majestic fire-horse, with all its grace and polish, moved up to a station, stopped, and snorted, as its mighty power was curbed, then slowly gathered up its forces again and moved swiftly on — "be jabers," says Pat, "there's muscle for you. What are we beside that giant?" They watched it intently till out of sight, seemingly with real envy, as if oppressed with a feeling of weakness and poverty before this unknown power; but rallying at last, one says to the other: "No matter, Pat; let it snort and dash on — it can't vote, after all."

Poor human nature wants something to look down on. No privileged order ever did see the wrongs of its own victims, and why expect the "white male citizen" to enfranchise woman without a struggle — by a scratch of the pen to place themselves on a dead level with their lowest order? And what a fall would that be, my countrymen. In none of the nations of modern Europe is there a class of women so degraded politically as are the women of these Northern States. In the Old World, where the government is the aristocracy, where it is considered a mark of nobility to share its offices and powers — there women of rank have certain hereditary rights which raise them above a majority of the men, certain honors and privileges not granted to serfs or peasants. In England woman may be Queen, hold office, vote on some questions. In the southern States even the women were not degraded below their working population, they were not humiliated in seeing their coachmen, gardeners and waiters go to the polls to legislate on their interests; hence there was a pride and dignity in their bearing not found in the women of the North, and a pluck in the chivalry before which northern doughfaceism has ever cowered. But here, where the ruling class, the aristocracy, is "male," no matter whether washed or unwashed, lettered or unlettered, rich or poor, black or white, here in this boasted northern civilization, under the shadow of Bunker Hill and Faneuil Hall, which Mr. Phillips proposes to cram down the throat of South Carolina — here women of wealth and education, who pay taxes and are amenable to law, who may be hung, even though not permitted to choose the judge, the juror, or the sheriff who does the dismal deed, women who are your peers in art, science and literature — already close upon your heels in the whole world of thought — are thrust outside the pale of political consideration with traitors, idiots, minors, with those guilty of bribery, larceny and infamous crime. What a category is this in which to place your mothers, wives and daughters. "I ask you, men of the Empire State, where on the footstool do you find such a class of citizens politically so degraded? Now, we ask you, in the coming Constitutional Convention, to so amend the Second Article of our State Constitution as to wipe out this record of our disgrace.

"But," say you, "women themselves do not make the demand." Mr. Phillips said on this platform, a year ago, that "the singularity of this cause is, that it has to be carried on against the wishes and purposes of its victims," and he has been echoed by nearly every man who has spoken on this subject during the past year. Suppose the assertion true, is it a peculiarity of this reform?

We established free schools opposed to the will and wishes of the children playing in the sunshine on the highway. We press temperance, opposed to the will and wishes of drunkards and rumsellers. It has always been opposed to the will and wishes of working men that inventors should apply machinery to labor, and thus lift the burdens of life from the shoulders of the race. Ignorant classes have always resisted innovations. Women looked on the sewing-machine as a rival for a long time. Years ago the laboring classes of England asked bread; but the Cobdens, the Brights, the Gladstones, the Mills have taught them there is a power behind bread, and to-day they ask the ballot. But they were taught its power first, and so must woman be. Again, do not those far-seeing philosophers who comprehend the wisdom, the beneficence, the morality of free trade urge this law of nations against the will and wishes of the victims of tariffs and protective duties? If you can prove to us that women do not wish to vote, that is no argument against our demand. There are many duties in life that ignorant, selfish, unthinking women do not desire to do, and this may be one of them.

"But," says a distinguished Unitarian clergyman, in a recent sermon on this subject, "they who first assume political responsibilities must necessarily lose something of the feminine element." In the education and elevation of woman we are yet to learn the true manhood and womanhood, the true masculine and feminine elements. Dio Lewis is rapidly changing our ideas of feminine beauty. In the large waists and strong arms of the girls under his training, some dilettant gentleman may mourn a loss of feminine delicacy. So in the wise, virtuous, self-supporting, common-sense women we propose as the mothers of the future republic, the reverend gentleman may see a lack of what he considers the feminine element. In the development of sufficient moral force to entrench herself on principle, need a woman necessarily lose any grace, dignity or perfection of character? Are not those who have advocated the rights of women in this country for the last twenty years as delicate and refined, as moral, high-toned, educated, just and generous as any women in the land? I have seen women in many countries and classes, in public and private; but have found none more pure and noble than those I meet on this platform. I have seen our venerable President in converse with the highest of English nobility, and even the Duchess of Sutherland did not eclipse her in grace, dignity and conversational power. Where are there any women, as wives and mothers, more beautiful in their home life than Lucretia Mott and Lucy Stone, or Antoinette Brown Blackwell? Let the freedmen of the South Sea Islands testify to the faithfulness, the devotion, the patience and tender mercy of Frances D. Gage, who watched over their interests, teaching them to read and work for two long years. Some on our platform have struggled with hardship and poverty — been slaves even in "the land of the free and the home of the brave," and bear the scars of life's battle. But is a self-made woman less honorable than a self-made man? Answer our arguments. When the Republic is in danger, no matter for our manners. When our soldiers came back from the war, wan, weary, and worn, maimed, halt, blind, wrinkled and decrepit — their banners torn, their garments stained with blood — who, with a soul to feel, thought of anything but the glorious work they had done? What if their mothers on this platform be angular, old, wrinkled and gray? They, too, have fought a good fight for freedom, and proudly bear the scars of the battle. We alone have struck the key-note of reconstruction. While man talks of "equal, impartial, manhood suffrage," we give the certain sound, "universal suffrage." While he talks of the rights of races, we exalt the higher, the holier idea proclaimed by the Fathers, and now twice baptized in blood, "individual rights." To woman it is given to save the Republic. You have seen, no doubt, an engraving of that beautiful conception of the artist, Beatrice and Dante. On a slight elevation stands the ideal woman, her whole attitude expressive of conscious power and dignity. Erect, self-poised, she gazes into the heavens as if to draw inspiration and life from the great soul of truth. The man, on a lower plane, looks up with admiration and reverence, with a chaste and holy love; and thus the poet tells us, by the law of attraction woman leads man upward and onward, even through the hells, to heaven. I have sometimes thought, in gazing on this picture, that it was suggestive of what might be our future position. But, for this stage of civilization, I would draw a line half way between our poets and law-makers — between Dante and Blackstone — and place woman neither at man's feet nor above his head, but on an even platform by his side.

25. Man the Reformer[*]

Ralph Waldo Emerson

Mr. President and Gentlemen: —

I wish to offer to your consideration some thoughts on the particular and general relations of man as a reformer. I shall assume that the aim of each young man in this association is the very highest that belongs to a rational mind. Let it be granted that our life, as we lead it, is common and mean; that some of those offices and functions for which we were mainly created are grown so rare in society, that the memory of them is only kept alive in old books and in dim traditions; that prophets and poets, that beautiful and perfect men, we are not now, no, nor have even seen such; that some sources of human instruction are almost unnamed and unknown among us; that the community in which we live will hardly bear to be told that every man should be open to ecstasy or a divine illumination, and his daily walk elevated by intercourse with the spiritual world. Grant all this, as we must, yet I suppose none of my auditors will deny that we ought to seek to establish ourselves in such disciplines and courses as will deserve that guidance and clearer communication with the spiritual nature. And further, I will not dissemble my hope, that each person whom I address has felt his own call to cast aside all evil customs, timidities, and limitations, and to be in his place a free and helpful man, a reformer, a benefactor, not content to slip along through the world like a footman or a spy, escaping by his nimbleness and apologies as many knocks as he can, but a brave and upright man, who must find or cut a straight road to everything excellent on the earth, and not only go honorably himself, but make it easier for all who follow him, to go in honor and with benefit.

In the history of the world the doctrine of Reform had never such scope as at the present hour. Lutherans, Hernhutters, Jesuits, Monks, Quakers, Knox, Wesley, Swedenborg, Bentham, in their accusations of society, all respected something, — church

[*] Ralph Waldo Emerson delivered 'Man the Reformer' as a lecture to the Mechanics' Apprentices' Library Association on January 25, 1841, in Boston. It appeared in print in 1849 in *Nature: Addresses and Lectures*. This particular selection was taken from Emerson, *Works of Ralph Waldo Emerson*, Vol. V., *Miscellanies: Embracing Nature, Addresses, and Lectures* (Boston: Houghton, Mifflin and Company, 1882), 185–207.

or state, literature or history, domestic usages, the market town, the dinner-table, coined money. But now all these and all things else hear the trumpet, and must rush to judgment, — Christianity, the laws, commerce, schools, the farm, the laboratory; and not a kingdom, town, statute, rite, calling, man, or woman, but is threatened by the new spirit.

What if some of the objections whereby our institutions are assailed are extreme and speculative, and the reformers tend to idealism; that only shows the extravagance of the abuses which have driven the mind into the opposite extreme. It is when your facts and persons grow unreal and fantastic by too much falsehood, that the scholar flies for refuge to the world of ideas, and aims to recruit and replenish nature from that source. Let ideas establish their legitimate sway again in society, let life be fair and poetic, and the scholars will gladly be lovers, citizens, and philanthropists.

It will afford no security from the new ideas, that the old nations, the laws of centuries, the property and institutions of a hundred cities, are built on other foundations. The demon of reform has a secret door into the heart of every law-maker, of every inhabitant of every city. The fact that a new thought and hope have dawned in your breast, should apprise you that in the same hour a new light broke in upon a thousand private hearts. That secret which you would fain keep, — as soon as you go abroad, lo! there is one standing on the doorstep, to tell you the same. There is not the most bronzed and sharpened money-catcher, who does not, to your consternation, almost quail and shake the moment he hears a question prompted by the new ideas. We thought he had some semblance of ground to stand upon, that such as he at least would die hard; but he trembles and flees. Then the scholar says, 'Cities and coaches shall never impose on me again; for, behold every solitary dream of mine is rushing to fulfilment. That fancy I had, and hesitated to utter because you would laugh, — lo, the broker, the attorney, the market-man are saying the same thing. Had I waited a day longer to speak, I had been too late. Behold, State Street thinks, and Wall Street doubts, and begins to prophesy!'

It cannot be wondered at, that this general inquest into abuses should arise in the bosom of society, when one considers the practical impediments that stand in the way of virtuous young men. The young man, on entering life, finds the way to lucrative employments blocked with abuses. The ways of trade are grown selfish to the borders of theft, and supple to the borders (if not beyond the borders) of fraud. The employments of commerce are not intrinsically unfit for a man, or less genial to his faculties, but these are now in their general course so vitiated by derelictions and abuses at which all connive, that it requires more vigor and resources than can be expected of every young man, to right himself in them; he is lost in them; he cannot move hand or foot in them. Has he genius and virtue? the less does he find them fit for him to grow in, and if he would thrive in them, he must sacrifice all the brilliant dreams of boyhood and youth as dreams; he must forget the prayers of his childhood; and must take on him the harness of routine and obsequiousness. If not so minded, nothing is left him but to begin the world anew, as he does who puts the spade into the ground for food. We are all implicated, of course, in this charge; it is only necessary to ask a few questions as to the progress of the articles of commerce from the fields where they grew, to our houses, to become aware that we eat and drink and wear perjury and fraud in a hundred commodities. How many articles of daily consumption are furnished us from the West Indies; yet it is said, that, in the Spanish islands, the venality of the officers of the government has passed into usage, and that no article passes into our ships which has not been fraudulently cheapened. In the

Spanish islands, every agent or factor of the Americans, unless he be a consul, has taken oath that he is a Catholic, or has caused a priest to make that declaration for him. The abolitionist has shown us our dreadful debt to the Southern negro. In the island of Cuba, in addition to the ordinary abominations of slavery, it appears, only men are bought for the plantations, and one dies in ten every year, of these miserable bachelors, to yield us sugar. I leave for those who have the knowledge the part of sifting the oaths of our custom-houses; I will not inquire into the oppression of the sailors; I will not pry into the usages of our retail trade. I content myself with the fact, that the general system of our trade (apart from the blacker traits, which, I hope, are exceptions denounced and unshared by all reputable men) is a system of selfishness; is not dictated by the high sentiments of human nature; is not measured by the exact law of reciprocity; much less by the sentiments of love and heroism, but is a system of distrust, of concealment, of superior keenness, not of giving but of taking advantage. It is not that which a man delights to unlock to a noble friend; which he meditates on with joy and self-approval in his hour of love and aspiration; but rather what he then puts out of sight, only showing the brilliant result, and atoning for the manner of acquiring, by the manner of expending it. I do not charge the merchant or the manufacturer. The sins of our trade belong to no class, to no individual. One plucks, one distributes, one eats. Everybody partakes, everybody confesses, — with cap and knee volunteers his confession, yet none feels himself accountable. He did not create the abuse; he cannot alter it. What is he? an obscure private person who must get his bread. That is the vice, — that no one feels himself called to act for man, but only as a fraction of man. It happens therefore that all such ingenuous souls as feel within themselves the irrepressible strivings of a noble aim, who by the law of their nature must act simply, find these ways of trade unfit for them, and they come forth from it. Such cases are becoming more numerous every year.

But by coming out of trade you have not cleared yourself. The trail of the serpent reaches into all the lucrative professions and practices of man. Each has its own wrongs. Each finds a tender and very intelligent conscience a disqualification for success. Each requires of the practitioner a certain shutting of the eyes, a certain dapperness and compliance, an acceptance of customs, a sequestration from the sentiments of generosity and love, a compromise of private opinion and integrity. Nay, the evil custom reaches into the whole institution of property, until our laws which establish and protect it seem not to be the issue of love and reason, but of selfishness. Suppose a man is so unhappy as to be born a saint, with keen perceptions, but with the conscience and love of an angel, and he is to get his living in the world; he finds himself excluded from all lucrative works; he has no farm, and he cannot get one; for, to earn money enough to buy one, requires a sort of concentration toward money, which is the selling himself for a number of years, and to him the present hour is as sacred and inviolable as any future hour. Of course, whilst another man has no land, my title to mine, your title to yours, is at once vitiated. Inextricable seem to be the twinings and tendrils of this evil, and we all involve ourselves in it the deeper by forming connections, by wives and children, by benefits and debts.

Considerations of this kind have turned the attention of many philanthropic and intelligent persons to the claims of manual labor, as a part of the education of every young man. If the accumulated wealth of the past generations is thus tainted, — no matter how much of it is offered to us, — we must begin to consider if it were not the nobler part to renounce it, and to put ourselves into primary relations with the soil and nature, and, abstaining from whatever is dishonest and unclean, to take each of us bravely his part, with his own hands, in the manual labor of the world.

But it is said, 'What! will you give up the immense advantages reaped from the division of labor, and set every man to make his own shoes, bureau, knife, wagon, sails, and needle? This would be to put men back into barbarism by their own act.' I see no instant prospect of a virtuous revolution; yet I confess, I should not be pained at a change which threatened a loss of some of the luxuries or conveniences of society, if it proceeded from a preference of the agricultural life out of the belief that our primary duties as men could be better discharged in that calling. Who could regret to see a high conscience and a purer taste exercising a sensible effect on young men in their choice of occupation, and thinning the ranks of competition in the labors of commerce, of law, and of state? It is easy to see that the inconvenience would last but a short time. This would be great action, which always opens the eyes of men. When many persons shall have done this, when the majority shall admit the necessity of reform in all these institutions, their abuses will be redressed, and the way will be open again to the advantages which arise from the division of labor, and a man may select the fittest employment for his peculiar talent again, without compromise.

But quite apart from the emphasis which the times give to the doctrine, that the manual labor of society ought to be shared among all the members, there are reasons proper to every individual, why he should not be deprived of it. The use of manual labor is one which never grows obsolete, and which is inapplicable to no person. A man should have a farm or a mechanical craft for his culture. We must have a basis for our higher accomplishments, our delicate entertainments of poetry and philosophy, in the work of our hands. We must have an antagonism in the tough world for all the variety of our spiritual faculties, or they will not be born. Manual labor is the study of the external world. The advantage of riches remains with him who procured them, not with the heir. When I go into my garden with a spade, and dig a bed, I feel such an exhilaration and health, that I discover that I have been defrauding myself all this time in letting others do for me what I should have done with my own hands. But not only health, but education is in the work. Is it possible that I who get indefinite quantities of sugar, hominy, cotton, buckets, crockery-ware, and letter-paper, by simply signing my name once in three months to a check in favor of John Smith & Co., traders, get the fair share of exercise to my faculties by that act, which nature intended for me in making all these far-fetched matters important to my comfort? It is Smith himself, and his carriers, and dealers, and manufacturers, it is the sailor, the hide-drogher, the butcher, the negro, the hunter, and the planter, who have intercepted the sugar of the sugar, and the cotton of the cotton. They have got the education, I only the commodity. This were all very well if I were necessarily absent, being detained by work of my own, like theirs, work of the same faculties; then should I be sure of my hands and feet, but now I feel some shame before my wood-chopper, my ploughman, and my cook, for they have some sort of self-sufficiency, they can contrive without my aid to bring the day and year round, but I depend on them, and have not earned by use a right to my arms and feet.

Consider further the difference between the first and second owner of property. Every species of property is preyed on by its own enemies, as iron by rust; timber by rot; cloth by moths; provisions by mould, putridity, or vermin; money by thieves; an orchard by insects; a planted field by weeds and the inroad of cattle; a stock of cattle by hunger; a road by rain and frost; a bridge by freshets. And whoever takes any of these things into his possession, takes the charge of defending them from this troop of enemies, or of keeping them in repair. A man who supplies his own want, who builds a raft or a boat to go a-fishing, finds it easy to calk it, or put in a thole-pin, or mend the rudder. What he gets only as fast as he wants for his own ends, does not embarrass him, or take away his sleep with looking after. But when he comes to give all the goods he has year after year collected, in one estate to his son, — house, orchard, ploughed land, cattle, bridges, hardware, wooden-ware, carpets, cloths, provisions, books, money, — and cannot give him the skill and experience which made or collected these, and the method and place they have in his own life, the son finds his hands full, — not to use these things, — but to look after them and defend them from their natural enemies. To him they are not means, but masters. Their enemies will not remit; rust, mould, vermin, rain, sun, freshet, fire, all seize their own, fill him with vexation, and he is converted from the owner into a watchman or a watch-dog to this magazine of old and new chattels. What a change! Instead of the masterly good-humor, and sense of power, and fertility of resource in himself; instead of those strong and learned hands, those piercing and learned eyes, that supple body, and that mighty and prevailing heart, which the father had, whom nature loved and feared, whom snow and rain, water and land, beast and fish, seemed all to know and to serve, we have now a puny, protected person, guarded by walls and curtains, stoves and down beds, coaches, and men-servants and women-servants from the earth and the sky, and who, bred to depend on all these, is made anxious by all that endangers those possessions, and is forced to spend so much time in guarding them, that he has quite lost sight of their original use, namely, to help him to his ends, — to the prosecution of his love; to the helping of his friend, to the worship of his God, to the enlargement of his knowledge, to the serving of his country, to the indulgence of his sentiment, and he is now what is called a rich man, — the menial and runner of his riches.

Hence it happens that the whole interest of history lies in the fortunes of the poor. Knowledge, Virtue, Power, are the victories of man over his necessities, his march to the dominion of the world. Every man ought to have this opportunity to conquer the world for himself. Only such persons interest us, Spartans, Romans, Saracens, English, Americans, who have stood in the jaws of need, and have by their own wit and might extricated themselves, and made man victorious.

I do not wish to overstate this doctrine of labor, or insist that every man should be a farmer, any more than that every man should be a lexicographer. In general, one may say, that the husbandman's is the oldest, and most universal profession, and that where a man does not yet discover in himself any fitness for one work more than another, this may be preferred. But the doctrine of the Farm is merely this, that every man ought to stand in primary relations with the work of the world, ought to do it himself, and not to suffer the accident of his having a purse in his pocket, or his having been bred to some dishonorable and injurious craft, to sever him from those duties; and for this reason, that labor is God's education; that he only is a sincere learner, he only can become a master, who learns the secrets of labor, and who by real cunning extorts from nature its sceptre.

Neither would I shut my ears to the plea of the learned professions, of the poet, the priest, the lawgiver, and men of study generally; namely, that in the experience of all men of that class, the amount of manual labor which is necessary to the maintenance of a family indisposes and disqualifies for intellectual exertion. I know, it often, perhaps usually, happens, that where there is a fine organization apt for poetry and philosophy, that individual finds himself compelled to wait on his thoughts, to waste several days that he may enhance and glorify one; and is better taught by a moderate and dainty exercise, such as rambling in the fields, rowing, skating, hunting, than by the downright drudgery of the farmer and the smith. I would not quite forget the venerable counsel of the Egyptian mysteries, which declared that "there were two pairs of eyes in man, and it is requisite that the pair which are beneath should be closed, when the pair that are above them perceive, and that when the pair above are closed, those which are beneath should be opened." Yet I will suggest that no separation from labor can be without some loss of power and of truth to the seer himself; that, I doubt not, the faults and vices of our literature and philosophy, their too great fineness, effeminacy, and melancholy, are attributable to the enervated and sickly habits of the literary class. Better that the book should not be quite so good, and the bookmaker abler and better, and not himself often a ludicrous contrast to all that he has written.

But granting that for ends so sacred and dear, some relaxation must be had, I think, that if a man find in himself any strong bias to poetry, to art, to the contemplative life, drawing him to these things with a devotion incompatible with good husbandry, that man ought to reckon early with himself, and, respecting the compensations of the Universe, ought to ransom himself from the duties of economy, by a certain rigor and privation in his habits. For privileges so rare and grand, let him not stint to pay a great tax. Let him be a cænobite, a pauper, and if need be, celibate also. Let him learn to eat his meals standing, and to relish the taste of fair water and black bread. He may leave to others the costly conveniences of housekeeping, and large hospitality, and the possession of works of art. Let him feel that genius is a hospitality, and that he who can create works of art needs not collect them. He must live in a chamber, and postpone his self-indulgence, forewarned and forearmed against that frequent misfortune of men of genius, — the taste for luxury. This is the tragedy of genius, — attempting to drive along the ecliptic with one horse of the heavens and one horse of the earth, there is only discord and ruin and downfall to chariot and charioteer.

The duty that every man should assume his own vows, should call the institutions of society to account, and examine their fitness to him, gains in emphasis, if we look at our modes of living. Is our housekeeping sacred and honorable? Does it raise and inspire us, or does it cripple us instead? I ought to be armed by every part and function of my household, by all my social function, by my economy, by my feasting, by my voting, by my traffic. Yet I am almost no party to any of these things. Custom does it for me, gives me no power therefrom, and runs me in debt to boot. We spend our incomes for paint and paper, for a hundred trifles, I know not what, and not for the things of a man. Our expense is almost all for conformity. It is for cake that we run in debt; 't is not the intellect, not the heart, not beauty, not worship, that costs so much. Why needs any man be rich? Why must he have horses, fine garments, handsome apartments, access to public houses, and places of amusement? Only for want of thought. Give his mind a new image, and he flees into a solitary garden or garret to enjoy it, and is richer with that dream, than the fee of a county could make him. But we are first thoughtless, and then find that we are moneyless. We are first sensual, and then must be rich. We dare not trust our wit for making our house pleasant to our friend, and so we buy ice-creams. He is accustomed to carpets, and we have not sufficient character to put floor-cloths out of his mind whilst he stays in the house, and so we pile the floor with carpets. Let the house rather be a temple of the Furies of Lacedæmon, formidable and holy to all, which none but a Spartan may enter or so much as behold. As soon as there is faith, as soon as there is society, comfits and cushions will be left to slaves. Expense will be inventive and heroic. We shall eat hard and lie hard, we shall dwell like the ancient Romans in narrow tenements, whilst our public edifices, like theirs, will be worthy, for their proportion, of the landscape in which we set them, for conversation, for art, for music, for worship. We shall be rich to great purposes; poor only for selfish ones.

Now what help for these evils? How can the man who has learned but one art, procure all the conveniences of life honestly? Shall we say all we think? — Perhaps with his own hands. Suppose he collects or makes them ill; — yet he has learned their lesson. If he cannot do that. — Then perhaps he can go without. Immense wisdom and riches are in that. It is better to go without, than to have them at too great a cost. Let us learn the meaning of economy. Economy is a high, humane office, a sacrament, when its aim is grand; when it is the prudence of simple tastes, when it is practised for freedom, or love, or devotion. Much of the economy which we see in houses is of a base origin, and is best kept out of sight. Parched corn eaten to-day that I may have roast fowl to my dinner on Sunday, is a baseness; but parched corn and a house with one apartment, that I may be free of all perturbations, that I may be serene and docile to what the mind shall speak, and girt and road-ready for the lowest mission of knowledge or good-will, is frugality for gods and heroes.

Can we not learn the lesson of self-help? Society is full of infirm people, who incessantly summon others to serve them. They contrive everywhere to exhaust for their single comfort the entire means and appliances of that luxury to which our invention has yet attained. Sofas, ottomans, stoves, wine, game-fowl, spices, perfumes, rides, the theatre, entertainments, — all these they want, they need, and whatever can be suggested more than these, they crave also, as if it was the bread which should keep them from starving; and if they miss any one, they represent themselves as the most wronged and most wretched persons on earth. One must have been born and bred with them to know how to prepare a meal for their learned stomach. Meantime, they never bestir themselves to serve another person; not they! they have a great deal more to do for themselves than they can possibly perform, nor do they once perceive the cruel joke of their lives, but the more odious they grow, the sharper is the tone of their complaining and craving. Can anything be so elegant as to have few wants and to serve them one's self, so as to have somewhat left to give, instead of being always prompt to grab? It is more elegant to answer one's own needs, than to be richly served; inelegant perhaps it may look to-day, and to a few, but it is an elegance forever and to all.

I do not wish to be absurd and pedantic in reform. I do not wish to push my criticism on the state of things around me to that extravagant mark, that shall compel me to suicide, or to an absolute isolation from the advantages of civil society. If we suddenly plant our foot, and say, — I will neither eat nor drink nor wear nor touch any food or fabric which I do not know to be innocent, or deal with any person whose whole manner of life is not clear and rational, we shall stand still. Whose is so? Not mine; not thine; not his. But I think we must clear ourselves each one by the interrogation, whether we have earned our bread to-day by the hearty contribution of our energies to the common benefit? and we must not cease to *tend* to the correction of flagrant wrongs, by laying one stone aright every day.

But the idea which now begins to agitate society has a wider scope than our daily employments, our households, and the institutions of property. We are to revise the whole of our social structure, the state, the school, religion, marriage, trade, science, and explore their foundations in our own nature; we are to see that the world not only fitted the former men, but fits us, and to clear ourselves of every usage which has not its roots in our own mind. What is a man born for but to be a Reformer, a Re-maker of what man has made; a renouncer of lies; a restorer of truth and good, imitating that great Nature which embosoms us all, and which sleeps no moment on an old past, but every hour repairs herself, yielding us every morning a new day, and with every pulsation a new life? Let him renounce everything which is not true to him, and put all his practices back on their first thoughts, and do nothing for which he has not the whole world for his reason. If there are inconveniences, and what is called ruin in the way, because we have so enervated and maimed ourselves, yet it would be like dying of perfumes to sink in the effort to re-attach the deeds of every day to the holy and mysterious recesses of life.

The power, which is at once spring and regulator in all efforts of reform, is the conviction that there is an infinite worthiness in man which will appear at the call of worth, and that all particular reforms are the removing of some impediment. Is it not the highest duty that man should be honored in us? I ought not to allow any man, because he has broad lands, to feel that he is rich in my presence. I ought to make him feel that I can do without his riches, that I cannot be bought, — neither by comfort, neither by pride, — and though I be utterly penniless, and receiving bread from him, that he is the poor man beside me. And if, at the same time, a woman or a child discovers a sentiment of piety, or a juster way of thinking than mine, I ought to confess it by my respect and obedience, though it go to alter my whole way of life.

The Americans have many virtues, but they have not Faith and Hope. I know no two words whose meaning is more lost sight of. We use these words as if they were as obsolete as Selah and Amen. And yet they have the broadest meaning, and the most cogent application to Boston in this year. The Americans have little faith. They rely on the power of a dollar; they are deaf to a sentiment. They think you may talk the north-wind down as easily as raise society; and no class more faithless than the scholars or intellectual men. Now if I talk with a sincere wise man, and my friend, with a poet, with a conscientious youth who is still under the dominion of his own wild thoughts, and not yet harnessed in the team of society to drag with us all in the ruts of custom, I see at once how paltry is all this generation of unbelievers, and what a house of cards their institutions are, and I see what one brave man, what one great thought executed might effect. I see that the reason of the distrust of the practical man in all theory is his inability to perceive the means whereby we work. Look, he says, at the tools with which this world of yours is to be built. As we cannot make a planet, with atmosphere, rivers, and forests, by means of the best carpenters' or engineers' tools, with chemist's laboratory and smith's forge to boot, — so neither can we ever construct that heavenly society you prate of, out of foolish, sick, selfish men and women, such as we know them to be. But the believer not only beholds his heaven to be possible, but already to begin to exist, — not by the men or materials the statesman uses, but by men transfigured and raised above themselves by the power of principles. To principles something else is possible that transcends all the power of expedients.

Every great and commanding moment in the annals of the world is the triumph of some enthusiasm. The victories of the Arabs after Mahomet, who, in a few years, from a small and mean beginning, established a larger empire than that of Rome, is an example. They did they knew not what. The naked Derar, horsed on an idea, was found an overmatch for a troop of Roman cavalry. The women fought like men, and conquered the Roman men. They were miserably equipped, miserably fed. They were Temperance troops. There was neither brandy nor flesh needed to feed them. They conquered Asia, and Africa, and Spain, on barley. The Caliph Omar's walking-stick struck more terror into those who saw it, than another man's sword. His diet was barley bread; his sauce was salt; and oftentimes by way of abstinence he ate his bread without salt. His drink was water. His palace was built of mud; and when he left Medina to go to the conquest of Jerusalem, he rode on a red camel, with a wooden platter hanging at his saddle, with a bottle of water and two sacks, one holding barley, and the other dried fruits.

But there will dawn erelong on our politics, on our modes of living, a nobler morning than that Arabian faith, in the sentiment of love. This is the one remedy for all ills, the panacea of nature. We must be lovers, and at once the impossible becomes possible. Our age and history, for these thousand years, has not been the history of kindness, but of selfishness. Our distrust is very expensive. The money we spend for courts and prisons is very ill laid out. We make, by distrust, the thief, and burglar, and incendiary, and by our court and jail we keep him so. An acceptance of the sentiment of love throughout Christendom for a season, would bring the felon and the outcast to our side in tears, with the devotion of his faculties to our service. See this wide society of laboring men and women. We allow ourselves to be served by them, we live apart from them, and meet them without a salute in the streets. We do not greet their talents, nor rejoice in their good fortune, nor foster their hopes, nor in the assembly of the people vote for what is dear to them. Thus we enact the part of the selfish noble and king from the foundation of the world. See, this tree always bears one fruit. In every household, the peace of a pair is poisoned by the malice, slyness, indolence, and alienation of domestics. Let any two matrons meet, and observe how soon their conversation turns on the troubles from their "*help*," as our phrase is. In every knot of laborers, the rich man does not feel himself among his friends, — and at the polls he finds them arrayed in a mass in distinct opposition to him. We complain that the politics of masses of the people are controlled by designing men, and led in opposition to manifest justice and the common weal, and to their own interest. But the people do not wish to be represented or ruled by the ignorant and base. They only vote for these, because they were asked with the voice and semblance of kindness. They will not vote for them long. They inevitably prefer wit and probity. To use an Egyptian metaphor, it is not their will for any long time "to raise the nails of wild beasts, and to depress the heads of the sacred birds." Let our affection flow out to our fellows; it would operate in a day the greatest of all revolutions. It is better to work on institutions by the sun than by the wind. The state must consider the poor man, and all voices must speak for him. Every child that is born must have a just chance for his bread. Let the amelioration in our laws of property proceed from the concession of the rich, not from the grasping of the poor. Let us begin by habitual imparting. Let us understand that the equitable rule is, that no one should take more than his share, let him be ever so rich. Let me feel that I am to be a lover. I am to see to it that the world is the better for me, and to find my reward in the act. Love would put a new face on this weary old world in which we dwell as pagans and enemies too long, and it would warm the heart to see how fast the vain diplomacy of statesmen, the impotence of armies, and navies, and lines of defence, would be superseded by this unarmed child. Love will creep where it cannot go, will accomplish that by imperceptible methods, — being its own lever, fulcrum, and power, — which force could never achieve. Have you not seen in the woods, in a late autumn morning, a poor fungus or mushroom, — a plant without any solidity, nay, that seemed nothing but a soft mush or jelly, — by its constant, total, and inconceivably gentle pushing, manage to break its way up through the frosty ground, and actually to lift a hard crust on its head? It is the symbol of the power of kindness. The virtue of this principle in human society in application to great interests is obsolete and forgotten. Once or twice in history it has been tried in illustrious instances, with signal success. This great, overgrown, dead Christendom of ours still keeps alive at least the name of a lover of mankind. But one day all men will be lovers; and every calamity will be dissolved in the universal sunshine.

Will you suffer me to add one trait more to this portrait of man the reformer? The mediator between the spiritual and the actual world should have a great prospective prudence. An Arabian poet describes his hero by saying,

> "Sunshine was he
> In the winter day;
> And in the midsummer
> Coolness and shade."

He who would help himself and others, should not be a subject of irregular and interrupted impulses of virtue, but a continent, persisting, immovable person, — such as we have seen a few scattered up and down in time for the blessing of the world; men who have in the gravity of their nature a quality which answers to the fly-wheel in a mill, which distributes the motion equably over all the wheels, and hinders it from falling unequally and suddenly in destructive shocks. It is better that joy should be spread over all the day in the form of strength, than that it should be concentrated into ecstasies, full of danger and followed by reactions. There is a sublime prudence, which is the very highest that we know of man, which, believing in a vast future, — sure of more to come than is yet seen, — postpones always the present hour to the whole life; postpones talent to genius, and special results to character. As the merchant gladly takes money from his income to add to his capital, so is the great man willing to lose particular powers and talents, so that he gain in the elevation of his life. The opening of the spiritual senses disposes men ever to greater sacrifices, to leave their signal talents, their means and skill of procuring a present success, their power and their fame, — to cast all things behind, in the insatiable thirst for divine communications. A purer fame, a greater power, rewards the sacrifice. It is the conversion of our harvest into seed. As the farmer casts into the ground the finest ears of his grain, the time will come when we too shall hold nothing back, but shall eagerly convert more than we now possess into means and powers, when we shall be willing to sow the sun and the moon for seeds.

26. Democracy and Education*

John Dewey

Chapter VII
The Democratic Conception in Education

For the most part, save incidentally, we have hitherto been concerned with education as it may exist in any social group. We have now to make explicit the differences in the spirit, material, and method of education as it operates in different types of community life. To say that education is a social function, securing direction and development in the immature through their participation in the life of the group to which they belong, is to say in effect that education will vary with the quality of life which prevails in a group. Particularly is it true that a society which not only changes but which has the ideal of such change as will improve it, will have different standards and methods of education from one which aims simply at the perpetuation of its own customs. To make the general ideas set forth applicable to our own educational practice, it is, therefore, necessary to come to closer quarters with the nature of present social life.

   1. **The Implications of Human Association.** — Society is one word, but many things. Men associate together in all kinds of ways and for all kinds of purposes. One man is concerned in a multitude of diverse groups, in which his associates may be quite different. It often seems as if they had nothing in common except that they are modes of associated life. Within every larger social organization there are numerous minor groups: not only political subdivisions, but industrial, scientific, religious, associations. There are political parties with differing aims, social sets, cliques, gangs, corporations, partnerships,

*John Dewey published *Democracy and Education: An Introduction to the Philosophy of Education* in 1916. This particular selection was taken from Dewey, *Democracy and Education: An Introduction to the Philosophy of Education*, Chapter VII (New York: Macmillan Company, 1922), 94–116.

groups bound closely together by ties of blood, and so in endless variety. In many modern states, and in some ancient, there is great diversity of populations, of varying languages, religions, moral codes, and traditions. From this standpoint, many a minor political unit, one of our large cities, for example, is a congeries of loosely associated societies, rather than an inclusive and permeating community of action and thought.

The terms society, community, are thus ambiguous. They have both a eulogistic or normative sense, and a descriptive sense; a meaning *de jure* and a meaning *de facto*. In social philosophy, the former connotation is almost always uppermost. Society is conceived as one by its very nature. The qualities which accompany this unity, praiseworthy community of purpose and welfare, loyalty to public ends, mutuality of sympathy, are emphasized. But when we look at the facts which the term *denotes* instead of confining our attention to its intrinsic *connotation*, we find not unity, but a plurality of societies, good and bad. Men banded together in a criminal conspiracy, business aggregations that prey upon the public while serving it, political machines held together by the interest of plunder, are included. If it is said that such organizations are not societies because they do not meet the ideal requirements of the notion of society, the answer, in part, is that the conception of society is then made so "ideal" as to be of no use, having no reference to facts; and in part, that each of these organizations, no matter how opposed to the interests of other groups, has something of the praiseworthy qualities of "Society" which hold it together. There is honor among thieves, and a band of robbers has a common interest as respects its members. Gangs are marked by fraternal feeling, and narrow cliques by intense loyalty to their own codes. Family life may be marked by exclusiveness, suspicion, and jealousy as to those without, and yet be a model of amity and mutual aid within. Any education given by a group tends to socialize its members, but the quality and value of the socialization depends upon the habits and aims of the group.

Hence, once more, the need of a measure for the worth of any given mode of social life. In seeking this measure, we have to avoid two extremes. We cannot set up, out of our heads, something we regard as an ideal society. We must base our conception upon societies which actually exist, in order to have any assurance that our ideal is a practicable one. But, as we have just seen, the ideal cannot simply repeat the traits which are actually found. The problem is to extract the desirable traits of forms of community life which actually exist, and employ them to criticize undesirable features and suggest improvement. Now in any social group whatever, even in a gang of thieves, we find some interest held in common, and we find a certain amount of interaction and coöperative intercourse with other groups. From these two traits we derive our standard. How numerous and varied are the interests which are consciously shared? How full and free is the interplay with other forms of association? If we apply these considerations to, say, a criminal band, we find that the ties which consciously hold the members together are few in number, reducible almost to a common interest in plunder; and that they are of such a nature as to isolate the group from other groups with respect to give and take of the values of life. Hence, the education such a society gives is partial and distorted. If we take, on the other hand, the kind of family life which illustrates the standard, we find that there are material, intellectual, æsthetic interests in which all participate and that the progress of one member has worth for the experience of other members — it is readily communicable — and that the family is not an isolated whole, but enters intimately into relationships with business groups, with schools, with all the agencies of culture, as well as with other similar groups, and that it plays a due part in the political organization and in return receives support from it. In short, there are many interests consciously communicated and shared; and there are varied and free points of contact with other modes of association.

I. Let us apply the first element in this criterion to a despotically governed state. It is not true there is no common interest in such an organization between governed and governors. The authorities in command must make some appeal to the native activities of the subjects, must call some of their powers into play. Talleyrand said that a government could do everything with bayonets except sit on them. This cynical declaration is at least a recognition that the bond of union is not merely one of coercive force. It may be said, however, that the activities appealed to are themselves unworthy and degrading — that such a government calls into functioning activity simply capacity for fear. In a way, this statement is true. But it overlooks the fact that fear need not be an undesirable factor in experience. Caution, circumspection, prudence, desire to foresee future events so as to avert what is harmful, these desirable traits are as much a product of calling the impulse of fear into play as is cowardice and abject submission. The real difficulty is that the appeal to fear is *isolated*. In evoking dread and hope of specific tangible reward — say comfort and ease — many other capacities are left untouched. Or rather, they are affected, but in such a way as to pervert them. Instead of operating on their own account they are reduced to mere servants of attaining pleasure and avoiding pain.

This is equivalent to saying that there is no extensive number of common interests; there is no free play back and forth among the members of the social group. Stimulation and response are exceedingly one sided. In order to have a large number of values in common, all the members of the group must have an equable opportunity to receive and to take from others. There must be a large variety of shared undertakings and experiences. Otherwise, the influences which educate some into masters, educate others into slaves. And the experience of each party loses in meaning, when the free interchange of varying modes of life-experience is arrested. A separation into a privileged and a subject-class prevents social endosmosis. The evils thereby affecting the superior class are less material and less perceptible, but equally real. Their culture tends to be sterile, to be turned back to feed on itself; their art becomes a showy display and artificial; their wealth luxurious; their knowledge overspecialized; their manners fastidious rather than humane.

Lack of the free and equitable intercourse which springs from a variety of shared interests makes intellectual stimulation unbalanced. Diversity of stimulation means novelty, and novelty — means challenge to thought. The more activity is restricted to a few definite lines — as it is when there are rigid class lines preventing adequate interplay of experiences — the more action tends to become routine on the part of the class at a disadvantage, and capricious, aimless, and explosive on the part of the class having the materially fortunate position. Plato defined a slave as one who accepts from another the purposes which control his conduct. This condition obtains even where there is no slavery in the legal sense. It is found wherever men are engaged in activity which is socially serviceable, but whose service they do not understand and have no personal interest in. Much is said about scientific management of work. It is a narrow view which restricts the science which secures efficiency of operation to movements of the muscles. The chief opportunity for science is the discovery of the relations of a man to his work — including his relations to others who take part — which will enlist his intelligent interest in what he is doing. Efficiency in production often demands division of labor. But it is reduced to a mechanical routine unless workers see the technical, intellectual, and social relationships involved in what they do, and engage in their work because of the motivation furnished by such perceptions. The tendency to reduce such things as efficiency of activity and scientific management to purely technical externals is evidence of the one-sided stimulation of thought given to those in control of industry — those who supply its aims. Because of their lack of all-round and well-balanced social interest, there is not sufficient stimulus for attention to the human factors and relationships in industry. Intelligence is narrowed to the factors concerned with technical production and marketing of goods. No doubt, a very acute and intense intelligence in these narrow lines can be developed, but the failure to take into account the significant social factors means none the less an absence of mind, and a corresponding distortion of emotional life.

II. This illustration (whose point is to be extended to all associations lacking reciprocity of interest) brings us to our second point. The isolation and exclusiveness of a gang or clique brings its antisocial spirit into relief. But this same spirit is found wherever one group has interests 'of its own' which shut it out from full interaction with other groups, so that its prevailing purpose is the protection of what it has got, instead of reorganization and progress through wider relationships. It marks nations in their isolation from one another; families which seclude their domestic concerns as if they had no connection with a larger life; schools when separated from the interest of home and community; the divisions of rich and poor; learned and unlearned. The essential point is that isolation makes for rigidity and formal institutionalizing of life, for static and selfish ideals within the group. That savage tribes regard aliens and enemies as synonymous is not accidental. It springs from the fact that they have identified their experience with rigid adherence to their past customs. On such a basis it is wholly logical to fear intercourse with others, for such contact might dissolve custom. It would certainly occasion reconstruction. It is a commonplace that an alert and expanding mental life depends upon an enlarging range of contact with the physical environment. But the principle applies even more significantly to the field where we are apt to ignore it — the sphere of social contacts.

Every expansive era in the history of mankind has coincided with the operation of factors which have tended to eliminate distance between peoples and classes previously hemmed off from one another. Even the alleged benefits of war, so far as more than alleged, spring from the fact that conflict of peoples at least enforces intercourse between them and thus accidentally enables them to learn from one another, and thereby to expand their horizons. Travel, economic and commercial tendencies, have at present gone far to break down external barriers; to bring peoples and classes into closer and more perceptible connection with one another. It remains for the most part to secure the intellectual and emotional significance of this physical annihilation of space.

2. The Democratic Ideal. — The two elements in our criterion both point to democracy. The first signifies not only more numerous and more varied points of shared common interest, but greater reliance upon the recognition of mutual interests as a factor in social control. The second means not only freer interaction between social groups (once isolated so far as intention could keep up a separation) but change in social habit — its continuous readjustment through meeting the new situations produced by varied intercourse. And these two traits are precisely what characterize the democratically constituted society.

Upon the educational side, we note first that the realization of a form of social life in which interests are mutually interpenetrating, and where progress, or readjustment, is an important consideration, makes a democratic community more interested than other communities have cause to be in deliberate and systematic education. The devotion of democracy to education is a familiar fact. The superficial explanation is that a government resting upon popular suffrage cannot be successful unless those who elect and who obey their governors are educated. Since a democratic society repudiates the principle of external authority, it must find a substitute in voluntary disposition and interest; these can be created only by education. But there is a deeper explanation. A democracy is more than a form of government; it is primarily a mode of associated living, of conjoint communicated experience. The extension in space of the number of individuals who participate in an interest so that each has to refer his own action to that of others, and to consider the action of others to give point and direction to his own, is equivalent to the breaking down of those barriers of class, race, and national territory which kept men from perceiving the full import of their activity. These more numerous and more varied points of contact denote a greater diversity of stimuli to which an individual has to respond; they consequently put a premium on variation in his action. They secure a liberation of powers which remain suppressed as long as the incitations to action are partial, as they must be in a group which in its exclusiveness shuts out many interests.

The widening of the area of shared concerns, and the liberation of a greater diversity of personal capacities which characterize a democracy, are not of course the product of deliberation and conscious effort. On the contrary, they were caused by the development of modes of manufacture and commerce, travel, migration, and intercommunication which flowed from the command of science over natural energy. But after greater individualization on one hand, and a broader community of interest on the other have come into existence, it is a matter of deliberate effort to sustain and extend them. Obviously a society to which stratification into separate classes would be fatal, must see to it that intellectual opportunities are accessible to all on equable and easy terms. A society marked off into classes need be specially attentive only to the education of its ruling elements. A society which is mobile, which is full of channels for the distribution of a change occurring anywhere, must see to it that its members are educated to personal initiative and adaptability. Otherwise, they will be overwhelmed by the changes in which they are caught and whose significance or connections they do not perceive. The result will be a confusion in which a few will appropriate to themselves the results of the blind and externally directed activities of others.

3. The Platonic Educational Philosophy. — Subsequent chapters will be devoted to making explicit the implications of the democratic ideas in education. In the remaining portions of this chapter, we shall consider the educational theories which have been evolved in three epochs when the social import of education was especially conspicuous. The first one to be considered is that of Plato. No one could better express than did he the fact that a society is stably organized when each individual is doing that for which he has aptitude by nature in such a way as to be useful to others (or to contribute to the whole to which he belongs); and that it is the business of education to discover these aptitudes and progressively to train them for social use. Much which has been said so far is borrowed from what Plato first consciously taught the world. But conditions which he could not intellectually control led him to restrict these ideas in their application. He never got any conception of the indefinite plurality of activities which may characterize an individual and a social group, and consequently limited his view to a limited number of *classes* of capacities and of social arrangements.

Plato's starting point is that the organization of society depends ultimately upon knowledge of the end of existence. If we do not know its end, we shall be at the mercy of accident and caprice. Unless we know the end, the good, we shall have no criterion for rationally deciding what the possibilities are which should be promoted, nor how social arrangements are to be ordered. We shall have no conception of the proper limits and distribution of activities — what he called justice — as a trait of both individual and social organization. But how is the knowledge of the final and permanent good to be achieved? In dealing with this question we come upon the seemingly insuperable obstacle that such knowledge is not possible save in a just and harmonious social order. Everywhere else the mind is distracted and misled by false valuations and false perspectives. A disorganized and factional society sets up a number of different models and standards. Under such conditions it is impossible for the individual to attain consistency of mind. Only a complete whole is fully self-consistent. A society which rests upon the supremacy of some factor over another irrespective of its rational or proportionate claims, inevitably leads thought astray. It puts a premium on certain things and slurs over others, and creates a mind whose seeming unity is forced and distorted. Education proceeds ultimately from the patterns furnished by institutions, customs, and laws. Only in a just state will these be such as to give the right education; and only those who have rightly trained minds will be able to recognize the end, and ordering principle of things. We seem to be caught in a hopeless circle. However, Plato suggested a way out. A few men, philosophers or lovers of wisdom — or truth — may by study learn at least in outline the proper patterns of true existence. If a powerful ruler should form a state after these patterns, then its regulations could be preserved. An education could be given which would sift individuals, discovering what they were good for, and supplying a method of assigning each to the work in life for which his nature fits him. Each doing his own part, and never transgressing, the order and unity of the whole would be maintained.

It would be impossible to find in any scheme of philosophic thought a more adequate recognition on one hand of the educational significance of social arrangements and, on the other, of the dependence of those arrangements upon the means used to educate the young. It would be impossible to find a deeper sense of the function of education in discovering and developing personal capacities, and training them so that they would connect with the activities of others. Yet the society in which the theory was propounded was so undemocratic that Plato could not work out a solution for the problem whose terms he clearly saw.

While he affirmed with emphasis that the place of the individual in society should not be determined by birth or wealth or any conventional status, but by his own nature as discovered in the process of education, he had no perception of the uniqueness of individuals. For him they fall by nature into classes, and into a very small number of classes at that. Consequently the testing and sifting function of education only shows to which one of three classes an individual belongs. There being no recognition that each individual constitutes his own class, there could be no recognition of the infinite diversity of active tendencies and combinations of tendencies of which an individual is capable.

There were only three types of faculties or powers in the individual's constitution. Hence education would soon reach a static limit in each class, for only diversity makes change and progress.

In some individuals, appetites naturally dominate; they are assigned to the laboring and trading class, which expresses and supplies human wants. Others reveal, upon education, that over and above appetites, they have a generous, outgoing, assertively courageous disposition. They become the citizen-subjects of the state; its defenders in war; its internal guardians in peace. But their limit is fixed by their lack of reason, which is a capacity to grasp the universal. Those who possess this are capable of the highest kind of education, and become in time the legislators of the state — for laws are the universals which control the particulars of experience. Thus it is not true that in intent, Plato subordinated the individual to the social whole. But it is true that lacking the perception of the uniqueness of every individual, his incommensurability with others, and consequently not recognizing that a society might change and yet be stable, his doctrine of limited powers and classes came in net effect to the idea of the subordination of individuality.

We cannot better Plato's conviction that an individual is happy and society well organized when each individual engages in those activities for which he has a natural equipment, nor his conviction that it is the primary office of education to discover this equipment to its possessor and train him for its effective use. But progress in knowledge has made us aware of the superficiality of Plato's lumping of individuals and their original powers into a few sharply marked-off classes; it has taught us that original capacities are indefinitely numerous and variable. It is but the other side of this fact to say that in the degree in which society has become democratic, social organization means utilization of the specific and variable qualities of individuals, not stratification by classes. Although his educational philosophy was revolutionary, it was none the less in bondage to static ideals. He thought that change or alteration was evidence of lawless flux; that true reality was unchangeable. Hence while he would radically change the existing state of society, his aim was to construct a state in which change would subsequently have no place. The final end of life is fixed; given a state framed with this end in view, not even minor details are to be altered. Though they might not be inherently important, yet if permitted they would inure the minds of men to the idea of change, and hence be dissolving and anarchic. The breakdown of his philosophy is made apparent in the fact that he could not trust to gradual improvements in education to bring about a better society which should then improve education, and so on indefinitely. Correct education could not come into existence until an ideal state existed, and after that education would be devoted simply to its conservation. For the existence of this state he was obliged to trust to some happy accident by which philosophic wisdom should happen to coincide with possession of ruling power in the state.

4. The "Individualistic" Ideal of the Eighteenth Century. — In the eighteenth-century philosophy we find ourselves in a very different circle of ideas. "Nature" still means something antithetical to existing social organization; Plato exercised a great influence upon Rousseau. But the voice of nature now speaks for the diversity of individual talent and for the need of free development of individuality in all its variety. Education in accord with nature furnishes the goal and the method of instruction and discipline. Moreover, the native or original endowment was conceived, in extreme cases, as nonsocial or even as antisocial. Social arrangements were thought of as mere external expedients by which these nonsocial individuals might secure a greater amount of private happiness for themselves.

Nevertheless, these statements convey only an inadequate idea of the true significance of the movement. In reality its chief interest was in progress and in social progress. The seeming antisocial philosophy was a somewhat transparent mask for an impetus toward a wider and freer society — towards cosmopolitanism. The positive ideal was humanity. In membership in humanity, as distinct from a state, man's capacities would be liberated; while in existing political organizations his powers were hampered and distorted to meet the requirements and selfish interests of the rulers of the state. The doctrine of extreme individualism was but the counterpart, the obverse, of ideals of the indefinite perfectibility of man and of a social organization having a scope as wide as humanity. The emancipated individual was to become the organ and agent of a comprehensive and progressive society.

The heralds of this gospel were acutely conscious of the evils of the social estate in which they found themselves. They attributed these evils to the limitations imposed upon the free powers of man. Such limitation was both distorting and corrupting. Their impassioned devotion to emancipation of life from external restrictions which operated to the exclusive advantage of the class to whom a past feudal system consigned power, found intellectual formulation in a worship of nature. To give "nature" full swing was to replace an artificial, corrupt, and inequitable social order by a new and better kingdom of humanity. Unrestrained faith in Nature as both a model and a working power was strengthened by the advances of natural science. Inquiry freed from prejudice and artificial restraints of church and state had revealed that the world is a scene of law. The Newtonian solar system, which expressed the reign of natural law, was a scene of wonderful harmony, where every force balanced with every other. Natural law would accomplish the same result in human relations, if men would only get rid of the artificial man-imposed coercive restrictions.

Education in accord with nature was thought to be the first step in insuring this more social society. It was plainly seen that economic and political limitations were ultimately dependent upon limitations of thought and feeling. The first step in freeing men from external chains was to emancipate them from the internal chains of false beliefs and ideals. What was called social life, existing institutions, were too false and corrupt to be intrusted with this work. How could it be expected to undertake it when the undertaking meant its own destruction? "Nature" must then be the power to which the enterprise was to be left. Even the extreme sensationalistic theory of knowledge which was current derived itself from this conception. To insist that mind is originally passive and empty was one way of glorifying the possibilities of education. If the mind was a wax tablet to be written upon by objects, there were no limits to the possibility of education by means of the natural environment. And since the natural world of objects is a scene of harmonious "truth," this education would infallibly produce minds filled with the truth.

5. Education as National and as Social. — As soon as the first enthusiasm for freedom waned, the weakness of the theory upon the constructive side became obvious. Merely to leave everything to nature was, after all, but to negate the very idea of education; it was to trust to the accidents of circumstance. Not only was some method required but also some positive organ, some administrative agency for carrying on the process of instruction. The "complete and harmonious development of all powers," having as its social counterpart an enlightened and progressive humanity, required definite organization for its realization. Private individuals here and there could proclaim the gospel; they could not execute the work. A Pestalozzi could try experiments and exhort philanthropically inclined persons having wealth and power to follow his example. But even Pestalozzi saw that any effective pursuit of the new educational ideal required the support of the state. The realization of the new education destined to produce a new society was, after all, dependent upon the activities of existing states. The movement for the democratic idea inevitably became a movement for publicly conducted and administered schools.

So far as Europe was concerned, the historic situation identified the movement for a state-supported education with the nationalistic movement in political life — a fact of incalculable significance for subsequent movements. Under the influence of German thought in particular, education became a civic function and the civic function was identified with the realization of the ideal of the national state. The "state" was substituted for humanity; cosmopolitanism gave way to nationalism. To form the citizen, not the "man," became the aim of education.[1] The historic situation to which reference is made is the after-effects of the Napoleonic conquests, especially in Germany. The German states felt (and subsequent events demonstrate the correctness of the belief) that systematic attention to education was the best means of recovering and maintaining their political integrity and power. Externally they were weak and divided. Under the leadership of Prussian statesmen they made this condition a stimulus to the development of an extensive and thoroughly grounded system of public education.

This change in practice necessarily brought about a change in theory. The individualistic theory receded into the background. The state furnished not only the instrumentalities of public education but also its goal. When the actual practice was such that the school system, from the elementary grades through the university faculties, supplied the patriotic citizen and soldier and the future state official and administrator and furnished the means for military, industrial, and political defense and expansion, it was impossible for theory not to emphasize the aim of social efficiency. And with the immense importance attached to the nationalistic state, surrounded by other competing and more or less hostile states, it was equally impossible to interpret social efficiency in terms of a vague cosmopolitan humanitarianism. Since the maintenance of a particular national sovereignty required subordination of individuals to the superior interests of the state both in military defense and in struggles for international supremacy in commerce, social efficiency was understood to imply a like subordination. The educational process was taken to be one of disciplinary training rather than of personal development. Since, however, the ideal of culture as complete development of personality persisted, educational philosophy attempted a reconciliation of the two ideas. The reconciliation took the form of the conception of the 'organic' character of the state. The individual in his isolation is nothing; only in and through an absorption of the aims and meaning of organized institutions does he attain true personality. What appears to be his subordination to political authority and the demand for sacrifice of himself to the commands of his superiors is in reality but making his own the objective reason manifested in the state — the only way in which he can become truly rational. The notion of development which we have seen to be characteristic of institutional idealism (as in the

Hegelian philosophy) was just such a deliberate effort to combine the two ideas of complete realization of personality and thoroughgoing 'disciplinary' subordination to existing institutions.

The extent of the transformation of educational philosophy which occurred in Germany in the generation occupied by the struggle against Napoleon for national independence, may be gathered from Kant, who well expresses the earlier individual-cosmopolitan ideal. In his treatise on Pedagogics, consisting of lectures given in the later years of the eighteenth century, he defines education as the process by which man becomes man. Mankind begins its history submerged in nature — not as Man who is a creature of reason, while nature furnishes only instinct and appetite. Nature offers simply the germs which education is to develop and perfect. The peculiarity of truly human life is that man has to create himself by his own voluntary efforts; he has to make himself a truly moral, rational, and free being. This creative effort is carried on by the educational activities of slow generations. Its acceleration depends upon men consciously striving to educate their successors not for the existing state of affairs but so as to make possible a future better humanity. But there is the great difficulty. Each generation is inclined to educate its young so as to get along in the present world instead of with a view to the proper end of education: the promotion of the best possible realization of humanity as humanity. Parents educate their children so that they may get on; princes educate their subjects as instruments of their own purposes.

Who, then, shall conduct education so that humanity may improve? We must depend upon the efforts of enlightened men in their private capacity. "All culture begins with private men and spreads outward from them. Simply through the efforts of persons of enlarged inclinations, who are capable of grasping the ideal of a future better condition, is the gradual approximation of human nature to its end possible. . . . Rulers are simply interested in such training as will make their subjects better tools for their own intentions." Even the subsidy by rulers of privately conducted schools must be carefully safeguarded. For the rulers' interest in the welfare of their own nation instead of in what is best for humanity, will make them, if they give money for the schools, wish to draw their plans. We have in this view an express statement of the points characteristic of the eighteenth century individualistic cosmopolitanism. The full development of private personality is identified with the aims of humanity as a whole and with the idea of progress. In addition we have an explicit fear of the hampering influence of a state-conducted and state-regulated education upon the attainment of these ideas. But in less than two decades after this time, Kant's philosophic successors, Fichte and Hegel, elaborated the idea that the chief function of the state is educational; that in particular the regeneration of Germany is to be accomplished by an education carried on in the interests of the state, and that the private individual is of necessity an egoistic, irrational being, enslaved to his appetites and to circumstances unless he submits voluntarily to the educative discipline of state institutions and laws. In this spirit, Germany was the first country to undertake a public, universal, and compulsory system of education extending from the primary school through the university, and to submit to jealous state regulation and supervision all private educational enterprises.

Two results should stand out from this brief historical survey. The first is that such terms as the individual and the social conceptions of education are quite meaningless taken at large, or apart from their context. Plato had the ideal of an education which should equate individual realization and social coherency and stability. His situation forced his ideal into the notion of a society organized in stratified classes, losing the individual in the class. The eighteenth century educational philosophy was highly individualistic in form, but this form was inspired by a noble and generous social ideal: that of a society organized to include humanity, and providing for the indefinite perfectibility of mankind. The idealistic philosophy of Germany in the early nineteenth century endeavored again to equate the ideals of a free and complete development of cultured personality with social discipline and political subordination. It made the national state an intermediary between the realization of private personality on one side and of humanity on the other. Consequently, it is equally possible to state its animating principle with equal truth either in the classic terms of "harmonious development of all the powers of personality" or in the more recent terminology of "social efficiency." All this reënforces the statement which opens this chapter: The conception of education as a social process and function has no definite meaning until we define the kind of society we have in mind.

These considerations pave the way for our second conclusion. One of the fundamental problems of education in and for a democratic society is set by the conflict of a nationalistic and a wider social aim. The earlier cosmopolitan and 'humanitarian' conception suffered both from vagueness and from lack of definite organs of execution and agencies of administration. In Europe, in the Continental states particularly, the new idea of the importance of education for human welfare and progress was captured by national interests and harnessed to do a work whose social aim was definitely narrow and exclusive. The social aim of education and its national aim were identified, and the result was a marked obscuring of the meaning of a social aim.

This confusion corresponds to the existing situation of human intercourse. On the one hand, science, commerce, and art transcend national boundaries. They are largely international in quality and method. They involve interdependencies and coöperation among the peoples inhabiting different countries. At the same time, the idea of national sovereignty has never been as accentuated in politics as it is at the present time. Each nation lives in a state of suppressed hostility and incipient war with its neighbors. Each is supposed to be the supreme judge of its own interests, and it is assumed as matter of course that each has interests which are exclusively its own. To question this is to question the very idea of national sovereignty which is assumed to be basic to political practice and political science. This contradiction (for it is nothing less) between the wider sphere of associated and mutually helpful social life and the narrower sphere of exclusive and hence potentially hostile pursuits and purposes, exacts of educational theory a clearer conception of the meaning of 'social' as a function and test of education than has yet been attained.

Is it possible for an educational system to be conducted by a national state and yet the full social ends of the educative process not be restricted, constrained, and corrupted? Internally, the question has to face the tendencies, due to present economic conditions, which split society into classes some of which are made merely tools for the higher culture of others. Externally, the question is concerned with the reconciliation of national loyalty, of patriotism, with superior devotion to the things which unite men in common ends, irrespective of national political boundaries. Neither phase of the problem can be worked out by merely negative means. It is not enough to see to it that education is not actively used as an instrument to make easier the exploitation of one class by another. School facilities must be secured of such amplitude and efficiency as will in fact and not simply in name discount the effects of economic inequalities, and secure to all the wards of the nation equality of equipment for their future careers. Accomplishment of this end demands not only adequate administrative provision of school facilities, and such supplementation of family resources as will enable youth to take advantage of them, but also such modification of traditional ideals of culture, traditional subjects of study and traditional methods of teaching and discipline as will retain all the youth under educational influences until they are equipped to be masters of their own economic and social careers. The ideal may seem remote of execution, but the democratic ideal of education is a farcical yet tragic delusion except as the ideal more and more dominates our public system of education.

The same principle has application on the side of the considerations which concern the relations of one nation to another. It is not enough to teach the horrors of war and to avoid everything which would stimulate international jealousy and animosity. The emphasis must be put upon whatever binds people together in coöperative human pursuits and results, apart from geographical limitations. The secondary and provisional character of national sovereignty in respect to the fuller, freer, and more fruitful association and intercourse of all human beings with one another must be instilled as a working disposition of mind. If these applications seem to be remote from a consideration of the philosophy of education, the impression shows that the meaning of the idea of education previously developed has not been adequately grasped. This conclusion is bound up with the very idea of education as a freeing of individual capacity in a progressive growth directed to social aims. Otherwise a democratic criterion of education can only be inconsistently applied.

Summary. — Since education is a social process, and there are many kinds of societies, a criterion for educational criticism and construction implies a *particular* social ideal. The two points selected by which to measure the worth of a form of social life are the extent in which the interests of a group are shared by all its members, and the fullness and freedom with which it interacts with other groups. An undesirable society, in other words, is one which internally and externally sets up barriers to free intercourse and communication of experience. A society which makes provision for participation in its good of all its members on equal terms and which secures flexible readjustment of its institutions through interaction of the different forms of associated life is in so far democratic. Such a society must have a type of education which gives individuals a personal interest in social relationships and control, and the habits of mind which secure social changes without introducing disorder.

Three typical historic philosophies of education were considered from this point of view. The Platonic was found to have an ideal formally quite similar to that stated, but which was compromised in its working out by making a class rather than an individual the social unit. The so-called individualism of the eighteenth-century enlightenment was found to involve the notion of a society as broad as humanity, of whose progress the individual was to be the organ. But it lacked any agency for securing the development of its ideal as was evidenced in its falling back upon Nature. The institutional idealistic philosophies of the nineteenth century supplied this lack by making the national state the agency, but in so doing narrowed the conception of the social aim to those who were members of the same political unit, and reintroduced the idea of the subordination of the individual to the institution.

Note

[1] There is a much neglected strain in Rousseau tending intellectually in this direction. He opposed the existing state of affairs on the ground that it formed *neither* the citizen nor the man. Under existing conditions, he preferred to try for the latter rather than for the former. But there are many sayings of his which point to the formation of the citizen as ideally the higher, and which indicate that his own endeavor, as embodied in the "Émile," was simply the best makeshift the corruption of the times permitted him to sketch.

Part V
Challenges to Authority

27. A Defence of Liberty against Tyrants*

Philippe Duplessis-Mornay

The third question.

Whether it be lawfull to resist a Prince which doth oppresse or ruine a publike State, and how far such resistance may be extended, by whom, how, and by what right, or law it is permitted.

…We have shewed already, that in the establishing of the King, there were two alliances or covenants contracted: the first between God, the King, and the people, of which wee have formerly treated: the second between the King and the people, of which wee must now say some-what.…

It is certain then, that the people by way of stipulation, require a performance of covenants, the King promises it. Now the condition of a Stipulator is in termes of law more worthy than of a promiser. The people asketh the King, whether he will govern justly and according to the lawes? He promiseth he will. Then the people answereth, and not before, that whilest he governes uprightly, they will obey faithfully. The King therefore promiseth simply and absolutely, the people upon condition: the which failing to be accomplished, the people rest according to equity and reason, quit from their promise.

In the first covenant, or contract, there is only an obligation to piety: in the second, to justice. In that the King promiseth to serve God religiously: in this, to rule the people

* *Vindiciæ contra Tyrannos* was first published in 1579 under the pseudonym Junius Brutus. Many scholars attribute this treatise to Philippe Duplessis-Mornay (1549–1623), while others credit Hubert Languet (1518–1581). This particular selection was excerpted from the third question in Junius Brutus, *Vindiciæ contra Tyrannos: A Defence of Liberty against Tyrants. Or, of the Lawfull Power of the Prince over the People, and of the People over the Prince* (London: Printed by Matthew Simmons and Robert Ibbitson, in Smithfield, near the Queens-head Tavern, 1648).

justly. By the one he is obliged with the utmost of his endeavours to procure the glory of God: by the other, the profit of the people. In the first there is a condition expressed, If thou keep my commandments: in the second, If thou distribute justice equally to every man. God is the proper revenger of deficiency in the former, and the whole people the lawfull punisher of delinquency in the latter, or the Estates, the representative body thereof, who have assumed to themselves the protection of the people. This hath been always practised in all well-governed Estates....

If we take into our consideration the condition of the Empires, Kingdomes and States of times, there is not any of them worthy of those names, where there is not some such covenant or confederacy between the people and the Prince....

Briefly, there is not any man can denie, but that there is a contract mutually obligatorie between the King and the Subjects, which requires the people to obey faithfully, and the King to governe lawfully, for the performance whereof the King sweares first, and after the people....

And what if all these ceremonies, solemne oaths, nay sacramentall promises had never been taken? Doth not nature her selfe sufficiently teach that Kings were on this condition ordained by the people, that they should governe well? Judges that they should distribute justice uprightly? Captaines in the warre, that they should lead their Armes against their enemies: If on the contrary, they themselves forrage and spoile their subjects, and instead of governors become enemies, as they leave indeed the true and essentiall qualities of a King, so neither ought the people to acknowledge them for lawfull Princes. But what if a people (you will reply) subdued by force, be compeld by the King to take an oath of servitude? And what if a robber, pirate, or tyrant, (I will answer) with whom no bond of humane societie can be effectuall, holding his dagger to your throate, constraine you presently to become bound in a great sum of money? Is it not an unquestionable Maxime in Law, that a promise exacted by violence cannot binde? especially if any thing be promised against common reason, or the law of nature? Is there any thing more repugnant to nature and reason, than that a people should manicle and fetter themselves; and to be obliged by promise to the Prince, with their own hands and weapons to be their own executioners? There is therefore a mutuall obligation between the King and the people, which whether it be civill or naturall onely, whether tacite, or expressed in words, it cannot by any meanes be annihilated, nor by any Law be abrogated, much lesse by force made voyde. And this obligation is of such power, that the Prince which wilfully violates it, is a tyrant: and the people which purposely breakes it, may be justly termed seditious.

Hitherto we have treated of a King, it now rests wee doe some-what more fully describe a Tyrant. Wee have shewed that he is a King, which lawfully governes a Kingdome, either derived to him by succession, or committed to him by Election. It followes therefore that he is reputed a tyrant, which as opposite to a King, either gaines a kingdome by violence, or indirect meanes, or being invested therewith by lawfull election or succession, governes it not according to law and equitie, or neglects those contracts and agreements, to the observation whereof he was strictly obliged at his reception. All which may very well occurre in one and the same person. The first is commonly called a tyrant without title: the second a tyrant by practise. Now it may well so come to passe, that he which possesseth himselfe of a kingdome by force, to governe justly, and he on whom it descends by a lawfull title, to rule unjustly. But for so much as a kingdome is rather a right than an inheritance, and an office than a possession: he seemes rather worthy the name of a tyrant, which unworthily acquits himselfe of his charge, than he which entered into his place by a wrong dore. In the same sence is the Pope called an intruder which entered by indirect means into the papacy: and he an abuser which governs il in it.

Pithagoras sayes, *That a worthy stranger is to be prefer'd before an unworthy Citizen, yea though he be a Kinsman.* Let it be lawfull also for us to say, that a Prince which gained his Principality by indirect courses, provided hee governe according to law, and administer justice equally, is much to be preferred before him, which carrieth himselfe tyrannously, although hee were legally invested into his government with all the Ceremonies and Rites thereunto appertaining.

For seeing that Kings were instituted to feede, to judge, to cure the diseases of the people: Certainely I had rather that a Thiefe should feede me, than a Shepherd devoure me: I had rather receive justice from a Robber, than out-rage from a Judge: I had better be healed by an Empirick, than poysoned by a Doctor in Physicke. It were much more profitable for me to have my estate carefully managed by an intruding Guardian, than to have it wasted and dissipated by one legally appointed....

Concerning Tyrants by practise, it is not so easie to describe them as true Kings. For reason rules the one, and selfe-will the other: the first prescribes bounds to his affections, the second confines his desires within no limits, what is the proper rights of Kings may be easily declared, but the outragious insolencies of Tyrants cannot without much difficulty be express'd. And as a right angle is uniforme, and like to it selfe one and the same, so an oblique diversifies it selfe into various and sundry species: In like manner is justice and equity simple, and may be deciphered in few words: but injustice and injury are divers, and for their sundry accidents not to be so easily defin'd; but that more will be omitted than express'd. Now although there be certaine rules by which these Tyrants may be represented (though not absolutely to the life:) yet notwithstanding there is not any more certaine than by conferring and comparing a Tyrants fraudulent sleights with a Kings vertuous actions....

But seeing the condition of men is such, that a King is with much difficulty to be found, that in all his actions only agreeth at the publique good, and yet cannot long subsist without expression of some speciall care thereof, we will conclude that where the Common-wealths advantage is most preferr'd, there is both a lawfull King and Kingdome; and where particular designes and private ends prevaile against the publique profit, there questionlesse is a Tyrant and tiranny....

Now at the last we are come as it were by degrees to the chiefe and principall point of the question. We have seene how that Kings have beene chosen by God, either with relation to their Families or their persons only, and after installed by the people: In like manner what is the duty of the King, and of the Officers of the Kindome, how farre the authority, power, and duty both of the one & the other extends, and what and how sacred are the Covenants and contracts which are made at the inauguration of Kings, and what conditions are intermixt, both tacite and express'd; finally who is a Tyrant without title, and who by practise, seeing it is a thing unquestionable that we are bound to obey a lawfull King, which both to God and people carrieth himselfe according to those Covenants whereunto he stands obliged, as it were to God himselfe, seeing in a sort he represents his divine Majestie: It now followes that we treate, how, and by whom a Tyrant may be lawfully resisted, and who are the persons who ought to be chiefely actors therein, and what course is to be held, that the action may be managed according to right and reason....

First, The law of nature teacheth, and commandeth us to maintaine and defend our lives and liberties, without which life is scant worth the enjoying, against all injury and violence....There is besides this, the civill law, or municipal laws of severall Countreyes which governs the societies of men, by certaine rules, some in one manner, some in another; some submit themselves to the government of one man, some to more; others are ruled by a whole Communalty, some absolutely exclude women from the Royall Throne, others admit them, these here chuse their King descended of such a family, those there make election of whom they please, besides other customes practised amongst severall Nations. If therefore any offer either by fraud or force to violate this law, wee are all bound to resist him, because he wrongs that society to which wee owe all that we have, and would runne our Countrey, to the preservation whereof, all men by nature; by law and by solemne oath are strictly obliged: insomuch that feare or negligence, or bad purposes, make us omit this dutie, wee may justly be accounted breakers of the Lawes, betrayers of our Countrey, and contemners of Religion. Now as the Law of Nature, of Nations, and the civill commands us to take Armes against such Tyrants: so is there not any manner of reason that should perswade us to the contrary; neither is there any oath, covenant, or obligation, publike or private, of power justly to restraine us; therefore the meanest private man may resist and lawfully oppose such an intruding tyrant....

Thus much concerning Tyrants without title.

But for Tyrants by practise, whether they at first gained their authoritie by the sword, or were legally invested therewith by a generall consent: It behooves us to examine this point with much wary circumspection. In the first place we must remember, that all Princes are born men, and therefore reason and passion are as hardly to be separated in them, as the soule is from the body whilest the man liveth: We must not then expect Princes absolute in perfection, but rather repute our selves happy if those that govern us be indifferently good. And therefore although the prince observe not exact mediocrity in State-affaires, if sometimes passion over-rule his reason, if some carelesse omission make him neglect the publick utility, or if he doe not alwayes carefully execute justice with equality, or repulse not with ready valour an invading enemy; he must not therefore be presently declared a tyrant. And certainly, seeing he rules not as a God over men, nor as men over beasts, but is a man composed of the same matter, and of the same nature with the rest: as we would questionlesse judge that prince unreasonably insolent, that should insult over and abuse his subjects, as if they were bruit beasts; so those people are doubtlesse as much void of reason, which imagine a prince should be compleat in perfection, or expect divine abilities in a nature so frail and subject to imperfections. But if a prince purposely ruine the Common-weale, if he presumptuously pervert and resist legall proceedings, or lawfull rights, if he make no reckoning of faith, covenants, justice nor piety, if he prosecute his subjects as enemies; briefly, if he expresse all or the chiefest of those wicked practices we have formerly spoken of; then we may certainly declare him a tyrant, which is as much as an enemy both to God and men. We doe not therefore speak of a prince lesse good, but of one absolute bad; not of one lesse wise, but of one malicious and treacherous; not of one lesse able judiciously to discusse legall differences, but of one perversly bent to pervert justice and equity; not of an unwarlick, but of one furiously disposed to ruine the people, and ransack the State....

Furthermore, as the Princes pleasure is not alwayes law, so many times it is not expedient that the people doe all that which may lawfully be done: for it may often-times chance, that the medicine proves more dangerous than the disease. Therefore it becomes wise men to try all wayes before they come to blowes, to use all other remedies before they suffer the sword to decide the controversie. If then those which represent the body of the people, foresee any innovation or machination against the State, or that it be already imbarked into a course of perdition, their duty is, first to admonish the Prince, and not to attend, that the disease by accession of time, and accidents, becomes unrecoverable. For tyranny may be properly resembled unto a Feaver Hectick, the which at the first is easie to be cured, but with much difficulty to be known; but after it is sufficiently known, it becomes uncurable. Therefore small beginnings are to be carefully observed, and by those whom it concernes diligently prevented.

If the Prince therefore persist in his violent courses, and contemne frequent admonitions, addressing his designes onely to that end, that he may oppresse at his pleasure, and effect his own desires without feare or restraint, he then doubtlesse makes himselfe liable to that detested crime of *Tyranny*: and whatsoever either the law, or lawfull authority permits against a tyrant, may be lawfully practised against him. Tyrany is not onely a will, but the chiefe, and as it were the complement and abstract of vices. A Tyrant subverts the State, pillages the people, layes stratagems to intrap their lives, breaks promise with all, scoffes at the sacred obligation of a solemne oath, and therefore is he so much more vile than the vilest of usuall malefactors, by how much offences committed against a generality, are worthy of greater punishment than those which concern onely particular and private persons. If Theeves and those that commit sacriledge, be declared infamous; nay, if they justly suffer corporall punishment by death, can we invent any that may be worthily equivalent for so outragious a crime?

Furthermore, we have already proved, that all Kings receive their Royall authority from the people, that the whole people considered in one body, is above and greater than the King: and that the King and Emperour are onely the prime and supreme governours and ministers of the Kingdome and Empire; but the people the absolute Lord and owner thereof. It therefore necessarily followes, that a tyrant is in the same manner guilty of rebellion against the Majesty of the people, as the Lord of a fee which felloniously transgresse the conditions of his investitures, & is liable to the same punishment, yea and certainly deserves much more greater than the equity of those lawes inflict on the delinquents. Therefore as *Barclus* says, He may either be deposed by those which are Lords in Soveraignty over him, or else justly punished according to the Law *Julia*, which condemnes those which offer violence to the publick. The body of the people must needs be the Soveraigne of those which represent it, which in some places are the Electors, Palatines, Peeres; in other, the Assembly of the generall Estates. And if the tyranny have gotten such sure footing, as there is no other meanes but force to remove him; then is it lawful for them to call the people to Arms, to inroll and raise forces, and to imploy the utmost of their power, and use against him all advantages and stratagems of warre, as against the enemy of the Common-wealth, and the disturber of the publick peace....

The Officers of the Kingdome cannot for this be rightly taxed of sedition: for in a sedition there must necessarily concurre but two parts, or sides, the which peremptorily contest together, so that it is necessary that the one be in the right, and the other in the wrong: That part undoubtedly hath the right on their side, which defends the Lawes, and strives to advance the publick profit of the Kingdome. And those on the contrary are questionlesse in the wrong, which breake the Lawes, and protect those that violate justice, and oppresse the Common-wealth. Those are certainly in the right way, as saith *Bartolus*, which endeavour to suppresse tyrannicall government, and those in the wrong which oppose lawfull authority. And that must ever be accounted just, which is intended only for the publique benefit, and that unjust, which aimes chiefly at private commodity. Wherefore *Thomas Aquinas* saith, *That a tyrannicall rule having no proper addresse for the publique welfare, but only to satisfie a private will, with increase of particular profit to the ruler, cannot in any reasonable construction be accounted lawfull, and therefore the disturbance of such a government cannot be esteemed seditious, much less traytors*; for that offence hath proper relation only to a lawfull Prince, who indeed is an inanimated or speaking law; therefore seeing that he which employes the utmost of his meanes and power to annihilate the lawes, and quell their vertue and vigour, can no wayes be justly intitled therewith: So neither likewise can those which oppose and take armes against him, be branded with so notorious a crime. Also this offence is committed against the Common-wealth: but for so much as the Common-wealth is there only where the lawes are in force, and not where a Tyrant devoures the State at his owne pleasure and liking, he certainly is quit of that crime which ruines the Majesty of the publique State, and those questionlesse are worthily protectors and preservers of the Common-wealth, who confident in the lawfulness of their authority, and summoned thereunto by their duty, do couragiously resist the unjust proceedings of the Tyrant.

And in this their action wee must not esteeme them as private men and Subjects, but as the representative body of the people, yea and as the Soveraignty it selfe, which demands of his Minister an account of his administration. Neither can we in any good reason account the Officers of the Kingdome disloyall, who in this manner acquit themselves of their charge.

There is ever, and in all places, a mutuall and reciprocall obligation betweene the people and the Prince, the one promiseth to be a good and wise Prince, the other to obey faithfully, provided he govern justly. The people therefore is obliged to the Prince under condition: the Prince to the people simply and purely. Therefore if the Prince faile in his promise, the people is exempt from obedience, the contract is made void, the right of obligation of no force. Then the King if he governe unjustly is perjur'd, and the people likewise forsworne if they obey not his lawfull commands: but that people is truly acquit from all perfidiousnesse, which publiquely renounce the unjust dominion of a Tyrant, or he striving unjustly by strong hand to continue the possession, doe constantly endeavour to expulse him by force of armes.

It is therefore permitted the Officers of a Kingdome, either all, or some good number of them to suppresse a Tyrant; And it is not only lawfull for them to doe it, but their duty expressely requires it: and if they doe it not, they can by no excuse colour their basenesse....

Those officers must also remember, that the King holds truly the first place in the administration of the State, but they the second; and so following according to their ranks; not that they should follow his courses, if he transgresse the lawes of equity and justice, not that if he oppresse the Common-wealth, they should connive to his wickednesse. For the Common-wealth was as well committed to their care as to his, so that it is not sufficient for them to discharge their owne duty in particular, but it behoves them also to containe the Prince within the limits of reason. Briefly they have both joyntly and severally promised with solemn oaths, to advance and procure the profit of the Common-wealth: ....If they deliver not the Common-wealth from tiranny, they may be truly ranckt in the number of Tyrants: as on the contrary they are protectors, tutors, and in a sort Kings, if they keepe and maintain the State safe and intire, which is also recommended to their care and custody....

But let us suppose that in this our Ship of State, the Pilot is drunke, the most of his associates are asleepe, or after large and unreasonable tipling together, they regard their imminent danger in approaching a rocke with idle and negligent jollitie; the Ship in the meane season in stead of following her right course, that might serve for the best advantage of the owners profit, is ready rather to split her selfe. What should then a Masters-mate or some other under-Officer doe, who is vigilant and carefull to performe his dutie? Shall it be thought sufficient for him to pinch or poule them which are asleepe? without daring in the meane time to put his helping hand to preserve the Vessell, which runnes on a course to destruction, least he should be thought to intermeddle with that which he hath no authoritie nor warrant to doe? What mad discretion, nay rather notorious impietie were this?...Nay rather than let such a one cheerefully call one, and command the Mariners to the performance of their dutie: let him carefully and constantly take order that the Common-wealth be not indamaged, and if need so require, even in despite of the King, preserve the Kingdome, without which the kingly title were idle and frivolous, and if by no other meanes it can be effected, let him take the King and binde him hand and foote, that so he may be more conveniently cured of his frensie and madnesse. For as wee have already said, all the administration of the Kingdome, is not by the people absolutely resigned into the hands of the King; as neither the Bishopricke, nor care of the universall Church, is totally committed to the Pope: but also to the care and custody of all the principall Officers of the Kingdome. Now for the preserving of peace and concord amongst those which governe, and for the preventing of jealousies, factions, and distrusts amongst men of equall ranke and dignitie, the King was created as prime and principall Superintendent in the government of the Common-wealth. The King sweares that his most speciall care shall be for the welfare of the Kingdome; and the Officers of the Crowne take all the same oath. If then the King, or divers of them falsifying their faith, ruine the Common-wealth, or abandon her in her greatest necessitie, must the rest also fashion themselves to their base courses, and quit all care of the States safetie; as if the bad example of their companions, absolved them from their oath of fidelitie? Nay, rather on the contrary, in seeing them neglect their promise, they shall best advantage the Common-wealth in carefully observing theirs: chiefly because for this reason they were instituted, as in the steads of *Ephori*, or publick Controllers, and for that every thing gaines the better estimation of just and right in that it is mainly and principally addressed to that end for which it was first ordained....

Therefore those which are obliged to serve a whole Empire or Kingdome, as the Constable, Marshals, Peeres and others, or those which have particular obligations to some Provinces, or Cities, which make a part or portion of the Kingdome, as Dukes,

Marquisses, Earles, Sheriffes, Mayors, and the rest, are bound by the dutie of their place, to succour the Common-wealth, and to free it from the burden of Tyrants, according to the ranke and place which they hold of the people next after the King. The first ought to deliver the whole Kingdome from tyrannous oppression: the other as tutors, that part of the Kingdome whose protection they have undertaken: the dutie of the former is to suppresse the Tyrant: that of the latter, to drive him from their confines....

Every Magistrate is bound to relieve, and as much as in him lies, to redresse the miseries of the Common-wealth, if he shall see the Prince, or the principall Officers of State his associates, by their weaknesse or wickednesse, to hazard the ruine thereof. Briefly, he must either free the whole kingdome, or at least that portion especially recommended to his care, from their imminent and incroaching tyranny. But hath this duty proper relation to every one: Shall it be permitted...to a meere private person, to present the bonnet to slaves, put Armes into the hands of subjects, or to joyn battell with the prince, although he oppresse the people with tyranny? No certainly: The Common wealth was not given in charge to particular persons....God nor the people have not put the sword into the hands of particular persons: Therefore if without commandment they draw the sword, they are seditious, although the cause seem never so just.

Furthermore, the prince is not establisht by private and particular persons, but by all in generall considered in one intire body; whereupon it followes, that they are bound to attend the commandment of all, to wit, of those which are the representative body of a kingdom, or of a Province, or of a Citie, or at the least of some one of them, before they undertake any thing against the prince. For as a Papist cannot bring an action, but being avowd in the name of his Tutor, although the pupill be indeed the true proprietor of the estate, and the tutor onely owner with reference to the charge committed unto him: so likewise the people may not enterprise actions of such nature, but by the command of those, into whose hands they have resigned their power and authority, whether they be ordinary Magistrates, or extraordinary, created in the Assembly of the Estates; whom, if I may so say, for that purpose, they have girded with their sword, and invested with authority, both to govern and defend them, establisht in the same kind as the Pretor at *Rome*, who determined all differences between masters and their servants, to the end that if any controversie happened between the King and the subjects, they should be Judges and preservers of the right, lest the subjects should assume power to themselves to be judges in their own causes. And therefore if they were opprest with tributes, and unreasonable imposts, if any thing were attempted contrary to covenant and oath, and no Magistrate opposed those unjust proceedings, they must rest quiet, and suppose that many times the best Physitians both to prevent and cure some grievous disease, do appoint both letting blood, evacuation of humors, & lancing of the flesh; and that the affaires of this world are of that nature, that with much difficulty one evill cannot be remedied without the adventuring if not the suffering of another, nor any good be achieved, without great pains....

If the Magistrates themselves manifestly favour the tyranny, or at the least doe not formally oppose it; let private men remember the saying of *Job, That for the sinnes of the people God permits hypocrites to reigne,* whom it is impossible either to convert or subvert, if men repent not of their wayes, to walk in obedience to Gods commandments; so that there is no other weapons to be used, but bended knees and humble hearts. Briefly, let them bear with bad princes, and pray for better, perswading themselves, that an outragious tyranny is to be supported as patiently, as some exceeding dammage done by the violence of tempests, or some excessive over-flowing waters, or some such naturall accidents unto the fruits of the earth, if they like not better to change their habitations, by retiring themselves into some other countries....

But if all the principall Officers of State, or divers of them, or but one, endeavour to suppresse a manifest tyranny, or if a Magistrate seek to free that province, or portion of the kingdome from oppression, which is committed to his care and custody, provided under colour of freedome he bring not in a new tyranny, then must all men with joynt courage and alacrity, run to Armes, and take part with him or them, and assist with body and goods, as if God himselfe from heaven had proclaimed warres, and meant to joyn battell against tyrants, and by all wayes and means endevour to deliver their Countrey and Common-wealth from their tyrannous oppression. For as God doth oftentimes chastise a people by the cruelty of tyrants: so also doth he many times punish tyrants by the hands of the people....

Finally, that we may come to some period of this third question; Princes are chosen by God, and establisht by the people: As all particulars considered one by one are inferiour to the Prince: so the whole body of the people and Officers of State which represent that body, are the Princes superiors. In the receiving and inauguration of a Prince, there are Covenants and contracts passed between him and the people, which are tacite and expressed, naturall or civill: to wit, to obey him faithfully whilst he commands justly, that he serving the Common-wealth, all men shal serve him, that whilst he governs according to Law, all shall be submitted to his government, &c. The Officers of the Kingdome are the Guardians and Protectors of these Covenants and contracts. He that maliciously or wilfully violates these conditions, is questionlesse a Tyrant by practice. And therefore the Officers of State may judge him according to the lawes: and if he support his tyranny by strong hands, their duty bindes them, when by no other meanes it can be effected, by force of armes to suppresse him.

Of these Officers there be two kindes, those which have generally undertaken the protection of the Kingdome: as the Constable, Marshalls, Peers, Palatines, and the rest, every one of which, although all the rest doe either connive or consort with the tyranny, are bound to oppose and represse the Tyrant: and those which have undertaken the government of any Province; Citie, or part of the Kingdome, as Dukes, Marquesses, Earles, Consuls, Mayors, Sheriffes, &c. they may according to right expell and drive tyranny and Tyrants from their Cities, Confines, and governments.

But particular and private persons may not unsheath the sword against Tyrants by practise, because they were not establisht by particulars, but by the whole body of the people. But for Tyrants which without title intrude themselves for so much as there is no contract or agreement betweene them and the people, it is indifferently permitted all to oppose and depose them; and in this rank of Tyrants may those be rang'd, who, abusing the weaknesse and sloath of a lawfull Prince, tyrannously insult over his Subjects. Thus much for this, to which for a more full resolution may be added that which hath beene formerly discoursed in the second question....

28. Manifesto of the Communist Party[*]

Karl Marx and Frederick Engels

A spectre is haunting Europe — the spectre of Communism. All the Powers of old Europe have entered into a holy alliance to exorcise this spectre; Pope and Czar, Metternich and Guizot, French Radicals and German police-spies.

Where is the party in opposition that has not been decried as communistic by its opponents in power? Where the Opposition that has not hurled back the branding reproach of Communism, against the more advanced opposition parties, as well as against its re-actionary adversaries?

Two things result from this fact.

I. Communism is already acknowledged by all European Powers to be itself a Power.

II. It is high time that Communists should openly, in the face of the whole world, publish their views, their aims, their tendencies, and meet this nursery tale of the Spectre of Communism with a Manifesto of the party itself.

To this end, Communists of various nationalities have assembled in London, and sketched the following manifesto, to be published in the English, French, German, Italian, Flemish and Danish languages.

[*] Karl Marx and Frederick Engels published the *Manifest der Kommunistischen Partei* in 1848, and it was translated into English and published as the *Manifesto of the Communist Party* in 1888. This particular selection is from Marx and Engels, *Manifesto of the Communist Party*, edited and annotated by Frederick Engels and translated by Samuel Moore (Chicago: Charles H. Kerr and Company, 1906), 11–47.

I. Bourgeois and Proletarians.[1]

The history of all hitherto existing society[2] is the history of class struggles.

Freeman and slave, patrician and plebeian, lord and serf, guild-master[3] and journeyman, in a word, oppressor and oppressed, stood in constant opposition to one another, carried on an uninterrupted, now hidden, now open fight, a fight that each time ended, either in a revolutionary re-constitution of society at large, or in the common ruin of the contending classes.

In the earlier epochs of history, we find almost everywhere a complicated arrangement of society into various orders, a manifold gradation of social rank. In ancient Rome we have patricians, knights, plebeians, slaves; in the middle ages, feudal lords, vassals, guild-masters, journeymen, apprentices, serfs; in almost all of these classes, again, subordinate gradations.

The modern bourgeois society that has sprouted from the ruins of feudal society, has not done away with class antagonisms. It has but established new classes, new conditions of oppression, new forms of struggle in place of the old ones.

Our epoch, the epoch of the bourgeoisie, possesses, however, this distinctive feature; it has simplified the class antagonisms. Society as a whole is more and more splitting up into two great hostile camps, into two great classes directly facing each other: Bourgeoisie and Proletariat.

From the serfs of the middle ages sprang the chartered burghers of the earliest towns. From these burgesses the first elements of the bourgeoisie were developed.

The discovery of America, the rounding of the Cape, opened up fresh ground for the rising bourgeoisie. The East-Indian and Chinese markets, the colonisation of America, trade with the colonies, the increase in the means of exchange and in commodities generally, gave to commerce, to navigation, to industry, an impulse never before known, and thereby, to the revolutionary element in the tottering feudal society, a rapid development.

The feudal system of industry, under which industrial production was monopolised by close guilds, now no longer sufficed for the growing wants of the new markets. The manufacturing system took its place. The guild-masters were pushed on one side by the manufacturing middle-class; division of labour between the different corporate guilds vanished in the face of division of labour in each single workshop.

Meantime the markets kept ever growing, the demand, ever rising. Even manufacture no longer sufficed. Thereupon, steam and machinery revolutionised industrial production. The place of manufacture was taken by the giant, Modern Industry, the place of the industrial middle-class, by industrial millionaires, the leaders of whole industrial armies, the modern bourgeois.

Modern industry has established the world-market, for which the discovery of America paved the way. This market has given an immense development to commerce, to navigation, to communication by land. This development has, in its turn, reacted on the extension of industry; and in proportion as industry, commerce, navigation, railways extended, in the same proportion the bourgeoisie developed, increased its capital, and pushed into the background every class handed down from the Middle Ages.

We see, therefore, how the modern bourgeoisie is itself the product of a long course of development, of a series of revolutions in the modes of production and of exchange.

Each step in the development of the bourgeoisie was accompanied by a corresponding political advance of that class. An oppressed class under the sway of the feudal nobility, an armed and self-governing association in the mediaeval commune,[4] here independent urban republic (as in Italy and Germany), there taxable "third estate" of the monarchy (as in France), afterwards, in the period of manufacture proper, serving either the semi-feudal or the absolute monarchy as a counterpoise against the nobility, and, in fact, corner stone of the great monarchies in general, the bourgeoisie has at last, since the establishment of Modern Industry and of the world-market, conquered for itself, in the modern representative State, exclusive political sway. The executive of the modern State is but a committee for managing the common affairs of the whole bourgeoisie.

The bourgeoisie, historically, has played a most revolutionary part.

The bourgeoisie, wherever it has got the upper hand, has put an end to all feudal, patriarchal, idyllic relations. It has pitilessly torn asunder the motley feudal ties that bound man to his "natural superiors," and has left remaining no other nexus between man and man than naked self-interest, than callous "cash payment." It has drowned the most heavenly ecstacies of religious fervour, of chivalrous enthusiasm, of philistine sentimentalism, in the icy water of egotistical calculation. It has resolved personal worth into exchange value, and in place of the numberless indefeasible chartered freedoms, has set up that single, unconscionable freedom — Free Trade. In one word, for exploitation, veiled by religious and political illusions, it has substituted naked, shameless, direct, brutal exploitation.

The bourgeoisie has stripped of its halo every occupation hitherto honoured and looked up to with reverent awe. It has converted the physician, the lawyer, the priest, the poet, the man of science, into its paid wage-labourers.

The bourgeoisie has torn away from the family its sentimental veil, and has reduced the family relation to a mere money relation.

The bourgeoisie has disclosed how it came to pass that the brutal display of vigour in the Middle Ages, which Reactionists so much admire, found its fitting complement in the most slothful indolence. It has been the first to shew what man's activity can bring about. It has accomplished wonders far surpassing Egyptian pyramids, Roman aqueducts, and Gothic cathedrals; it has conducted expeditions that put in the shade all former Exoduses of nations and crusades.

The bourgeoisie cannot exist without constantly revolutionising the instruments of production, and thereby the relations of production, and with them the whole relations of society. Conservation of the old modes of production in unaltered form, was, on the contrary, the first condition of existence for all earlier industrial classes. Constant revolutionising of production, uninterrupted disturbance of all social conditions, everlasting uncertainty and agitation distinguish the bourgeois epoch from all earlier ones. All fixed, fast-frozen relations, with their train of ancient and venerable prejudices and opinions, are swept away, all new-formed ones become antiquated before they can ossify. All that is solid melts into air, all that is holy is profaned, and man is at last compelled to face with sober senses, his real conditions of life, and his relations with his kind.

The need of a constantly expanding market for its products chases the bourgeoisie over the whole surface of the globe. It must nestle everywhere, settle everywhere, establish connexions everywhere.

The bourgeoisie has through its exploitation of the world-market given a cosmopolitan character to production and consumption in every country. To the great chagrin of Reactionists, it has drawn from under the feet of industry the national ground on which it stood. All old-established national industries have been destroyed or are daily being destroyed. They are dislodged by new industries, whose introduction becomes a life and death question for all civilised nations, by industries that no longer work up indigenous raw material, but raw material drawn from the remotest zones; industries whose products are consumed, not only at home, but in every quarter of the globe. In place of the old wants, satisfied by the productions of the country, we find new wants, requiring for their satisfaction the products of distant lands and climes. In place of the old local and national seclusion and self-sufficiency, we have intercourse in every direction, universal interdependence of nations: And as in material, so also in intellectual production. The intellectual creations of individual nations become common property. National onesidedness and narrow-mindedness become more and more impossible, and from the numerous national and local literatures there arises a world-literature.

The bourgeoisie, by the rapid improvement of all instruments of production, by the immensely facilitated means of communication, draws all, even the most barbarian, nations into civilisation. The cheap prices of its commodities are the heavy artillery with which it batters down all Chinese walls, with which it forces the barbarians' intensely obstinate hatred of foreigners to capitulate. It compels all nations, on pain of extinction, to adopt the bourgeois mode of production; it compels them to introduce what it calls civilisation into their midst, i.e., to become bourgeois themselves. In a word, it creates a world after its own image.

The bourgeoisie has subjected the country to the rule of the towns. It has created enormous cities, has greatly increased the urban population as compared with the rural, and has thus rescued a considerable part of the population from the idiocy of rural life. Just as it has made the country dependent on the towns, so it has made barbarian and semi-barbarian countries dependent on the civilised ones, nations of peasants on nations of bourgeois, the East on the West.

The bourgeoisie keeps more and more doing away with the scattered state of the population, of the means of production, and of property. It has agglomerated population, centralised means of production, and has concentrated property in a few hands. The necessary consequence of this was political centralisation. Independent, or but loosely connected provinces, with separate interests, laws, governments and systems of taxation, became lumped together in one nation, with one government, one code of laws, one national class-interest, one frontier and one customs-tariff.

The bourgeoisie, during its rule of scarce one hundred years, has created more massive and more colossal productive forces than have all preceding generations together. Subjection of Nature's forces to man, machinery, application of chemistry to industry and agriculture, steam-navigation, railways, electric telegraphs, clearing of whole continents for cultivation, canalization of rivers, whole populations conjured out of the ground — what earlier century had even a presentiment that such productive forces slumbered in the lap of social labour?

We see then: the means of production and of exchange on whose foundation the bourgeoisie built itself up, were generated in feudal society. At a certain stage in the development of these means of production and of exchange, the conditions under which feudal society produced and exchanged, the feudal organisation of agriculture and manufacturing industry, in one word, the feudal relations of property became no longer compatible with the already developed productive forces; they became so many fetters. They had to burst asunder; they were burst asunder.

[handwritten margin note: We had to invent new ways of production]

Into their places stepped free competition, accompanied by a social and political constitution adapted to it, and by the economical and political sway of the bourgeois class.

A similar movement is going on before our own eyes. Modern bourgeois society with its relations of production, of exchange and of property, a society that has conjured up such gigantic means of production and of exchange, is like the sorcerer, who is no longer able to control the powers of the nether world whom he has called up by his spells. For many a decade past the history of industry and commerce is but the history of the revolt of modern productive forces against modern conditions of production, against the property relations that are the conditions for the existence of the bourgeoisie and of its rule. It is enough to mention the commercial crises that by their periodical return put on its trial, each time more threateningly, the existence of the entire bourgeois society. In these crises a great part not only of the existing products, but also of the previously created productive forces, are periodically destroyed. In these crises there breaks out an epidemic that, in all earlier epochs, would have seemed an absurdity — the epidemic of over-production. Society suddenly finds itself put back into a state of momentary barbarism; it appears as if a famine, a universal war of devastation had cut off the supply of every means of subsistence; industry and commerce seem to be destroyed; and why? Because there is too much civilisation, too much means of subsistence, too much industry, too much commerce. The productive forces at the disposal of society no longer tend to further the development of the conditions of bourgeois property; on the contrary, they have become too powerful for these conditions, by which they are fettered, and so soon as they overcome these fetters, they bring disorder into the whole of bourgeois society, endanger the existence of bourgeois property. The conditions of bourgeois society are too narrow to comprise the wealth created by them. And how does the bourgeoisie get over these crises? On the one hand by enforced destruction of a mass of productive forces; on the other, by the conquest of new markets, and by the more thorough exploitation of the old ones. That is to say, by paving the way for more extensive and more destructive crises, and by diminishing the means whereby crises are prevented.

[handwritten margin note: war]

The weapons with which the bourgeoisie felled feudalism to the ground are now turned against the bourgeoisie itself.

But not only has the bourgeoisie forged the weapons that bring death to itself; it has also called into existence the men who are to wield those weapons — the modern working-class — the proletarians.

In proportion as the bourgeoisie, i.e., capital, is developed, in the same proportion is the proletariat, the modern working-class, developed, a class of labourers, who live only so long as they find work, and who find work only so long as their labour increases capital. These labourers, who must sell themselves piecemeal, are a commodity, like every other article of commerce, and are consequently exposed to all the vicissitudes of competition, to all the fluctuations of the market.

Owing to the extensive use of machinery and to division of labour, the work of the proletarians has lost all individual character, and, consequently, all charm for the workman. He becomes an appendage of the machine, and it is only the most simple, most monotonous, and most easily acquired knack that is required of him. Hence, the cost of production of a workman is restricted, almost entirely, to the means of subsistence that he requires for his maintenance, and for the propagation of his race. But the price of a commodity, and also of labour, is equal to its cost of production. In proportion, therefore, as the repulsiveness of the work increases, the wage decreases. Nay more, in proportion as the use of machinery and division of labour increases, in the same proportion the burden of toil also increases, whether by prolongation of the working hours, by increase of the work enacted in a given time, or by increased speed of the machinery, etc.

Modern industry has converted the little workshop of the patriarchal master into the great factory of the industrial capitalist. Masses of labourers, crowded into the factory, are organised like soldiers. As privates of the industrial army they are placed under the command of a perfect hierarchy of officers and sergeants. Not only are they the slaves of the bourgeois class, and of the bourgeois State, they are daily and hourly enslaved by the machine, by the over-looker, and, above all, by the individual bourgeois manufacturer himself. The more openly this despotism proclaims gain to be its end and aim, the more petty, the more hateful and the more embittering it is.

The less the skill and exertion or strength implied in manual labour, in other words, the more modern industry becomes developed, the more is the labour of men superseded by that of women. Differences of age and sex have no longer any distinctive social validity for the working class. All are instruments of labour, more or less expensive to use, according to their age and sex.

No sooner is the exploitation of the labourer by the manufacturer, so far, at an end, that he receives his wages in cash, than he is set upon by the other portions of the bourgeoisie, the landlord, the shopkeeper, the pawnbroker, etc.

The lower strata of the Middle class — the small tradespeople, shopkeepers, and retired tradesmen generally, the handicraftsmen and peasants — all these sink gradually into the proletariat, partly because their diminutive capital does not suffice for the scale on which Modern Industry is carried on, and is swamped in the competition with the large capitalists, partly because their specialised skill is rendered worthless by new methods of production. Thus the proletariat is recruited from all classes of the population.

The proletariat goes through various stages of development. With its birth begins its struggle with the bourgeoisie. At first the contest is carried on by individual labourers, then by the workpeople of a factory, then by the operatives of one trade, in one locality, against the individual bourgeois who directly exploits them. They direct their attacks not against the bourgeois conditions of production, but against the instruments of production themselves; they destroy imported wares that compete with their labour, they smash to pieces machinery, they set factories ablaze, they seek to restore by force the vanished status of the workman of the Middle Ages.

At this stage the labourers still form an incoherent mass scattered over the whole country, and broken up by their mutual competition. If anywhere they unite to form more compact bodies, this is not yet the consequence of their own active union, but of the union of the bourgeoisie, which class, in order to attain its own political ends, is compelled to set the whole proletariat in motion, and is moreover yet, for a time, able to do so. At this stage, therefore, the proletarians do not fight their enemies, but the enemies of their enemies, the remnants of absolute monarchy, the landowners, the nonindustrial bourgeois, the petty bourgeoisie. Thus the whole historical movement is concentrated in the hands of the bourgeoisie; every victory so obtained is a victory for the bourgeoisie.

But with the development of industry the proletariat not only increases in number; it becomes concentrated in greater masses, its strength grows, and it feels that strength more. The various interests and conditions of life within the ranks of the proletariat are more and more equalised, in proportion as machinery obliterates all distinctions of labour, and nearly everywhere reduces wages to the same low level. The growing competition among the bourgeois, and the resulting commercial crises, make the wages of the workers ever more fluctuating. The unceasing improvement of machinery, ever more rapidly developing, makes their livelihood more and more precarious; the collisions between individual workmen and individual bourgeois take more and more the character of collisions between two classes. Thereupon the workers begin to form combinations (Trades' Unions) against the bourgeois; they club together in order to keep up the rate of wages; they found permanent associations in order to make provision beforehand for these occasional revolts. Here and there the contest breaks out into riots.

Now and then the workers are victorious, but only for a time. The real fruit of their battles lies, not in the immediate result, but in the ever expanding union of the workers. This union is helped on by the improved means of communication that are created by modern industry, and that place the workers of different localities in contact with one another. It was just this contact that was needed to centralise the numerous local struggles, all of the same character, into one national struggle between classes. But every class struggle is a political struggle. And that union, to attain which the burghers of the Middle Ages, with their miserable highways, required centuries, the modern proletarians, thanks to railways, achieve in a few years.

This organisation of the proletarians into a class, and consequently into a political party, is continually being upset again by the competition between the workers themselves. But it ever rises up again, stronger, firmer, mightier. It compels legislative recognition of particular interests of the workers, by taking advantage of the divisions among the bourgeoisie itself. Thus the ten-hours'-bill in England was carried.

Altogether collisions between the classes of the old society further, in many ways, the course of development of the proletariat. The bourgeoisie finds itself involved in a constant battle. At first with the aristocracy; later on, with those portions of the bourgeoisie itself, whose interests have become antagonistic to the progress of industry; at all times, with the bourgeoisie of foreign countries. In all these battles it sees itself compelled to appeal to the proletariat, to ask for its help, and thus, to drag it into the political arena. The bourgeoisie itself, therefore, supplies the proletariat with its own elements of political and general education, in other words, it furnishes the proletariat with weapons for fighting the bourgeoisie.

Further, as we have already seen, entire sections of the ruling classes are, by the advance of industry, precipitated into the proletariat, or are at least threatened in their conditions of existence. These also supply the proletariat with fresh elements of enlightenment and progress.

Finally, in times when the class-struggle nears the decisive hour, the process of dissolution going on within the ruling class, in fact within the whole range of old society, assumes such a violent, glaring character, that a small section of the ruling class cuts itself adrift, and joins the revolutionary class, the class that holds the future in its hands. Just as, therefore, at an earlier period, a section of the nobility went over to the bourgeoisie, so now a portion of the bourgeoisie goes over to the proletariat, and in particular, a portion of the bourgeois ideologists, who have raised themselves to the level of comprehending theoretically the historical movements as a whole.

Of all the classes that stand face to face with the bourgeoisie to-day, the proletariat alone is a really revolutionary class. The other classes decay and finally disappear in the face of modern industry; the proletariat is its special and essential product.

The lower middle-class, the small manufacturer, the shopkeeper, the artisan, the peasant, all these fight against the bourgeoisie, to save from extinction their existence as fractions of the middle class. They are therefore not revolutionary, but conservative. Nay more, they are reactionary, for they try to roll back the wheel of history. If by chance they are revolutionary, they are so, only in view of their impending transfer into the proletariat, they thus defend not their present, but their future interests, they desert their own standpoint to place themselves at that of the proletariat.

The "dangerous class," the social scum, that passively rotting mass thrown off by the lowest layers of old society, may, here and there, be swept into the movement by a proletarian revolution; its conditions of life, however, prepare it far more for the part of a bribed tool of reactionary intrigue.

In the conditions of the proletariat, those of old society at large are already virtually swamped. The proletarian is without property; his relation to his wife and children has no longer anything in common with the bourgeois family-relations; modern industrial labour, modern subjection to capital, the same in England as in France, in America as in Germany, has stripped him of every trace of national character. Law, morality, religion, are to him so many bourgeois prejudices, behind which lurk in ambush just as many bourgeois interests.

All the preceding classes that got the upper hand, sought to fortify their already acquired status by subjecting society at large to their conditions of appropriation. The proletarians cannot become masters of the productive forces of society, except by abolishing their own previous mode of appropriation, and thereby also every other previous mode of appropriation. They have nothing of their own to secure and to fortify; their mission is to destroy all previous securities for, and insurances of, individual property.

All previous historical movements were movements of minorities, or in the interest of minorities. The proletarian movement is the self-conscious, independent movement of the immense majority, in the interest of the immense majority. The proletariat, the lowest stratum of our present society, cannot stir, cannot raise itself up, without the whole superincumbent strata of official society being sprung into the air.

Though not in substance, yet in form, the struggle of the proletariat with the bourgeoisie is at first a national struggle. The proletariat of each country must, of course, first of all settle matters with its own bourgeoisie.

In depicting the most general phases of the development of the proletariat, we traced the more or less veiled civil war, raging within existing society, up to the point where that war breaks out into open revolution, and where the violent overthrow of the bourgeoisie, lays the foundation for the sway of the proletariat.

Hitherto, every form of society has been based, as we have already seen, on the antagonism of oppressing and oppressed classes. But in order to oppress a class, certain conditions must be assured to it under which it can, at least, continue its slavish existence. The serf, in the period of serfdom, raised himself to membership in the commune, just as the petty bourgeois, under the yoke of feudal absolutism, managed to develop into a bourgeois. The modern labourer, on the contrary, instead of rising with the progress of industry, sinks deeper and deeper below the conditions of existence of his own class. He becomes a pauper, and pauperism develops more rapidly than population and wealth. And here it becomes evident, that the bourgeoisie is unfit any longer to be the ruling class in society, and to impose its conditions of existence upon society as an over-riding law. It is unfit to rule, because it is incompetent to assure an existence to its slave within his slavery, because it cannot help letting him sink into such a state, that it has to feed him, instead of being fed by him. Society can no longer live under this bourgeoisie, in other words, its existence is no longer compatible with society.

The essential condition for the existence, and for the sway of the bourgeois class, is the formation and augmentation of capital; the condition for capital is wage-labour. Wage-labour rests exclusively on competition between the labourers. The advance of industry, whose involuntary promoter is the bourgeoisie, replaces the isolation of the labourers, due to competition, by their involuntary combination, due to association. The development of Modern Industry, therefore, cuts from under its feet the very foundation on which the bourgeoisie produces and appropriates products. What the bourgeoisie therefore produces, above all, are its own grave-diggers. Its fall and the victory of the proletariat are equally inevitable.

II. Proletarians and Communists.

In what relation do the Communists stand to the proletarians as a whole?

The Communists do not form a separate party opposed to other working-class parties.

They have no interests separate and apart from those of the proletariat as a whole.

They do not set up any sectarian principles of their own, by which to shape and mould the proletarian movement.

The Communists are distinguished from the other working class parties by this only: 1. In the national struggles of the proletarians of the different countries, they point out and bring to the front the common interests of the entire proletariat, independently of all nationality. 2. In the various stages of development which the struggle of the working class against the bourgeoisie has to pass through, they always and everywhere represent the interests of the movement as a whole.

The Communists, therefore, are on the one hand, practically, the most advanced and resolute section of the working class parties of every country, that section which pushes forward all others; on the other hand, theoretically, they have over the great mass of the proletariat the advantage of clearly understanding the line of march, the conditions, and the ultimate general results of the proletarian movement.

The immediate aim of the Communists is the same as that of all the other proletarian parties: formation of the proletariat into a class, overthrow of the bourgeois supremacy, conquest of political power by the proletariat.

The theoretical conclusions of the Communists are in no way based on ideas or principles that have been invented, or discovered, by this or that would-be universal reformer.

They merely express, in general terms, actual relations springing from an existing class struggle, from a historical movement going on under our very eyes. The abolition of existing property-relations is not at all a distinctive feature of Communism.

All property relations in the past have continually been subject to historical change consequent upon the change in historical conditions.

The French Revolution, for example, abolished feudal property in favour of bourgeois property.

The distinguishing feature of Communism is not the abolition of property generally, but the abolition of bourgeois property. But modern bourgeois private property is the final and most complete expression of the system of producing and appropriating products, that is based on class antagonism, on the exploitation of the many by the few.

In this sense, the theory of the Communists may be summed up in the single sentence: Abolition of private property.

We Communists have been reproached with the desire of abolishing the right of personally acquiring property as the fruit of a man's own labour, which property is alleged to be the ground work of all personal freedom, activity and independence.

Hard-won, self-acquired, self-earned property! Do you mean the property of the petty artizan and of the small peasant, a form of property that preceded the bourgeois form? There is no need to abolish that; the development of industry has to a great extent already destroyed it, and is still destroying it daily.

Or do you mean modern bourgeois private property?

But does wage-labour create any property for the labourer? Not a bit. It creates capital, i.e., that kind of property which exploits wage-labour, and which cannot increase except upon condition of getting a new supply of wage-labour for fresh exploitation. Property, in its present form, is based on the antagonism of capital and wage-labour. Let us examine both sides of this antagonism.

To be a capitalist, is to have not only a purely personal, but a social status in production. Capital is a collective product, and only by the united action of many members, nay, in the last resort, only by the united action of all members of society, can it be set in motion.

Capital is therefore not a personal, it is a social power.

When, therefore, capital is converted into common property, into the property of all members of society, personal property is not thereby transformed into social property. It is only the social character of the property that is changed. It loses its class-character.

Let us now take wage-labour.

The average price of wage-labour is the minimum wage, i.e., that quantum of the means of subsistence, which is absolutely requisite to keep the labourer in bare existence as a labourer. What, therefore, the wage-labourer appropriates by means of his labour, merely suffices to prolong and reproduce a bare existence. We by no means intend to abolish this personal appropriation of the products of labour, an appropriation that is made for the maintenance and reproduction of human life, and that leaves no surplus wherewith to command the labour of others. All that we want to do away with is the miserable character of this appropriation, under which the labourer lives merely to increase capital, and is allowed to live only in so far as the interest of the ruling class requires it.

In bourgeois society, living labour is but a means to increase accumulated labour. In Communist society, accumulated labour is but a means to widen, to enrich, to promote the existence of the labourer.

In bourgeois society, therefore, the past dominates the present; in communist society, the present dominates the past. In bourgeois society capital is independent and has individuality, while the living person is dependent and has no individuality.

And the abolition of this state of things is called by the bourgeois, abolition of individuality and freedom! And rightly so. The abolition of bourgeois, individuality, bourgeois independence, and bourgeois freedom is undoubtedly aimed at.

By freedom is meant, under the present bourgeois conditions of production, free trade, free selling and buying.

But if selling and buying disappears, free selling and buying disappears also. This talk about free selling and buying, and all the other "brave words" of our bourgeoisie about freedom in general, have a meaning, if any, only in contrast with restricted selling and buying, with the fettered traders of the Middle Ages, but have no meaning when opposed to the Communistic abolition of buying and selling, of the bourgeois conditions of production, and of the bourgeoisie itself.

You are horrified at our intending to do away with private property. But in your existing society, private property is already done away with for nine-tenths of the population; its existence for the few is solely due to its non-existence in the hands of those nine-tenths. You reproach us, therefore, with intending to do away with a form of property, the necessary condition for whose existence is, the non-existence of any property for the immense majority of society.

In one word, you reproach us with intending to do away with your property. Precisely so: that is just what we intend.

From the moment when labour can no longer be converted into capital, money, or rent, into a social power capable of being monopolised, i.e., from the moment when individual property can no longer be transformed into bourgeois property, into capital, from that moment, you say, individuality vanishes.

You must, therefore, confess that by "individual" you mean no other person than the bourgeois, than the middle-class owner of property. This person must, indeed, be swept out of the way, and made impossible.

Communism deprives no man of the power to appropriate the products of society: all that it does is to deprive him of the power to subjugate the labour of others by means of such appropriation.

It has been objected, that upon the abolition of private property all work will cease, and universal laziness will overtake us.

According to this, bourgeois society ought long ago to have gone to the dogs through sheer idleness; for those of its members who work, acquire nothing, and those who acquire anything, do not work. The whole of this objection is but another expression of the tautology: that there can no longer be any wage-labour when there is no longer any capital.

All objections urged against the Communistic mode of producing and appropriating material products, have, in the same way, been urged against the Communistic modes of producing and appropriating intellectual products. Just as, to the bourgeois, the disappearance of class property is the disappearance of production itself, so the disappearance of class culture is to him identical with the disappearance of all culture.

That culture, the loss of which he laments, is, for the enormous majority, a mere training to act as a machine.

But don't wrangle with us so long as you apply, to our intended abolition of bourgeois property, the standard of your bourgeois notions of freedom, culture, law, etc. Your very ideas are but the outgrowth of the conditions of your bourgeois production and bourgeois property, just as your jurisprudence is but the will of your class made into a law for all, a will, whose essential character and direction are determined by the economical conditions of existence of your class.

The selfish misconception that induces you to transform into eternal laws of nature and of reason, the social forms springing from your present mode of production and form of property — historical relations that rise and disappear in the progress of production — this misconception you share with every ruling class that has preceded you. What you see clearly in the case of ancient property, what you admit in the case of feudal property, you are of course forbidden to admit in the case of your own bourgeois form of property.

Abolition of the family! Even the most radical flare up at this infamous proposal of the Communists.

On what foundation is the present family, the bourgeois family, based? On capital, on private gain. In its completely developed form this family exists only among the bourgeoisie. But this state of things finds its complement in the practical absence of the family among the proletarians, and in public prostitution.

The bourgeois family will vanish as a matter of course when its complement vanishes, and both will vanish with the vanishing of capital.

Do you charge us with wanting to stop the exploitation of children by their parents? To this crime we plead guilty.

But, you will say, we destroy the most hallowed of relations, when we replace home education by social.

And your education! Is not that also social, and determined by the social conditions under which you educate, by the intervention, direct or indirect, of society by means of schools, &c.? The Communists have not invented the intervention of society in education; they do but seek to alter the character of that intervention, and to rescue education from the influence of the ruling class.

The bourgeois clap-trap about the family and education, about the hallowed co-relation of parent and child, become all the more disgusting, the more, by the action of Modern Industry, all family ties among the proletarians are torn asunder, and their children transformed into simple articles of commerce and instruments of labour.

But you Communists would introduce community of women, screams the whole bourgeoisie in chorus.

The bourgeois sees in his wife a mere instrument of production. He hears that the instruments of production are to be exploited in common, and, naturally, can come to no other conclusion, than that the lot of being common to all will likewise fall to the women.

He has not even a suspicion that the real point aimed at is to do away with the status of women as mere instruments of production.

For the rest, nothing is more ridiculous than the virtuous indignation of our bourgeois at the community of women which, they pretend, is to be openly and officially established by the Communists. The Communists have no need to introduce community of women; it has existed almost from time immemorial.

Our bourgeois, not content with having the wives and daughters of their proletarians at their disposal, not to speak of common prostitutes, take the greatest pleasure in seducing each others' wives.

Bourgeois marriage is in reality a system of wives in common and thus, at the most, what the Communists might possibly be reproached with, is that they desire to introduce, in substitution for a hypocritically concealed, an openly legalised community of women. For the rest, it is self-evident, that the abolition of the present system of production must bring with it the abolition of the community of women springing from that system, i.e., of prostitution both public and private.

The Communists are further reproached with desiring to abolish countries and nationalities.

The working men have no country. We cannot take from them what they have not got. Since the proletariat must first of all acquire political supremacy, must rise to be the leading class of the nation, must constitute itself the nation, it is, so far, itself national, though not in the bourgeois sense of the word.

National differences, and antagonisms between peoples, are daily more and more vanishing, owing to the development of the bourgeoisie, to freedom of commerce, to the world-market, to uniformity in the mode of production and in the conditions of life corresponding thereto.

The supremacy of the proletariat will cause them to vanish still faster. United action, of the leading civilised countries at least, is one of the first conditions for the emancipation of the proletariat.

In proportion as the exploitation of one individual by another is put an end to, the exploitation of one nation by another will also be put an end to. In proportion as the antagonism between classes within the nation vanishes, the hostility of one nation to another will come to an end.

The charges against Communism made from a religious, a philosophical, and generally, from an ideological standpoint, are not deserving of serious examination.

Does it require deep intuition to comprehend that man's ideas, views, and conceptions, in one word, man's consciousness, changes with every change in the conditions of his material existence, in his social relations and in his social life?

What else does the history of ideas prove, than that intellectual production changes in character in proportion as material production is changed? The ruling ideas of each age have ever been the ideas of its ruling class.

When people speak of ideas that revolutionize society, they do but express the fact, that within the old society, the elements of a new one have been created, and that the dissolution of the old ideas keeps even pace with the dissolution of the old conditions of existence.

When the ancient world was in its last throes, the ancient religions were overcome by Christianity. When Christian ideas succumbed in the 18th century to rationalist ideas, feudal society fought its death-battle with the then revolutionary bourgeoisie. The ideas of religious liberty and freedom of conscience, merely gave expression to the sway of free competition within the domain of knowledge.

"Undoubtedly," it will be said, "religious, moral, philosophical and juridical ideas have been modified in the course of historical development. But religion, morality, philosophy, political science, and law, constantly survived this change."

"There are, besides, eternal truths, such as Freedom, Justice, etc., that are common to all states of society. But Communism abolishes eternal truths, it abolishes all religion, and all morality, instead of constituting them on a new basis; it therefore acts in contradiction to all past historical experience."

What does this accusation reduce itself to? The history of all past society has consisted in the development of class antagonisms, antagonisms that assumed different forms at different epochs.

But whatever form they may have taken, one fact is common to all past ages, viz., the exploitation of one part of society by the other. No wonder, then, that the social consciousness of past ages, despite all the multiplicity and variety it displays, moves within certain common forms, or general ideas, which cannot completely vanish except with the total disappearance of class antagonisms.

The Communist revolution is the most radical rupture with traditional property-relations; no wonder that its development involves the most radical rupture with traditional ideas.

But let us have done with the bourgeois objections to Communism.

We have seen above, that the first step in the revolution by the working class, is to raise the proletariat to the position of ruling class, to win the battle of democracy.

The proletariat will use its political supremacy, to wrest, by degrees, all capital from the bourgeoisie, to centralise all instruments of production in the hands of the State, i.e., of the proletariat organised as the ruling class; and to increase the total of productive forces as rapidly as possible.

Of course, in the beginning, this cannot be effected except by means of despotic

tyrannical

inroads on the rights of property, and on the conditions of bourgeois production; by means of measures, therefore, which appear economically insufficient and untenable, but which, in the course of the movement, outstrip themselves, necessitate further inroads upon the old social order, and are unavoidable as a means of entirely revolutionising the mode of production.

These measures will of course be different in different countries.

Nevertheless in the most advanced countries the following will be pretty generally applicable:

1. Abolition of property in land and application of all rents of land to public purposes.

2. A heavy progressive or graduated income tax.

3. Abolition of all right of inheritance.

4. Confiscation of the property of all emigrants and rebels.

5. Centralisation of credit in the hands of the State, by means of a national bank with State capital and an exclusive monopoly.

6. Centralisation of the means of communication and transport in the hands of the State.

7. Extension of factories and instruments of production owned by the State; the bringing into cultivation of waste lands, and the improvement of the soil generally in accordance with a common plan.

8. Equal liability of all to labour. Establishment of industrial armies, especially for agriculture.

9. Combination of agriculture with manufacturing industries; gradual abolition of the distinction between town and country, by a more equable distribution of the population over the country.

10. Free education for all children in public schools. Abolition of children's factory labour in its present form. Combination of education with industrial production, etc., etc.

When, in the course of development, class distinctions have disappeared, and all production has been concentrated in the hands of a vast association of the whole nation, the public power will lose its political character. Political power, properly so called, is merely the organised power of one class for oppressing another. If the proletariat during its contest with the bourgeoisie is compelled, by the force of circumstances, to organise itself as a class, if, by means of a revolution, it makes itself the ruling class, and, as such, sweeps away by force the old conditions of production, then it will, along with these conditions, have swept away the conditions for the existence of class antagonisms, and of classes generally, and will thereby have abolished its own supremacy as a class.

In place of the old bourgeois society, with its classes and class antagonisms, we shall have an association, in which the free development of each is the condition for the free development of all.

Notes

[1] By bourgeoisie is meant the class of modern Capitalists, owners of the means of social production and employers of wage-labour. By proletariat, the class of modern wage-labourers who,

having no means of production of their own, are reduced to selling their labour-power in order to live.

[2] That is, all written history. In 1847, the prehistory of society, the social organization existing previous to recorded history, was all but unknown. Since then, Haxthausen discovered common ownership of land in Russia, Maurer proved it to be the social foundation from which all Teutonic races started in history, and by and bye village communities were found to be, or to have been, the primitive form of society everywhere from India to Ireland. The inner organization of this primitive Communistic society was laid bare, in its typical form, by Morgan's crowning discovery of the true nature of the gens and its relation to the tribe. With the dissolution of these primæval communities society begins to be differentiated into separate and finally antagonistic classes. I have attempted to retrace this process of dissolution in: "Der Ursprung der Familie, des Privateigenthums und des Staats," 2nd edit., Stuttgart 1886.

[3] Guild-master, that is a full member of a guild, a master within, not a head of, a guild.

[4] "Commune" was the name taken, in France, by the nascent towns even before they had conquered from their feudal lords and masters, local self-government and political rights as "the Third Estate." Generally speaking, for the economical development of the bourgeoisie, England is here taken as the typical country, for its political development, France.

29. David Walker's Appeal[*]

David Walker

Article III.

Our Wretchedness in Consequence of the Preachers of the Religion of Jesus Christ.

Religion, my brethren, is a substance of deep consideration among all nations of the earth. The Pagans have a kind, as well as the Mahometans, the Jews and the Christians. But pure and undefiled religion, such as was preached by Jesus Christ and his apostles, is hard to be found in all the earth. God, through his instrument, Moses, handed a dispensation of his Divine will, to the children of Israel after they had left Egypt for the land of Canaan or of Promise, who through hypocrisy, oppression and unbelief, departed from the faith. — He then, by his apostles, handed a dispensation of his, together with the will of Jesus Christ, to the Europeans in Europe, who, in open violation of which, have made *merchandise* of us, and it does appear as though they take this very dispensation to aid them in their *infernal* depredations upon us. Indeed, the way in which religion was and is conducted by the Europeans and their descendants, one might believe it was a plan fabricated by themselves and the *devils* to oppress us. But hark! My master has taught me better than to believe it — he has taught me that his gospel as it was preached by himself and his apostles remains the same, notwithstanding Europe has tried to mingle blood and opression with it.

It is well known to the Christian world, that Bartholomew Las Casas, that very very notoriously avaricious Catholic priest or preacher, and adventurer with Columbus in his second voyage, proposed to his countrymen, the Spaniards in Hispaniola to import the Africans from the Portuguese settlement in Africa, to dig up gold and silver, and work their plantations for them, to effect which, he made a voyage thence to Spain, and opened

[*] David Walker published *Walker's Appeal, in Four Articles* on September 28, 1829, in Boston, Massachusetts. This particular selection was taken from Walker, *David Walker's Appeal, in Four Articles; Together with a Preamble, to the Coloured Citizens of the World, but in Particular, and Very Expressly, to Those of the United States of America*, Article III, edited and with an introduction by Charles M. Wiltse (New York: Hill and Wang, 1965), 35–43.

the subject to his master, Ferdinand then in declining health, who listened to the plan: but who died soon after, and left it in the hand of his successor, Charles V.[1] This wretch, ("Las Casas, the Preacher,") succeeded so well in his plans of oppression, that in 1503, the first blacks had been imported into the new world. Elated with this success, and stimulated by sordid avarice only, he importuned Charles V. in 1511, to grant permission to a Flemish merchant, to import 4000 blacks at one time.[2] Thus we see, through the instrumentality of a pretended preacher of the gospel of Jesus Christ our common master, our wretchedness first commenced in America — where it has been continued from 1503, to this day, 1829. A period of three hundred and twenty-six years. But two hundred and nine, from 1620 [1619] — when twenty of our fathers were brought into Jamestown, Virginia, by a Dutch man of war, and sold off like brutes to the highest bidders; and there is not a doubt in my mind, but that tyrants are in hope to perpetuate our miseries under them and their children until the final consumation of all things. — But if they do not get dreadfully deceived, it will be because God has forgotten them.

The Pagans, Jews and Mahometans try to make proselytes to their religions, and whatever human beings adopt their religions they extend to them their protection. But Christian Americans, not only hinder their fellow creatures, the Africans, but thousands of them *will absolutely beat a coloured person nearly to death, if they catch him on his knees, supplicating the throne of grace.* This barbarous cruelty was by all the heathen nations of antiquity, and is by the Pagans, Jews and Mahometans of the present day, left entirely to Christian Americans to inflict on the Africans and their descendants, that their cup which is nearly full may be completed. I have known tyrants or usurpers of human liberty in different parts of this country to take their fellow creatures, the coloured people, and beat them until they would scarcely leave life in them; what for? Why they say "The black devils had the audacity to be found *making prayers and supplications to the God who made them! ! ! !*" Yes, I have known small collections of coloured people to have convened together, for no other purpose than to worship God Almighty, in spirit and in truth, to the best of their knowledge; when tyrants, calling themselves *patrols*, would also convene and wait almost in breathless silence for the poor coloured people to commence singing and praying to the Lord our God, as soon as they had commenced, the wretches would burst in upon them and drag them out and commence beating them as they would rattle-snakes — many of whom, they would beat so unmercifully, that they would hardly be able to crawl for weeks and sometimes for months. Yet the American ministers send out missionaries to convert the heathen, while they keep us and our children sunk at their feet in the most abject ignorance and wretchedness that ever a people was afflicted with since the world began. Will the Lord suffer this people to proceed much longer? Will he not stop them in their career? Does he regard the heathens abroad, more than the heathens among the Americans? Surely the Americans must believe that God is partial, notwithstanding his Apostle Peter, declared before Cornelius and others that he has no respect to persons, but in every nation he that feareth God and worketh righteousness is accepted with him. — "The word," said he, "which God sent unto the children of Israel, preaching peace, by Jesus Christ, (he is Lord of all."[3]) Have not the Americans the Bible in their hands? Do they believe it? Surely they do not. See how they treat us in open violation of the Bible! ! They no doubt will be greatly offended with me, but if God does not awaken them, it will be, because they are superior to other men, as they have represented themselves to be. Our divine Lord and Master said, "all things whatsoever ye would that men should do unto you, do ye even so unto them." But an American minister, with the Bible in his hand, holds us and our children in the most abject slavery and wretchedness. Now I ask them, would they like for us to hold them and their children in abject slavery and wretchedness? No, says one, that never can be done — you are too abject and ignorant to do it — you are not men — you were made to be slaves to us, to dig up gold and silver for us and our children. Know this, my dear sirs, that although you treat us and our children now, as you do your domestic beast — yet the final result of all future events are known but to God Almighty alone, who rules in the armies of heaven and among the inhabitants of the earth, and who dethrones one earthly king and sits up another, as it seemeth good in his holy sight. We may attribute these vicissitudes to what we please, but the God of armies and of justice rules in heaven and in earth, and the whole American people shall see and know it yet, to their satisfaction. I have known pretended preachers of the gospel of my Master, who not only held us as their natural inheritance, but treated us with as much rigor as any Infidel or Deist in the world — just as though they were intent only on taking our blood and groans to glorify the Lord Jesus Christ. The wicked and ungodly, seeing their preachers treat us with so much cruelty, they say: our preachers, who must be right, if any body are, treat them like brutes, and why cannot we? — They think it is no harm to keep them in slavery and put the whip to them, and why cannot we do the same! — They being preachers of the gospel of Jesus Christ, if it were any harm, they would surely preach against their oppression and do their utmost to erase it from the country; not only in one or two cities, but one continual cry would be raised in all parts of this confederacy, and would cease only with the complete overthrow of the system of slavery, in every part of the country. But how far the American preachers are from preaching against slavery and oppression, which have carried their country to the brink of a precipice; to save them from plunging down the side of which, will hardly be affected, will appear in the sequel of this paragraph, which I shall narrate just as it transpired. I remember a Camp Meeting in South Carolina, for which I embarked in a Steam Boat at Charleston, and having been five or six hours on the water, we at last arrived at the place of hearing, where was a very great concourse of people, who were no doubt, collected together to hear the word of God, (that some had collected barely as spectators to the scene, I will not here pretend to doubt, however, that is left to themselves and their God.) Myself and boat companions, having been there a little while, we were all called up to hear; I among the rest went up and took my seat — being seated, I fixed myself in a complete position to hear the word of my Saviour and to receive such as I thought was authenticated by the Holy Scriptures; but to my no ordinary astonishment, our Reverend gentleman got up and told us (coloured people) that slaves must be obedient to their masters — must do their duty to their masters or be whipped — the whip was made for the backs of fools, &c. Here I pause for a moment, to give the world time to consider what was my surprise, to hear such preaching from a minister of my Master, whose very gospel is that of peace and not of blood and whips, as this pretended preacher tried to make us believe. What the American preachers can think of us, I aver this day before my God, I have never been able to define. They have newspapers and monthly periodicals, which they receive in continual succession, but on the pages of which, you will scarcely ever find a paragraph respecting slavery, which is ten thousand times more injurious to this country than all the other evils put together; and which will be the final overthrow of its government, unless something is very speedily

done; for their cup is nearly full. — Perhaps they will laugh at or make light of this; but I
tell you Americans ! that unless you speedily alter your course, *you* and your *Country are*
gone!!!!! For God Almighty will tear up the very face of the earth! ! ! Will not that
very remarkable passage of Scripture be fulfilled on Christian Americans? Hear it
Americans! ! "He that is unjust, let him be unjust still: — and he which is filthy, let him
be filthy still: and he that is righteous, let him be righteous still: and he that is holy, let
him be holy still."[4] I hope that the Americans may hear, but I am afraid that they have
done us so much injury, and are so firm in the belief that our Creator made us to be an
inheritance to them for ever, that their hearts will be hardened, so that their destruction
may be sure. This language, perhaps is too harsh for the American's delicate ears. But Oh
Americans! Americans! ! I warn you in the name of the Lord, (whether you will hear, or
forbear,) to repent and reform, or you are ruined! ! ! Do you think that our blood is hidden
from the Lord, because you can hide it from the rest of the world, by sending out
missionaries, and by your charitable deeds to the Greeks, Irish, &c.? Will he not publish
your secret crimes on the house top? Even here in Boston, pride and prejudice have got to
such a pitch, that in the very houses erected to the Lord, they have built little places for
the reception of coloured people, where they must sit during meeting, or keep away from
the house of God, and the preachers say nothing about it — much less go into the hedges
and highways seeking the lost sheep of the house of Israel, and try to bring them in to
their Lord and Master. There are not a more wretched, ignorant, miserable, and abject set
of beings in all the world, than the blacks in the Southern and Western sections of this
country, under tyrants and devils. The preachers of America cannot see them, but they
can send out missionaries to convert the heathens, notwithstanding. Americans! unless
you speedily alter your course of proceeding, if God Almighty does not stop you, I say it
in his name, that you may go on and do as you please for ever, both in time and eternity
— never fear any evil at all! ! ! ! ! ! ! !

ADDITION. — The preachers and people of the United States form societies against
Free Masonry and Intemperance, and write against Sabbath breaking, Sabbath mails,
Infidelity, &c. &c. But the fountain head,[5] compared with which, all those other evils are
comparatively nothing, and from the bloody and murderous head of which, they receive
no trifling support, is hardly noticed by the Americans. This is a fair illustration of the
state of society in this country — it shows what a bearing *avarice* has upon a people,
when they are nearly given up by the Lord to a hard heart and a reprobate mind, in
consequence of afflicting their fellow creatures. God suffers some to go on until they are
ruined for ever! ! ! ! Will it be the case with the whites of the United States of America?
— We hope not — we would not wish to see them destroyed notwithstanding, they have
and do now treat us more cruel than any people have treated another, on this earth since it
came from the hands of its Creator (with the exceptions of the French and the Dutch, they
treat us nearly as bad as the Americans of the United States.) The will of God must
however, in spite of us, *be done*.

The English are the best friends the coloured people have upon earth. Though they
have oppressed us a little and have colonies now in the West Indies, which oppress us
sorely. — Yet notwithstanding they (the English) have done one hundred times more for
the melioration of our condition, than all the other nations of the earth put together. The
blacks cannot but respect the English as a nation, notwithstanding they have treated us a
little cruel.

There is no intelligent *black man* who knows any thing, but esteems a real Englishman, let him see him in what part of the world he will — for they are the greatest benefactors we have upon earth. We have here and there, in other nations, good friends. But as a nation, the English are our friends.

How can the preachers and people of America believe the Bible? Does it teach them any distinction on account of a man's colour? Hearken, Americans! to the injunctions of our Lord and Master, to his humble followers.

⁶ "And Jesus came and spake unto them, saying, all power is given unto me in Heaven and in earth.

"Go ye, therefore, and teach all nations, baptizing them in the name of the Father, and of the Son, and of the Holy Ghost.

"Teaching them to observe all things whatsoever I have commanded you; and lo, I am with you alway, even unto the end of the world. Amen."

I declare, that the very face of these injunctions appear to be of God and not of man. They do not show the slightest degree of distinction. "Go ye therefore," (says my divine Master) "and teach all nations," (or in other words, all people) "baptizing them in the name of the Father, and of the Son, and of the Holy Ghost." Do you understand the above, Americans? We are a people, notwithstanding many of you doubt it. You have the Bible in your hands, with this very injunction. — Have you been to Africa, teaching the inhabitants thereof the words of the Lord Jesus? "Baptizing them in the name of the Father, and of the Son and of the Holy Ghost." Have you not, on the contrary, entered among us, and learnt us the art of throat-cutting, by setting us to fight, one against another, to take each other as prisoners of war, and sell to you for small bits of calicoes, old swords, knives, &c. to make slaves for you and your children? This being done, have you not brought us among you, in chains and hand-cuffs, like brutes, and treated us with all the cruelties and rigour your ingenuity could invent, consistent with the laws of your country, which (for the blacks) are tyrannical enough? Can the American preachers appeal unto God, the Maker and Searcher of hearts, and tell him, with the Bible in their hands, that they make no distinction on account of men's colour? Can they say, O God! thou knowest all things — thou knowest that we make no distinction between thy creatures, to whom we have to preach thy Word? Let them answer the Lord; and if they cannot do it in the affirmative, have they not departed from the Lord Jesus Christ, their master? But some may say, that they never had, or were in possession of religion, which made no distinction, and of course they could not have departed from it. I ask you then, in the name of the Lord, of what kind can your religion be? Can it be that which was preached by our Lord Jesus Christ from Heaven? I believe you cannot be so wicked as to tell him that his Gospel was that of *distinction*. What can the American preachers and people take God to be? Do they believe his words? If they do, do they believe that he will be mocked? Or do they believe, because they are whites and we blacks, that God will have respect to them? Did not God make us all as it seemed best to himself? What right, then, has one of us, to despise another, and to treat him cruel, on account of his colour, which none, but the God who made it can alter? Can there be a greater absurdity in nature, and particularly in a free republican country? But the Americans, having introduced slavery among them, their hearts have become almost seared, as with an hot iron, and God has nearly given them up to believe a lie in preference to the truth! ! ! And

I am awfully afraid that pride, prejudice, avarice and blood, will, before long prove the final ruin of this happy republic, or land of *liberty! ! ! !* Can any thing be a greater mockery of religion than the way in which it is conducted by the Americans? It appears as though they are bent only on daring God Almighty to do his best — they chain and handcuff us and our children and drive us around the country like brutes, and go into the house of the God of justice to return him thanks for having aided them in their infernal cruelties inflicted upon us. Will the Lord suffer this people to go on much longer, taking his holy name in vain? Will he not stop them, PREACHERS and all? O Americans! Americans! ! I call God — I call angels — I call men, to witness, that your DESTRUCTION *is at hand*, and will be speedily consummated unless you REPENT.

Notes

[1] See Butler's History of the United States, vol. 1, page 24. — See also, page 25. [The citation is to Frederick Butler, *A Complete History of the United States of America, Embracing the Whole Period from the Discovery of North America, down to the Year 1820.* 3 vols., Hartford, 1821. Ed.]

[2] It is not unworthy of remark, that the Portuguese and Spaniards, were among, if not the very first Nations upon Earth, about three hundred and fifty or sixty years ago — But see what those *Christians* have come to now in consequence of afflicting our fathers and us, who have never molested, or disturbed them or any other of the white *Christians*, but have they received one quarter of what the Lord will yet bring upon them, for the murders they have inflicted upon us? — They have had, and in some degree have now, sweet times on our blood and groans, the time however, of bitterness have sometime since commenced with them. — There is a God the Maker and preserver of all things, who will as sure as the world exists, give all his creatures their just recompense of reward in this and in the world to come, — we may fool or deceive, and keep each other in the most profound ignorance, beat murder and keep each other out of what is our lawful rights, or the rights of man, yet it is impossible for us to deceive or escape the Lord Almighty.

[3] See Acts of the Apostles, chap. x. v. — 25–27. [The citation should be to Acts 10:36. Ed.]

[4] See Revelation, chap. xxii. 11.

[5] Slavery and oppression. [The allusion to Free Masonry refers to the furor following the threatened revelation of Masonic secrets by William Morgan in 1826, and Morgan's subsequent murder. Ed.]

[6] See St. Matthew's Gospel, chap. xxviii. 18, 19, 20. After Jesus was risen from the dead.

30. Civil Disobedience[*]

Henry David Thoreau

I heartily accept the motto, — "That government is best which governs least;" and I should like to see it acted up to more rapidly and systematically. Carried out, it finally amounts to this, which also I believe, — "That government is best which governs not at all;" and when men are prepared for it, that will be the kind of government which they will have. Government is at best but an expedient; but most governments are usually, and all governments are sometimes, inexpedient. The objections which have been brought against a standing army, and they are many and weighty, and deserve to prevail, may also at last be brought against a standing government. The standing army is only an arm of the standing government. The government itself, which is only the mode which the people have chosen to execute their will, is equally liable to be abused and perverted before the people can act through it. Witness the present Mexican war, the work of comparatively a few individuals using the standing government as their tool; for, in the outset, the people would not have consented to this measure.

This American government, — what is it but a tradition, though a recent one, endeavoring to transmit itself unimpaired to posterity, but each instant losing some of its integrity? It has not the vitality and force of a single living man; for a single man can bend it to his will. It is a sort of wooden gun to the people themselves. But it is not the less necessary for this; for the people must have some complicated machinery or other, and hear its din, to satisfy that idea of government which they have. Governments show thus how successfully men can be imposed on, even impose on themselves, for their own

[*] Henry David Thoreau delivered 'The Rights and the Duties of the Individual in Relation to Government' as a two-part lecture on the evenings of January 26 and February 16 of 1848 in Concord, Massachusetts. It first appeared in print form under the title 'Resistance to Civil Government' in the periodical *Aesthetic Papers* in the year 1849. This same piece was published posthumously in 1866 in *A Yankee in Canada, with Anti-Slavery and Reform Papers* (a collection of Thoreau's essays) under the title by which it is now known, 'Civil Disobedience.' This particular selection was taken from Thoreau, *Miscellanies*, with a biographical sketch by Ralph Waldo Emerson, Vol. 10, *The Writings of Henry David Thoreau* (Boston: Houghton Mifflin Company, 1893), 131–170.

advantage. It is excellent, we must all allow. Yet this government never of itself furthered any enterprise, but by the alacrity with which it got out of its way. *It* does not keep the country free. *It* does not settle the West. *It* does not educate. The character inherent in the American people has done all that has been accomplished; and it would have done somewhat more, if the government had not sometimes got in its way. For government is an expedient by which men would fain succeed in letting one another alone; and, as has been said, when it is most expedient, the governed are most let alone by it. Trade and commerce, if they were not made of India-rubber, would never manage to bounce over the obstacles which legislators are continually putting in their way; and, if one were to judge these men wholly by the effects of their actions and not partly by their intentions, they would deserve to be classed and punished with those mischievous persons who put obstructions on the railroads.

But, to speak practically and as a citizen, unlike those who call themselves no-government men, I ask for, not at once no government, but *at once* a better government. Let every man make known what kind of government would command his respect, and that will be one step toward obtaining it.

After all, the practical reason why, when the power is once in the hands of the people, a majority are permitted, and for a long period continue, to rule is not because they are most likely to be in the right, nor because this seems fairest to the minority, but because they are physically the strongest. But a government in which the majority rule in all cases cannot be based on justice, even as far as men understand it. Can there not be a government in which majorities do not virtually decide right and wrong, but conscience? — in which majorities decide only those questions to which the rule of expediency is applicable? Must the citizen ever for a moment, or in the least degree, resign his conscience to the legislator? Why has every man a conscience, then? I think that we should be men first, and subjects afterward. It is not desirable to cultivate a respect for the law, so much as for the right. The only obligation which I have a right to assume is to do at any time what I think right. It is truly enough said, that a corporation has no conscience; but a corporation of conscientious men is a corporation *with* a conscience. Law never made men a whit more just; and, by means of their respect for it, even the well-disposed are daily made the agents of injustice. A common and natural result of an undue respect for law is, that you may see a file of soldiers, colonel, captain, corporal, privates, powder-monkeys, and all, marching in admirable order over hill and dale to the wars, against their wills, ay, against their common sense and consciences, which makes it very steep marching indeed, and produces a palpitation of the heart. They have no doubt that it is a damnable business in which they are concerned; they are all peaceably inclined. Now, what are they? Men at all? or small movable forts and magazines, at the service of some unscrupulous man in power? Visit the Navy-Yard, and behold a marine, such a man as an American government can make, or such as it can make a man with its black arts, — a mere shadow and reminiscence of humanity, a man laid out alive and standing, and already, as one may say, buried under arms with funeral accompaniments, though it may be, —

> "Not a drum was heard, not a funeral note,
>   As his corse to the rampart we hurried;

Not a soldier discharged his farewell shot
O'er the grave where our hero we buried."

The mass of men serve the state thus, not as men mainly, but as machines, with their bodies. They are the standing army, and the militia, jailers, constables, posse comitatus, etc. In most cases there is no free exercise whatever of the judgment or of the moral sense; but they put themselves on a level with wood and earth and stones; and wooden men can perhaps be manufactured that will serve the purpose as well. Such command no more respect than men of straw or a lump of dirt. They have the same sort of worth only as horses and dogs. Yet such as these even are commonly esteemed good citizens. Others — as most legislators, politicians, lawyers, ministers, and office-holders — serve the state chiefly with their heads; and, as they rarely make any moral distinctions, they are as likely to serve the Devil, without *intending* it, as God. A very few, as heroes, patriots, martyrs, reformers in the great sense, and *men*, serve the state with their consciences also, and so necessarily resist it for the most part; and they are commonly treated as enemies by it. A wise man will only be useful as a man, and will not submit to be "clay," and "stop a hole to keep the wind away," but leave that office to his dust at least: —

"I am too high-born to be propertied,
To be a secondary at control,
Or useful serving-man and instrument
To any sovereign state throughout the world."

He who gives himself entirely to his fellowmen appears to them useless and selfish; but he who gives himself partially to them is pronounced a benefactor and philanthropist.

How does it become a man to behave toward this American government to-day? I answer, that he cannot without disgrace be associated with it. I cannot for an instant recognize that political organization as *my* government which is the *slave's* government also.

All men recognize the right of revolution; that is, the right to refuse allegiance to, and to resist, the government, when its tyranny or its inefficiency are great and unendurable. But almost all say that such is not the case now. But such was the case, they think, in the Revolution of '75. If one were to tell me that this was a bad government because it taxed certain foreign commodities brought to its ports, it is most probable that I should not make an ado about it, for I can do without them. All machines have their friction; and possibly this does enough good to counterbalance the evil. At any rate, it is a great evil to make a stir about it. But when the friction comes to have its machine, and oppression and robbery are organized, I say, let us not have such a machine any longer. In other words, when a sixth of the population of a nation which has undertaken to be the refuge of liberty are slaves, and a whole country is unjustly overrun and conquered by a foreign army, and subjected to military law, I think that it is not too soon for honest men to rebel and revolutionize. What makes this duty the more urgent is the fact that the country so overrun is not our own, but ours is the invading army.

Paley, a common authority with many on moral questions, in his chapter on the "Duty of Submission to Civil Government," resolves all civil obligation into expediency; and he proceeds to say, "that so long as the interest of the whole society requires it, that is, so long as the established government cannot be resisted or changed without public inconveniency, it is the will of God that the established government be obeyed, and no longer. . . . This principle being admitted, the justice of every particular case of resistance is reduced to a computation of the quantity of the danger and grievance on the one side, and of the probability and expense of redressing it on the other." Of this, he says, every man shall judge for himself. But Paley appears never to have contemplated those cases to which the rule of expediency does not apply, in which a people, as well as an individual, must do justice, cost what it may. If I have unjustly wrested a plank from a drowning man, I must restore it to him though I drown myself. This, according to Paley, would be inconvenient. But he that would save his life, in such a case, shall lose it. This people must cease to hold slaves, and to make war on Mexico, though it cost them their existence as a people.

In their practice, nations agree with Paley; but does any one think that Massachusetts does exactly what is right at the present crisis?

> "A drab of state, a cloth-o'-silver slut,
> To have her train borne up, and her soul trail in the dirt."

Practically speaking, the opponents to a reform in Massachusetts are not a hundred thousand politicians at the South, but a hundred thousand merchants and farmers here, who are more interested in commerce and agriculture than they are in humanity, and are not prepared to do justice to the slave and to Mexico, *cost what it may*. I quarrel not with far-off foes, but with those who, near at home, coöperate with, and do the bidding of, those far away, and without whom the latter would be harmless. We are accustomed to say, that the mass of men are unprepared; but improvement is slow, because the few are not materially wiser or better than the many. It is not so important that many should be as good as you, as that there be some absolute goodness somewhere; for that will leaven the whole lump. There are thousands who are *in opinion* opposed to slavery and to the war, who yet in effect do nothing to put an end to them; who, esteeming themselves children of Washington and Franklin, sit down with their hands in their pockets, and say that they know not what to do, and do nothing; who even postpone the question of freedom to the question of free-trade, and quietly read the prices-current along with the latest advices from Mexico, after dinner, and, it may be, fall asleep over them both. What is the price-current of an honest man and patriot to-day? They hesitate, and they regret, and sometimes they petition; but they do nothing in earnest and with effect. They will wait, well disposed, for others to remedy the evil, that they may no longer have it to regret. At most, they give only a cheap vote, and a feeble countenance and Godspeed, to the right, as it goes by them. There are nine hundred and ninety-nine patrons of virtue to one virtuous man. But it is easier to deal with the real possessor of a thing than with the temporary guardian of it.

All voting is a sort of gaming, like checkers or backgammon, with a slight moral tinge to it, a playing with right and wrong, with moral questions; and betting naturally accompanies it. The character of the voters is not staked. I cast my vote, perchance, as I think right; but I am not vitally concerned that that right should prevail. I am willing to leave it to the majority. Its obligation, therefore, never exceeds that of expediency. Even voting *for the right* is *doing* nothing for it. It is only expressing to men feebly your desire that it should prevail. A wise man will not leave the right to the mercy of chance, nor wish it to prevail through the power of the majority. There is but little virtue in the action of masses of men. When the majority shall at length vote for the abolition of slavery, it will be because they are indifferent to slavery, or because there is but little slavery left to be abolished by their vote. *They* will then be the only slaves. Only *his* vote can hasten the abolition of slavery who asserts his own freedom by his vote.

I hear of a convention to be held at Baltimore, or elsewhere, for the selection of a candidate for the Presidency, made up chiefly of editors, and men who are politicians by profession; but I think, what is it to any independent, intelligent, and respectable man what decision they may come to? Shall we not have the advantage of his wisdom and honesty, nevertheless? Can we not count upon some independent votes? Are there not many individuals in the country who do not attend conventions? But no: I find that the respectable man, so called, has immediately drifted from his position, and despairs of his country, when his country has more reason to despair of him. He forthwith adopts one of the candidates thus selected as the only *available* one, thus proving that he is himself *available* for any purposes of the demagogue. His vote is of no more worth than that of any unprincipled foreigner or hireling native, who may have been bought. O for a man who is a *man*, and, as my neighbor says, has a bone in his back which you cannot pass your hand through! Our statistics are at fault: the population has been returned too large. How many *men* are there to a square thousand miles in this country? Hardly one. Does not America offer any inducement for men to settle here? The American has dwindled into an Odd Fellow, — one who may be known by the development of his organ of gregariousness, and a manifest lack of intellect and cheerful self-reliance; whose first and chief concern, on coming into the world, is to see that the Almshouses are in good repair; and, before yet he has lawfully donned the virile garb, to collect a fund for the support of the widows and orphans that may be; who, in short, ventures to live only by the aid of the Mutual Insurance company, which has promised to bury him decently.

It is not a man's duty, as a matter of course, to devote himself to the eradication of any, even the most enormous wrong; he may still properly have other concerns to engage him; but it is his duty, at least, to wash his hands of it, and, if he gives it no thought longer, not to give it practically his support. If I devote myself to other pursuits and contemplations, I must first see, at least, that I do not pursue them sitting upon another man's shoulders. I must get off him first, that he may pursue his contemplations too. See what gross inconsistency is tolerated. I have heard some of my townsmen say, "I should like to have them order me out to help put down an insurrection of the slaves, or to march to Mexico; — see if I would go;" and yet these very men have each, directly by their allegiance, and so indirectly, at least, by their money, furnished a substitute. The soldier is applauded who refuses to serve in an unjust war by those who do not refuse to sustain the unjust government which makes the war; is applauded by those whose own act and authority he disregards and sets at naught; as if the state were penitent to that degree that it hired one to scourge it while it sinned, but not to that degree that it left off sinning for a moment. Thus, under the name of Order and Civil Government, we are all made at last to pay homage to and support our own meanness. After the first blush of sin comes its indifference; and from immoral it becomes, as it were, *un*moral, and not quite unnecessary to that life which we have made.

The broadest and most prevalent error requires the most disinterested virtue to sustain it. The slight reproach to which the virtue of patriotism is commonly liable, the noble are most likely to incur. Those who, while they disapprove of the character and measures of a government, yield to it their allegiance and support are undoubtedly its most conscientious supporters, and so frequently the most serious obstacles to reform. Some are petitioning the state to dissolve the Union, to disregard the requisitions of the President. Why do they not dissolve it themselves, — the union between themselves and the state, — and refuse to pay their quota into its treasury? Do not they stand in the same relation to the state that the state does to the Union? And have not the same reasons prevented the state from resisting the Union which have prevented them from resisting the state?

How can a man be satisfied to entertain an opinion merely, and enjoy *it*? Is there any enjoyment in it, if his opinion is that he is aggrieved? If you are cheated out of a single dollar by your neighbor, you do not rest satisfied with knowing that you are cheated, or with saying that you are cheated, or even with petitioning him to pay you your due; but you take effectual steps at once to obtain the full amount, and see that you are never cheated again. Action from principle, the perception and the performance of right, changes things and relations; it is essentially revolutionary, and does not consist wholly with anything which was. It not only divides states and churches, it divides families; ay, it divides the *individual*, separating the diabolical in him from the divine.

Unjust laws exist: shall we be content to obey them, or shall we endeavor to amend them, and obey them until we have succeeded, or shall we transgress them at once? Men generally, under such a government as this, think that they ought to wait until they have persuaded the majority to alter them. They think that, if they should resist, the remedy would be worse than the evil. But it is the fault of the government itself that the remedy *is* worse than the evil. *It* makes it worse. Why is it not more apt to anticipate and provide for reform? Why does it not cherish its wise minority? Why does it cry and resist before it is hurt? Why does it not encourage its citizens to be on the alert to point out its faults, and *do* better than it would have them? Why does it always crucify Christ, and excommunicate Copernicus and Luther, and pronounce Washington and Franklin rebels?

One would think, that a deliberate and practical denial of its authority was the only offense never contemplated by government; else, why has it not assigned its definite, its suitable and proportionate penalty? If a man who has no property refuses but once to earn nine shillings for the state, he is put in prison for a period unlimited by any law that I know, and determined only by the discretion of those who placed him there; but if he should steal ninety times nine shillings from the state, he is soon permitted to go at large again.

If the injustice is part of the necessary friction of the machine of government, let it go, let it go: perchance it will wear smooth, — certainly the machine will wear out. If the injustice has a spring, or a pulley, or a rope, or a crank, exclusively for itself, then perhaps you may consider whether the remedy will not be worse than the evil; but if it is of such a nature that it requires you to be the agent of injustice to another, then, I say, break the law. Let your life be a counter friction to stop the machine. What I have to do is to see, at any rate, that I do not lend myself to the wrong which I condemn.

As for adopting the ways which the state has provided for remedying the evil, I know not of such ways. They take too much time, and a man's life will be gone. I have other affairs to attend to. I came into this world, not chiefly to make this a good place to live in, but to live in it, be it good or bad. A man has not everything to do, but something; and because he cannot do *everything*, it is not necessary that he should do *something* wrong. It is not my business to be petitioning the Governor or the Legislature any more than it is theirs to petition me; and if they should not hear my petition, what should I do then? But in this case the state has provided no way: its very Constitution is the evil. This may seem to be harsh and stubborn and unconciliatory; but it is to treat with the utmost kindness and consideration the only spirit that can appreciate or deserves it. So is all change for the better, like birth and death, which convulse the body.

I do not hesitate to say, that those who call themselves Abolitionists should at once effectually withdraw their support, both in person and property, from the government of Massachusetts, and not wait till they constitute a majority of one, before they suffer the right to prevail through them. I think that it is enough if they have God on their side, without waiting for that other one. Moreover, any man more right than his neighbors constitutes a majority of one already.

I meet this American government, or its representative, the state government, directly, and face to face, once a year — no more — in the person of its tax-gatherer; this is the only mode in which a man situated as I am necessarily meets it; and it then says distinctly, Recognize me; and the simplest, the most effectual, and, in the present posture of affairs, the indispensablest mode of treating with it on this head, of expressing your little satisfaction with and love for it, is to deny it then. My civil neighbor, the tax-gatherer, is the very man I have to deal with, — for it is, after all, with men and not with parchment that I quarrel, — and he has voluntarily chosen to be an agent of the government. How shall he ever know well what he is and does as an officer of the government, or as a man, until he is obliged to consider whether he shall treat me, his neighbor, for whom he has respect, as a neighbor and well-disposed man, or as a maniac and disturber of the peace, and see if he can get over this obstruction to his neighborliness without a ruder and more impetuous thought or speech corresponding with his action. I know this well, that if one thousand, if one hundred, if ten men whom I could name, — if ten *honest* men only, — ay, if *one* HONEST man, in this State of Massachusetts, *ceasing to hold slaves*, were actually to withdraw from this copartnership, and be locked up in the county jail therefor, it would be the abolition of slavery in America. For it matters not how small the beginning may seem to be: what is once well done is done forever. But we love better to talk about it: that we say is our mission. Reform keeps many scores of newspapers in its service, but not one man. If my esteemed neighbor, the State's ambassador, who will devote his days to the settlement of the question of human rights in the Council Chamber, instead of being threatened with the prisons of Carolina, were to sit down the prisoner of Massachusetts, that State which is so anxious to foist the sin of slavery upon her sister, — though at present she can discover only an act of inhospitality to be the ground of a quarrel with her, — the Legislature would not wholly waive the subject the following winter.

Under a government which imprisons any unjustly, the true place for a just man is also a prison. The proper place to-day, the only place which Massachusetts has provided for her freer and less desponding spirits, is in her prisons, to be put out and locked out of the State by her own act, as they have already put themselves out by their principles. It is there that the fugitive slave, and the Mexican prisoner on parole, and the Indian come to plead the wrongs of his race should find them; on that separate, but more free and honorable ground, where the State places those who are not *with* her, but *against* her, — the only house in a slave State in which a free man can abide with honor. If any think that their influence would be lost there, and their voices no longer afflict the ear of the State, that they would not be as an enemy within its walls, they do not know by how much truth is stronger than error, nor how much more eloquently and effectively he can combat injustice who has experienced a little in his own person. Cast your whole vote, not a strip of paper merely, but your whole influence. A minority is powerless while it conforms to the majority; it is not even a minority then; but it is irresistible when it clogs by its whole weight. If the alternative is to keep all just men in prison, or give up war and slavery, the State will not hesitate which to choose. If a thousand men were not to pay their tax-bills this year, that would not be a violent and bloody measure, as it would be to pay them, and enable the State to commit violence and shed innocent blood. This is, in fact, the definition of a peaceable revolution, if any such is possible. If the tax-gatherer, or any other public officer, asks me, as one has done, "But what shall I do?" my answer is, "If you really wish to do anything, resign your office." When the subject has refused allegiance, and the officer has resigned his office, then the revolution is accomplished. But even suppose blood should flow. Is there not a sort of blood shed when the conscience is wounded? Through this wound a man's real manhood and immortality flow out, and he bleeds to an everlasting death. I see this blood flowing now.

I have contemplated the imprisonment of the offender, rather than the seizure of his goods, — though both will serve the same purpose, — because they who assert the purest right, and consequently are most dangerous to a corrupt State, commonly have not spent much time in accumulating property. To such the State renders comparatively small service, and a slight tax is wont to appear exorbitant, particularly if they are obliged to earn it by special labor with their hands. If there were one who lived wholly without the use of money, the State itself would hesitate to demand it of him. But the rich man — not to make any invidious comparison — is always sold to the institution which makes him rich. Absolutely speaking, the more money, the less virtue; for money comes between a man and his objects, and obtains them for him; and it was certainly no great virtue to obtain it. It puts to rest many questions which he would otherwise be taxed to answer; while the only new question which it puts is the hard but superfluous one, how to spend it. Thus his moral ground is taken from under his feet. The opportunities of living are diminished in proportion as what are called the "means" are increased. The best thing a man can do for his culture when he is rich is to endeavor to carry out those schemes which he entertained when he was poor. Christ answered the Herodians according to their condition. "Show me the tribute-money," said he; — and one took a penny out of his pocket; — if you use money which has the image of Cæsar on it, and which he has made current and valuable, that is, *if you are men of the State*, and gladly enjoy the advantages of Cæsar's government, then pay him back some of his own when he demands it. "Render therefore to Cæsar that which is Cæsar's, and to God those things which are God's," — leaving them no wiser than before as to which was which; for they did not wish to know.

When I converse with the freest of my neighbors, I perceive that, whatever they may say about the magnitude and seriousness of the question, and their regard for the public tranquillity, the long and the short of the matter is, that they cannot spare the protection of the existing government, and they dread the consequences to their property and families of disobedience to it. For my own part, I should not like to think that I ever rely on the protection of the State. But, if I deny the authority of the State when it presents its tax-bill, it will soon take and waste all my property, and so harass me and my children without end. This is hard. This makes it impossible for a man to live honestly, and at the same time comfortably, in outward respects. It will not be worth the while to accumulate property; that would be sure to go again. You must hire or squat somewhere, and raise but a small crop, and eat that soon. You must live within yourself, and depend upon yourself always tucked up and ready for a start, and not have many affairs. A man may grow rich in Turkey even, if he will be in all respects a good subject of the Turkish government. Confucius said: "If a state is governed by the principles of reason, poverty and misery are subjects of shame; if a state is not governed by the principles of reason, riches and honors are the subjects of shame." No: until I want the protection of Massachusetts to be extended to me in some distant Southern port, where my liberty is endangered, or until I am bent solely on building up an estate at home by peaceful enterprise, I can afford to refuse allegiance to Massachusetts, and her right to my property and life. It costs me less in every sense to incur the penalty of disobedience to the State than it would to obey. I should feel as if I were worth less in that case.

Some years ago, the State met me in behalf of the Church, and commanded me to pay a certain sum toward the support of a clergyman whose preaching my father attended, but never I myself. "Pay," it said, "or be locked up in the jail." I declined to pay. But, unfortunately, another man saw fit to pay it. I did not see why the schoolmaster should be taxed to support the priest, and not the priest the schoolmaster; for I was not the State's schoolmaster, but I supported myself by voluntary subscription. I did not see why the lyceum should not present its tax-bill, and have the State to back its demand, as well as the Church. However, at the request of the selectmen, I condescended to make some such statement as this in writing: — "Know all men by these presents, that I, Henry Thoreau, do not wish to be regarded as a member of any incorporated society which I have not joined." This I gave to the town clerk; and he has it. The State, having thus learned that I did not wish to be regarded as a member of that church, has never made a like demand on me since; though it said that it must adhere to its original presumption that time. If I had known how to name them, I should then have signed off in detail from all the societies which I never signed on to; but I did not know where to find a complete list.

I have paid no poll-tax for six years. I was put into a jail once on this account, for one night; and, as I stood considering the walls of solid stone, two or three feet thick, the door of wood and iron, a foot thick, and the iron grating which strained the light, I could not help being struck with the foolishness of that institution which treated me as if I were mere flesh and blood and bones, to be locked up. I wondered that it should have concluded at length that this was the best use it could put me to, and had never thought to avail itself of my services in some way. I saw that, if there was a wall of stone between me and my townsmen, there was a still more difficult one to climb or break through before they could get to be as free as I was. I did not for a moment feel confined, and the walls seemed a great waste of stone and mortar. I felt as if I alone of all my townsmen had paid my tax. They plainly did not know how to treat me, but behaved like persons who are underbred. In every threat and in every compliment there was a blunder; for they thought that my chief desire was to stand the other side of that stone wall. I could not but smile to see how industriously they locked the door on my meditations, which followed them out again without let or hindrance, and *they* were really all that was dangerous. As they could not reach me, they had resolved to punish my body; just as boys, if they cannot come at some person against whom they have a spite, will abuse his dog. I saw that the State was half-witted, that it was timid as a lone woman with her silver spoons, and that it did not know its friends from its foes, and I lost all my remaining respect for it, and pitied it.

Thus the State never intentionally confronts a man's sense, intellectual or moral, but only his body, his senses. It is not armed with superior wit or honesty, but with superior physical strength. I was not born to be forced. I will breathe after my own fashion. Let us see who is the strongest. What force has a multitude? They only can force me who obey a higher law than I. They force me to become like themselves. I do not hear of *men* being *forced* to live this way or that by masses of men. What sort of life were that to live? When I meet a government which says to me, "Your money or your life," why should I be in haste to give it my money? It may be in a great strait, and not know what to do: I cannot help that. It must help itself; do as I do. It is not worth the while to snivel about it. I am not responsible for the successful working of the machinery of society. I am not the son of the engineer. I perceive that, when an acorn and a chestnut fall side by side, the one does not remain inert to make way for the other, but both obey their own laws, and spring and grow and flourish as best they can, till one, perchance, overshadows and destroys the other. If a plant cannot live according to its nature, it dies; and so a man.

The night in prison was novel and interesting enough. The prisoners in their shirt-sleeves were enjoying a chat and the evening air in the doorway, when I entered. But the jailer said, "Come, boys, it is time to lock up;" and so they dispersed, and I heard the sound of their steps returning into the hollow apartments. My room-mate was introduced to me by the jailer as "a first-rate fellow and a clever man." When the door was locked, he showed me where to hang my hat, and how he managed matters there. The rooms were whitewashed once a month; and this one, at least, was the whitest, most simply furnished, and probably the neatest apartment in the town. He naturally wanted to know where I came from, and what brought me there; and, when I had told him, I asked him in my turn how he came there, presuming him to be an honest man, of course; and, as the world goes, I believe he was. "Why," said he, "they accuse me of burning a barn; but I never did it." As near as I could discover, he had probably gone to bed in a barn when drunk, and smoked his pipe there; and so a barn was burnt. He had the reputation of being a clever man, had been there some three months waiting for his trial to come on, and would have to wait as much longer; but he was quite domesticated and contented, since he got his board for nothing, and thought that he was well treated.

He occupied one window, and I the other; and I saw that if one stayed there long, his principal business would be to look out the window. I had soon read all the tracts that were left there, and examined where former prisoners had broken out, and where a grate had been sawed off, and heard the history of the various occupants of that room; for I found that even here there was a history and a gossip which never circulated beyond the walls of the jail. Probably this is the only house in the town where verses are composed, which are afterward printed in a circular form, but not published. I was shown quite a long list of verses which were composed by some young men who had been detected in an attempt to escape, who avenged themselves by singing them.

I pumped my fellow-prisoner as dry as I could, for fear I should never see him again; but at length he showed me which was my bed, and left me to blow out the lamp.

It was like traveling into a far country, such as I had never expected to behold, to lie there for one night. It seemed to me that I never had heard the town-clock strike before, nor the evening sounds of the village; for we slept with the windows open, which were inside the grating. It was to see my native village in the light of the Middle Ages, and our Concord was turned into a Rhine stream, and visions of knights and castles passed before me. They were the voices of old burghers that I heard in the streets. I was an involuntary spectator and auditor of whatever was done and said in the kitchen of the adjacent village-inn, — a wholly new and rare experience to me. It was a closer view of my native town. I was fairly inside of it. I never had seen its institutions before. This is one of its peculiar institutions; for it is a shire town. I began to comprehend what its inhabitants were about.

In the morning, our breakfasts were put through the hole in the door, in small oblong-square tin pans, made to fit, and holding a pint of chocolate, with brown bread, and an iron spoon. When they called for the vessels again, I was green enough to return what bread I had left; but my comrade seized it, and said that I should lay that up for lunch or dinner. Soon after he was let out to work at haying in a neighboring field, whither he went every day, and would not be back till noon; so he bade me good-day, saying that he doubted if he should see me again.

When I came out of prison, — for some one interfered, and paid that tax, — I did not perceive that great changes had taken place on the common, such as he observed who went in a youth and emerged a tottering and gray-headed man; and yet a change had to my eyes come over the scene, — the town, and State, and country, — greater than any that mere time could effect. I saw yet more distinctly the State in which I lived. I saw to what extent the people among whom I lived could be trusted as good neighbors and friends; that their friendship was for summer weather only; that they did not greatly propose to do right; that they were a distinct race from me by their prejudices and superstitions, as the Chinamen and Malays are; that in their sacrifices to humanity they ran no risks, not even to their property; that after all they were not so noble but they treated the thief as he had treated them, and hoped, by a certain outward observance and a few prayers, and by walking in a particular straight though useless path from time to time, to save their souls. This may be to judge my neighbors harshly; for I believe that many of them are not aware that they have such an institution as the jail in their village.

It was formerly the custom in our village, when a poor debtor came out of jail, for his acquaintances to salute him, looking through their fingers, which were crossed to represent the grating of a jail window, "How do ye do?" My neighbors did not thus salute me, but first looked at me, and then at one another, as if I had returned from a long journey. I was put into jail as I was going to the shoemaker's to get a shoe which was mended. When I was let out the next morning, I proceeded to finish my errand, and, having put on my mended shoe, joined a huckleberry party, who were impatient to put themselves under my conduct; and in half an hour, — for the horse was soon tackled, —

was in the midst of a huckleberry field, on one of our highest hills, two miles off, and then the State was nowhere to be seen.

This is the whole history of "My Prisons."

I have never declined paying the highway tax, because I am as desirous of being a good neighbor as I am of being a bad subject; and as for supporting schools, I am doing my part to educate my fellow-countrymen now. It is for no particular item in the tax-bill that I refuse to pay it. I simply wish to refuse allegiance to the State, to withdraw and stand aloof from it effectually. I do not care to trace the course of my dollar, if I could, till it buys a man or a musket to shoot one with, — the dollar is innocent, — but I am concerned to trace the effects of my allegiance. In fact, I quietly declare war with the State, after my fashion, though I will still make what use and get what advantage of her I can, as is usual in such cases.

If others pay the tax which is demanded of me, from a sympathy with the State, they do but what they have already done in their own case, or rather they abet injustice to a greater extent than the State requires. If they pay the tax from a mistaken interest in the individual taxed, to save his property, or prevent his going to jail, it is because they have not considered wisely how far they let their private feelings interfere with the public good.

This, then, is my position at present. But one cannot be too much on his guard in such a case, lest his action be biased by obstinacy or an undue regard for the opinions of men. Let him see that he does only what belongs to himself and to the hour.

I think sometimes, Why, this people mean well, they are only ignorant; they would do better if they knew how: why give your neighbors this pain to treat you as they are not inclined to? But I think again, This is no reason why I should do as they do, or permit others to suffer much greater pain of a different kind. Again, I sometimes say to myself, When many millions of men, without heat, without ill will, without personal feeling of any kind, demand of you a few shillings only, without the possibility, such is their constitution, of retracting or altering their present demand, and without the possibility, on your side, of appeal to any other millions, why expose yourself to this overwhelming brute force? You do not resist cold and hunger, the winds and the waves, thus obstinately; you quietly submit to a thousand similar necessities. You do not put your head into the fire. But just in proportion as I regard this as not wholly a brute force, but partly a human force, and consider that I have relations to those millions as to so many millions of men, and not of mere brute or inanimate things, I see that appeal is possible, first and instantaneously, from them to the Maker of them, and, secondly, from them to themselves. But if I put my head deliberately into the fire, there is no appeal to fire or to the Maker of fire, and I have only myself to blame. If I could convince myself that I have any right to be satisfied with men as they are, and to treat them accordingly, and not according, in some respects, to my requisitions and expectations of what they and I ought to be, then, like a good Mussulman and fatalist, I should endeavor to be satisfied with things as they are, and say it is the will of God. And, above all, there is this difference between resisting this and a purely brute or natural force, that I can resist this with some effect; but I cannot expect, like Orpheus, to change the nature of the rocks and trees and beasts.

I do not wish to quarrel with any man or nation. I do not wish to split hairs, to make fine distinctions, or set myself up as better than my neighbors. I seek rather, I may say, even an excuse for conforming to the laws of the land. I am but too ready to conform to them. Indeed, I have reason to suspect myself on this head; and each year, as the tax-gatherer comes round, I find myself disposed to review the acts and position of the general and State governments, and the spirit of the people, to discover a pretext for conformity.

> "We must affect our country as our parents,
> And if at any time we alienate
> Our love or industry from doing it honor,
> We must respect effects and teach the soul
> Matter of conscience and religion,
> And not desire of rule or benefit."

I believe that the State will soon be able to take all my work of this sort out of my hands, and then I shall be no better a patriot than my fellow-countrymen. Seen from a lower point of view, the Constitution, with all its faults, is very good; the law and the courts are very respectable; even this State and this American government are, in many respects, very admirable, and rare things, to be thankful for, such as a great many have described them; but seen from a point of view a little higher, they are what I have described them; seen from a higher still, and the highest, who shall say what they are, or that they are worth looking at or thinking of at all?

However, the government does not concern me much, and I shall bestow the fewest possible thoughts on it. It is not many moments that I live under a government, even in this world. If a man is thought-free, fancy-free, imagination-free, that which *is not* never for a long time appearing *to be* to him, unwise rulers or reformers cannot fatally interrupt him.

I know that most men think differently from myself; but those whose lives are by profession devoted to the study of these or kindred subjects content me as little as any. Statesmen and legislators, standing so completely within the institution, never distinctly and nakedly behold it. They speak of moving society, but have no resting-place without it. They may be men of a certain experience and discrimination, and have no doubt invented ingenious and even useful systems, for which we sincerely thank them; but all their wit and usefulness lie within certain not very wide limits. They are wont to forget that the world is not governed by policy and expediency. Webster never goes behind government, and so cannot speak with authority about it. His words are wisdom to those legislators who contemplate no essential reform in the existing government; but for thinkers, and those who legislate for all time, he never once glances at the subject. I know of those whose serene and wise speculations on this theme would soon reveal the limits of his mind's range and hospitality. Yet, compared with the cheap professions of most reformers, and the still cheaper wisdom and eloquence of politicians in general, his are almost the only sensible and valuable words, and we thank Heaven for him. Comparatively, he is always strong, original, and, above all, practical. Still, his quality is not wisdom, but prudence. The lawyer's truth is not Truth, but consistency or a consistent expediency. Truth is always in harmony with herself, and is not concerned chiefly to reveal the justice that may consist with wrong-doing. He well deserves to be called, as he has been called, the Defender of the Constitution. There are really no blows to be given by him but defensive ones. He is not a leader, but a follower. His leaders are the men of '87. "I have never made an effort," he says, "and never propose to make an effort; I have never countenanced an effort, and never mean to countenance an effort, to disturb the arrangement as originally made, by which the various States came into the Union." Still thinking of the sanction which the Constitution gives to slavery, he says, "Because it was a part of the original compact, — let it stand." Notwithstanding his special acuteness and ability, he is unable to take a fact out of its merely political relations, and behold it as it lies absolutely to be disposed of by the intellect, — what, for instance, it behooves a man to do here in America to-day with regard to slavery, — but ventures, or is driven, to make some such desperate answer as the following, while professing to speak absolutely, and as a private man, — from which what new and singular code of social duties might be inferred? "The manner," says he, "in which the governments of those States where slavery exists are to regulate it is for their own consideration, under their responsibility to their constituents, to the general laws of propriety, humanity, and justice, and to God. Associations formed elsewhere, springing from a feeling of humanity, or any other cause, have nothing whatever to do with it. They have never received any encouragement from me, and they never will."[1]

They who know of no purer sources of truth, who have traced up its stream no higher, stand, and wisely stand, by the Bible and the Constitution, and drink at it there with reverence and humility; but they who behold where it comes trickling into this lake or that pool, gird up their loins once more, and continue their pilgrimage toward its fountain-head.

No man with a genius for legislation has appeared in America. They are rare in the history of the world. There are orators, politicians, and eloquent men, by the thousand; but the speaker has not yet opened his mouth to speak who is capable of settling the much-vexed questions of the day. We love eloquence for its own sake, and not for any truth which it may utter, or any heroism it may inspire. Our legislators have not yet learned the comparative value of free-trade and of freedom, of union, and of rectitude, to a nation. They have no genius or talent for comparatively humble questions of taxation and finance, commerce and manufactures and agriculture. If we were left solely to the wordy wit of legislators in Congress for our guidance, uncorrected by the seasonable experience and the effectual complaints of the people, America would not long retain her rank among the nations. For eighteen hundred years, though perchance I have no right to say it, the New Testament has been written; yet where is the legislator who has wisdom and practical talent enough to avail himself of the light which it sheds on the science of legislation?

The authority of government, even such as I am willing to submit to, — for I will cheerfully obey those who know and can do better than I, and in many things even those who neither know nor can do so well, — is still an impure one: to be strictly just, it must have the sanction and consent of the governed. It can have no pure right over my person and property but what I concede to it. The progress from an absolute to a limited monarchy, from a limited monarchy to a democracy, is a progress toward a true respect for the individual. Even the Chinese philosopher was wise enough to regard the individual as the basis of the empire. Is a democracy, such as we know it, the last improvement possible in government? Is it not possible to take a step further towards recognizing and organizing the rights of man? There will never be a really free and enlightened State until the State comes to recognize the individual as a higher and independent power, from which all its own power and authority are derived, and treats him accordingly. I please myself with imagining a State at last which can afford to be just to all men, and to treat the individual with respect as a neighbor; which even would not think it inconsistent with its own repose if a few were to live aloof from it, not meddling with it, nor embraced by it, who fulfilled all the duties of neighbors and fellowmen. A State which bore this kind of fruit, and suffered it to drop off as fast as it ripened, would prepare the way for a still more perfect and glorious State, which also I have imagined, but not yet anywhere seen.

Note

[1] These extracts have been inserted since the lecture was read.

31. The Souls of Black Folk[*]

W.E.B. Du Bois

VI

Of the Training of Black Men

> Why, if the Soul can fling the Dust aside,
> And naked on the Air of Heaven ride,
> Were't not a Shame — were't not a Shame for him
> In this clay carcase crippled to abide?
>
> OMAR KHAYYÁM (FITZGERALD).

From the shimmering swirl of waters where many, many thoughts ago the slave-ship first saw the square tower of Jamestown, have flowed down to our day three streams of thinking: one swollen from the larger world here and over-seas, saying, the multiplying of human wants in culture-lands calls for the world-wide coöperation of men in satisfying them. Hence arises a new human unity, pulling the ends of earth nearer, and all men, black, yellow, and white. The larger humanity strives to feel in this contact of living Nations and sleeping hordes a thrill of new life in the world, crying, "If the contact of Life and Sleep be Death, shame on such Life." To be sure, behind this thought lurks the afterthought of force and dominion, — the making of brown men to delve when the temptation of beads and red calico cloys.

The second thought streaming from the death-ship and the curving river is the thought of the older South, — the sincere and passionate belief that somewhere between men and cattle, God created a *tertium quid*, and called it a Negro, — a clownish, simple creature,

---

[*] W.E.B. Du Bois published *The Souls of Black Folk: Essays and Sketches* in 1903. This particular selection was taken from Du Bois, *The Souls of Black Folk: Essays and Sketches*, Chapter VI (London: Archibald Constable and Co., Ltd., 1905), 88–109.

at times even lovable within its limitations, but straitly foreordained to walk within the Veil. To be sure, behind the thought lurks the afterthought, — some of them with favoring chance might become men, but in sheer self-defence we dare not let them, and we build about them walls so high, and hang between them and the light a veil so thick, that they shall not even think of breaking through.

And last of all there trickles down that third and darker thought, — the thought of the things themselves, the confused, half-conscious mutter of men who are black and whitened, crying "Liberty, Freedom, Opportunity — vouchsafe to us, O boastful World, the chance of living men!" To be sure, behind the thought lurks the afterthought, — suppose, after all, the World is right and we are less than men? Suppose this mad impulse within is all wrong, some mock mirage from the untrue?

So here we stand among thoughts of human unity, even through conquest and slavery; the inferiority of black men, even if forced by fraud, a shriek in the night for the freedom of men who themselves are not yet sure of their right to demand it. This is the tangle of thought and afterthought wherein we are called to solve the problem of training men for life.

Behind all its curiousness, so attractive alike to sage and *dilettante*, lie its dim dangers, throwing across us shadows at once grotesque and awful. Plain it is to us that what the world seeks through desert and wild we have within our threshold, — a stalwart laboring force, suited to the semi-tropics; if, deaf to the voice of the Zeitgeist, we refuse to use and develop these men, we risk poverty and loss. If, on the other hand, seized by the brutal afterthought, we debauch the race thus caught in our talons, selfishly sucking their blood and brains in the future as in the past, what shall save us from national decadence? Only that saner selfishness, which Education teaches men, can find the rights of all in the whirl of work.

Again, we may decry the color-prejudice of the South, yet it remains a heavy fact. Such curious kinks of the human mind exist and must be reckoned with soberly. They cannot be laughed away, nor always successfully stormed at, nor easily abolished by act of legislature. And yet they must not be encouraged by being let alone. They must be recognized as facts, but unpleasant facts; things that stand in the way of civilization and religion and common decency. They can be met in but one way, — by the breadth and broadening of human reason, by catholicity of taste and culture. And so, too, the native ambition and aspiration of men, even though they be black, backward, and ungraceful, must not lightly be dealt with. To stimulate wildly weak and untrained minds is to play with mighty fires; to flout their striving idly is to welcome a harvest of brutish crime and shameless lethargy in our very laps. The guiding of thought and the deft coordination of deed is at once the path of honor and humanity.

And so, in this great question of reconciling three vast and partially contradictory streams of thought, the one panacea of Education leaps to the lips of all: — such human training as will best use the labor of all men without enslaving or brutalizing; such training as will give us poise to encourage the prejudices that bulwark society, and to stamp out those that in sheer barbarity deafen us to the wail of prisoned souls within the Veil, and the mounting fury of shackled men.

But when we have vaguely said that Education will set this tangle straight, what have we uttered but a truism? Training for life teaches living; but what training for the profitable living together of black men and white? A hundred and fifty years ago our task would have seemed easier. Then Dr. Johnson blandly assured us that education was needful solely for the embellishments of life, and was useless for ordinary vermin. To-day we have climbed to heights where we would open at least the outer courts of knowledge to all, display its treasures to many, and select the few to whom its mystery of Truth is revealed, not wholly by birth or the accidents of the stock market, but at least in part according to deftness and aim, talent and character. This programme, however, we are sorely puzzled in carrying out through that part of the land where the blight of slavery fell hardest, and where we are dealing with two backward peoples. To make here in human education that ever necessary combination of the permanent and the contingent — of the ideal and the practical in workable equilibrium — has been there, as it ever must be in every age and place, a matter of infinite experiment and frequent mistakes.

In rough approximation we may point out four varying decades of work in Southern education since the Civil War. From the close of the war until 1876, was the period of uncertain groping and temporary relief. There were army schools, mission schools, and schools of the Freedman's Bureau in chaotic disarrangement seeking system and coöperation. Then followed ten years of constructive definite effort toward the building of complete school systems in the South. Normal schools and colleges were founded for the freedmen, and teachers trained there to man the public schools. There was the inevitable tendency of war to underestimate the prejudices of the master and the ignorance of the slave, and all seemed clear sailing out of the wreckage of the storm. Meantime, starting in this decade yet especially developing from 1885 to 1895, began the industrial revolution of the South. The land saw glimpses of a new destiny and the stirring of new ideals. The educational system striving to complete itself saw new obstacles and a field of work ever broader and deeper. The Negro colleges, hurriedly founded, were inadequately equipped, illogically distributed, and of varying efficiency and grade; the normal and high schools were doing little more than common-school work, and the common schools were training but a third of the children who ought to be in them, and training these too often poorly. At the same time the white South, by reason of its sudden conversion from the slavery ideal, by so much the more became set and strengthened in its racial prejudice, and crystallized it into harsh law and harsher custom; while the marvellous pushing forward of the poor white daily threatened to take even bread and butter from the mouths of the heavily handicapped sons of the freedmen. In the midst, then, of the larger problem of Negro education sprang up the more practical question of work, the inevitable economic quandary that faces a people in the transition from slavery to freedom, and especially those who make that change amid hate and prejudice, lawlessness and ruthless competition.

The industrial school springing to notice in this decade, but coming to full recognition in the decade beginning with 1895, was the proffered answer to this combined educational and economic crisis, and an answer of singular wisdom and timeliness. From the very first in nearly all the schools some attention had been given to training in handiwork, but now was this training first raised to a dignity that brought it in direct touch with the South's magnificent industrial development, and given an emphasis which reminded black folk that before the Temple of Knowledge swing the Gates of Toil.

Yet after all they are but gates, and when turning our eyes from the temporary and the contingent in the Negro problem to the broader question of the permanent uplifting and civilization of black men in America, we have a right to inquire, as this enthusiasm for material advancement mounts to its height, if after all the industrial school is the final and sufficient answer in the training of the Negro race; and to ask gently, but in all sincerity, the ever-recurring query of the ages, Is not life more than meat, and the body more than raiment? And men ask this today all the more eagerly because of sinister signs in recent educational movements. The tendency is here, born of slavery and quickened to renewed life by the crazy imperialism of the day, to regard human beings as among the material resources of a land to be trained with an eye single to future dividends. Race-prejudices, which keep brown and black men in their "places," we are coming to regard as useful allies with such a theory, no matter how much they may dull the ambition and sicken the hearts of struggling human beings. And above all, we daily hear that an education that encourages aspiration, that sets the loftiest of ideals and seeks as an end culture and character rather than bread-winning, is the privilege of white men and the danger and delusion of black.

Especially has criticism been directed against the former educational efforts to aid the Negro. In the four periods I have mentioned, we find first, boundless, planless enthusiasm and sacrifice; then the preparation of teachers for a vast public-school system; then the launching and expansion of that school system amid increasing difficulties; and finally the training of workmen for the new and growing industries. This development has been sharply ridiculed as a logical anomaly and flat reversal of nature. Soothly we have been told that first industrial and manual training should have taught the Negro to work, then simple schools should have taught him to read and write, and finally, after years, high and normal schools could have completed the system, as intelligence and wealth demanded.

That a system logically so complete was historically impossible, it needs but a little thought to prove. Progress in human affairs is more often a pull than a push, a surging forward of the exceptional man, and the lifting of his duller brethren slowly and painfully to his vantage-ground. Thus it was no accident that gave birth to universities centuries before the common schools, that made fair Harvard the first flower of our wilderness. So in the South: the mass of the freedmen at the end of the war lacked the intelligence so necessary to modern workingmen. They must first have the common school to teach them to read, write, and cipher; and they must have higher schools to teach teachers for the common schools. The white teachers who flocked South went to establish such a common-school system. Few held the idea of founding colleges; most of them at first would have laughed at the idea. But they faced, as all men since them have faced, that central paradox of the South, — the social separation of the races. At that time it was the sudden volcanic rupture of nearly all relations between black and white, in work and government and family life. Since then a new adjustment of relations in economic and political affairs has grown up, — an adjustment subtle and difficult to grasp, yet singularly ingenious, which leaves still that frightful chasm at the color-line across which men pass at their peril. Thus, then and now, there stand in the South two separate worlds; and separate not simply in the higher realms of social intercourse, but also in church and school, on railway and street-car, in hotels and theatres, in streets and city sections, in books and newspapers, in asylums and jails, in hospitals and graveyards. There is still enough of contact for large economic and group coöperation, but the separation is so thorough and deep that it absolutely precludes for the present between the races anything like that sympathetic and effective group-training and leadership of the one by the other, such as the American Negro and all backward peoples must have for effectual progress.

This the missionaries of '68 soon saw; and if effective industrial and trade schools were impracticable before the establishment of a common-school system, just as certainly no adequate common schools could be founded until there were teachers to teach them. Southern whites would not teach them; Northern whites in sufficient numbers could not be had. If the Negro was to learn, he must teach himself, and the most effective help that could be given him was the establishment of schools to train Negro teachers. This conclusion was slowly but surely reached by every student of the situation until simultaneously, in widely separated regions, without consultation or systematic plan, there arose a series of institutions designed to furnish teachers for the untaught. Above the sneers of critics at the obvious defects of this procedure must ever stand its one crushing rejoinder: in a single generation they put thirty thousand black teachers in the South; they wiped out the illiteracy of the majority of the black people of the land, and they made Tuskegee possible.

Such higher training-schools tended naturally to deepen broader development: at first they were common and grammar schools, then some became high schools. And finally, by 1900, some thirty-four had one year or more of studies of college grade. This development was reached with different degrees of speed in different institutions: Hampton is still a high school, while Fisk University started her college in 1871, and Spelman Seminary about 1896. In all cases the aim was identical, — to maintain the standards of the lower training by giving teachers and leaders the best practicable training; and above all, to furnish the black world with adequate standards of human culture and lofty ideals of life. It was not enough that the teachers of teachers should be trained in technical normal methods; they must also, so far as possible, be broad-minded, cultured men and women, to scatter civilization among a people whose ignorance was not simply of letters, but of life itself.

It can thus be seen that the work of education in the South began with higher institutions of training, which threw off as their foliage common schools, and later industrial schools, and at the same time strove to shoot their roots ever deeper toward college and university training. That this was an inevitable and necessary development, sooner or later, goes without saying; but there has been, and still is, a question in many minds if the natural growth was not forced, and if the higher training was not either overdone or done with cheap and unsound methods. Among white Southerners this feeling is widespread and positive. A prominent Southern journal voiced this in a recent editorial.

"The experiment that has been made to give the colored students classical training has not been satisfactory. Even though many were able to pursue the course, most of them did so in a parrot-like way, learning what was taught, but not seeming to appropriate the truth and import of their instruction, and graduating without sensible aim or valuable occupation for their future. The whole scheme has proved a waste of time, efforts, and the money of the state."

While most fair-minded men would recognize this as extreme and overdrawn, still without doubt many are asking, Are there a sufficient number of Negroes ready for college training to warrant the undertaking? Are not too many students prematurely forced into this work? Does it not have the effect of dissatisfying the young Negro with his environment? And do these graduates succeed in real life? Such natural questions cannot be evaded, nor on the other hand must a Nation naturally skeptical as to Negro ability assume an unfavorable answer without careful inquiry and patient openness to conviction. We must not forget that most Americans answer all queries regarding the Negro *a priori*, and that the least that human courtesy can do is to listen to evidence.

The advocates of the higher education of the Negro would be the last to deny the incompleteness and glaring defects of the present system: too many institutions have attempted to do college work, the work in some cases has not been thoroughly done, and quantity rather than quality has sometimes been sought. But all this can be said of higher education throughout the land; it is the almost inevitable incident of educational growth, and leaves the deeper question of the legitimate demand for the higher training of Negroes untouched. And this latter question can be settled in but one way, — by a first-hand study of the facts. If we leave out of view all institutions which have not actually graduated students from a course higher than that of a New England high school, even though they be called colleges; if then we take the thirty-four remaining institutions, we may clear up many misapprehensions by asking searchingly, What kind of institutions are they? what do they teach? and what sort of men do they graduate?

And first we may say that this type of college, including Atlanta, Fisk, and Howard, Wilberforce and Claflin, Biddle, Shaw, and the rest, is peculiar, almost unique. Through the shining trees that whisper before me as I write, I catch glimpses of a boulder of New England granite, covering a grave, which graduates of Atlanta University have placed there, —

> "IN GRATEFUL MEMORY OF THEIR FORMER TEACHER AND FRIEND AND OF THE UNSELFISH LIFE HE LIVED, AND THE NOBLE WORK HE WROUGHT; THAT THEY, THEIR CHILDREN, AND THEIR CHILDREN'S CHILDREN MIGHT BE BLESSED."

This was the gift of New England to the freed Negro: not alms, but a friend; not cash, but character. It was not and is not money these seething millions want, but love and sympathy, the pulse of hearts beating with red blood; — a gift which to-day only their own kindred and race can bring to the masses, but which once saintly souls brought to their favored children in the crusade of the sixties, that finest thing in American history, and one of the few things untainted by sordid greed and cheap vainglory. The teachers in these institutions came not to keep the Negroes in their place, but to raise them out of the defilement of the places where slavery had wallowed them. The colleges they founded were social settlements; homes where the best of the sons of the freedmen came in close and sympathetic touch with the best traditions of New England. They lived and ate together, studied and worked, hoped and harkened in the dawning light. In actual formal content their curriculum was doubtless old-fashioned, but in educational power it was supreme, for it was the contact of living souls.

From such schools about two thousand Negroes have gone forth with the bachelor's degree. The number in itself is enough to put at rest the argument that too large a proportion of Negroes are receiving higher training. If the ratio to population of all Negro students throughout the land, in both college and secondary training, be counted, Commissioner Harris assures us "it must be increased to five times its present average" to equal the average of the land.

Fifty years ago the ability of Negro students in any appreciable numbers to master a modern college course would have been difficult to prove. To-day it is proved by the fact that four hundred Negroes, many of whom have been reported as brilliant students, have received the bachelor's degree from Harvard, Yale, Oberlin, and seventy other leading colleges. Here we have, then, nearly twenty-five hundred Negro graduates, of whom the crucial query must be made, How far did their training fit them for life? It is of course extremely difficult to collect satisfactory data on such a point, — difficult to reach the men, to get trustworthy testimony, and to gauge that testimony by any generally acceptable criterion of success. In 1900, the Conference at Atlanta University undertook to study these graduates, and published the results. First they sought to know what these graduates were doing, and succeeded in getting answers from nearly two-thirds of the living. The direct testimony was in almost all cases corroborated by the reports of the colleges where they graduated, so that in the main the reports were worthy of credence. Fifty-three per cent of these graduates were teachers, — presidents of institutions, heads of normal schools, principals of city school-systems, and the like. Seventeen per cent were clergymen; another seventeen per cent were in the professions, chiefly as physicians. Over six per cent were merchants, farmers, and artisans, and four per cent were in the government civil-service. Granting even that a considerable proportion of the third unheard from are unsuccessful, this is a record of usefulness. Personally I know many hundreds of these graduates, and have corresponded with more than a thousand; through others I have followed carefully the lifework of scores; I have taught some of them and some of the pupils whom they have taught, lived in homes which they have builded, and looked at life through their eyes. Comparing them as a class with my fellow students in New England and in Europe, I cannot hesitate in saying that nowhere have I met men and women with a broader spirit of helpfulness, with deeper devotion to their life-work, or with more consecrated determination to succeed in the face of bitter difficulties than among Negro college-bred men. They have, to be sure, their proportion of ne'er-do-weels, their pedants and lettered fools, but they have a surprisingly small proportion of them; they have not that culture of manner which we instinctively associate with university men, forgetting that in reality it is the heritage from cultured homes, and that no people a generation removed from slavery can escape a certain unpleasant rawness and *gaucherie*, despite the best of training.

With all their larger vision and deeper sensibility, these men have usually been conservative, careful leaders. They have seldom been agitators, have withstood the temptation to head the mob, and have worked steadily and faithfully in a thousand communities in the South. As teachers, they have given the South a commendable system of city schools and large numbers of private normal-schools and academies. Colored college-bred men have worked side by side with white college graduates at Hampton; almost from the beginning the backbone of Tuskegee's teaching force has been formed of graduates from Fisk and Atlanta. And to-day the institute is filled with college graduates, from the energetic wife of the principal down to the teacher of agriculture, including nearly half of the executive council and a majority of the heads of departments. In the professions, college men are slowly but surely leavening the Negro church, are healing and preventing the devastations of disease, and beginning to furnish legal protection for the liberty and property of the toiling masses. All this is needful work. Who would do it if Negroes did not? How could Negroes do it if they were not trained carefully for it? If white people need colleges to furnish teachers, ministers, lawyers, and doctors, do black people need nothing of the sort?

If it is true that there are an appreciable number of Negro youth in the land capable by character and talent to receive that higher training, the end of which is culture, and if the two and a half thousand who have had something of this training in the past have in the main proved themselves useful to their race and generation, the question then comes, What place in the future development of the South ought the Negro college and college-bred man to occupy? That the present social separation and acute race-sensitiveness must eventually yield to the influences of culture, as the South grows civilized, is clear. But such transformation calls for singular wisdom and patience. If, while the healing of this vast sore is progressing, the races are to live for many years side by side, united in economic effort, obeying a common government, sensitive to mutual thought and feeling, yet subtly and silently separate in many matters of deeper human intimacy, — if this unusual and dangerous development is to progress amid peace and order, mutual respect and growing intelligence, it will call for social surgery at once the delicatest and nicest in modern history. It will demand broad-minded, upright men, both white and black, and in its final accomplishment American civilization will triumph. So far as white men are concerned, this fact is to-day being recognized in the South, and a happy renaissance of university education seems imminent. But the very voices that cry hail to this good work are, strange to relate, largely silent or antagonistic to the higher education of the Negro.

Strange to relate! for this is certain, no secure civilization can be built in the South with the Negro as an ignorant, turbulent proletariat. Suppose we seek to remedy this by making them laborers and nothing more: they are not fools, they have tasted of the Tree of Life, and they will not cease to think, will not cease attempting to read the riddle of the world. By taking away their best equipped teachers and leaders, by slamming the door of opportunity in the faces of their bolder and brighter minds, will you make them satisfied with their lot? or will you not rather transfer their leading from the hands of men taught to think to the hands of untrained demagogues? We ought not to forget that despite the pressure of poverty, and despite the active discouragement and even ridicule of friends, the demand for higher training steadily increases among Negro youth: there were, in the years from 1875 to 1880, 22 Negro graduates from Northern colleges; from 1885 to 1890 there were 43, and from 1895 to 1900, nearly 100 graduates. From Southern Negro colleges there were, in the same three periods, 143, 413, and over 500 graduates. Here, then, is the plain thirst for training; by refusing to give this Talented Tenth the key to knowledge, can any sane man imagine that they will lightly lay aside their yearning and contentedly become hewers of wood and drawers of water?

No. The dangerously clear logic of the Negro's position will more and more loudly assert itself in that day when increasing wealth and more intricate social organization preclude the South from being, as it so largely is, simply an armed camp for intimidating black folk. Such waste of energy cannot be spared if the South is to catch up with civilization. And as the black third of the land grows in thrift and skill, unless skilfully guided in its larger philosophy, it must more and more brood over the red past and the creeping, crooked present, until it grasps a gospel of revolt and revenge and throws its new-found energies athwart the current of advance. Even to-day the masses of the Negroes see all too clearly the anomalies of their position and the moral crookedness of yours. You may marshal strong indictments against them, but their counter-cries, lacking though they be in formal logic, have burning truths within them which you may not wholly ignore, O Southern Gentlemen! If you deplore their presence here, they ask, Who brought us? When you cry, Deliver us from the vision of intermarriage, they answer that legal marriage is infinitely better than systematic concubinage and prostitution. And if in just fury you accuse their vagabonds of violating women, they also in fury quite as just may reply: The rape which your gentlemen have done against helpless black women in defiance of your own laws is written on the foreheads of two millions of mulattoes, and written in ineffaceable blood. And finally, when you fasten crime upon this race as its peculiar trait, they answer that slavery was the arch-crime, and lynching and lawlessness its twin abortion; that color and race are not crimes, and yet they it is which in this land receives most unceasing condemnation, North, East, South, and West.

I will not say such arguments are wholly justified, — I will not insist that there is no other side to the shield; but I do say that of the nine millions of Negroes in this nation, there is scarcely one out of the cradle to whom these arguments do not daily present themselves in the guise of terrible truth. I insist that the question of the future is how best to keep these millions from brooding over the wrongs of the past and the difficulties of the present, so that all their energies may be bent toward a cheerful striving and co-operation with their white neighbors toward a larger, juster, and fuller future. That one wise method of doing this lies in the closer knitting of the Negro to the great industrial possibilities of the South is a great truth. And this the common schools and the manual training and trade schools are working to accomplish. But these alone are not enough. The foundations of knowledge in this race, as in others, must be sunk deep in the college and university if we would build a solid, permanent structure. Internal problems of social advance must inevitably come, — problems of work and wages, of families and homes, of morals and the true valuing of the things of life; and all these and other inevitable problems of civilization the Negro must meet and solve largely for himself, by reason of his isolation; and can there be any possible solution other than by study and thought and an appeal to the rich experiece of the past? Is there not, with such a group and in such a crisis, infinitely more danger to be apprehended from half-trained minds and shallow thinking than from over-education and over-refinement? Surely we have wit enough to found a Negro college so manned and equipped as to steer successfully between the *dilettante* and the fool. We shall hardly induce black men to believe that if their stomachs be full, it matters little about their brains. They already dimly perceive that the paths of peace winding between honest toil and dignified manhood call for the guidance of skilled thinkers, the loving, reverent comradeship between the black lowly and the black men emancipated by training and culture.

The function of the Negro college, then, is clear: it must maintain the standards of popular education, it must seek the social regeneration of the Negro, and it must help in the solution of problems of race contact and co-operation. And finally, beyond all this, it must develop men. Above our modern socialism, and out of the worship of the mass, must persist and evolve that higher individualism which the centres of culture protect; there must come a loftier respect for the sovereign human soul that seeks to know itself and the world about it; that seeks a freedom for expansion and self-development; that will love and hate and labor in its own way, untrammeled alike by old and new. Such souls aforetime have inspired and guided worlds, and if we be not wholly bewitched by our Rhine-gold, they shall again. Herein the longing of black men must have respect: the rich and bitter depth of their experience, the unknown treasures of their inner life, the strange rendings of nature they have seen, may give the world new points of view and make their loving, living, and doing precious to all human hearts. And to themselves in these the days that try their souls, the chance to soar in the dim blue air above the smoke is to their finer spirits boon and guerdon for what they lose on earth by being black.

I sit with Shakespeare and he winces not. Across the color line I move arm in arm with Balzac and Dumas, where smiling men and welcoming women glide in gilded halls. From out the caves of evening that swing between the strong-limbed earth and the tracery of the stars, I summon Aristotle and Aurelius and what soul I will, and they come all graciously with no scorn nor condescension. So, wed with Truth, I dwell above the Veil. Is this the life you grudge us, O knightly America? Is this the life you long to change into the dull red hideousness of Georgia? Are you so afraid lest peering from this high Pisgah, between Philistine and Amalekite, we sight the Promised Land?

Name Index